George Barrell Cheever

The pilgrim's progress

and the life and times of John Bunyan

George Barrell Cheever

The pilgrim's progress
and the life and times of John Bunyan

ISBN/EAN: 9783741143519

Manufactured in Europe, USA, Canada, Australia, Japa

Cover: Foto ©ninafisch / pixelio.de

Manufactured and distributed by brebook publishing software (www.brebook.com)

George Barrell Cheever

The pilgrim's progress

THE PILGRIM'S PROGRESS

AND

THE LIFE AND TIMES OF JOHN BUNYAN.

A Series of Lectures

BY

THE REV. GEORGE B. CHEEVER, D.D.,
NEW YORK.

LONDON:
T. NELSON AND SONS, PATERNOSTER ROW;
EDINBURGH; AND NEW YORK.

1872.

PREFACE.

This work attempts to trace the footsteps of a great circumnavigator in the Divine Life, somewhat as an open boat might follow in the wake of the ships of Columbus into a New World. And yet it is not new, but as old as the grace of God in the heart of sinful man; and now, so many have crossed the sea, and prepared charts and maps of their passage for the use of others, that there is scarcely a league over which some compass has not been drawn, or into which some fathoming line has not been let down; though there is scenery still hidden, and there are depths never yet sounded, nor ever will be, inasmuch as the grace of God in the heart of man is unfathomable; and in sailing over this ocean, we can often do no more than cry out with the Apostle Paul, "O the depths!" There is always much that is peculiar with every individual mind in crossing this sea; and likewise in following the traces of so experienced and wise a navigator as Bunyan, every individual will find something new to remark upon; so that these lectures, though on an old subject, will not necessarily be found commonplace, or monotonous, or superfluous.

It ought probably to be mentioned, that a former essay by the author, printed in the North American Review, has been, in one or two of these lectures, worked up anew. A greater space also is occupied by that division of the work on the life and times of Bunyan, than was originally contemplated; but in the Providence of God, Bunyan himself in his own lifetime, furnished as much matter for profitable meditation and instruction, as his own Pilgrim, in his beautiful Allegory. Of course the first division is more particularly biographical and historical, the second more meditative and expository.

The world of Christian Pilgrims may in general be divided into two classes, the cheerful and the depressed; those who have joy in the Lord, and those whose joy is overborne and kept down by cares and doubts, unbelief and many sins, fallings by the way and broodings over them. Indeed, there is a sad want, in our present Christian experience, of that joy of the Lord, which is our strength; and to give the reasons for this would by itself require a volume. There must be more of this joy, and it must be more habitual, if the church of Christ would be strong to convert the world, would be prepared to teach transgressors the way of the Lord, so that sinners may be converted unto him; for that is the meaning of the Psalmist, taking what is individual, and applying it, as we must, to the church universal, as the source of her power.

The importance of this joy for the strength of the church is manifest not only from the fifty-first Psalm, but from those remarkable words of our blessed Lord to his disciples, "These things have I spoken unto you, that my joy might remain in you, and that your joy might be full." The Saviour's own joy! What a depth of blissful meaning is contained in these words, as the portion of his people! It is not a doubting, weak, depressed piety, that is here recognized.

And yet there is provision in the same gospel for those who do not attain to this joy. There is mention made of those, "whose hands hang down," and of "the feeble knees;" and the arrangements made in the gospel for the sustaining and comforting of such do shew that there will always continue to be, more or less, in the Christian race, and in the Christian church, hands that hang down and feeble knees.

Now it is at once a proof of the wisdom of the delineations of Christian character in the Pilgrim's Progress, and a source of the usefulness of that book to all classes, that it is not a picture of abstract perfections, nor drawn from any one extreme or exclusive point of view. It recognizes both divisions of the Christian world, of which we have spoken. Nay, it recognizes them at different times in the different experience of the same persons, which is in accordance with the examples of Scripture. For the same great saint who says, "I have rejoiced in the way of thy testimonies," and, "I will delight myself in thy statutes," says also, a few verses afterwards, "My soul cleaveth unto the dust," and "My soul melteth for heaviness."

There is in general more of this cleaving unto the dust, than of this rejoicing; but it is not always to be concluded, because the soul thus seems bound up in dust and heaviness, that therefore there is nothing of the Christian life in it. The straight lines of light and joy in the gospel falling into such a dense medium of cares and anxieties in this world, are refracted and broken, so to speak, and the reflection of the gospel comes from troubled waters,—waters ruffled and stirred,—and not from still lakes, where halcyon birds of calm sit brooding on the surface.

The Christian life is represented as a race, a work, a labour, a conflict, a warfare. It needs a strong, constant, unwavering purpose, along with the constant, ever present omnipotent grace of God. God is one all in all. Christ's strength must be made perfect in our weakness. So David says, "I will run in the way of thy commandments when thou shalt enlarge my heart." Here is the purpose, "I will run;" here is the way, "thy commandments;" here is the soul's dependence, "when thou shalt enlarge my heart;" and here is the source of power, the grace of God in the heart, in the deep heart. To this Paul answers, "Work out your own salvation with fear and trembling, for it is God that worketh in you, both to will and to do." Blessed harmony of God's working and man's working, of God's grace and man's obedience!

The Pilgrim's Progress is constructed throughout on this divine harmony, never losing sight of either side of the arrangement. So must our individual progress through life, in grace, be of the same divine harmony, a perpetual strife on our part, and God striving in us. So says Paul of this progress in his own person, "Whereunto I also labour, striving according to his working, which worketh in me mightily." When these two things are kept together, then there is joy, —joy even amidst great trials and discouragements. Because we are cast down, it is not necessary to be destroyed; and the same Apostle who says, "Rejoice in the Lord alway," says also, with Barnabas, who was the son of consolation, that we must "through much tribulation enter into the kingdom of God."

In all things we are brought to Christ, and thrown upon him; and this is the sweet voice of the Pilgrim's Progress, as of the gospel, "Come unto me, all ye that labour and are heavy laden, and I will give you rest." One consolation amidst our distresses is this, that "we have not an High Priest who cannot be touched with the feeling of our infirmities, but was in all points tempted like as we are, yet without sin. Let us therefore come boldly unto the throne of grace, that we may obtain mercy, and find grace to help in time of need." And "unto Him that is able to keep us from falling, and to present us faultless before the presence of his glory with exceeding joy, to the only wise God our Saviour, be glory and majesty, dominion and power, both now and ever. Amen."

Contents.

I.	BUNYAN AND HIS TIMES,	9
II.	BUNYAN'S TEMPTATIONS,	39
III.	BUNYAN'S EXAMINATION,	74
IV.	BUNYAN IN PRISON,	104
V.	PROVIDENCE, GRACE, AND GENIUS, IN BUNYAN AND THE PILGRIM'S PROGRESS,	137
VI.	THE CITY OF DESTRUCTION AND SLOUGH OF DESPOND,	171
VII.	CHRISTIAN IN THE HOUSE OF THE INTERPRETER,	195
VIII.	CHRISTIAN ON THE HILL DIFFICULTY,	216
IX.	CHRISTIAN'S FIGHT WITH APOLLYON IN THE VALLEY OF HUMILIATION,	232
X.	CHRISTIAN IN THE VALLEY OF THE SHADOW OF DEATH,	256
XI.	CHRISTIAN AND FAITHFUL IN VANITY FAIR,	279
XII.	DOUBTING CASTLE AND GIANT DESPAIR,	300
XIII.	THE DELECTABLE MOUNTAINS AND ENCHANTED GROUND, WITH THE CHARACTERS OF IGNORANCE AND LITTLE-FAITH,	321
XIV.	THE LAND BEULAH AND THE RIVER OF DEATH,	345
XV.	CHRISTIANA, MERCY, AND THE CHILDREN,	369

LECTURE FIRST.

Bunyan and his Times.

Historical sketch of the period.—Bunyan's contemporaries.—His boyhood and convictions of sin.—The Providence and Grace of God illustrated in his life and conversion.—The characters he met with.—His Evangelist.—His spiritual and intellectual discipline.—Necessity of experimental piety, for a full appreciation and understanding of the Pilgrim's Progress.

IF a man were to look about the world, or over all the world's history, for that one of his race, in whose life there should be found the completest illustration of the providence and grace of God, he could hardly fix upon a more perfect instance than that of John Bunyan. The detailed biography of this man I shall not attempt to present, in so short a sketch as that to which I must of necessity confine myself. But there are points in his life, where the Divine Providence is unfolded so gloriously, and junctures where the Divine grace comes out so clearly and so brightly, that nothing could be more simple, beautiful, and deeply interesting, than their illustration. On some of these points I shall dwell, premising, in order to a right view of them, a rapid but important glance at the age in which he lived.

It was an age of great revolutions, great excitement, great genius, great talent; great extremes both in good and evil; great piety and great wickedness; great freedom and great tyranny and oppression. Under Cromwell there was great liberty and prosperity; under the Charleses there was great oppression and disgrace. Bunyan's life, continuing from 1628 to 1688, embraces the most revolutionary and stirring period in English history. There pass before the mind within this period the oppressive reign of Charles First; the characters of Laud and Strafford; the Star Chamber, and the king's tyrannical men, courts, and measures; the noble defence of liberty in the House of Commons; Hampden and Pym; the war between the King and Parliament; the King's defeat, and death upon the scaffold; the glorious protectorate of Cromwell, few years, but grand and prosperous, a freedom and prosperity united, such as England had never known; then comes the hasty, unconditional restoration of a Prince who cared for nothing but his own pleasure, the dissolute, tyrannical reign of Charles Second, one of the most promising, lying, unprincipled, worthless, selfish, corrupted and corrupting kings, that ever sat upon the throne of England; in the terribly severe language of the Edinburgh Review, a king, "who superseded the reign of the saints by the reign of strumpets; who was crowned in his youth with the Covenant in his hand, and died with the Host sticking in his throat, after a life spent in dawdling suspense between Hobbism and Popery;" a king and a reign, of which one of the grand climacterics in wickedness embraced the royal murders of the noble patriots Russell and Algernon Sydney; immortal be their names, and honoured ever be their memories; a reign the very beginning of which, threw John Bunyan into prison, and produced a Bartholomew's day to thousands of the conscientious ministers of the Church of England.

The king's reign from the time of the Restoration, began in contempt of all religion, and continued in debauchery and drunkenness. Even those persons who may have taken their views of the history of this period simply from the pages of Hume, may, if they will look narrowly, gather so much as this. "Agreeable to the present prosperity of public affairs," says Hume, "was the universal joy and festivity diffused throughout the nation. The melancholy austerity of the fanatics fell into discredit, together with their principles. The royalists, who had ever affected a contrary disposition, found in their recent success new motives for mirth and gaiety; and it now belonged to them to give repute and fashion to their manners.

From past experience it had sufficiently appeared that gravity was very distinct from wisdom, formality from virtue, and hypocrisy from religion. The king himself, who bore a strong propensity to pleasure, served, by his powerful and engaging example, to banish those sour and malignant humours, which had hitherto engendered such confusion And though the just bounds were undoubtedly passed, when once returned from their former extreme, yet was the public happy in exchanging vices, pernicious to society, for disorders, hurtful chiefly to the individuals themselves who were guilty of them."

This means simply that the nation, under the example of the king and the royalists, having thrown off the *vices* and vicious restraints of gravity, formality, and hypocrisy, so generally pernicious to society, became almost entirely abandoned to the more individual "*disorders*" of profligacy and sensual licentiousness. They were happy in exchanging "those sour and malignant humours" for the more luscious and generous qualities of sin. The Restoration, says Bishop Burnet, brought with it the throwing off the very professions of virtue and piety; and all ended in entertainments and drunkenness, which overran the three kingdoms.

As the reign began so it continued; and it was a period when just such men, as God had been preparing in the case of Bunyan, were most needed; just such men also, as he had ready in Baxter, Owen, Howe, and a multitude of others, perhaps quite equal in piety, though not so distinguished as these. So was fulfilled the great principle, that when the Enemy cometh in like a flood, then the Spirit of the Lord shall lift up a standard against him.

As to the measures of this reign for the destruction of religious liberty, with which more especially we are now concerned, it opened with what is called the Corporation Act, by which, in defiance of all the king's previous stipulations, all persons, whose religious principles constrained them conscientiously to refuse conformity to the established Episcopal Church, were at once expelled and excluded from every branch of the magistracy, and rendered incapable of serving their country in the meanest civil offices.

Next followed the memorable statute against the Society of Friends, by which upwards of four thousand persons were cast into prison for their religious scruples, and treated with the utmost cruelty, with even a savage barbarity.

In the second year of this reign, 1662, came the Act of Uniformity, suppressing by force all diversity of religious opinions, imposing the book of Common Prayer, and reviving for this purpose the whole terrific penal laws of preceding reigns. This was to take effect from the feast day of St Bartholomew, in 1662; the day of a former well-known dreadful massacre of Protestants in Paris, and other French cities, the 24th of August 1572, nearly an hundred years previous; and a day, on which more than two thousand conscientious ministers were silenced, ejected from their pulpits, and thrown into persecution and poverty. For these men to preach, or conduct public worship, was made a penal offence against the state; and among these men are such names as those of Owen, Bates, Manton, Goodwin, Baxter, and Howe; towards whom that very cruelty was enacted by the Established Church of England, which, in the case of the Jewish Church, is said to have filled up the measure of its crimes, and prepared the Jewish people for the divine vengeance; "forbidding the apostles to speak to the Gentiles, that they might be saved." No matter how holy, nor how eminently useful the body of the non-conforming clergy might be; the act would have passed, it has truly been said, though the measure had involved the eternal misery of half the nation.

Of this act Hume himself says (and I like to take authorities of which it may be said, *our enemies themselves being judges*); Hume himself says that in it the Church party gladly laid hold of the prejudices (the conscientious scruples) which prevailed among the Presbyterians, "in order to eject them from their livings. By the Bill of Uniformity it was required that every clergyman should be reordained, if he had not before received Episcopal ordination; should declare his assent to every thing contained in the book of Common Prayer; should take the oath of canonical obedience; should abjure the Solemn League and Covenant; and should renounce the principle of taking arms, on any pretence whatsoever, against the king. This bill reinstated the Church in the same condition in which it stood before the commencement of the Civil Wars; and as the old persecuting laws of Elizabeth still subsisted in their full vigour, and new clauses of a like nature were now enacted, all the king's promises of toleration and of indulgence to tender consciences were thereby eluded and broken." The same historian observes, that the ecclesiastical form of government, according to the Presbyterian discipline, is "more favourable to *liberty* than to *royal power;*" and hence the readiness of Charles to break all promises of tolerance which he had made for the gaining of the throne, and to produce an iron uniformity of ecclesiastical subjection, in which he might break down all the defences raised against regal encroachments. The spirit of religious liberty always has been, and ever must be, the world's greatest safeguard against the oppression of political tyranny.

Two years after this statute came the memorable Conventicle Act, in 1664. It was found that these holy clergymen, though banished from their own pulpits, would preach, and that people would hear; preach any where, and hear any where; in dens and caves of the earth, in barns and private houses, so it were but the gospel. To put a stop to this, and to extirpate all public worship not within the walls of Episcopal consecration, the barbarous statute of a preceding reign was declared in force, which condemned all persons refusing to attend the public worship appointed by the State to banishment; and in case of return, to death without benefit of clergy. It was then enacted, that if any person should be present at any assembly, conventicle, or meeting, under colour or pretence of any exercise of religion in other manner than is allowed by the Liturgy or practice of the Church of England; or if any person shall suffer any such meeting in his house, barn, yard, woods, or grounds; they should, for the first and second offence, be thrown into jail or fined; for the third offence, transported for seven years, or fined a hundred pounds; and in case of return of escape after such transportation, death without benefit of clergy! Troops of horse and foot were on the alert, to break up such meetings; the ravages and forfeitures for this crime of religious worship according to conscience became very great; the jails were filled with prisoners; others were transported as convicts; other whole families emigrated; informers were multiplied, and the defence and security of life, liberty, and property, in the trial by jury, were broken down.

Next came the Great Plague, in which the Non-conformist clergy, having before been driven from their pulpits by power of persecution, the Established clergy fled from theirs through fear of death. But when men fled who feared death more than God, then those men entered their places who feared nothing but God. They came, those same persecuted and silenced clergy, when the Court and Parliament had removed to Oxford, and the hirelings had fled from their flocks, they came, in defiance of law and contagion, and ministered the bread of life to pale multitudes, at altars from which they would have been driven with penal inflictions in the season of health. But this too must be stopped; and therefore, by this very Parliament sitting in Oxford through fear of the plague in London, and to shut out those men who entered with the gospel where others dared not enter, a fresh penal law was enacted, by which, unless they would take an oath that the Earl of Southampton declared in parliament no honest man could take, all Non-conformist ministers were banished five miles from any city, town, or borough that sent members to parliament, and five miles from any place whatsoever where they had, at any time in a number of years past, preached. This savage act produced, of course, great suffering; but it also called into exercise great endurance and patience for Christ's sake. Ministers who would not sacrifice their duty to God and their people, and who had to be concealed at a distance, sometimes rode thirty or forty miles to preach to their flocks in the night, fleeing again from their persecutors before the dawn of day.

In 1670, the barbarous Conventicle Act was renewed with still greater severity; the trial by jury in case of offenders was destroyed; no warrant to be reversed by reason of any default in the form; persons to be seized wherever they could be found, informers encouraged and rewarded; and justices punished who would not execute the law. Archbishop Sheldon addressed a circular letter to all the bishops of his province, commanding them to take notice of all offenders, and to aid in bringing them to punishment. The Bishop of Peterborough declared publicly concerning this law, that "It hath done its business against all fanatics, except the Quakers; but when the parliament sits again, a stronger law will be made, not only to take away their lands and goods, *but also to sell them for bond slaves.*" The magistracy became, it has been truly remarked, under this law, an encouragement to *evil doers*, and a punishment of those *who did well.*

We shall pursue no further the history of political and ecclesiastical cruelty in this arbitrary persecuting reign. It is enough to make the very name of the union of Church and State abhorred in the mind of every man who has a spark of generosity or freedom in his composition. Thus much was absolutely necessary to illustrate the life of Bunyan, and the providence and grace of God in the age where God placed him. It was an age for the formation and intrepid action of great minds; it was also an age for the development of apostolic piety, and endurance of suffering, on the part of men and ministers who chose to obey God rather than man. If great qualities and great capacities of virtue existed, there were great flames to try them; sharp tools and terrible, to cut and polish the hidden jewels of the Saviour.

Into this age Bunyan was thrown; a great pearl, sunk in deep and troubled waters, out of which God's Spirit would in due time draw it, and place it in a setting where its glorious lustre should attract the admiration of the world. There were along with him great men, and men of great piety, both in the Established Church and out of it. He was born in the village of Elstow, in the year 1628—thirty years after the death of Spenser, twelve years after the death of Shakspeare, when Milton was in his twentieth year, and three years before the birth of Dryden. Bunyan's life and times were also Baxter's, Baxter being but thirteen years the oldest. Bunyan died in 1688, Milton in 1674, Baxter in 1691. Owen was another contemporary, 1616–1683. John Howe was another, born 1630. Philip Henry was another, born 1631. The sweet poet George Herbert should be named as another. Matthew Poole was another, born 1623. Thomas Goodwin was another, born in 1600. Lord Chief-Justice Hale was another, born in 1609. Cudworth was born in 1617; Henry More was born in 1614, and died in 1687, a year before the death of Bunyan; Archbishop Usher and Bishop Hall both of them died in 1656. Taking these names together, you have a striking picture of the great richness of the age, both in piety and genius—an ascending series of great minds and good men from every rank and party.

But, for complete originality of genius, Bunyan, all things considered, stands foremost amongst them all. The form of his work, the nature of the subject, and its creation so completely out of the depths of his own soul, unaided by learning or art, place it before every other uninspired production. Without the teaching of the Spirit of God, the genius of the poet, though he were Shakspeare himself, could no more have pourtrayed the inward life of the soul by external images and allegories, than a man born blind could paint the moon and the stars, the flowers, the forests, and the foliage. The education of Bunyan was an education for eternity, under the power of the Bible and the schooling of the Holy Spirit. This is all that the pilgrims in this world really need to make them good, great, powerful. But, set aside the Bible, and in Bunyan's education there was not one of the elements out of which the genius and learning of his contemporaries gathered strength and richness. Baxter was not, any more than Bunyan, a child of the universities; but Baxter's intellect was sharpened by a great exercise with the schoolmen; though, even if this discipline had been entirely wanting in Baxter's development, the result, on the whole, might not have been less happy, nay, it might have been richer. He would not have preached with less fervour, nor less scriptural power and beauty; and, though he might not have been so keen a disputant, so subtle a casuist, yet we cannot believe that his Saint's Rest would have lost one ray of its heavenly glory. Neither would the Pilgrim's Progress have gained in its beauty or its truth,—it would have lost in both,—had Bunyan's soul been steeped in that scholastic discipline, without which, the learned Selden used to say, a divine knows nothing logically; just as if the Bible were not the best logic in the world! Bunyan never heard of Thomas Aquinas, it is true, and he scarcely knew the philosophical meaning of the word Logic any more than a breathing child, whose pulse beats freely, knows the place of its heart, or the movement of its lungs; but Bunyan wrote the Pilgrim's Progress for all that; which, indeed, is itself the sweet logic of Celestial Love.

Bunyan's own life is an illustration of the guidance of Divine Providence, as clearly as his Pilgrim's Progress is a delineation of the work of the Divine Spirit. And perhaps the Providence of God, in the education of this man, may be traced quite as distinctly in the things from which he shut out Bunyan's soul, in order to prepare him for his mission, as in the influences by which he surrounded him. The fountains from which he was prevented drinking, though other men drank to the full, and almost worshipped the springs, it was better to keep sealed from his soul, if the pure river of the water of life was to flow through his pages. This peculiarity of his training fitted him to be one of the most original writers in the world. Almost the only books Bunyan ever read, at least before he wrote the Pilgrim's Progress, were the Bible, the Book of Martyrs, a copy of Luther on Galatians, and two volumes, the Plain Man's Path-way to Heaven, and the Practice of Piety, which formed the marriage portion of his wife. Foxe's old Book of Martyrs had, next to the Bible, a great and thrilling power over Bunyan's spirit.

Bunyan has given an account of his own conversion and life, especially of the workings of the grace of God, and the guidance of his providence, in a little work entitled Grace Abounding to the Chief of Sinners. It is powerfully written, though with extreme and studied plainness; and almost all the material obtained and worked into various shapes by his various biographers was gained in that book. It is deeply interesting, and in following its delineation I shall mark some successive particulars, in which the providence and grace of God are clearly illustrated, and which, on a comparison with the Pilgrim's Progress, make it evident at once that in that work Bunyan was following his own experience, and that in such experience, God was so ordering all things as to fit Bunyan for that work.

As you read the Grace Abounding you are ready to say at every step, Here is the future author of Pilgrim's Progress. It is as if you stood beside some great sculptor, and watched every movement of his chisel, having had his design described to you beforehand, so that at every blow some new trait of beauty in the future statue comes clearly into view. In the Grace Abounding you see at every step the work of the Divine Artist on one of the most precious living stones that ever his wisdom and mercy selected in this world to shine in the glory of his living temple. Nay, to lay aside every figure but that employed by the Holy Spirit, you see the refiner's fire, and the crucible, and the gold in it, and the Heavenly Refiner himself sitting by it, and bending over it, and carefully removing the dross, and tempering the heat, and watching and waiting for his own perfect image. How beautiful, how sacred, how solemn, how interesting, how thrilling the process!

But with Bunyan it begins in dreams. Would you think it? Indeed it is no illusion, but the very beginning of God's refining work on Bunyan's soul. The future dreamer for others was himself visited with dreams, and this is the first point which I mark, where the providence and grace of God are illustrated together; for it is the first point which Bunyan himself has noted down, after describing the iniquity of his childhood, " in cursing, swearing, lying, and blaspheming the holy name of God." "Yea," says he, "so settled and rooted was I in these things, that they became as a second nature to me; the which, as I have also with soberness considered since, did so offend the Lord, that even in my childhood he did scare and affrighten me with fearful dreams, and did terrify me with fearful visions. For often after I had spent this and the other day in sin, I have in my bed been greatly afflicted while asleep, with the apprehensions of devils and wicked spirits, who still, as I then thought, laboured to draw me away with them, of which I never could be rid." If now you would have a glimpse of the nature of these terrifying dreams, with which Bunyan's sinful childhood was visited, you have only to turn to your Pilgrim's Progress, and there read the powerful description of the last sight shewn to Christian in the House of the Interpreter. There you have the manner in which, even in Bunyan's childish soul, his partly awakened conscience, with his vivid imagination, and the word and the Spirit of God, wrestled together. And now, before leaving this point for another, let me call your attention to a text strikingly illustrative of it, which I marvel that Bunyan himself had not used, to which none of his biographers, that I am aware of, save one, in dwelling upon his early experience, have referred, but which, in the unconverted state of a man made afterwards by God's grace so signally useful, receives, as well as reflects, a very striking illustration. It is that remarkable passage in Job, where the Divine Spirit is recounting the discipline of God with his creatures for the salvation of their souls. "For God speaketh once, yea twice, yet man perceiveth it not. In a dream, in a vision of the night, when deep sleep falleth upon men, in slumberings upon the bed; then he openeth the ears of men, and sealeth their instruction, that he may withdraw man from his purpose, and hide pride from man." You may find this in the thirty-third chapter, and the whole is worthy of studying. Bunyan not only in his childhood, but all his life, was made the subject of such discipline.

The next point which I shall select as an illustration of Divine Providence in Bunyan's life, sets us down with him in the Parliamentary army, as a soldier. It was probably in 1645, at the siege of Leicester. He was drawn to be one of the besiegers; but when he was just ready to go upon this perilous service, one of the company desired to go in his room; "to which," says Bunyan, "when I had consented, he took my place; and coming to the siege, as he stood sentinel, he was shot in the head with a musket bullet, and died." At this time he was seventeen years of age. "Here," says Bunyan, "were judgments and mercy, but neither of them did awaken my soul to righteousness; wherefore I sinned still, and grew more and more rebellious against God, and careless of my own salvation." The providence of God in Bunyan's case was wonderfully similar to the instances recorded in the early life of John Newton; so were the recklessness and habits of profaneness, in which, notwithstanding these remarkable interpositions, he still persisted.

The next important point is Bunyan's marriage, at the time of which event he could not have been more than nineteen years of age. Upon this point we would not lay so much stress as to say with some, that it constituted Bunyan's salvation; but it was certainly a great step towards it. Being with a woman who had received from a godly father a religious education, it gave him a quiet, well-ordered home; and through the instrumentality of two excellent books, which his wife brought to him as her only marriage portion (the Plain Man's Pathway to Heaven, and the Practice of Piety), it begat in him some desires to reform his vicious life. He and his wife would read together in these books, and then young Mrs Bunyan would bring her own recollections of the godly life of her father in aid of her husband's better impulses. All these things together wrought upon him for an external reformation at least, and produced certain church-going habits, to fall in, as Bunyan says, "very eagerly with the religion of the times; to wit, to go to church twice a-day, and that too with the foremost; and there should very devoutly both say and sing, as others did, yet retaining my wicked life; but withal I was so overrun with the spirit of superstition, that I adored, and that with great devotion, even all things, both the high place, priest, clerk, vestment-service, and what else, belonging to the church; counting all things holy that were therein contained, and especially the priest and clerk most happy, and without doubt greatly blessed." "This conceit grew so strong in a little time upon my spirit, that, had I but seen a priest, though never so sordid and debauched in his life, I should find my spirit fall under him, reverence him, and knit unto him; yea, I thought for the love I did bear unto them, supposing they were the ministers of God, I could have laid down at their feet, and have been trampled on by them; their name, their garb, and work did so intoxicate and bewitch me."

This stage in Bunyan's experience is exceedingly curious and instructive; his mind seems to have been in that state of bondage which we call *priest-ridden;* heartily as he afterwards hated the pope, it would not have taken much, at this time, to have carried him completely over to Rome. Had he lived in our day, with such an experience, he would assuredly have made what some might be disposed to call a thorough-going Puseyite. Such was the intoxicating effect of the glare of religious formalism upon his soul, that he adored, and that with great devotion, all things belonging to the church. Mark the phraseology, and see if it does not wonderfully characterize some in our day. He did not adore God, but the church, and the things in it, and the forms of it, its altar, priest, clerk, vestments. Never was described more to the life that sentimental mixture of superstition and devotion, which, borrowing something from the Spirit, but bewildered and carried into ecstasies by the beauty of religious rites, rests in and worships, not the Saviour, but the form. In this state of mind, if Bunyan had seen a babe baptized, the holy water and the white robe of the priest, and the sign of the cross, would have made a much deeper impression on his soul, than the name of Father, Son, and Holy Ghost, named upon an immortal spirit. And now mark the intimate connection between this ecstatic reverence for priests and forms, and the belief that church membership, though merely by the apostolical succession of birth, constitutes salvation. Bunyan, finding in Scripture that the Israelites were once the peculiar people of God, concluded that if he could be found to have sprang from that race, his soul must needs be happy. He asked his father about it, but received an answer which destroyed all his hopes, for neither he nor his family were of the lineage of Israel.

It has been conjectured from this passage, that Bunyan's family were Gypsies, and that this was the reason why he asked his father if they were not descended from the Israelites, intending, if he found they were so descended, to have considered himself as belonging to the only true church, and all the rest of the world as entitled only to God's uncovenanted mercies, that is, to remediless perdition. There is no knowing to what extreme this state of mind might have carried Bunyan, had it lasted. As it was, it gave him an insight into the nature, power, and danger of formalism, which nothing else could have taught him, neither discipline nor instruction. "For all this while," he says, "I was not sensible of the danger and evil of sin; I was kept from considering that sin would damn me whatsoever religion I followed, unless I was found in Christ; nay, I never thought of him, nor whether there were such an one or no." There is no telling, I say, what might have been the end of this in Bunyan's soul; but now comes,—

A fourth point, specially illustrating the providence and grace of God, namely, a sermon which Bunyan heard on the holiness of the Sabbath, and the evil of breaking it. This ran directly athwart one of Bunyan's besetting sins; for notwithstanding his thorough Churchism, he says he took much delight in all manner of vice, and did solace himself especially therewith on the Sabbath day. He went home from this sermon to his dinner with a great load upon his conscience, but he soon shook it off, and after dinner went out with all zest to his sports and gaming. As suddenly as a miracle his convictions returned upon him. That very same day, as he was "in the midst of a game of cat, and having struck it one blow from the hole, just as I was about to strike it a second time, a voice did suddenly dart from heaven into my soul, which said, Wilt thou leave thy sins and go to heaven, or have thy sins and go to hell? At this I was put to an exceeding amaze; wherefore, leaving my cat upon the ground, I looked up to heaven, and was as if I had seen with the eyes of my understanding, the Lord Jesus looking down upon me, as being very hotly displeased with me, and as if he did severely threaten me with some grievous punishment for these and other ungodly practices."

"I had no sooner thus conceived in my mind, but suddenly this conclusion was fastened upon my spirit (for the former hint did set my sins again before my face), that I had been a great and grievous sinner, and that it was now too late for me to look after heaven; for Christ would not forgive me, nor pardon my transgressions. Then I fell to musing on this also; and while I was thinking of it, and fearing lest it should be so, I felt my heart sink in despair, concluding it was too late; and therefore I resolved in my mind to go on in sin; for, thought I, if the case be thus, my state is surely miserable; miserable if I leave my sins, and but miserable if I follow them; I can but be damned, and if I must be so, I had as good be damned for many sins, as damned for few. Thus I stood in the midst of my play, before all that then were present; but yet I told them nothing: but I say, having made this conclusion, I returned desperately to my sport again. The good Lord, whose mercy is unsearchable, forgive my transgressions!"

We should like to see a picture by the hand of a master, representing Bunyan in the midst of his game of cat, arrested thus suddenly by the fire of conviction flashing up in his soul, and thrown into this appalling reverie in the midst of his wondering companions, with the thoughts of his past life and of the coming judgment, flying through his awakened mind swifter than the lightning. What a scene was this, and how little could Bunyan's merry playmates have imagined the commotion in his soul! This rapid crowded moment must have been as a year to Bunyan; it was like those dreams, in which the soul lives a life-time in an hour. The words that were kindled with such power in Bunyan's conscience, that he seemed to hear them, may have been spoken to him in the very sermon to which he listened in the morning. But returning desperately from this dream of conscience to his sport, he shook off his convictions, resisted the Holy Ghost, and afterwards fell to cursing and swearing, and playing the madman at such a fearful rate, that even wicked people were astonished at him.

On one occasion, while he was garnishing his discourses, as he termed it, with oaths at the beginning and the end, an abandoned woman, who stood by, severely reproved him, and told his companions to quit his conversation, or he would make them as bad as himself. This strange and unexpected reproof of the bold blasphemer reached the child's heart, that still lived within him. He stood by the shop-window, and hung his head in silence; and the language, in which he has told the effect of this rebuke upon him, is a most exquisitely beautiful revelation of the simplicity of his nature, yet undestroyed amidst all his evil habits. "While I stood there," says he, "I wished with all my heart that I might be a little child again, that my father might learn me to speak without this wicked way of swearing." He thought himself so accustomed to it that he could not leave it off; but he did from that moment.

Bunyan's character was not unlike that of Peter. They seemed both to have been profane swearers; for the sudden outbreak of this devil in Peter, at the time of his denial of Christ, we take to be the reproduction of an early habit, and not a new one, assumed for the moment. The change wrought by divine grace in the character of Peter, of Bunyan, and of Christian in the Pilgrim's Progress, seems marvellously similar. Southey has observed, apparently by way of some excuse for the arrest of Bunyan by the Establishment, that his office of preaching may well be deemed incompatible with his calling. Perhaps the poet and historian had forgotten, or might never have had his attention directed to a passage, which he could have found in the Acts of the Apostles, descriptive of the early teachers and preachers of Christianity: "And because he was of the same craft, he abode with them and wrought: for by their occupation they were tent-makers." John Bunyan had no more need to be ashamed of his temporal, than of his spiritual calling; nor was there any such inconsistency between the two, as could form the most distant shadow of justification to a persecuting hierarchy for forbidding him to speak in the name of Christ, to the people. Indeed, had the tinker of Bedford been pursuing his humble occupation when

Matthew, Peter, and John were upon earth, his was a character of such native elements, that he might have been chosen as one of their associates in the work of the primitive Gospel ministry. Our Saviour committed the Gospel to unlearned, but not to ignorant men; and Bunyan, though illiterate, was not ignorant; no man is so, who believing with the heart in him who is the Light of the World, beholds spiritual realities, and acts with reference to them. "The fears," says Mr Coleridge in his Aids to Reflection, "the hopes, the remembrances, the anticipations, the inward and outward experience, the belief and the faith of a Christian, form of themselves a philosophy and a sum of knowledge, which a life spent in the grove of Academus or the painted Porch, could not have attained or collected."

The fifth point which I shall mention as illustrating both the providence and grace of God in preparing Bunyan for his great work, not only in converting his soul, and fitting him for the ministry, but preparing him for the painting of that beautiful map of the divine life in the Pilgrim's Progress, is the succession of characters he met with in his own experience. He worked his way, you are well aware, by the Spirit of God, out of the ignorance and vice by which he was surrounded, against much opposition, and with very little aid from any of his fellow-creatures. And yet, all along in his own experience, you meet the germ of those characters afterwards so fully developed, so vigorously painted, in the progress of his pilgrim. His mind was as a magic lantern, or camera obscura, through which every form and figure that fell upon it was revealed again in glowing life and beauty on the canvass. The first that I shall name is his own Mr Legality, who, however, afterwards became, in Bunyan's words, a devilish ranter, giving himself over to all manner of sin and wickedness. Under the influence of this man, and his pleasant talk of the Scriptures and the matter of religion, Bunyan, like his own Christian at first setting out, went to Mount Sinai. "Wherefore," he says, "I fell to some outward reformation, both in my words and life, and did set the commandments before me for my way to heaven; which commandments I also did strive to keep, and, as I thought, did keep them pretty well sometimes, and then I should have comfort; yet now and then should break one, and so afflict my conscience: but then I should repent, and say I was sorry for it, and promised God to do better next time, and then got help again; for then I thought I pleased God as well as any man in England. Thus I continued about a year; all which time our neighbours did take me to be a very godly man, a new and religious man, and did marvel much to see such a great and famous alteration in my life and manners, and indeed so it was, though I knew not Christ, nor grace, nor faith, nor hope; for, as I have well since seen, had I then died, my state had then been most fearful."

"But I say my neighbours were amazed at this my great conversion from prodigious profaneness to something like a moral life; and truly so they well might; for this my conversion was as great, as for Tom of Bedlam to become a sober man. Now therefore they began to praise, to commend, and to speak well of me, both to my face and behind my back. Now I was, as they said, become godly; now I was become a right honest man. But oh, when I understood these were their words and opinions of me, it pleased me mighty well. For though as yet I was nothing but a poor painted hypocrite, yet I loved to be talked of as one that was truly godly. I was proud of my godliness, and indeed I did all I did, either to be seen of, or to be well spoken of by men; and thus I continued for about a twelvemonth, or more."

Here he was, according to Mr Worldly Wiseman's directions, under Mount Sinai. But now the mountain began to quake and thunder at a dreadful rate, and flames came out of it, and threatened to consume him. He saw more of this afterwards; "But, poor wretch as I was," he says, "I was all this while ignorant of Jesus Christ, and going about to establish my own righteousness, and had perished therein, had not God in mercy shewed me more of my own state by nature."

At this very time, one of the happiest impulses and most remarkable helps he ever received in his spiritual conflicts, came from the conversation of three or four godly women sitting at a door in the sun, and talking joyfully of the things of God. Bunyan, busy at his occupation, drew near and listened like a child to all they said. "Methought," he says, "they spake as if joy did make them speak. They spake with much pleasantness of scripture language, and with such appearance of grace in all they said, that they were to me as if I had found a new world; as if they were a people that dwelt alone, and were not to be reckoned among their neighbours." These holy, happy women, sitting in the sun, may have dwelt as a sun-lit picture in Bunyan's imagination, till the vision was transfigured into that beautiful incident of the Three Shining Ones, who met Christian at the Cross, and gave him his robe and his roll. There were other incidents also, and lights in his experience, which contributed to form that picture; for Bunyan's was that great quality of genius, as well as of piety, which all unconsciously generalizes, and then combines into unity, even the most distant and separate events and experiences, that have a secret affinity, that spring from one principle or cause. The conversation of these holy, happy women, who evidently possessed an experience, such as he knew nothing of, set Bunyan at this time to questioning his own condition, and gave him an insight into the wickedness of his own heart, and the nature of true religion, and produced in him a longing desire after its blessedness, such as he never before possessed. The state and happiness of these poor people presented a lovely vision to him; and at length, after much conflict and inward temptation, he was persuaded to break his mind to them, and tell them his condition. And here he found sweet sympathy and guidance, for they were humble, happy, kind-hearted Christians, and as soon as they heard Bunyan's recital of his troubles, they ran and told their pastor, Mr Gifford, about him, and with how much joy we may well conceive. We may, perhaps, be reminded by these holy happy women of the three heavenly maidens, Prudence, Piety, and Charity, whose discourse with Christian was so rich, who shewed him the rarities of the House Beautiful, and who placed him for rest in a large upper chamber, whose windows opened to the sun-rising; the name of the chamber was Peace, where he slept till break of day, and then he awoke and sang.

And now came a new and blessed era in his religious life, for this "holy Mr Gifford" was a remarkable man, a man of deep piety and joy, and well prepared, by his own spiritual conflicts, to guide Bunyan through his. This man took Bunyan under his careful charge, and invited him to his house, where he could hear him converse with others about the dealings of God with their souls. This man was, indeed, the original of that delightful portrait of Evangelist in the Pilgrim's Progress, a character drawn from real life, being such an one as met Bunyan himself on his wandering way from the City of Destruction, "and expounded unto him the way of God more perfectly." Of this man, Bunyan afterwards says, "I sat under the ministry of holy Mr Gifford, whose doctrine, by God's grace, was much for my stability. This man made it much his business to deliver the people of God from all those hard and unsound tests, that by nature we are prone to. He would bid us take special heed that we took not up any truth upon trust, as from this or that, or any other man or men; but cry mightily to God that he would convince us of the reality thereof, and set us down therein, by his own Spirit in the holy word; for, said he, if you do otherwise, when temptation comes, if strongly upon you, you not having received them with evidence from heaven, will find you want that help and strength now to resist, which once you thought you had." This, Bunyan says, was "as seasonable to my soul as the former and latter rain in their season." The Spirit of God led Bunyan to act according to these directions; and this was, as we shall see, one great cause of his wonderful power in the scriptures.

Into this Baptist Church of Christ, under this holy pastor, Bunyan was received in the year 1653, when about twenty-five years of age. And now having traced him to this point, let me say a word in regard to that work, Grace Abounding, from which I have drawn my illustrations of Divine Providence and grace in Bunyan's life. I cannot close without recommending it to the very careful perusal of all, who would have a deeper relish and more thorough understanding of the beauties of the Pilgrim's Progress. It is a marvellous book, and cannot but be a precious book to every soul that reads it with a sober, prayerful spirit. Its pages are, next to the Pilgrim's Progress, invaluable. It is condensed, severe, and naked in its style, beneath the pent fire of Bunyan's feelings, and the pressure of his conscience, forbidding him to seek for beauty. He says of it himself; "I could have stepped into a style much higher than this, in which I have here discoursed, and could have adorned all things more than I have seemed to do ; but I dare not. God did not play in tempting of me ; neither did I play when the pangs of hell caught hold upon me, wherefore I may not play in relating of them ; but be plain and simple, and lay down the thing as it was. He that liketh it, let him receive it ; and he that doth not, let him produce a better." The very extreme plainness of this work adds to its power ; never was the inward life of any being depicted with more vehement and burning language ; it is an intensely interesting description of the workings of a mind of the keenest sensibility and most fervid imagination, convinced of guilt, and fully awake to all the dread realities of eternity.

Sometimes, with all its plainness and solemnity, it is almost comic, like Luther's own humour, as in the dialogues of Bunyan's soul with the Tempter. It possesses, indeed, the elements of a great spiritual drama. The Faust of Goethe is not to be compared with it for truth and depth and vividness. There are but few actors, but those how solemn, how grand, how awful ! An immortal spirit, and its great adversary the devil, are in almost unceasing conflict ; but such a stamp of reality, such discrimination, such flashing of lights, such crossing of the swords of Michael and of Satan, such a revelation of the power of divine truth, and of the blessed ministration of the Spirit of God, you can find nowhere else out of the Bible. It is a great battle ; heaven and hell are contending ; you have the gleam of armour, the roar of artillery, fire and smoke and blood-red vapour, in which ofttimes the combatants themselves are lost from your view.

You follow with intense interest the movements of Bunyan's

soul. You seem to see a lonely bark driving across the ocean in a hurricane. By the flashes of the lightning you can just discern her through the darkness, plunging and labouring fearfully in the midnight tempest, and you think that all is lost; but there again you behold her in the quiet sunshine; or the moon and the stars look down upon her, as the wind breathes softly; or, in a fresh and favourable gale, she flies across the flying waters. Now it is clouds and rain and hail and rattling thunder, storms coming down as sudden, almost, as the lightning; and now again her white sails glitter in heaven's light, like an Albatross in the spotless horizon. The last glimpse you catch of her, she is gloriously entering the harbour, the haven of eternal rest; yea, you see her like a star, that in the morning of eternity dies into the light of Heaven. Can there be any thing more interesting, than thus to follow the perilous course of an immortal soul, from danger to safety, from conflict to victory, from temptation to triumph, from suffering to blessedness, from the City of Destruction to the City of God?

Bunyan's genius I had almost said was *created* by his piety; the fervour and depth of his religious feelings formed its most important elements of power, and its materials to work upon. His genius also pursued a path dictated by his piety, and one that no other being in the world ever pursued before him. The light that first broke through his darkness was light from heaven. It found him, even that being who wrote the Pilgrim's Progress, coarse, profane, boisterous, and almost brutal. It shone before him, and with a single eye he followed it, till his native City of Destruction could no longer be seen in the distance, till his moral deformities fell from him, and his garments became purity and light. The Spirit of God was his teacher; the very discipline of his intellect was a spiritual discipline; the conflicts that his soul sustained with the powers of darkness were the very sources of his intellectual strength.

Southey called the experience of this man, in one stage of it, a burning and feverish enthusiasm. The poet Cowper, in one of his beautiful letters to Lady Hesketh, after describing his own feelings, remarks. " What I have written would appear like enthusiasm to many, for we are apt to give that name to every warm affection of the mind in others, which we have not experienced in ourselves." It would have been the truth, as well as the better philosophy, if Southey had said that the Spirit of God was preparing Bunyan, by that severe discipline, to send forth into the world the Pilgrim's Progress. And when he was at length prepared for the task, then an overruling Providence placed him, through the instrumentality of his own enemies, in the prison of Bedford to accomplish it.

Bunyan's imagination was powerful enough, in connection with his belief in God's superintending providence, to array his inward trials with a sensible shape, and external events with a light reflected from his own experience; hopes and fears were friends and enemies, acting in concert with them; all things he met with in the world were friends or enemies likewise, according as they aided or opposed his spiritual life. He acted always under one character, the Christian soldier, realizing in his own conflicts and conquests the progress of his own Pilgrim. Therefore his book is a perfect reality in oneness as a whole, and in every page a book not of imagination and shadows, but of realities experienced. To those who have never set out on this pilgrimage, nor encountered its dangers, it is interesting, as would be a book powerfully written of travels in an unknown romantic land. Regarded as a work of original genius simply, without taking into view its spiritual meaning, it is a wonder to all, and cannot cease to be. Though a book of personification and allegory, it enchants the simplest child, as powerfully, almost, as the story of Aladdin and his Lamp, or the Adventures of Sinbad the Sailor, or the history of Robinson Crusoe himself. It is interesting to all who have any taste for poetical beauty, in the same manner as Spenser's Fairy Queen, or we might mention, especially for the similar absorbing interest we take in all that happens to the hero, the Odyssey of Homer.

And yet its interest for the imagination is in reality the smallest portion of its power; and it will be pleasing to the imagination just in proportion as the mind of the reader has been accustomed to interpret the things of this life by their connection with another, and by the light that comes from that world to this. A reader who has not formed this habit, nor ever felt that he is a stranger and pilgrim in a world of temptations and snares, can see but half the beauty of such poetry as fills this work, because it cannot make its appeal to his own experience; for him there is nothing within, that tells more certainly than any process of judgment or criticism the truth and sweetness of the picture; there is no reflection of its images, nor interpretation of its meaning in his own soul. The Christian, the actual pilgrim, reads it with another eye. It comes to his heart. It is like a painting meant to be exhibited by fire-light; the common reader sees it by day. To the Christian it is a glorious transparency; and the light that shines through it, and gives its incidents such life, its colours such depth, and the whole scene such a surpassing glory, is light from eternity, the meaning of heaven.

I repeat it, therefore, as truth very evident, that the true beauty of the allegory in the Pilgrim's Progress can be felt only by a religious mind. No one, indeed, can avoid admiring it. The honest nature in the characters, their homely truth, the simplicity and good sense of the conversations, the beauty of the incidents, the sweetness of the scenery through which the reader is conducted, the purity of the language,

"The humorous vein, strong sense, and simple style,
To teach the gayest, make the gravest smile;"

all these things to the eye of the severest critic are beautiful, and he who loves to read Shakspeare will admire them, and on common ground. But such a reader, in respect to the veiled beauty of the allegory, is like a deaf man, to whom you speak of the sweetness of musical sounds. Of the faithfulness with which Bunyan has depicted the inward trials of the Christian conflict; of the depth and power of the appeal which that book makes to the Christian's heart; of the accuracy and beauty of the map therein drawn of the dealings of the Spirit of God in leading the sinner from the City of Destruction to Mount Zion above; he knows and can conceive nothing. It is like Milton's daughters reading aloud from his Hebrew Bible to the blind poet, while they could only pronounce the words, but were ignorant of the sacred meaning, nor could divine the nature of the inspiration it excited in his soul. Little can such a reader see

> "Of all that power of prospect,
> Whereof many thousands tell."

And I might go on to express, in Wordsworth's delightful poetry, what is the utmost of the admiration excited by a common, and not a Christian perusal of the Pilgrim's Progress :—

> "The western sky did recompense us well
> With Grecian Temple, minaret and bower;
> And in one part a minster with its tower
> Substantially expressed.
>   Many a glorious pile
> Did we beheld; fair sights that might repay
> All disappointment. And as such the eye
> Delighted in them; but we felt the while
> We should forget them.
> The grove, the sky-built temple, and the dome
> Though clad in colours beautiful and pure,
> Find in the heart of man no natural home.
> The immortal mind craves objects that endure."

Yes! it is perfectly true that no critical admiration of this work, overlooking its immortal meaning, sees any thing of its enduring beauty; to look at it aright, we need a portion of the same spiritual faith by which it was inspired, by which only it can be explained.

> "Who scoffs these sympathies
> Makes mock of the Divinity within."

In the light of eternity, this book is as far superior to a common poem of this world, or of man's temporal being and affections, as the soul of man is superior to the clod it inhabits. Whatever connects itself with man's spiritual being, turns his attention to spiritual interest and realities, and rouses his imagination to take hold on eternity, possesses, the mere philosopher would say, a dignity and power with which nothing else can be invested. Religion does this. In her range of contemplation there is truer and deeper poetry, than in the whole world, and all man's being else. Dr Johnson, in his Life of Waller, advances the strange opinion, that devotion is not a fit subject for poetry, and in his dogmatical way dedicates some space to an inquiry why it is so. "Contemplative poetry," he says, "or the intercourse between God and the human soul, cannot be poetical. Man, admitted to implore the mercy of his Creator, is already in a higher state than poetry can confer. The essence of poetry is invention; such invention as, by producing something unexpected, surprises and delights. The topics of devotion are few, and being few, are universally known; but few as they are, they can be made no more; they can receive no grace from novelty of sentiment, and very little from novelty of expression." In this sweeping style Johnson proceeds with criticism that, notwithstanding our deference for his great intellect, might be shewn, on philosophical grounds, to be as poor, as the assertions are authoritative. The very definition of poetry is a most degrading one; and it is the only one to which the reasoning will at all apply; the whole passage shews what a low estimate and false views the "wits" of the "Augustan Age" of English literature possessed of the greatest of all intellectual subjects. It would not have been thought that a being who could admire the Pilgrim's Progress as Johnson did, would have reasoned in this manner. That book itself is a refutation of the sentiment quoted; so is Cowper's Task; so is Blair's Grave; so is even George Herbert's little volume of Devotional Poetry.

And how can it be otherwise? If man is not a mere creature of this world; if his vision is not restricted to the shadows that have closed around him; if he is connected with another, an eternal world, a world of higher intelligences, of angels, and arch-angels, and beings free from sin—a world, where the Creator of this and of all worlds manifests his immediate presence, where the veil of flesh will no longer be held before the eye of the soul;—and if, by the revelation which God has made, and by communion with his Maker through Him who is the Way, the Truth, and the Life, man becomes acquainted by inward experience, and by that faith which is the soul's spiritual vision, with the powers of that world to come;—then will those far-seen visions, and all the objects of this world on which light from that world falls, and all man's thoughts, affections, and movements in regard to that world, possess an interest, and wear a glory, that makes them more appropriately the province of the poetical imagination than any other subjects in the universe. And the poetry of this world will rise in magnificence, in proportion as it borrows or reflects the light from that.

> "From worlds not quickened by the sun
> A portion of the gift is won:
> An intermingling of Heaven's pomp is spread
> On ground which British shepherds tread!"

All truth, to the humble mind, is poetry: spiritual truth is eminently so. We long to witness a better understanding of its sublime laws, an acknowledgment of its great fountain, and a more worthy appreciation of its nature ; to have it felt and acknowledged that there is poetry in this world, only because light from heaven shines upon it ; because it is full of hieroglyphics, whose meaning points to the eternal world ; because man is immortal, and this world is only the habitation of his infancy, and possesses power to rouse his imagination only in proportion as it is invested with moral grandeur by his own wonderful destiny; and by the light reflected down upon it from the habitation of angels. All on earth is shadow, and all in heaven is substance. Truly as well as feelingly did Burke exclaim, "What shadows we are, and what shadows we pursue!" We are encompassed by shadows and flitting apparitions and semi-transparencies, that wear the similitude of greatness, only because they are near us, and interposed between our vision and the world of eternal reality and light. Man of the world! you know not what poetry is, till you know God, and can hail in every created thing the manifestation of omnipresent Deity! Look at the highest creations of the art, and behold how they owe their power over the human soul to the presence of the idea of that Being, the thought of whom transfigures the movements of the imagination with glory, and makes language itself almost divine! What is it that gives to Coleridge's Hymn before Sunrise in the Vale of Chamouney, the deep, unutterable sublimity, that awes the soul into worship, and suffuses the eye with swelling tears? What, but the thought of Him, to whose praise that stupendous mountain, with its sky-pointing peaks and robe of silent cataracts, rises like a cloud of incense from the earth ?—

> " Motionless torrents! silent cataracts!
> Who made you glorious as the gates of heaven
> Beneath the keen, full moon? Who bade the sun
> Clothe you with rainbows? Who, with living flowers,
> Of loveliest blue, spread garlands at your feet?
> God! Let the torrents, like a shout of nations,
> Answer—and let the ice-plains echo, God!
> And they too have a voice, yon piles of snow,
> And in their perilous fall shall thunder, God!"

There is a spiritual world, and it is a world of light and grandeur! Man's relation to it is the greatest theme that poet or philosopher ever yet exercised his powers upon. It broods over him like the day, a master o'er a slave.

> " A presence which is not to be put by!"

The truths that man is fallen, exposed because of sin to the just indignation of God, in peril of his soul for ever, the object of all the stupendous histories and scenes of revelation recorded in the Bible, surrounded by dangers, and directed how to avoid them, pointed to heaven, and told what to do that he may enter there, and watched in all his course with anxiety by heavenly spirits, do, rightly considered, throw round every spiritual movement a thrilling, absorbing interest; an interest, for the individual who knows and feels it personally, too deep and awful, till he is in a place of safety, to be the subject of poetry. He can no more command attention to the sublimity of his situation, than Lot, hurried by the hand of the angel to Zoar, with the storm of fire rushing after him, could have stood to admire burning Sodom and Gomorrah. It was not amidst his distressing conflicts with the enemy, when it seemed as if his soul would be wrested from his body, that a thought of the Pilgrim's Progress came in upon the Author's mind. It was when the Fiend had spread his dragon wings and fled for ever, and the hand came to him with leaves from the Tree of Life, and the presence of God gladdened him, and on the mountain summit, light shone around him, and a blessed prospect stretched before him, with the Celestial City at its close, that that sweet vision rose upon his view. To the Pilgrim, looking back from a safe resting-place, all the way is fraught with poetical recollections and associations. His imagination now sees a spiritual life full of beauty. In the new light that shines upon him, he loves to retrace it again and again, and to lift his hands in grateful, speechless wonder at the unutterable goodness of the Lord of the Way. He is like Jacob, sleeping in the open air of Padan-aram, and dreaming of heaven. Angels of God are ascending and descending continually before his sight. His are no longer the

> "Blank misgivings of a creature
> Moving about in worlds not realized,"

but the rejoicings of a weary Pilgrim, on whose forehead the mark of Heaven has been placed, and who sees close at hand his everlasting rest. Once within the strait gate, and in the holy confidence of being a Pilgrim bound from the City of Destruction to the City of Immanuel, and all past circumstances of trial or danger, or of unexpected relief and security, wear a charmed aspect. Light from a better world shines upon them. Distance softens and lends enchantment to the view. Proof from experience as well as warnings from above, shew how many dangerous places he has passed, how many concealed and malignant enemies were here and there lying in ambush around him, and in how many instances there were hairbreadth escapes from ruin. There were the Slough of Despond, the fiery darts at the entrance to the Wicket Gate, the hill Difficulty, that pleasant arbour where he lost his roll of assurance, the lions that so terrified him, when in the darkness of evening he could not see that they were chained; there was that dark valley of the Shadow of Death, and that dread conflict with Apollyon before it. There were those fearful days and nights passed in the Dungeon of the Castle of Giant Despair, and the joyful escape from his territories. There were the Land Beulah, and the Delectable Mountains, and the Enchanted Ground, and all the glimpses of the Holy City, not dream-like, but distinct and full of glory, breaking in upon the vision, to last in the savour of them, for many days and nights of the blessed pilgrimage! Ingenious Dreamer, who could invest

a life of such realities with a colouring so full of Heaven!
Who can wonder at the affectionate sympathy, with which
a heart like Cowper's was wont to turn to thee?

> " And e'en in transitory life's late day
> That mingled all his brown with sober gray,
> Revere the man, whose PILGRIM marks the road,
> And guides the PROGRESS of the soul to God."

LECTURE SECOND.

Bunyan's Temptations.

The Valley of the Shadow of Death in Bunyan's experience—Blasphemous suggestions of Satan—Bunyan's meeting with Luther—Conflict of scripture with scripture in his mind—The fiery darts of the Wicked One—Power of conscience by the aid of memory—Bunyan's intense study of the Bible—Secret of his power in preaching—Of the purity and simplicity of his style—Bunyan's call to the ministry—Existence and agency of Satan as the Tempter and Adversary of Mankind.

WE come now to a great and important subject—Bunyan's temptations. In the midst of deep and terrible convictions of sin, he received great comfort and joy on hearing a sermon preached on the love of Christ. He was so taken with the love and mercy of God, as he says, that he could scarcely contain himself till he got home. To use his own graphic language, "I thought I could have spoken of his love, and have told of his mercy to me, even to the crows that sat upon the ploughed lands before me, had they been capable to have understood me; wherefore I said to my soul with much gladness, Well, I would I had a pen and ink here, I would write this down before I go any farther; for surely I will not forget this forty years hence." But now very speedily began to be renewed the great power of inward temptation upon him. I must tell the warning he had of it, and the beginning of it, in his own words. "Now, about a week or fortnight after this, I was much followed by this scripture—*Simon, Simon, behold Satan hath desired to have you ;* and sometimes it would sound so loud within me, yea, and as it were call so strongly after me, that once, above all the rest, I turned my head over my shoulder, thinking verily that some man behind me had called me ; being at a great distance, methought he called so loud. It came, as I have thought since, to have stirred me up to watchfulness ; it came to acquaint me that a cloud and a storm was coming down upon me. But so foolish was I and ignorant, that I knew not the reason of this sound, only I mused and wondered in my mind that at this rate, so often and so loud, it should still be sounding and rattling in mine ears. But I soon perceived the end of God therein.

" For about the space of a month after, a very great storm came down upon me, which handled me twenty times worse than all I had met with before ; it came stealing upon me, now by one piece, then by another ; first, all my comfort was taken from me ; then darkness seized upon me, after which whole floods of blasphemies, both against God, Christ, and the Scriptures, were poured upon my spirit, to my great confusion and astonishment." He was tempted to question the very being of God and of Christ, and, in burning language, he continues the description of these fearful suggestions, many of which he says he dare not utter, neither by word nor pen, which nevertheless for the space of a whole year did, with their number, continuance, and fiery force, seize upon and overweigh his heart. " Now I thought, surely I am possessed of the devil ; again I thought I should be bereft of my wits ; for instead of lauding and magnifying God the Lord with others, if I have heard him spoken of, presently some most horrible blasphemous thought or other would bolt out of my heart against him ; which things did sink me into very deep despair, for I concluded that such things could not possibly be found amongst them that loved God."

The provocations by which he was beset are indeed almost too terrible to be spoken of. It is a wonder that he was kept from absolute despair. He was especially distressed in this manner whenever he attempted an attendance on any of the ordinances of God, when he was at

prayer, when he was labouring to compose his mind, and fix it upon God; such distracting temptations would rush upon him as are almost inconceivable. Sometimes, in the midst of all this, his heart was so hard, that if he could have given a thousand pounds for a tear, he could not have shed one. Yet at times he had strong and heart-affecting apprehensions of God and divine truth; and then, oh! with what eagerness, in such intervals of relief, did his soul pour itself forth with inexpressible groanings for God's mercy; his whole soul in every word. And then again the Tempter would be upon him with such discouragements as these:—
"'You are very hot after mercy, but I will cool you; this frame shall not last always; many have been as hot as you for a season, but I have quenched their zeal.' And with this such and such who were fallen off would be set before mine eyes. Then would I be afraid that I should do so too; but, thought I, I am glad this comes into my mind; well, I will watch and take what care I can. 'Though you do,' said Satan, 'I shall be too hard for you: I will cool you insensibly by degrees, by little and little. What care I,' saith he, 'though I be seven years in chilling your heart, if I can do it at last? Continual rocking will lull a crying child asleep; I will ply it close, but I will have my end accomplished. Though you be burning hot at present, yet I can pull you from this fire; I shall have you cold before it be long.'"

Was ever anything more natural than this? Was ever more solemn truth couched in such a dialogue, of which the very sarcasm and humour is awful? It was the taunting of the devil; but Bunyan's heart, once set on fire by divine grace, was not so easy to cool as Satan at this time thought for. The poor Pilgrim was well nigh in despair under his fierce enemy, but he kept up his crying and pleading with God. Little did he think at this time how gracious and powerful a friend was near him, for he could not see the Heavenly Refiner watching over this child, his jewel, guarding the furnace and tempering its heat. Neither could his great adversary see him, or surely he would have left his devilish work in despair. The passage reminds me of a place in the Pilgrim's Progress, of which it is so evidently the germ, that I must refer you to it. It is one of those instructive sights which Christian was indulged with, and instructed by, in the house of the Interpreter. You recollect that the "Interpreter took Christian by the hand, and led him into a place where was a fire burning against a wall, and one standing by it always casting much water upon it to quench it; yet did the fire burn brighter and hotter. Then said Christian, What means this? The Interpreter answered, This fire is the work of grace that is wrought in the heart; he that casts water upon it to extinguish and put it out, is the devil; but in that thou seest the fire notwithstanding burn higher and hotter, thou shalt also see the reason of that. So he had him about to the backside of the wall, where he saw a man with a vessel of oil in his hand, of which he did also continually cast, but secretly, into the fire. Then said Christian, What means this? The Interpreter answered, This is Christ, who continually, with the oil of his grace, maintains the work already begun in the heart, by the means of which, notwithstanding what the devil can do, the souls of his people prove gracious still; and in that thou sawest that the man stood behind the wall to maintain the fire, this is to teach thee that it is hard for the tempted to see how this work of grace is maintained in the soul."

You will also read, if you wish to see another passage of great beauty that grew out of these dreadful temptations, the account of Christian's fight with Apollyon in the Valley of Humiliation. "In this combat no man can imagine, unless he had seen and heard, as I did, what yelling and hideous roaring Apollyon made all the time of the fight; he spake like a dragon; and on the other side, what sighs and groans burst from Christian's heart. I never saw him all the while give so much as one pleasant look, till he perceived he had wounded Apollyon with his two-edged sword; then indeed he did smile and look upward. But it was the dreadfullest fight that ever I saw." Ay! and this is so vivid, because the Dreamer himself was gazing back upon his own fearful experience. He sees himself, describes himself, as in his Grace Abounding, beneath the horrible assaults of Satan, during this long and murky year of temptation,—a year passed beneath a continual storm of the fiery darts of the Wicked One. But now came an interval of mercy; a hand came to poor exhausted Bunyan, with the leaves from the Tree of Life for his healing; his comfort and deliverance he always obtained from the word of God, which would come into his soul with the power of an immediate voice from heaven. "The Lord," he says, "did more fully and graciously discover himself unto me, the temptation was removed, and I was put into my right mind again, as other Christians were." The glory of God's word was now at times so weighty upon Bunyan, that he was ready to swoon away with solid joy and peace. This was the Tree of Life after the conflict. And now he had a season of great delight under holy Mr Gifford's ministry, and now did God set him down in all the things of Christ, and did open unto him his words, and cause them to shine before him, and make them to dwell with him, talk with him, and comfort him. And now about this time, what was next to the very leaves from the Tree of Life for Bunyan's spirit, came into his hands by God's providence, while he was longing to see some ancient godly man's experience, an old tattered copy of Martin Luther's Comment on Galatians; in which he had but a little way perused, before he found his own condition in Luther's experience so largely and profoundly handled, as if the book had been written out of his own heart. Oh! with what joy did Bunyan, in the midst of his temptations, hail this trumpet voice of the old Reformer! He saw now that he was not alone. It was like that voice which his own Christian heard, when groping in the Valley of the Shadow of Death, and which caused his heart to leap for gladness to find that some other soul that feared God was in that valley with him, the voice as of a man going before and crying, Though I walk through the Valley of the Shadow of Death, I will fear no evil, for Thou art with me! I must, said Bunyan, declare before all men, that I do prefer this book of Martin Luther upon the Galatians before all the books, excepting the Holy Bible, that I ever have seen, as most fit for a wounded conscience.

Now was Bunyan in great blessedness in the love of Christ; but it lasted only for a little, and then again the Tempter rushed upon him with a dreadful violence for the space of another whole year, in which, if I should take the whole evening, I could not describe to you the twinings and wrestlings, the strivings and agonies of Bunyan's spirit. Strange as it may seem, the temptation presented was that of selling Christ, sell him, sell him, sell him, sell him, as fast as man can speak, which tortured Bunyan as upon the rack, and against which, with a morbid fear lest he should consent thereto, he bent the whole force of his being with a strife unutterable. At length, one morning there seemed to pass deliberately through his heart, as if he were tired of resisting the wickedness, this thought, "Let him go if he will," and from that moment down fell Bunyan, "as a bird that is shot from the top of a tree into great guilt and fearful despair."

And now commenced a great strife of scripture against scripture in his soul, the threatenings against the promises, the law against the gospel, a conflict of unbelief and terror, in which he was indeed in the Valley of the Shadow of Death, and not a glimpse of light through its darkness. Deep called unto deep at the noise of God's water-spouts; all the waves and billows seemed to have gone over him. And now, like a man seeking to escape from a labyrinth of fire, in which he was bewildered, he would run from scripture to scripture, from this avenue to that in the Bible, but found every door closed against him. With a dreadful perverseness and ingenuity of unbelief under the power of his adversary, who seemed now indeed to have gotten the victory, he would compare his case with that of all the greatest criminals recorded in the Bible, but always turned every comparison against himself. In this state of mind he met with that terrible book, the despairing death of the Apostate Francis Spira, which, he says, was to his troubled spirit as salt rubbed into a fresh wound; and so it must have been inevitably, such a picture of the sufferings of a soul in despair; and that sentence was frightful to him, "Man knows the beginning of sin, but who bounds the issues thereof?" And that scripture, which was pursuing his soul all this year like one of the avenging furies, fell continually as an hot thunderbolt upon his conscience : " For ye know how that afterwards, when he would have inherited the blessing, he was rejected ; for he found no place of repentance, though he sought it carefully with tears."

Now he is in the midst of his own Death-Valley, beset behind and before ; and if we compare the account of this Valley with Bunyan's own experience, we shall see that the picture is simply the elements of his own inward sufferings combined and reorganized. " Thus Christian went on a great while, yet still the flames would be reaching towards him ; also he heard doleful voices and rushings to and fro, so that sometimes he thought he should be torn to pieces, or trodden down like mire in the streets. This frightful sight was seen, and these dreadful voices were heard by him for several miles together ; and coming to a place where he thought he heard a company of fiends coming forward to meet him, he stopt and began to muse what he had best to do : sometimes he had a thought to go back ; then again he thought he might be half-way through the valley ; he remembered also how he had vanquished many a danger already ; and that the danger of going back might be much more than to go forward."

" One thing I would not let slip. I took notice that now poor Christian was so confounded, that he did not know his own voice ; and thus I perceived it ; just when he was come over against the mouth of the burning pit, one of the wicked ones got behind him, and stept up softly to him, and whisperingly suggested many grievous blasphemies to him, which he verily thought had proceeded from his own mind ! This put Christian more to it than any thing that he met with before, even to think that he should now blaspheme him that he loved so much before ; yet, if he could have helped it, he would not have done it. But he had not the discretion either to stop his ears, or to know from whence those blasphemies came."

Nothing could be more vividly descriptive than this passage from the Pilgrim's Progress, of the state of Bunyan's own mind, as from a point of calm and clear observation, he afterwards looked back upon it in light from Heaven. His obstinate unbelief, his entanglement in the wrathful places of God's word, his jealousy against all consolation, and his holding of the dagger to his heart, that he had sold Christ, these things in the Valley of the Shadow of Death, were as much the work of the unseen Devil, as the crowds of blasphemous suggestions that were shoaled upon him, well-nigh driving him distracted. And now you see his own thoughtful, deliberate, well considered judgment in regard to that state of mind. "He had not the discretion either to stop his ears, or to know whence those blasphemies came." And who would have had? Bunyan possessed a very strong mind; but let any man be thus assaulted of the Devil, and see if he will possess his soul in patience any better than Bunyan did? How tender was his conscience! How fearful of offending God! How pierced with anguish in the thought of such ingratitude to Christ! And how fervid and powerful his imagination at work amidst eternal realities? Ah! here were materials for Satan to work upon in order to persuade Bunyan that he had sinned irrecoverably, in order to make him endorse against himself the bill of blasphemy and unbelief presented by his implacable, malignant, hellish adversary! And he did endorse it, in all the anxiety, trembling, and agony of despair, he did endorse those bitter dreadful things against himself; but it was a forged bill; it was known in Heaven's Chancery; the Saviour himself denied it.

Upon a day when Bunyan was bemoaning and abhorring himself in this abyss of misery, there came as it were a voice from Heaven, in a sweet pleasant wind, that like the wings of angels rushed past him, with this question, "Didst thou ever refuse to be justified by the blood of Christ?" and Bunyan's heart, in spite of all the black clouds of guilt that Satan's malignity had rolled around his conscience, was compelled honestly to answer, No. Then fell with power that word of God upon him, See that ye refuse not Him that speaketh. This, says Bunyan, made a strange *seizure* upon my spirit; it brought light with it, and commanded a silence in my heart of all those tumultuous thoughts that did before use, like masterless hell-hounds, to roar and bellow and make a hideous noise within me.

Not Milton himself could have described this with more energy; nay, you may apply the very language of the great Poet of Heaven, Hell, and Satan; for the thunder now, "winged with red lightning and impetuous rage," had for a season spent his shafts, and ceased for a moment

"To bellow through the vast and boundless deep!"

Yea, says Bunyan, this was a kind of check for my proneness to desperation; a kind of threatening of me, if I did not, notwithstanding my sins, and the heinousness of them, venture my salvation upon the Son of God. But this providence was so strange, so wonderful to Bunyan, that for twenty years he could not make a judgment of it, would scarce dare give an opinion; only one thing he knew, it commanded a great calm in his soul; and another thing he knew, namely, that he laid not the stress of his salvation upon this wonderful interposition, of which he knew not what to say, but *upon the Lord Jesus in the promise.*

And here we see a remarkable trait in Bunyan's character, and that is, that with all the strength of his feelings, and the glowing, restless power of his imagination, he was so entirely free from fanaticism, so unwilling, except compelled, to refer his experience to any thing like personal miraculous interpositions. He was exceedingly cautious to rest upon nothing, to trust in nothing, but for which he had the warrant of God's word. This, as we have seen, was what holy Mr Gifford, as well as his own good sense, taught him; but there are few men who could have gone through Bunyan's experience, and not come out fanatics,—certainly none without the guidance of the Holy Spirit.

And we see here in a striking manner the distinction between fanaticism and true piety. Fanaticism interprets according to its own vagaries, and not according to God's word; fanaticism leaves the word, and rises into its own wild spirit. Fanaticism interprets God's providences as miracles for self; it says, God is working miracles for me, I am the favoured one of God, I have a special mission from

God, and all my enemies are God's enemies. Then it proceeds to say, I belong to the true church, and all that do not go with me are of God's uncovenanted mercies, heathen, uncircumcised, fit only, if I can get the power, for fire-and-faggot application. This indeed is the convulsive, Romish stage of fanaticism; but so it proceeds. Self and intolerance, pride and cruelty, are its constituent elements. But now how different these characteristics of Bunyan; as fearful, almost, of daring to appropriate any of God's miraculous interpositions in his own behalf, as he was of hiding himself from God under a false refuge. All Bunyan's hallucinations, if you please to call them such, were against himself, and made him remarkably gentle and humble; so here Satan overdid his own work; but the hallucinations of fanaticism are all in behalf of self, and make the subject of them proud, self-righteous, and intolerant. Bunyan's conscience was as tender, as sensitive, as quick to the evil and pain of sin, as the apostle John's; and Bunyan was writing bitter things against himself, when he was full of love, tenderness, and deference to others; but fanaticism is always writing proud things concerning itself, and despising others. "Two men went up into the temple to pray; the one a Pharisee, and the other a Publican. The Pharisee stood and prayed thus with himself; God, I thank thee that I am not as other men, extortioners, unjust, adulterers, or even as this Publican. I fast twice in the week. I give tithes of all that I possess." I belong to the true church. "And the Publican standing afar off, would not lift up so much as his eyes to heaven, but smote upon his breast, saying, God be merciful to me a sinner!"

I have said that these blasphemies and unbelief were Satan's work, and not Bunyan's; and now let us see another material, which Satan's devilish ingenuity had to work upon in Bunyan's composition, indeed in the very constitution of all our minds. There is a morbid disposition in the mind, when in an anxious state, or under great trials, to fasten upon any evil imagination, or conjecture, or suggestion which it dreads greatly, and to clasp it, as it were, and hold to it. There is a sort of feverish state of the mind, which holds these phantasms, as a fever does in the body. In such a state, evil suggestions, though rejected, have a most horrible pertinacity in cleaving to the mind; and the more the mind dreads them, and tries to avoid them, the more palpable they become. They really seem like fiends pursuing the soul, shouting over the shoulder, hissing in the ear. And I say the more direct and intense efforts a man makes to reject and avoid them, the more palpable and fiend-like they become.

This is in part our very constitution, in the memory as well as imagination; for, let a man try to forget any dreadful thing, of which he hates the remembrance, and the more he tries to forget it, the more surely he remembers it, the more he bodies it forth, and every thrust he makes at it causes it to glare up anew, reveals some new horror in it. Doubtless, this peculiarity in our mental constitution is destined to play a most terrific part in the punishment of men's sins in eternity; for there can be nothing so dreadful as the remembrance of sin, and nothing, which men will strive with more intense earnestness to hide from and forget, than the recollection of their sins; and yet every effort they make at such forgetfulness only gives to such sins a more terrible reality, and makes them blaze up in a more lurid light to the conscience. Oh, if they could but be forgotten! But the more intense is the earnestness of this wish, the more impossible becomes the forgetfulness, the more terribly the dreaded evil stands out. There are cases even in this life, in which men would give ten thousand worlds if they possessed them, could they only forget; but how much more in eternity! The man that has committed a secret midnight murder, how often, think you, though perhaps not a human being suspects it, would he give the riches of the material universe, if he had them at command, could he but forget that one moment's crime! But it is linked to his very constitution, and every time he tries to cut the chain, he does but rattle and rouse the crime out of its grave into a new existence. Did my hearers ever see Allston's picture of the bloody hand? It is a revelation of the power of sin through the combined agency of imagination, memory, and conscience—sin unrepented in the conscience, unpardoned in the soul.

Now all this Satan knew far better than Bunyan. Was not the lost archangel's own soul always and obstinately dwelling upon his own sins? Could he but forget his fall, his once blessed state, his holiness, his happiness, it would be almost heaven to him! But no! he might fly from heaven, and fly to the utmost limits of an external hell; but he could not fly from himself.

> "Me miserable! Which way shall I fly
> Infinite wrath, and infinite despair?
> Which way I fly is hell; myself am hell;
> And in the lowest deep a lower deep
> Still threatening to devour me opens wide
> To which the hell I suffer seems a heaven."

This is poetry, of the highest, sublimest kind; but it is not fiction; it is not deeper poetry than it is truth, terrific truth! It would seem as if Satan disgorged upon Bunyan the hell of his own soul more fully than ever he did upon any other mortal. Certainly, he made use of this morbid self-reproaching disposition of Bunyan's mind to the utmost. He plied him, vexed him, overwhelmed him with devilish suggestions, well knowing that Bunyan would start from them as if an adder stung him, and yet that they would possess a sort of fascinating, icy, paralyzing power, like that which dwells in the eye of a rattlesnake. Now, if Bunyan could but have had his attention turned away from the eye of the temptations, from the face of the Tempter, from the point of almost morbid lunacy, as it were, the horrid charm would be broken. If at this time Bunyan's mind could have been strongly arrested and filled by a presentation of Christ crucified, Satan would have found himself quite unnoticed, and all his temptations unnerved; but he succeeded in getting the morbid attention of Bunyan fixed on himself, and his own detestableness and diabolical malignity and blasphemy, and then he could fasten his serpent's fangs in him, and nothing but Christ by his word and Spirit ever did or could deliver him.

In regard to these temptations, Bunyan was sometimes just like a scared child, that thinks it sees a ghost, or like a timid person in a wood by twilight, that sees in the stump of a tree a man couched and lying in wait, and instead of daring to go boldly up to it, to see what it is, stands shivering and almost dead with terror. Who has not realized this in his own experience, timid or brave? And just so, Bunyan did not dare to go up to, and examine and look in the face, the shocking blasphemies, accusations, and wrathful passages, that Satan would be ever thrusting into his soul; but went cowering and shivering, and bowed down as a man in chains under the weight of them. There was a time when all that Satan said to him he seemed morbidly inclined to take upon trust; and if it were a fiery passage of God's word, so much the worse; for instead of coming up to it as a child of God to see what it was, and whether it were really against him, he fled from it at once, as from the fiery, flaming sword in the gate to Eden. And nothing can be more curious, more graphic, more affecting in its interest, more childlike in its simplicity, than the manner in which Bunyan describes the commencement and progress of his recovery out of this state of condemnation and terror; how timidly and cautiously, and as it were by stealth, he began to look these dreadful passages in the face, when they had ceased pursuing him; standing at first afar off, and gazing at them, and then, as a child, that cannot get rid of its fears, slowly drawing near, and at length daring to touch them, and to walk around them, and to see their true position and meaning, but always conscious of their awful power.

If ever there was a man who knew to the full the meaning of that passage, *The fiery darts of the Wicked One;* and of that, The word of God is sharper than any two-edged sword, *piercing even to the dividing asunder of soul and spirit;* it was John Bunyan. You cannot possibly tell, except you read it for yourself, the conflicts that his soul sustained between opposing passages of scripture, wielded on the one side by the Spirit of God, and on the other by his soul's malignant adversary; the blessed Spirit holding out some sweet, gracious, comprehensive promise, and then Satan flashing between it and Bunyan's soul the gleaming sword of a threat to keep him from it; and so, as I have said, the swords of Michael and of Satan are thus crossing and flashing continually in this protracted and fearful conflict.

There were two passages especially, that thus met and struggled for the mastery; and the one was that sweet promise, " My grace is sufficient for thee ;" and the other that most tremendous passage in regard to Esau selling his birthright, and after finding no place of repentance. " Oh," says Bunyan, " the combats and conflicts that I did meet with ! As I strove to hold by this word of promise, that of Esau would fly in my face like lightning. So my soul did hang as in a pair of scales, sometimes up, and sometimes down ; now in peace, and now again in terror. And I remember one day, as I was in divers frames of spirit, and considering that the frames were according to the nature of several scriptures that came in upon my mind, if this of grace, then I was quiet ; but if that of Esau, then tormented. Lord, thought I, if both these scriptures should meet in my heart at once, I wonder which of them would get the better of me. So methought I had a longing mind that they might come both together upon me ; yea, I desired of God they might. Well, about two or three days after, so they did indeed ; they bolted both upon me at a time, and did work and struggle strongly in me for a while ; at last that about Esau's birthright began to wax weak, and withdraw, and vanish, and this about the sufficiency of grace prevailed with power and joy. And as I was in a muse about this thing, that scripture came in upon me, *Mercy rejoiceth over judgment.* This was a wonderment to me, yet truly I am apt to think it was of God, for the word of the law and wrath must give place to the word of life and grace ; because, though the word of condemnation be glorious, yet the word of life and salvation doth far exceed in glory. Also, that Moses and Elias must both vanish, and leave Christ and his saints alone."

Now we may call this a conceit, if we please, but to some minds this use of scripture is inimitably sweet and beautiful. Nor can there be any thing more beautiful than to see this soldier of Jesus Christ escaped from the perils of the conflict, sitting down to trace, with so calm and skilful a hand,

and a heart so believing, joyous, and grateful, the evolutions and currents of the battle, the movements of his great Commander on the one side, and of his fierce Adversary on the other.

The consideration of Bunyan's temptations reveals to us three great secrets; the secret of his deep experimental knowledge of the power of God's word; the secret of his great skill and power in preaching; and the secret of his pure, idiomatic, energetic, English style. Every step he took in the word of God was experimental. The Bible was his book of all learning; for years he studied it as for his life. No bewildered mariner, in a crazy bark on an unknown sea, amidst sunken reefs and dangerous shallows, ever pondered his chart with half the earnestness. It was as if life or death depended on every time he opened it, and every line he read. The scriptures were wonderful things unto him; he saw that the truth and verity of them were the keys of the kingdom of heaven; those that the scriptures favour, they must inherit bliss; but those that they oppose and condemn must perish for evermore. "One sentence of the scripture did more afflict and terrify my mind, I mean those sentences that stood against me, as sometimes I thought they every one of them did, than an army of forty thousand men that might come against me. Wo be to him, against whom he scriptures bend themselves. This made me, with careful heart and watchful eye, with great fearfulness, to turn over every leaf, and with much diligence mixed with trembling, to consider every sentence, together with its natural force and latitude. Now would he leap into the bosom of that promise, that yet he feared did shut its heart against him. Now also I would labour to take the word as God hath laid it down, without restraining the natural force of one syllable thereof. Oh! what did I now see in that blessed sixth of John! 'And him that cometh unto me I will in nowise cast out.' Oh many a pull hath my heart had with Satan for that blessed sixth of John! A word, a word, to lean a weary soul upon, that it might not sink for ever! It was that I hunted for! Yea, often when I have been making for the promise, I have seen as if the Lord would refuse my soul for ever. I was often as if I had run upon the pikes, and as if the Lord had thrust at me, to keep me from him as with a flaming sword!"

Here we have the secret of Bunyan's experimental knowledge of the word of God; and this, coupled with the remembrance of the tenor of holy Mr Gifford's instructions to take nothing upon trust, but to labour to be set down by the Spirit of God in the word of God, and how faithfully Bunyan made this his practice, shews us how he came to be so rooted and grounded in divine truth, so consummate a master in it, in its living beauty and harmony. He was led from truth to truth by the Divine Spirit; every part of the gospel was thus revealed unto him; he could not express what he saw and felt of its glory, of the steadiness of Jesus Christ the Rock of man's salvation, and of the power, sweetness, light, and fitness of his word. It was as a fire and a hammer in his own soul, burning and beating. It was food and nourishment to his spiritual life, and a clothing of majesty and glory to his intellect. There never was a being more perfectly and entirely created out of the scriptures.

And here too, in his intense study of the Bible, you have the secret of the purity of his English style. How is it possible, it might have been asked, that this illiterate man, familiar with none of the acknowledged models of his native tongue, can have acquired a style which its most skilful and eloquent masters might envy, for its artless simplicity, purity, and strength! It was because his soul was baptized by the Spirit of God in its native idioms; because he *was* familiar as no other man of his age was, with *the* model, the very best model of the English tongue in existence, our common English Bible! Yes! that very Bible, which some modern infidel reformers would exclude from our schools, and from its blessed place of influence over the hearts and minds of our children! The fervour of the poet's soul, acting through the medium of such a language as he learned from our common translation of the scriptures, has produced some of the most admirable specimens in existence of the manly power and familiar beauty of the English tongue. There are passages even in the Grace Abounding, which for fervidness and power of expression might be placed side by side with any thing in the most admired authors, and not suffer in the comparison. Bunyan is not less to be praised than Shakspeare himself for the purity of his language, and the natural simplicity of his style. It comes even nearer indeed, to the common diction of good conversation. Its idioms are genuine English, in their most original state, unmingled with any external ornament, and of a beauty unborrowed from any foreign shades of expression.

Then too, Bunyan's imagination, his judgment, his taste, every faculty of his mind was developed, disciplined, and enriched at the same great fountain of the Scriptures. The poetry of the Bible was the source of his poetical power. His heart was not only made new by the Spirit of the Bible, but his whole intellectual being was penetrated and transfigured by its influence. He brought the spirit and power gathered from so long and exclusive a communion with the prophets and apostles to the composition of every page of the Pilgrim's Progress. To the habit of mind thus induced, and the workings of an imagination thus disciplined, may be traced the simplicity of all his imagery, and the great power of his personifications. The spirit of his work is Hebrew; we may trace the mingled influence both of David and Isaiah in the character of his genius; and as to the images in the sacred poets, he is lavish in the use of them, in the most natural and unconscious manner possible: his mind was imbued with them. He is indeed the only poet, whose genius was nourished entirely by the Bible. He felt and thought in scripture imagery.

Now here are great lessons for all our minds. We say to every young man, whose intellectual as well as moral habits are now formed, Do you wish to gain a mastery over your native language in its earliest, purest, freshest idioms, and to command a style, in which you may speak with power to the very hearts of the people? Study your Bible, your English Bible; study it with your feelings, your heart, and let its beautiful forms of expression entwine themselves around your sensibilities, your very habits of thinking, no more to be separated from them, than sensibility and thought itself can be separated from your existence. We stand in amazement at the blessed power of transfiguration which the Bible possesses for the human intellect. And yet we are not amazed, for the Bible is the voice of God, and the words of the Bible are the words of God, and he who will give himself up to them, who will feed upon them, and love them, and dwell amidst them, shall have his intellect and his soul transfigured with glory and blessedness by them. Do you ask for experience ? Do you desire life ? Hear our Saviour: "The words that I speak unto you, they are spirit and they are life!" But beware you let no mediator come between your soul and its immediate, electric contact with those lively oracles. Beware you let no church with its self-assumed authority of interpretation, hang up its darkening veil between your soul and the open face of God in the scriptures. Come to them for yourself. Say to yourself, This is my possession, and no church, and no priest, and no power in the universe shall wrest it from me. This is my God and my Saviour speaking to me; and he shall speak to me, though the whole church were against me, or though I were the only Christian in the world. "Yea," saith our Saviour, "if ye abide in me, and my words abide in you, ye shall ask what ye will, and it shall be done unto you." We say, Put your soul beneath the fire of God's word, and not beneath the winking tapers of the fathers, or the councils, or the traditions in the churches! And just so, if we could get the Roman Catholics within the sound of our voice in God's sanctuary, we would say to every Roman Catholic, How can you be willing, as a man and a Christian, to let any priest, or pope, or church, or daring council, or saint on earth, or saint in heaven, take from your soul your immediate personal communion with your God ? Come to him yourself, and live upon his words yourself, and all the anathemas of all the popes, councils, priests, and churches in the world, shall only strengthen and deepen in your soul the elements of eternal blessedness.

And to every Christian we would say, Mind the example of Bunyan and his wise Evangelist, "holy Mr Gifford," and when you study the Scriptures, study them as for your life, take fast hold upon them, bind them upon your neck, engrave them in your affections, seek to be set down in them by the Spirit of God, seek their experimental knowledge, the living, burning experience of their power. Let the Spirit of God lead you from truth to truth. So, and in no other way, you can be powerful as a Christian. Yea, this was the experience of Paul and Luther and Bunyan, and of all men mighty in the Scriptures. This is the experience that we need, in this very age into which we are thrown, in order to save the church and the world from destruction. This is the experience that must constitute a new era of power in the church, if we would meet the crisis that has come upon us, in the resurrection of old exploded errors under new forms. We must not let Christ be displaced by the church. We must enter, as Zuingle said, into God's thoughts in his own word; and we must dwell there, as in a tower of invincible strength and glory! Hear an old, noble, martyred saint, now in glory. "I had rather follow the *shadow* of Christ," said the blessed reformer and martyr, Bishop Hooper, "than the *body* of all the general councils or doctors since the death of Christ. It is mine opinion unto all the world, that the Scriptures solely, and the apostles' church, is to be followed, and no man's authority, be he Augustine, Tertullian, or even cherubim or seraphim!"

And to every unconverted person we would say, See how Bunyan entered the strait and narrow way, and rose to Heaven. He followed the word of God. Take you the word of God. Take that one sentence, Flee from the wrath to come; and let it point you to that other sentence, Believe in the Lord Jesus Christ. And if the world, seeing you so set out, ridicule you, shut your ears, like Christian, and run forward, and stay not, till the Wicket Gate opens before you, and you enter, and become a blessed Pilgrim from the City of Destruction to the City of Immanuel.

Here now is the secret of Bunyan's power in preaching. He became a preacher through his power in God's word. That word, so kindled in his soul by the Spirit of God, could not be repressed; it would blaze out; it was as a fire in his bones, if he restrained it, and it must burn. Unconsciously to himself, others first marked its power in him, and marked him as an instrument of God, for the instruction of his people and the conversion of men. Bunyan was pressed on, but never put himself forward. The gifts and graces of God in him shone so brightly, that men would have him for their minister. He was exceedingly retiring, humble, trembling, self-distrustful, and began to speak only to a few, in few words, in little meetings. But it was soon seen and felt that the Spirit and the word of God were speaking in him. And even before he became the ordained pastor of a people, he had that seal of God's ambassadors, which is better than all the consecrating oil of the Vatican, better than the hands of all the Bishops, better than all apostolical successions traced down through idolaters and adulterers in the House of God; he had the seal of the Spirit of God upon his preaching, bringing men to Christ. He could say, if he chose, " The seal of mine apostleship are YE IN THE LORD! Though I be not an apostle unto others, yet doubtless I am unto you." These things were, as well they might be, an argument unto Bunyan, that God had called him to, and stood by him in this work. Wherefore, says he, though of myself of all the saints the most unworthy, yet I, but with great fear and trembling at the sight of my own weakness, did set upon the work, and did, according to my gift, and the proportion of my faith, preach that blessed gospel that God has shewed me in the holy word of truth; which, when the country understood, they came in to hear the word by hundreds, and that from all parts, though upon divers and sundry accounts.

Bunyan was called to his ministry, and led into it, by God's word, though most unfortunately not in the regular line of the apostolical succession. He enumerates the passages which ran in his mind, and encouraged and strengthened him; and they are very striking, and all-sufficient for his justification. The first of them is that of Acts, viii. 4, " Therefore they that were scattered abroad, went every where preaching the word." Bunyan knew there was no apostolical succession there. Another passage was that in 1 Peter, iv. 10, " As every man hath received the gift, even so minister the same one to another, as good stewards of the manifold grace of God." Bunyan knew that being addressed to the strangers scattered throughout Pontus, Galatia, Cappadocia, Asia, and Bithynia, there was no apostolical succession there. He also knew that in the case of the household of Stephanus, who had addicted themselves to the ministry of the saints, there was no apostolical succession. And these passages all were as so many certificates to him from Jesus Christ, that he, being called by the Holy Ghost, might preach the gospel. And so he did preach it, and many and blessed were the seals of his faithful stewardship. He knew what the office of the ministry was. He had often read Paul's catalogue of its qualifications, and they suited the frame of his own intrepid spirit. " In all things approving ourselves as the ministers of God, in much patience, in afflictions, in necessities, in distresses, in stripes, in imprisonments, in tumults, in labours, in watchings, in fastings ; by pureness, by knowledge, by long-suffering, by kindness, by the Holy Ghost, by love unfeigned, by the word of truth, by the power of God, by the armour of righteousness on the right hand and on the left, by honour and dishonour, by evil report and good report : as deceivers, and yet true ; as unknown, and yet well known; as dying, and behold we live ; as chastened, and not killed ; as sorrowful, yet always rejoicing ; as poor, yet making many rich ; as having nothing, and yet possessing all things," 2 Cor. vi. 4-10. There is no apostolical succession here, nor prelatical nor episcopal consecration ; but a succession of adversities ; a consecration to the sacred fires of self-denial and of suffering for Christ's sake. Assuredly John Bunyan was as true, and regular, and heaven-commissioned a minister of Jesus Christ, as any bishop in lawn sleeves, under whose jurisdiction he was forbidden to preach, and was thrust into prison.

Bunyan's life and discipline, under the leadings of Divine Providence, were very much like those of some of the early Reformers of England. In his character and his preaching he resembled not a little the honesty and vigour, the straightforwardness and humour of Bishop Latimer. He had kindred qualities also with those of Luther ; and the perusal of Luther's Commentary on Galatians, we doubt not, exerted a great influence on the character of Bunyan's preaching.

Nevertheless, the little that Bunyan received from others became his own, as much as if it had originated with himself; being a process as natural and unconscious in his intellectual and moral being, as that in which the dews and light from heaven, falling on the plants, are worked into the nature of the fruits and foliage.

Bunyan always preached what he saw and felt, and so the character of his preaching varied with the aspect which divine truth, in the colouring of his personal hopes and fears, wore to his own soul. He enumerates three chief enclosures in the pastures of divine truth, in which he was detained by his own experience; for he dared not break through that hedge, and take things at second hand, as he might find them. He says, that he never endeavoured, nor durst make use of, other men's lives or tracings, though, he adds, I do not condemn all that do; for I verily thought, and found by experience, that what was taught me by the word and Spirit of Christ could be spoken, maintained, and stood to by the soundest and best established conscience. He could, in a great measure, say with the apostle, " I certify you, brethren, that the gospel which was preached of me is not after man ; for I neither received it of man, neither was I taught it, but by the revelation of Jesus Christ."

In the first years of his preaching, Bunyan had not advanced to that richness and blissfulness of religious experience, in the possession and command of which he wrote the Pilgrim's Progress. As a preacher, he was at first as a man flying from hell, and warning others to flee also, but not having reached the gates of heaven. He was as his own Pilgrim, trembling beneath the overhanging rocks of Sinai, stunned by the crashing peals of thunder, and wellnigh blinded by the lightning. He was passing through the Valley of the Shadow of Death, and knowing the terrors of the Lord, he persuaded men, pouring out upon them, as in a stream of fire, the intensity of his own convictions. How ne preached in the midst of such soul-torturing experience may be gathered from his own language:—" This part of my work," says he, " I fulfilled with great sense: for the terrors of the law, and guilt for my transgressions, lay heavy upon my conscience. I preached what I felt, what smartingly I did feel, even that under which my poor soul did groan and tremble to astonishment. Indeed, I have been as one sent to them from the dead. I WENT MYSELF IN CHAINS TO PREACH TO THEM IN CHAINS; AND CARRIED THAT FIRE IN MY OWN CONSCIENCE THAT I PERSUADED THEM TO BE AWARE OF. I can truly say, that when I have been to preach, I have gone full of guilt and terror to the pulpit door; and then it hath been taken off, and I have been at liberty in my mind until I have done my work; and then immediately, even before I could get down the pulpit stairs, I have been as bad as I was before. Yet God carried me on; but surely with a strong hand, for neither guilt nor hell could take me off my work." So Bunyan preached, and preaching so, it is no wonder that he made an impression both on men and devils. He describes with great nature and truth his various frames in preaching; sometimes with such enlargement of soul, that he could speak as in a very flame of fire; and then again so straitened in his utterance before the people, as if his head had been in a bag all the time of his exercise. The truth is, the heart of the preacher is more apt to be in the bag than his head is; and when his heart is there, then generally, as to effect, his head is there also. This experience of the bag, we are sorry to say, is rather more common than that of the seraphic enlargement of soul, which the love of Christ ought always to give us.

Thus Bunyan went on preaching, travelling through those special enclosures in the word of God of which he speaks, about the space of five years or more, when, says he, " I was caught in my then present practice, and cast into prison, where I have lain above as long again to confirm the truth by way of suffering, as I was before in testifying of it according to the Scriptures, in a way of preaching." Nor is it to be supposed that during all this time Bunyan was free from the temptations of Satan in his ministry; nay, he had them abundantly, but somewhat changed from inward to external; for " when Satan perceived that his thus tempting and assaulting me would not answer his design—to wit, to overthrow the ministry, and make it ineffectual as to the ends thereof—then he tried another way, which was to stir up the minds of the ignorant and malicious to load me with slanders and reproaches: now therefore I may say, that what the devil could devise, and his instruments invent, was whirled up and down the country against me, thinking, as I said, that by that means they should make my ministry to be abandoned. It began therefore to be rumoured up and down among the people that I was a witch, a Jesuit, a highwayman, a whoremonger, and the like. To all which I shall only say, God knows that I am innocent. I have a good conscience; and whereas they speak evil of me as an evil-doer, they shall be ashamed that falsely accuse my good conversation in Christ. So then, what shall I say to those who have thus bespattered me? Shall I threaten them? Shall I chide them? Shall I flatter them? Shall I entreat them to hold their tongues? No, not I. Were it not that these things make those ripe for damnation who are the authors and abettors, I would say unto them, Report it, because it will increase my glory. Therefore, I bind these lies and slanders to me as an ornament; it belongs to my Christian profession to be thus vilified, slandered, reproached, and reviled; and since all this is nothing else, as my God and conscience do bear me witness, I rejoice in reproaches for Christ's sake."

"Now, as Satan endeavoured by reproaches and slanders to make me vile among my countrymen, that if possible my preaching might be made of no more effect, so there was added hereto a long and tedious imprisonment, that thereby I might be frightened from the service of Christ, and the world terrified, and made afraid to hear me preach. Of which I shall, in the next place, give you a brief account."

Now, in this matter of Bunyan's imprisonment, it is evident that, so far as Satan had a share in it, he did, as we say, overshoot the mark; he was a clear illustration of that saying of Shakspeare's concerning

> "Vaulting ambition, which o'erleaps itself,
> And falls on t'other side."

Doubtless this enemy of souls, and this adversary of Bunyan, because of the great good he was doing in his preaching, supposed he had accomplished a great work when, through the tyranny of the Church Establishment, he had succeeded in silencing the preacher; and when he got him into prison, he thought within himself, There is an end of that man's usefulness; no more souls shall rise to glory through him. But what a signal mistake! Perhaps the greatest mistake but one or two that Satan ever committed! If this man, John Bunyan, had been permitted still to go at large and preach, the world, doubtless, would never have been blessed with the Pilgrim's Progress. But God permitted the wrath of Bunyan's adversaries to shut him up in prison just at that point, where the inward temptations of the devil, and the discipline of God's Spirit, and Bunyan's varied acquaintance with men, and knowledge of his own heart, and experience in the business of preaching, and experimental knowledge of the gospel, and of the power, blessedness, and fitness of God's word, had just fitted him for the composition of precisely such a work. I say, just at the point when God had fitted his chosen instrument for this work, he permitted the malice of his infernal enemy, and the wrath of his earthly adversaries, to put him in a quiet cell, where he would have heavenly retirement to meditate upon it, and uninterrupted leisure to accomplish it. Was there ever a more perfect and delightful illustration of that promise, "Surely thou wilt cause the wrath of man to praise thee, and the remainder of wrath thou wilt restrain?"

And now as to these satanic temptations:—Having followed Bunyan to prison, we must perforce leave him there till such time as we can, God willing, dwell more particularly on the manner in which he was brought there, and the way in which the light and loveliness of the creations of his Pilgrim arose like the sun in his soul out of that imprisoned darkness. But a few words as to these satanic temptations. It is a deeply interesting and important subject; one on which we would much rather devote a whole lecture. We do not suppose that any man who, in spite of the testimony of the Scriptures, is a disbeliever in the existence of the devil and his angels, will be brought to believe on the testi mony of Bunyan; and yet, in the providence of God there might be such a thing; at any rate, the strong and simple experience and testimony of Bunyan might lead such a man to review with more candour and less doubt the scripture argument and evidence. And we say, that the murky experience of Bunyan cannot philosophically be accounted for on any other principles than those laid down in the Scriptures, nor in any other way so rationally, so probably, so truly, as Bunyan himself under the light of the Scriptures has taken to illustrate it. Refer it to satanic agency, and all is plain, consistent, and full of the deepest, most solemn interest. Reject that agency, and all is unaccountable, absurd, prodigious; unless, indeed, you make Bunyan a downright madman—a lunatic; which conclusion, in regard to a man whose whole life, from the time when that madness commenced, was one bright career of goodness, and who in the midst of it wrote the most sensible, excellent, and delightful book in the language, would be the most absurd of all conclusions. Indeed, there was more "method in his madness" than there is in most other men's sanity. But his own deliberate conclusions concerning the workings of his mind, and the influences brought to bear upon him, formed fifteen years or more after his own personal passage through the Valley of the Shadow of Death; formed in the midst of light from heaven, formed with the most careful adherence to the words and principles of the Scriptures, formed with the help of much observance of the conflicts of others, and formed by a mind not at all inclined to fanaticism, but remarkably liberal, tolerant, free from extremes, and cautious in asserting a supernatural interposition, as in some remarkable cases we have seen he was; I say, the conclusions of such a mind, after such a period of thoughtful, prayerful examination, are invaluable, and to be relied upon.

They even form an important addition to our external testimony for the truth of the Scriptures, and the manner of their interpretation. How often do we have to resort to existing realities to explain texts of Scripture otherwise inexplicable, and which to the infidel vulgar—to men of the kin of Voltaire and Tom Paine—serve for ignorant and senseless ridicule? For example, to take one of the very simplest instances: if a man meet with the passage, "I am become like a bottle in the smoke," or the passage about putting new wine into old bottles, he must go to an external reality to determine its meaning; and if he does not know (as most infidel writers have not known enough even *about* the Scriptures *to* know) that bottles were made out of goatskins, he may, perhaps, like Voltaire or Tom Paine, exercise his wit upon these passages. But if he be a believer, and come for the first time upon such an illustration, he will say, How delightful is this! I bless God for this! Now I know the meaning of a passage of which before I was ignorant. And just so, if what is said in the Scriptures in many passages about the temptations of the devil, were perfectly inexplicable to one who had never met with those temptations, and he should for the first time meet the tale of Bunyan's trials, he would say, when he sees such experience, Now I know how to interpret those Scriptures; now I see the meaning of things which I did not see before; now I know the meaning of those fiery darts of the Wicked One. Poor Bunyan!—his suffering was, as it were, vicarious; he was tried, that I might be instructed.

Suffer me to illustrate this matter still further, for it is important. Among the difficulties brought against the Scriptures, it had, at one time, often been alleged as an objection to the historical accuracy of the New Testament, that it gave the title of Proconsul to the Governor of Cyprus (Acts, xiii. 7), when, in strict propriety, he could only have been styled Prætor of the Province. So strongly did this apparent inaccuracy weigh with Beza, observes Mr Benson, that he absolutely attempted to remove it by translation; and our own translators have used the term Deputy, instead of the correct title of Proconsul. Now, it is a fact, that a medal has since then been discovered, on which the very same title is assigned, about the same period, to the governor of the same province, and so that difficulty vanishes for ever. But, as Benson well remarks in his "Scripture Difficulties," it does not vanish without leaving stronger evidence for the truth. Now, as to these difficulties about satanic temptations, about the devil, and his agency with the mind, a man may say, it is inexplicable, incredible, not to be taken as strict history, but something figurative, a *mythos*. But suppose, in a really candid and inquiring frame of mind, this inexperienced man lights upon the personal history of Luther, or upon this thrilling story of Bunyan's temptations, a hundred years afterwards, is it not just as if he had found a medal, struck in the same sacred treasury where the words of Scripture were engraven, with the very image of the devil on one side, and the inscription SATANIC TEMPTER above it? And now ought not the difficulty to vanish for ever? And are not discoveries like these of incalculable importance to the believer in the evil hour of temptation? Yea, it is like Christian himself hearing a human voice before him in the Valley of the Shadow of Death, where it seemed as if no living creature ever could pass safely.

Now, on this point there is a wonderful coincidence between the experience of men recorded in the word of God, and those out of it; and these two things illustrate each other. Take Job, for example. If a man say, this experience of Bunyan is all a delusion, it is merly his own imagination tormenting him, there never was or could be such a reality. We say, beware; this experience of Bunyan has its original in the word of God itself; it is countersigned, as it were, in Job's own history. Or if a man say, this experience of Job is figurative; no man ever experienced such dealings in reality; we say, so far from this, other men *have* experienced such discipline; it is countersigned, as it were, and illustrated, in the experience of a modern Christian. It is true, that in the account of Job, the steps are marked by the Divine hand; but in the account of Bunyan, also, the steps are just as clear, with that single exception. They are almost as clear as if it had been said, as in the case of Job, There was a man in the land of England whom God would take and prepare for the greatest usefulness of all men living. And Satan said, let me take Bunyan, and I will tempt him from his integrity, and make him curse God, and deny his very being. And God said, Let Satan try his uttermost upon this man, and the awful discipline shall only prepare him for greater usefulness and glory. So Satan went forth, and by the space of two years filled the soul of Bunyan with distresses and temptations, and the fiery darts of the Wicked One. Is not this the very truth of the matter? You may say, that with Job, Satan's temptations were all external, while with Bunyan they were mostly inward. Yes, but let it be remembered that Job had a bosom companion, a treacherous, unbelieving, discontented wife, who would, in the place of the devil, do all the whisperings, and the blasphemous suggestions that were needed. Yea, while Job was passing through the valley of temptation, this woman was as a fiend at his ear, " Curse God and die," to make it as the Valley of the Shadow of Death! Bunyan, on the other hand, had a godly wife, who would do no part of the work of the tempter, but would shield her husband, and help him on to God. As to many matters the cases are wonderfully similar, especially if in Bunyan's imprisonment likewise you trace the malice of the devil, as assuredly you ought.

Now, if you pass from the Old Testament to the New, the very experience of our blessed Lord at the very outset confirms this view. Before entering on his great work, he was led of the Spirit into the wilderness, to be tempted of the Devil.

To be tempted of the Devil! And for what cause? What ineffable mystery is this! Nay, it is indeed a mystery, and yet in part it is so brightly, so sweetly, so lovingly explained to us, that nothing could be more delightful to the soul than this very fact. Turn, then, in your Bibles, to those precious passages in the Epistle to the Hebrews, which explain our blessed Lord's temptations, and the reason for them, and in some respects the manner of them. They tell us that it became Him, for whom are all things, and by whom are all things, in bringing many sons unto glory, to make the Captain of their salvation perfect through sufferings. And, therefore, as the children are partakers of flesh and blood, he also himself took part in the same, that through death he might destroy him that had the power of death, that is, the devil. Wherefore, in all things it behoved him to be made like unto his brethren, that he might be a merciful and faithful High Priest, to make reconciliation for the sins of the people. For IN THAT HE HIMSELF HATH SUFFERED, BEING TEMPTED, HE IS ABLE TO SUCCOUR THEM THAT ARE TEMPTED. Wherefore, people of God, rejoice! For we have not an High Priest which cannot be touched with the feeling of our infirmities, but was in all points tempted like as we are, yet without sin. Let us, therefore, come boldly unto the throne of grace, that we may obtain mercy, and find grace to help in time of need.

Now, is any further explanation needed than such a passage, so full of light, mercy, loveliness, in regard to that other passage, "Then was Jesus led up of the Spirit into the wilderness to be tempted of the devil?" And how could he be tempted with evil thoughts in any other way? They could not spring out of his own soul, for he was perfectly sinless. They could not come from his own imagination, for that imagination was invested with the splendours of heaven. They could not be the ravings of lunacy; for though, because of our Saviour's supremacy of goodness, because of the lightning of his countenance, his life, and his words against sin, and because of his irresistible power in casting out devils, his enemies asserted that he *had* a devil and was mad, yet no man now would dare the blasphemy. They could only come from the personal suggestions of the Evil One; and thus did our blessed Lord take part in our temptations; thus did that spotless being pass through a furnace of blasphemies and hell-born propositions, the very Valley of the Shadow of Death; and thus, at the very commencement of his ministry, did the Captain of our salvation begin to be made perfect through sufferings. Nor is there in all his ministry, nor, I had almost said, even in his death upon the cross, a greater, more wonderful, more affecting proof of his boundless compassion and love. The spotless Son of God consenting, for our sakes, at the very entrance on his ministry, to pass through so revolting, so awful, so hideous an ordeal; an ordeal ten thousand times worse to an infinitely holy mind than death itself! Consenting to be for forty days alone in the wilderness with Satan as a personal companion, with this blaspheming, daring, polluted, tortured fiend, dragon, devil, belching forth his hellish thoughts, and insulting our blessed Lord with the application even of sacred scripture! All this for us! that he might be in all points tempted like as we are, yet without sin! Oh, who can tell the smallest part of the infinite goodness and condescension of our Redeemer!

He was led up of the Spirit into the wilderness to be tempted of the devil. Now let me say, if you will read the opening of Milton's Paradise Regained, you will find there a marvellously probable and beautiful description of the manner in which Satan would enter on this work of temptation. Nor did his disappointment, and his utter discomfiture in it, prevent him from renewing it on the eminent disciples of our blessed Lord. There were some of them that, like Bunyan, were made to know the very " depths of Satan." There was Peter, of whom our blessed Lord forewarned him, that Satan would try him to the utmost of his malignity and power! " Simon, Simon, I say unto thee that Satan hath desired to have thee, that he may sift thee as wheat." Why! this is the very renewal of the scene in the Old Testament in regard to Job. Let me but lay my hand, says this sarcastic and malignant devil, upon this Peter, this disciple so hot and zealous for his Lord and Master, and I will make him blaspheme his very Saviour. I will make him curse God and die. Yes! and the devil did succeed in making him curse God! Awful, awful truth! Fearful revelation of the meaning of our Saviour in his warning to Peter, and of the dreadful power of this Tempter of mankind! But he did not succeed in making him die, not in utterly putting out the light of faith and life within him. No, there again was Satan disappointed, and out of evil still was brought forth good. But why, how, by what agency? Ah, how beautiful, how precious is the explanation! " Simon, Simon, Satan hath desired to have thee, that he may sift thee as wheat; *but I have prayed for thee, that thy faith fail not.*" So thou shalt yet be saved and strengthened, even though thou shalt deny thy Lord ; and when thou art converted, strengthen thy brethren! Ah yes, that was the reason, I HAVE PRAYED FOR THEE. And what saint is there that Christ does not pray for? So, if our trust be in him, we are all safe, but not otherwise. And now, who does not see that in Peter's case, just as in Bunyan's, these dreadful storms of temptation were permitted to overwhelm him, that even out of that terrible experience, out of these very "depths of Satan," the tempted and fallen disciple might gain a strength in the end, through the good Spirit of God, which not another of the brethren, except perhaps Paul, ever manifested. And hence you can trace in Peter's rich instructive epistles, a knowledge of the great adversary, and a warning and a vigilance against him, that sprung from Peter's own dreadful wrestlings with him. Yea, those very blasphemies that Satan made Peter utter, turned out to be the most effective weapons, in remembrance, against himself.

And now I should like to ask any man of common sense to contemplate that striking declaration of our Lord to Peter, "Satan hath desired to have thee, that he may sift thee as wheat;" and tell me in what possible way he would translate or interpret it, except as a manifest absurdity without recognising the existence and agency of fallen spirits? How, I say, shall we translate it, supposing it to mean merely an evil thought, impulse, principle of wickedness? Simon, Simon, I say unto thee, the principle of wickedness hath desired to have thee that it may sift thee as wheat? Could any thing be more ineffably absurd, paltering, emasculating, than such a mode of dealing with the Scriptures? But why desire to resort to such absurdity? Can any thing be more consistent, steadfast, and definite, than the voice of the whole Bible in regard to the personality and agency of Satan? In the very opening of the word of God he comes before us in that awful character, sustained ever since, as the Tempter of mankind, the Tempter, and by his dreadful power the conqueror of the first Adam; and in the opening of the New Testament, the very first thing we see of him again is as the great Tempter of mankind, in personal conflict with the Son of God, the Second Adam, to be by him thrown as lightning from heaven; and his very weapons are those which he used with Bunyan, a diabolical perversion of the word of God itself, and a suggestion of devilish blasphemies. And then in the closing up of all revelation, the same accursed being comes into view as the Dragon, the Serpent, the Devil and Satan, the Deceiver of the world, the Deceiver of the nations, the Tempter of mankind, the Accuser of our brethren!

I have referred you to the temptation of our blessed Lord, and to that beautiful work of Milton, in which, with so much verisimilitude, the character and reflections of the devil, in entering on that work of temptation, are drawn before us. And I say, that Satan would be likely to make the same reflections, and pursue the same measures, though on a smaller scale, whenever he saw men like Luther or Bunyan in such an attitude, under such a discipline, of such a make, that he might expect great danger to his own kingdom from their efforts. For it is characteristic of Satan, as of all the wicked, never to profit by his own experience; and though all the evil he ever did, recoils, and ever must recoil, upon his own head, still he goes on doing it, providing materials for God to display his own glory, and out of evil still to bring forth good. "Experience, like the stern-lights of a ship," only shews Satan the path that has been passed over, and on he goes, committing the same errors in crime again.

Passing, now, in this argument, from our Lord's temptation to our Lord's prayer, we find there a distinct recognition of the Satanic tempter; "Lead us not into temptation, but deliver us from the WICKED ONE." This is one of the few passages in which our translation of the Scriptures, incomparably excellent though it be, is peculiarly defective, not rendering the power and full meaning of the original. There is another passage, equally unfortunate, where the translation, in the opinion of almost all commentators, ancient and modern, ought to be the Evil One, or the Wicked One, the same word being used as in our Lord's prayer:—"But the Lord is faithful, who shall establish you, and keep you from the Wicked One," 2 Thess. iii. 3. And yet another passage in Ephesians, concerning which there cannot be a moment's doubt: "Above all taking the shield of faith, wherewith ye shall be able to quench all the fiery darts of the WICKED

ONE," Ephes. vi. 16. And this is a passage in which the phrase fiery darts is wonderfully expressive and powerful, being taken from the use in war of those slender arrows of cane, to which ignited combustible matter was attached, which, when shot, would set on fire wood-work, tents, whatever there was that would catch fire. Just so are the fiery darts of the WICKED ONE shot into the soul, or shot at the Christian, tipped, as it were, with damnation; and if there be wood, hay, stubble, in a Christian's works, instead of prayer, self-denial, labour for Christ, and in such a case these darts fall into the soul, then what a conflagration, perhaps what apostasy, what ruin, what death! Now in war it was the aim of persons so assailed to intercept and quench these burning arrows; and a most nimble and powerful exercise in the use of the shield did it require; and in the Christian warfare, it is nothing but the Shield of Faith, and an equally nimble and dexterous use of it, that can defend the Christian. And this Bunyan found to his cost; for his great adversary assailed him with a fierce fiery storm of those darts, when he had but very little faith; and his very experience in the use of his shield he had to gain in his conflicts with the enemy. Now, if you compare these passages with some others—such as, "I would have come to you once and again, but Satan hindered me;" "Lest Satan get an advantage of us, for we are not ignorant of his devices;" "Lest by any means the tempter may have tempted you, and our work be in vain;" and other passages of the like character, you will see delineated in the Scriptures the features of that fiend who tempted Bunyan; and you cannot doubt the meaning of the declaration that "your adversary the devil goeth about as a roaring lion, seeking whom he may devour."

Let it be marked that I have here confined myself to one class of passages in regard to Satan, those which present him in the character in which we have to do with him in the case of Bunyan. There are multitudes of passages, which I have not touched, and shall not. In the Revelation of St John the devil is said to be concerned in throwing saints into prison, that they may be tried there; and here is a new mark of identity between the adversary of Bunyan and the devil of the Scriptures; and a new proof that in every age his wiles and stratagems are the same. I could easily fill a whole volume with arguments drawn from Scripture, and another volume with proofs from experience, on this subject. There is one point of importance in Bunyan's experience of the wiles of the devil, which I have not noticed, and that is, the great advantage which early habits of sin give to the Tempter against our own souls. Perhaps we may note this in the case of Peter, in the readiness with which Satan could fill his mouth with profaneness in the recurrence of what were probably his oaths as a youthful passionate fisherman. You may note it much more clearly in the case of Bunyan, who used to swear so dreadfully in his childhood, so that when the devil in his manhood tempted him with blasphemies, he had a powerful advantage over him. God indeed often uses a man's own sins to be terrible scourges to him; and in this is realized what is said in Jeremiah, "Thine own wickedness shall correct thee, and thy backslidings shall reprove thee; know therefore and see that it is an evil and bitter thing that thou hast forsaken the Lord thy God." The truth of this Bunyan found to his great cost under the assaults of the Tempter, opening anew the sluices of his youthful wickedness.

LECTURE THIRD.

Bunyan's Examination.

Bunyan's use of his temptations.—The gloom of his mind in the early part of his imprisonment.—His faithfulness to Christ in the midst of it.—His perfect disinterestedness.—His little blind daughter.—Relation of his examination and imprisonment.—That old enemy Dr Lindale.—Bunyan's admirable answers and Christian deportment.—The nature and preciousness of religious liberty.—Parable by Dr Franklin.

THERE never was a man who made better use of his temptations, especially the temptations by his Great Adversary, than Bunyan. In the preface to his Grace Abounding, addressed to those whom God had counted him worthy to bring to the Redeemer by his ministry, he says, " I have sent you here enclosed a drop of the honey that I have taken out of the carcass of a lion. I have eaten thereof myself, and am much refreshed thereby. Temptations, when we meet them at first, are as the lion that roared upon Samson ; but if we overcome them, the next time we see them we shall find a nest of honey within them." Nor was there ever a man who traced the parental care, tenderness, and goodness of God more clearly, or with more gratitude, in those temptations, the designs of God in suffering such things to befall him, and the manner in which those designs were accomplished. It was for this, Bunyan said, that God suffered him to lie so long at Sinai, to see the fire, and the cloud, and the darkness, " that I might fear the Lord all the days of my life upon earth, and tell of his wondrous works to my children."

It was in the calm, clear light of heaven, in the light of divine mercy to his rescued soul, that Bunyan remembered his ways, his journeyings, the desert and the wilderness, the Rock that followed him, and the Manna that fed him. "Thou shalt remember all the ways which the Lord thy God led thee these forty years in the wilderness, to humble thee, and prove thee, and to know what was in thine heart, whether thou wouldst keep his commandments or no." The grace of God was above Bunyan's sins, and Satan's temptations too; he could remember his fears and doubts and sad months with comfort; they were "as the head of Goliah in his hand." He sang of God's grace as the children of Israel, with the Red Sea between them and the land of their enemies.

It is not to be supposed that the temptations of Satan departed entirely from Bunyan when he was thrown into prison. On the contrary, he was for a time assailed through the same spirit of unbelief, of which his Adversary had made such fearful use, when he was passing through the Valley of Humiliation, and of the Shadow of Death. It was in the early part of his imprisonment, when he was in a sad and low condition for many weeks. A pretty business he says it was; for he thought his imprisonment might end at the gallows, and if it did, and he should be so afraid to die when the time came, and so destitute of all evidence of preparation for a better state hereafter, what could he do! These thoughts, revolved in his mind in various shapes, greatly distressed him. He was afraid of dishonouring his Saviour, and though he prayed earnestly for strength, yet no comfort came; and the only encouragement he could get was this: that he should doubtless have an opportunity to speak to the great multitudes that would come to see him die, and if God would but use his last words for the conversion of one single soul, he would not count his life thrown away nor lost. How delightful is the evidence of Bunyan's disinterestedness, forgetfulness of self, and love to souls, even in the darkness and distress of his sore spiritual conflicts!

But still the things of God were kept out of his sight, and still the Tempter followed hard upon him; a desperate foe, and able still at times to overwhelm Bunyan's soul with anguish, although there remained only the hinder part of

the tempest, and the thunder was gone beyond him
" Whither must you go when you die?" was the gloomy,
moody, sullen question of unbelief in Bunyan's soul beneath
his temptation. What will become of you? Where will you
be found in another world? What evidence have you for
heaven and glory, and an inheritance among them that are
sanctified? For many weeks poor Bunyan knew not what
to do; till at length it came to him with great power, that
at all events, it being for the word and way of God that he
was in this condition of danger, perhaps in the path of death,
he was engaged not to flinch an hair's-breadth from it.
Bunyan thought, furthermore, that it was for God to choose
whether he would give him comfort then, or in the hour of
death, or whether he would or would not give him comfort
in either, comfort at all; but it was not for Bunyan to
choose whether to serve God or not, whether to hold fast his
profession or not, for to this he was bound. He was bound,
but God was free; "Yea," says he, "it was my duty to stand
to his word, whether he would ever look upon me, or save
me at the last, or not; wherefore, thought I, the point being
thus, I am for going on, and venturing my eternal state with
Christ, whether I have comfort here or no. If God doth not
come in, thought I, I will leap off the ladder even blindfold
into eternity; sink or swim, come heaven, come hell. Lord
Jesus, if thou wilt catch me, do; if not, I will venture for
thy name!"

Well done, noble Bunyan! Faithful even unto death, and
faithful even in darkness! Here was no imaginary temptation to sell thy Saviour, but a real inducement, by relinquishing thy confession of the truth, to escape from prison
and from death; a temptation accompanied by dreadful darkness in thy soul. And yet, amidst it all, he ventured every
thing upon Christ, yea, determined to die for him, even though
rejected by him! Was not this a noble triumph over the
Tempter? One would think that from this hour he would
have left Bunyan in utter despair, yea, that he would have
spread his dragon-wings, and Bunyan have seen him no more
for ever! And this indeed I believe that he did; for so soon
as Bunyan had come to this noble and steadfast resolution,

the word of the Tempter flashed across his soul, Doth Job serve God for nought? Hast thou not made an hedge about him? He serves God for benefits. Ah, thought Bunyan, then, even in the opinion of Satan, a man who will serve God when there is nothing to keep or to gain by it, is a renewed man, an upright man. Now, Satan, thou givest me a weapon against thyself. "Is this the sign of a renewed soul, to desire to serve God, when all is taken from him? Is he a godly man that will serve God for nothing, rather than give out? Blessed be God, then, I hope I have an upright heart; for I am resolved, God giving me strength, never to deny my profession, though I had nothing at all for my pains."

Here was a second fight with Apollyon, and a conquest of him for ever. Bunyan's perplexities, after this, were but as drops from the trees after a thunder-shower. He greatly rejoiced in this trial. It made his heart to be full of comfort, because he hoped it proved his heart sincere. And indeed it did; a man that resolves to serve Christ, come heaven, come hell, shews, whatever be his darkness, that God is with him; and Bunyan's noble resolution, amidst such deep gloom over his soul, was a remarkable instance of obedience to that word of God by the prophet, "Who is among you that feareth the Lord, that obeyeth the voice of his servant, that walketh in darkness and hath no light? Let him trust in the name of the Lord, and stay upon his God." Bunyan could now say, in a passage in the forty-fourth Psalm, brought powerfully to remembrance, "Though thou hast sore broken us in the place of dragons, and covered us with the shadow of death, yet our heart is not turned back, neither have our steps declined from thy way." This indeed, is the truest sign of conversion, to venture all on Christ, and resolve to serve him come what may.

When a soul comes to this determination, it always finds light. And so it was with Bunyan; and he says himself, "I would not have been without this trial for much. I am comforted every time I think of it; and I hope I shall bless God for ever for the teaching I have had by it." In this trial, Bunyan may in truth be said to have been added to the number of the witnesses in the Revelation, who overcame the Tempter by the blood of the Lamb, and the word of their testimony; *and they loved not their lives unto the death.* For Bunyan was as if he had been brought to the scaffold, and there taken the leap into eternity in the dark. This passage in Bunyan's prison experience reminds us powerfully of Christian's woeful confinement in the dungeon of Giant Despair's castle from Wednesday morning till Saturday night, and of his sudden and joyful deliverance; nor can there be any doubt that some of the lights and shades in that beautiful passage grew out of those melancholy weeks, when Bunyan's soul as well as his body was in prison. Afterwards, his soul was unfettered, and then what cared he for the confinement of his body? He could say, in an infinitely higher sense than some of his enemies in the celebrated song of his times,

> "Stone walls do not a prison make,
> Nor iron-bars a cage;
> Minds innocent and quiet take
> That for a hermitage."

In Bunyan's prison meditations, he describes most forcibly, in his own rude but vigorous rhymes, the freedom and triumph of his soul.

> "For though men keep my outward man
> Within their locks and bars,
> Yet by the faith of Christ I can
> Mount higher than the stars.
>
> 'Tis not the baseness of this state
> Doth hide us from God's face;
> He frequently, both soon and late,
> Doth visit us with grace.
>
> We change our drossy dust for gold,
> From death to life we fly;
> We let go shadows, and take hold
> Of immortality.
>
> These be the men that God doth count
> Of high and noble mind;
> These be the men that do surmount
> What you in nature find.
>
> First they do conquer their own hearts,
> All worldly fears, and then
> Also the Devil's fiery darts,
> And persecuting men.

> They conquer when they thus do fall.
> They kill when they do die;
> They overcome then most of all,
> And get the victory."

Such poetry would have been noble from any man of genius, but it came from Bunyan's heart; it was his own experience. "I never had in my life," he says, "so great an inlet into the word as now. Those scriptures that I saw nothing in before, are made in this place and state to shine upon me. Jesus Christ also was never more real and apparent than now; here I have seen and felt him indeed." Three or four sweet and thrilling scriptures were a great refreshment to him, especially that sweet fourteenth of John, "Let not your heart be troubled," &c., and that of John, xvi. 33, "In the world ye shall have tribulation; but be of good cheer, I have overcome the world;" and also that inspiring, animating word, "We are come unto Mount Zion," &c. Sometimes, when Bunyan was "in the savour" of these scriptures, he was able to laugh at destruction, and to fear neither the horse nor his rider. "I have had sweet sights of the forgiveness of my sins in this place, and of my being with Jesus in another world. O the Mount Zion, the heavenly Jerusalem, the innumerable company of angels, and God the Judge of all, and the spirits of just men made perfect, and Jesus the Mediator, have been sweet unto me in this place! I have seen that here, which I am persuaded I shall never, while in this world, be able to express. I have seen a truth in this scripture, 'Whom having not seen ye love; in whom, though now ye see him not, yet believing, ye rejoice with joy unspeakable, and full of glory.'

"I never knew what it was for God to stand by me at all times, and at every offer of Satan to afflict me, as I have found him since I came in hither; for look how fears have presented themselves, so have supports and encouragements; yea, when I have started even as it were at nothing else but my shadow, yet God, as being very tender of me, hath not suffered me to be molested, but would, with one scripture or another, strengthen me against all, insomuch that I have often said, Were it lawful, I could pray for greater trouble for the greater comfort's sake." Bunyan could now say with Paul, that as his sufferings *for* Christ abounded, so his consolation *in* Christ abounded likewise.

Bunyan had thought much upon these things before he went to prison; for he saw the storm coming, and had some preparatory considerations "warm upon his heart." Like a prudent, skilful, fearless mariner, he took in sail at the signs of the hurricane, and made all tight aloft, by prayer, and by consideration of the things which are unseen and eternal. He kept on his course, turning neither to the right hand nor the left, in his Master's service, but he made all ready for the tempest, and familiarized himself to the worst that might come, be it the prison, the pillory, or banishment, or death. With a magnanimity and grandeur of philosophy which none of the princes, or philosophers, or sufferers of this world ever dreamed of, he concluded that "the best way to go through suffering, is to trust in God through Christ as touching the world to come; and as touching this world, to be dead to it, to give up all interest in it, to have the sentence of death in ourselves and admit it, to count the grave my house, to make my bed in darkness, and to say to corruption, Thou art my father; and to the worm, Thou art my mother and sister; that is, to familiarize these things to me."

With this preparation, when the storm suddenly fell, though the ship at first bowed and laboured heavily under it, yet how, like a bird, did she afterwards flee before it! It reminds me of those two lines of Wesley,

> "The tempests that rise,
> Shall gloriously hurry our souls to the skies!"

So Bunyan's bark sped onward, amidst howling gales, with rattling hail and thunder; but onward, still onward, and upward, still upward, to heaven!

There is one passage in his experience at this time which is deeply affecting, as shewing what he had to break from and to leave, and in what difficult circumstances, as well as to encounter, in going to prison, and perhaps to death. "Notwithstanding these spiritual helps," he says, "I found myself a man encompassed with infirmities. The parting with my wife and poor children hath often been to me, in this place, as the pulling the flesh from my bones; and that not only because I am somewhat too fond of these mercies, but also because I should have often brought to my mind the many hardships, miseries, and wants that my poor family was likewise to meet with; *especially my poor blind child,* who lay nearer my heart than all I had beside. Oh, the thoughts of the hardships I thought my blind one might go under would break my heart to pieces! Poor child, thought I, what sorrow art thou like to have for thy portion in this world! Thou must be beaten, must beg, suffer hunger, cold, nakedness, and a thousand calamities, though I cannot now endure the wind shall blow upon thee! But yet recalling myself, thought I, I must venture you all with God, though it goeth to the quick to leave you. Oh, I saw in this condition I was as a man who is pulling down his house upon the head of his wife and children; yet, thought I, I must do it, I must do it. And now, I thought on those two milch kine, that were to carry the ark of God into another country, to leave their calves behind them."

Nothing could be more touching than this artless picture of Bunyan's domestic tenderness, especially of the father's affection for his poor blind child. If anything could have tempted him from duty; if anything could have allured him to *conform* against his conscience, it had been this. But the Scriptures and the love of Christ supported him; and he who could venture to die for Christ, even while his soul was in darkness, could also trust in the promise, "Leave thy fatherless children; I will preserve them alive; and let thy widow trust in me. Verily, it shall go well with thy remnant." So, by divine grace, Bunyan overcame this temptation also.

And now, having followed this instructive picture of Bunyan's conflicts, partly while under fear of prison and of death, laying our tracery, as it were, over his own deeply engraven lines to make it accurate, we come next to his own account of his commitment, which is one of the most humorous, characteristic, and instructive pieces in the English language. This is not to be found in the "Grace Abounding," but stands by itself in a tract entitled, "A Relation of the Imprisonment of Mr John Bunyan, Minister of the Gospel at Bedford, in November 1660; his Examination before the Justices; his Conference with the Clerk of the Peace; what passed between the Judges and his Wife, when she presented a Petition for his Deliverance, and so forth. Written by himself."

"I was indicted," says Bunyan, "for an upholder and maintainer of unlawful assemblies and conventicles, and for not conforming to the national worship of the Church of England; and after some conference there with the justices, they taking my plain dealing with them for a confession, as they termed it, of the indictment, did sentence me to a perpetual banishment, because I refused to conform. So being again delivered up to the jailor's hands, I was had home to prison, and there have lain now complete twelve years, *waiting to see what God would suffer these men to do with me.*"

It is a striking phraseology which Bunyan uses, he "was had *home* to prison;" it was indeed a home to him, for God made it such, sweeter, by divine grace, than any earthly home in his pilgrimage. He had been preaching for years when he was first taken, which was upon the 12th of November 1660. He had engaged, if the Lord permitted, to come and teach some of the people who desired it on that day; but the justice of the peace hearing of it, issued his warrant to take Bunyan, and mean time to keep a strong watch about the house, "as if," says Bunyan, "we that were to meet together in that place, did intend to do some fearful business to the destruction of the country." Yea, they could scarce have been more alarmed and vigilant, if there had been rumour of a Popish gunpowder plot on foot. "When, alas! the constable, when he came in, found us only with our Bibles in our hands, ready to speak and hear the word of God; for we were just about to begin our exercise. Nay, we had begun in prayer for the blessing of God upon our opportunity, intending to have preached the word of the Lord unto them there present; but the constable coming in, prevented us."

Bunyan might have escaped had he chosen, for he had fair warning; but he reasoned nobly that as he had shewed himself hearty and courageous in his preaching, and made it his business to encourage others, if he should now run, his weak and newly converted brethren would certainly think he was not so strong in deed as in word. " Also, I feared that if I should run, now that there was a warrant out for me, I might, by so doing, make them afraid to stand, when great words only should be spoken to them. Besides, I thought that seeing God of his mercy should choose me to go upon the forlorn hope in this country; that is, to be the first that should be opposed for the gospel; if I should fly, it might be a discouragement to the whole body that might follow after. And further, I thought the world thereby would take occasion at my cowardliness to have blasphemed the gospel, and to have had some grounds to suspect worse of me and my profession than I deserved." So Bunyan staid with full resolution, and began the meeting. And when brought before the Justice, and questioned as to what he did there, and why he did not content himself with following his calling, for it was against the law that such as he should be admitted to do as he did; he answered, that the intent of his coming thither, and to other places, was to instruct and counsel people to forsake their sins, and close in with Christ, lest they did miserably perish, and that he could do both these without confusion, to wit, follow his calling, and preach the word also.

" Now," says Bunyan, in a passage where you have the germ of many a character that afterwards figured in the pages of the Pilgrim's Progress, " Now, while my mittimus was a-making, the justice was withdrawn, and in comes an old enemy to the truth, Dr Lindale, who when he was come in, fell to taunting at me with many reviling terms. To whom I answered, that I did not come thither to talk with him, but with the Justice. Whereat he supposing that I had nothing to say for myself, triumphed as if he had got the victory, charging and condemning me for meddling with that for which I could shew no warrant, and asked me if I had taken the oaths, and if I had not, it was pity but that I should be sent to prison. I told him that if I was minded, I could answer to any sober question put to me. He then urged me again, how I could prove it lawful for me to preach, with a great deal of confidence of the victory. But at last, because he should see that I could answer him if I listed, I cited to him that in Peter, which saith, "As every man hath received the gift, even so let him minister the same."

Lindale. Ay, saith he, to whom is that spoken?

Bunyan. To whom? said I; why, to every man that hath received a gift from God. Mark, saith the apostle, as every man hath received the gift from God; and again, You may all prophecy one by one. Whereat the man was a little stopt, and went a softlier pace. But not being willing to lose the day, he began again, and said:

Lind. Indeed, I do remember that I have read of one Alexander a coppersmith, who did much oppose and disturb the apostles: (aiming, it is like, at me, because I was a tinker).

Bun. To which I answered, that I also had read of very many priests and Pharisees, that had their hands in the blood of our Lord Jesus Christ.

Lind. Ay, saith he, and you are one of those scribes and Pharisees, for you, with a pretence, make long prayers to devour widows' houses.

Bun. I answered, that if he got no more by preaching and praying than I had done, he would not be so rich as now he was. But that scripture coming into my mind, "Answer not a fool according to his folly," I was as sparing of my speech as I could without prejudice to the truth.

After this there was another examination with one Mr Foster of Bedford, who tried hard to persuade Bunyan to promise that he would leave off preaching, in which case he should be acquitted. Bunyan's honest, straightforward truth, good sense, and mother-wit, answered as good a purpose with this Mr Foster, as it did with that "old enemy," Dr Lindale. Mr Foster told Bunyan there were none that heard him but a company of foolish people.

Bun. I told him that there were the wise as well as the foolish that did hear me; and again, those that are most commonly counted foolish by the world, are the wisest before

God. Also, that God had rejected the wise and mighty and noble, and chosen the foolish and the base.

Foster. He told me that I made people neglect their calling; and that God hath commanded people to work six days, and serve him on the seventh.

Bun. I told him that it was the duty of people, rich and poor, to look out for their souls on those days, as well as their bodies; and that God would have his people exhort one another daily, while it is called to-day.

Fost. He said again, that there were none but a company of poor, simple, ignorant people that came.

Bun. I told him that the foolish and the ignorant had most need of teaching and information; and therefore it would be profitable for me to go on in that work.

Fost. Well, said he, to conclude, but will you promise that you will not call the people together any more, and then you may be released and go home?

Bun. I told him that I durst say no more than I had said; for I durst not leave off that work which God had called me to. If my preaching might be said to call the people together, I durst not say that I would not call them together.

Foster upon this told the justice that he must send Bunyan to prison; and so to prison he went, nothing daunted, but singing and making melody in his heart unto the Lord. After this follows an inimitably rich and humorous dialogue, which Bunyan called the Sum of my Examination before Justice Keelin, Justice Chester, Justice Blundale, Justice Beecher, and Justice Snagg. These men's names are immortalized in a way they never dreamed of; nor can any one read this scene, and compare it with the trial of Faithful in the Pilgrim's Progress, and not see what rich materials Bunyan was now gathering, in the providence of God, out of his own experience, for his future work. These persons are just as certainly to be detected in Bunyan's sketches of the court, in the town of Vanity Fair, as Sancho Panza whenever he appears in any part of Don Quixote. It was an almost unconscious operation of quiet, but keen satire, when this scene remoulded its materials afterwards in Bunyan's imagination. The extent of the indictment against Bunyan was as follows: That John Bunyan, of the town of Bedford, labourer, being a person of such and such conditions, he hath, since such a time, devilishly and perniciously abstained from coming to church to hear divine service, and is a common upholder of several unlawful meetings and conventicles, to the great disturbance and distraction of the good subjects of this kingdom, contrary to the laws of our sovereign Lord the King. When this was read, the clerk of the sessions said to Bunyan, What say you to this?

Bunyan. I said that as to the first part of it, I was a common frequenter of the church of God, and was also, by grace, a member with those people, over whom Christ was the head.

Keelin. But, saith Justice Keelin, who was the judge in that court—Do you come to church—you know what I mean —to the parish church, to hear divine service?

Bun. I answered no, I did not.

Keel. He asked me why.

Bun. I said, because I did not find it commanded in the word of God.

Keel. He said we were commanded to pray.

Bun. I said, but not by the Common Prayer Book.

Keel. He said, how then?

Bun. I said, with the Spirit. As the apostle saith, I will pray with the Spirit, with understanding.

Keel. He said, we might pray with the Spirit with understanding, and with the Common Prayer Book also.

Bun. I said that those prayers in the Common Prayer Book were such as were made by other men, and not by the motions of the Holy Ghost within our hearts; and as I said, the apostle saith he will pray with the Spirit and with understanding, not with the Spirit and the Common Prayer Book.

Another Justice. What do you count prayer? Do you think it is to say a few words over, before or among a people?

Bun. I said, not so; for men might have many elegant or excellent words, and yet not pray at all; but when a man prayeth, he doth, through a sense of those things which he wants, which sense is begotten by the Spirit, pour out his heart before God through Christ; though his words be not so many and so excellent as others.

Justices. They said that was true.

Bun. I said this might be done without the Common Prayer Book.

There was a strange mixture of candour and bitterness in these Justices, for they acknowledged the truth of some things that Bunyan said, and that very freely, while they were blasphemous in other things, as we shall see. Bunyan's own argument against the Common Prayer Book would not be admitted as valid by many out of the Episcopal Church as well as in it; but his argument against the enforcing of it on the conscience is incontrovertible, as well as his own candid and tolerant spirit towards those who preferred to use it. "Let them use it, if they choose," said he, "we would not keep them from it; only, for our part, we can pray to God without it; and all we ask is the liberty of so praying and preaching." Could any thing be more fair, equitable, or generous than this? The same we say now to those who assert, that we cannot worship God aright without episcopacy, confirmation, and a liturgy; and who arrogantly say, that without these things we are not of the true church, and are neither ministers nor flocks of Jesus Christ. We say to those who are guilty of such unchristian conduct, Use you your liturgy, and love it as much as you please, and we will agree with you, that for those who choose a liturgy, it is, with some great faults, an admirable composition; but dare not to impose it upon us; be not guilty of the great intolerance and wickedness of unchurching and anathematizing others, because they do not use a liturgy nor hold to episcopacy; stand not by yourselves and say, I am holier than thou by the apostolical succession, and episcopacy, and the liturgy! Above all, if you do these things, expect to be met with severity and indignation; and accuse no man of bitterness who defends, or because he defends, the church and the ministry of Christ from your unrighteous assumptions.

Bunyan's chief reason for not using the Common Prayer

Book was, that it is not commanded in the Scriptures. "Shew me," said he, "the place in the epistles where the Common Prayer Book is written, or one text of Scripture that commands me to read it, and I will use it. But yet, notwithstanding," said he, "they that have a mind to use it, they have their liberty; that is, I would not keep it from them, or them from it; but for our parts, we can pray to God without it. Blessed be his name."

With that one of them said, Who is your God, Beelzebub? Moreover they often said that I was possessed with the spirit of delusion and of the devil. All which sayings I passed over, the Lord forgive them! And further, I said, Blessed be the Lord for it, we are encouraged to meet together, and to pray, and exhort one another: for we have had the comfortable presence of God among us, for ever blessed be his holy name.

Justice Keelin called this pedler's French, saying that I must leave off my canting. The Lord open his eyes.

Bun. I said that we ought to exhort one another daily, while it is called to-day.

Keel. Justice Keelin said that I ought not to preach; and asked me where I had my authority?

Bun. I said that I would prove that it was lawful for me, and such as I am, to preach the word of God.

Keel. He said unto me, By what scripture?

Bun. I said, By that in the first epistle of Peter, the fourth chapter, the eleventh verse; and Acts the eighteenth, with other scriptures, which he would not suffer me to mention. But hold, said he, not so many; which is the first?

Bun. I said this: "As every man hath received the gift, so let him minister the same one to another, as good stewards of the manifold grace of God; if any man speak, let him speak as the oracles of God."

Keel. He said, Let me a little open that scripture to you. As every man hath received the gift; that is, said he, as every man hath received a trade, so let him follow it. If any man hath received a gift of tinkering, as thou hast done, let him follow his tinkering; and so other men their trades, and the divine his calling, &c.

Bun. Nay, sir, said I, but it is most clear that the apostle speaks here of preaching the word; if you do but compare both the verses together, the next verse explains this gift, what it is; saying, "If any man speak, let him speak as the oracles of God;" so that it is plain that the Holy Ghost doth not, in this place, so much exhort to civil callings, as to the exercising of those gifts that we have received from God. I would have gone on, but he would not give me leave.

Keel. He said, we might do it in our families, but not otherwise.

Bun. I said, if it was lawful to do good to some, it was lawful to do good to more. If it was a good duty to exhort our families, it is good to exhort others; but if they hold it a sin to meet together to seek the face of God, and exhort one another to follow Christ, I should sin still, for so we should do.

Keel. Then you confess the indictment, do you not?

Bun. This I confess, we have had many meetings together, both to pray to God and to exhort one another, and that we had the sweet comforting presence of the Lord among us, for our encouragement, blessed be his name therefore. I confess myself guilty no otherwise.

Keel. Then, said he, hear your judgment. You must be had back again to prison, and there lie for three months following; and at three months' end, if you do not submit to go to church to hear divine service, and leave your preaching, you must be banished the realm; and if, after such a day as shall be appointed you to be gone, you shall be found in this realm, or be found to come over again without special license from the king, you must stretch by the neck for it, I tell you plainly. And so he bid my jailer have me away.

Bun. I told him, as to this matter I was at a point with him; for if I was out of prison to-day, I would preach the gospel again to-morrow, by the help of God.

Thus ended the examination and commitment of John Bunyan. This answer of his is equal in nobleness to any thing recorded of Luther. IF I WAS OUT OF THE PRISON TO-DAY, I WOULD PREACH THE GOSPEL AGAIN TO-MORROW, BY THE HELP OF GOD. There was neither obstinacy nor vainglory in it, but a calm steadfast determination to obey God rather than man. Bunyan had good examples for his steadfastness and courage. The scene reminds us more than almost any thing else, of certain events in the Acts of the Apostles. What shall we do to these men? said the Jewish rulers. That it spread no further among the people, let us straitly threaten them, that they speak henceforth to no man in this name. And they called them, and commanded them not to speak at all, nor teach in the name of Jesus. But Peter and John answered and said unto them, Whether it be right in the sight of God to hearken unto you more than unto God, judge ye. For we cannot but speak the things which we have seen and heard. And again they spake; and again they were thrust into prison; and again they spake; and again the council and high priest charged them, Did we not straitly command you that ye should not teach in this name? So they beat the apostles, and commanded that they should not speak in the name of Jesus, and let them go. And what next? Why, just this: And daily in the temple, and in every house, they ceased not to teach, and to preach Jesus Christ.

In all these trying and vexing examinations, Bunyan appears to the greatest advantage, both as a man and a Christian. If he sometimes answered a fool according to his folly, it was never with railing or bitterness; and with all his prejudices against the Common Prayer Book, he has not one word to say against those who choose it, or conscientiously use it, or against their religion. And now, to those who may think it strange that so strong a prejudice should have prevailed against that book, so that men would rather go to prison than use it, we would simply say, What think you would be your feelings in regard to the Presbyterian Book of Discipline, if you were compelled by law to use it, and abide by it, or else have no religion at all? If the strong grasp of civil and ecclesiastical tyranny were laid upon you, and your face were pressed in the dust beneath that book, and it were said to you, Either abide by this and obey it, or you shall neither preach nor teach, nor hold any civil office; nay, you shall be thrust into prison, or banished, and if found returning, you shall be hanged by the neck till you are dead! I say, what think you would be your feelings towards that book? Why, if it were better than the Pilgrim's Progress itself, you would abhor it, and I had almost said, you would do well to hate it; and you would, as an instrument of pride and tyranny. Prejudice against the Common Prayer Book! If men wish to bring it into disgrace, let them persevere in their assumption that there is no true church, and no true ministry without it. The cross itself, the moment you erect it into a thing of worship, the moment you put the image in place of the thing signified, becomes an idol, a mark of sin instead of glory. Just so it was with the brazen serpent. There was a race of Romanists in that day, who kept it as an object of idolatrous adoration; had they been let go on in their absurdities, they would have passed a law that no person should worship without the brazen serpent. But good King Hezekiah, the noble old image-breaker, took it, and called it with the utmost contempt, *a piece of brass*, Nehushtan, and burned it in the fire, and ground it to powder.

Here I am reminded of a very beautiful remark by Mr Coleridge, taken partly from an old writer, that an appropriate and seemly religious ceremony is as a gold chain about the neck of faith; it at once adorns and secures it. Yes, says Mr Coleridge, but if you draw it too close, you strangle it. You strangle and destroy religion, if you make that which is not essential, and especially that which is not commanded in scripture, to be essential and inevitable. And just so with the Prayer Book, the Liturgy; if you seek to enforce it on men's consciences, if you make it essential to religion or to the true church, you suffocate and strangle your religion, and instead of finding in it a living seraph, it will be to you a dead corpse. Let no man judge you in regard to these things, saith Paul; let no man be admitted to spy out and destroy your liberty, which ye have in Christ Jesus. Give no place in subjection to such an one, no, not for an hour.

One of the most instructive and important lessons to be drawn from this part of Bunyan's history, and from the survey of his times, is the invaluable preciousness of that discipline of trial, which God, in infinite wisdom and mercy, has appointed for his people, as their pathway to the kingdom of heaven. We scarcely know how the church of Christ could have existed, or what she would have become, without the purifying and ennobling fires of persecution to burn upon her. The most precious of her literary and religious treasures have come out of this furnace. The most heavenly and inspiring names in the record of her living examples are the names of men whose souls were purged from their dross by just such discipline, and perhaps taken out of their bodies, and conveyed in a chariot of fire to heaven. The martyr literature of England, a possession like which, in glory and in value, no nation in the world can shew the counterpart, grew out of that fiery process upon men's souls; it is as gold seven-fold purified in the furnace. This book of Bunyan's, the heavenly Pilgrim's Progress, grew out of just such a process; for such is the nature of adversity in the hand of God, not only to refine and purify, but to bring out hidden virtue into exercise, and to give to all qualities so wrought, a power over the universal heart of man, such as no learning can sway, and no philosophy communicate. The best work of Baxter's was written on the borders of the grave, in weakness and suffering, having bidden the world adieu, and being raised by the magic of such discipline to a mount of vision, from whence he could take a broad and near survey of the glories of heaven. And perhaps self-denial, by the grace of God, is still more efficacious to raise a man's soul, impart to it power, and transfigure it with glory, than even adversity under the hand of God. At any rate, here is the true secret of greatness. Virtue, said Lord Bacon, is like precious odours, most fragrant when they are either burned or crushed. This is the power of adversity with noble natures, or, with the grace of God, even in a poor nature. But self-denial is a sort of self-burning, that makes a purer fire, and more surely separates the dross from a man's being, than temptation and affliction. Indeed, self-denial is the great end in this world, of which temptation and affliction are the means; a man being then most free and powerful, when most completely dead to self and absorbed in God the Saviour.

The importance of suffering and self-denial as elements of spiritual discipline, is never by us sufficiently considered. If we draw back from the baptism of suffering, we are not likely to be instrumental in the regeneration either of the soul or the literature of the world. How beautiful the language of the poet Cowper, wrung from him by his own experience of anguish!

> "The path of sorrow, and that path alone,
> Leads to the land where sorrow is unknown."

And Cowper's own intellectual being, Cowper's own poetry, derived a strength and a sacred fire of inspiration from his own sufferings, which nothing else could have communicated. Such has been the experience of multitudes; and it is true that the very best part of our literature has come out of that same furnace. And must not this be our experience if in our piety and intellect we would retain the elements of originality and vital power? It was a remark of Mr Coleridge, that cannot be too often quoted, that Death only supplies the oil for the inextinguishable lamp of life; a great truth, which is true even before our mortal dissolution; that death to self, which trial, by God's grace, produces, constituting, even in this world, the very essence of strength, life, and glory.

Another most important and instructive lesson to be drawn from this part of Bunyan's history, and from our survey of his times, is that of the invaluable preciousness of religious liberty, and the importance not only of the possession, but of the right understanding and use of this great blessing. The experience of ages has proved that there is no lesson so difficult for mankind to learn as that of true religious toleration; for almost every sect in turn, when tempted by the power, has resorted to the practice of religious persecution. Were it not for the seeming incongruity of the sentiment, we should say that good men have even taken turns in burning one another; though, to the credit of Rome, it must be said that the baptism of fire is almost exclusively *her* sacrament for heretics. Good men of almost all persuasions have been confined in prison for conscience' sake.

Bunyan was the first person in the reign of Charles II. *punished* for the *crime* of non-conformity. This, in part, is Southey's own language, *punished* is the phrase he uses ; it should have been, *persecuted* for the *virtue ;* for such it was in Bunyan : and any palliation which could be resorted to for the purpose of justifying the English Hierarchy for shutting up John Bunyan in prison, would also justify a Romish Hierarchy for burning Latimer and Ridley at the stake. Strange, that the lesson of religious toleration should be one of the last and hardest, even for liberal minds, to learn ! It cost long time, instruction, and discipline even for the disciples of Christ to learn it ; and they never would have learned it, had not the infant church been cut loose from the state, and deprived of all possibility of girding the secular arm with thunder in its behalf. John had not learned it, when he would have called down fire from heaven to destroy the Samaritans ; nor John nor his fellows, wher they forbade a faithful saint (some John Bunyan of those ays, belike), from casting out devils, because he followed ot *them*. And they never would have learned it had the union of church and state been sanctioned by the Saviour. Wherever one sect in particular is united to the state, the lesson of religious toleration will not be perfectly learned ; nay, who does not see that toleration itself, applied to religion, implies the assumption of a power that ought not to exist, that in itself is tyranny. It implies that you, an earthly authority, an earthly power, say to me, so condescendingly, I *permit* you the free exercise of your religion. You permit me ! And what authority have you to permit me, any more than I to permit you ? God permits me, God commands me ; and do you dare to say that you *tolerate* me ? Who is he that shall dare come in between me and God, either to say yea or nay ? Your toleration itself is tyranny, for you have no right to meddle with the matter. But wherever church and state are united, then there will be meddling with the matter ; and even in this country, if one particular sect were to get the patronage of the state, there would be an end to our perfect religious freedom. In the reign of Queen Elizabeth, the poet Southwell, who wrote one of the most exquisitely beautiful death-hymns in our language, and who seems to have been truly a devout man, was put to death violently and publicly, no other crime being proved against him, but what he honestly and proudly avowed, that he had come over into England simply and solely to preach the Roman Catholic religion. And he ought to have been left at liberty to preach it; for if the Protestant religion cannot stand against Roman Catholic preaching, it ought to go down; no religion is worth having, or worth supporting, that needs racks, or inquisitions, or fires and faggots to sustain it; that dare not or cannot meet its adversaries on the open battle-field of truth; no religion is worth supporting that needs any thing but the truth and Spirit of God to support it; and no establishment ought to be permitted to stand, that stands by persecuting others; nor any church to exist, that exists simply by unchurching others.

So, if the English Church Establishment dared not consider herself safe without shutting up John Bunyan and sixty other dissenters with him in prison, some of them ministers, and some laymen—some for preaching the gospel, and some for hearing it, the English Church Establishment was not worthy to *be* safe; the English Church Establishment was a disgrace and an injury to the gospel, and a disgrace and an injury to a free people. No church is worth saving from destruction, if it has to be saved by the destruction of other men's religious liberties; nay, if that be the case with it, it ought to go down, and the sooner the better. No church is worthy to stand that makes non-conformity to its rites and usages a penal crime. It becomes a persecuting church the moment it does this. For, supposing that every man, woman, and child in the kingdom is kept from non-conformity simply by that threat, and that through the power of such terror there comes to be never the need to put such penal laws in execution, and so never a single subject really molested or punished; still that church is a persecuting church, and that people a persecuted people, a terrified people, a people cowed down, a people in whose souls the sacred fire of liberty is fast extinguishing, a people bound to God's service by the fear of men's racks. Such a people can never be free; their cowardice will forge their fetters. A people who will sell themselves to a church through fear of punishment, will sell themselves to any tyrant through the same fear; nay, a people who will serve God through the fear of punishment, when they would not serve him otherwise, will serve Satan in the same way.

If you make *non-conformity* a crime, you are therefore a persecuting church, whether your name be Rome, or England, or America, even though there be not a single non-conformist found for you to exercise your wrath upon, not one against whom you may draw the sword of your penalty. But it *is* drawn, and drawn against the liberty of conscience, and every man whom in this way you keep from non-conformity, you make him a deceiver to his God; you make him barter his conscience for exemption from an earthly penalty; you make him put his conscience not into God's keeping, but into the keeping of your sword; you dry up the life-blood of liberty in his soul; you make him in his inmost conscience an imprisoned slave, a venal victim of your bribery and terror: and though he may still walk God's earth as others, it is with the iron in his soul—it is with your chain about his neck—it is as the shuffling fugitive from your penalties, and not as a man of noble soul, who, fearing God religiously, fears nothing else. There may, indeed, be no chain visible, but you have wound its invisible links around the man's spirit; you have bound the man within the man; you have fettered him, and laid him down in a cold dark dungeon; and until those fetters are taken off, and he stands erect and looks out from his prison to God, it is no man, but a slave that you have in your service; it is no disciple, but a Simon Magus that you have in your church. If a man obeys God through the fear of man, when he would not do it otherwise, he obeys not God, but man; and in that very obedience he becomes a dissembler and a coward. If he says, I do this, which I should not do otherwise, for fear of such or such a penalty ; or, I partake of this sacrament, which I should not otherwise touch, because the continuance of my office depends upon it, what is he but an acknowledged sacrilegious hypocrite ? And thus it is that your system of penalties for an established church inevitably makes hypocrites.

Let me now close what I have said on this point with a very beautiful parable by Dr Franklin, taken originally, it is said, from a Persian poet, and to be found in substance also in Jeremy Taylor. Its imitation of the scripture style is as exquisite as its lessons are admirable :—" And it came to pass, after these things, that Abraham sat in the door of his tent, about the going-down of the sun ; and behold a man bent with age coming from the way of the wilderness, leaning on a staff. And Abraham arose and met him, and said unto him, Turn in, I pray thee, and wash thy feet, and tarry all night ; and thou shalt arise early in the morning, and go thy way. And the man said, Nay ; for I will abide under this tree. But Abraham pressed him greatly : so he turned, and they went into the tent ; and Abraham baked unleavened bread, and they did eat. And when Abraham saw that the man blessed not God, he said unto him, Wherefore dost thou not worship the most high God, Creator of heaven and earth ? And the man answered and said, I do not worship thy God, neither do I call on his name ; for I have made to myself a god, which abideth always in my house, and provideth me with all things. And Abraham's zeal was kindled against the man, and he arose, and fell upon him, and drove him forth with blows into the wilderness. And God called unto Abraham, saying, Abraham, where is the stranger ? And Abraham answered and said, Lord, he would not worship thee, neither would he call upon thy name ; therefore have I driven him out from before my face into the wilderness. And God said, Have I borne with him these hundred and ninety and eight years, and nourished him and clothed him, notwithstanding his rebellion against me ; and couldst not thou, who art thyself a sinner, bear with him one night ?"

Now this supposed zeal of Abraham was far more natural,

though not more excusable, than most ebullitions of religious intolerance. But who are we, that dare take into our hands the prerogative of God over the conscience? Who are we, that we should punish with blows, or penalties of any kind, the fellow-creatures who differ from us, or because they differ from us, in their religious worship? Let us hope that the time is hastening, when that zeal divorced from love, which has produced such incalculable misery on earth, shall be banished from all human hearts, and its place forever supplied by the charity of the gospel. Out of God's holy word, I know of no brighter example of that charity on record than John Bunyan.

In the Grace Abounding to the Chief of Sinners, Bunyan published what he names, *A Brief Account of the Author's Call to the Work of the Ministry*. It is one of the most interesting and instructive portions of that remarkable work, shewing the deep exercises of his soul for others, in as vivid a light as the account of his conversion sheds upon his personal spiritual experience. We venture to say, that there was never in the world, since the time of the Apostle Paul, a more remarkable instance of a wrestling spirit in behalf of others. And this it was, that, by the blessing of God, made his preaching efficacious; it was the deep, powerful, soul-stirring intensity of interest with which he entered into it himself, preparing himself for it by fervent prayer, and following his own sermons with a restless importunity of supplication for the divine blessing. "In my preaching," he tells us himself, "I have really been in pain, and have as it were travailed to bring forth children to God; neither could I be satisfied unless some fruits did appear in my work. If it were fruitless, it mattered not who commended me; but if I were fruitful, I cared not who did condemn I have thought of that word, 'Lo! children are an heritage of the Lord; and the fruit of the womb is his reward. As arrows in the hands of a mighty man, so are children of the youth. Happy is the man that hath his quiver full of them; they shall not be ashamed, but shall speak with the enemies in the gate.'

"It pleased me nothing to see a people drink in my opinions, if they seemed ignorant of Jesus Christ, and the worth of their own salvation; sound conviction of sin, especially of unbelief, and an heart set on fire to be saved by Christ, with strong breathings after a truly sanctified soul, that it was that delighted me; those were the souls I counted blessed.

"If any of those who were awakened by my ministry did after that fall back (as sometimes too many did), I can truly say their loss hath been more to me than if my own children, begotten of my own body, had been going to the grave. I think verily I may speak it without any offence to the Lord, nothing has gone so near me as that; unless it was the fear of the loss of the salvation of my own soul. I have counted as if I had goodly buildings and lordships in those places where my children were born. My heart hath been so wrapped up in the glory of this excellent work, that I counted myself more blessed and honoured of God by this, than if he had made me emperor of the Christian world, or the lord of all the glory of the earth without it. Oh these words! He that converteth a sinner from the error of his ways doth save a soul from death. The fruit of the righteous is a tree of life; and he that winneth souls is wise. They that be wise shall shine as the brightness of the firmament, and they that turn many to righteousness as the stars for ever and ever. For what is our hope, our joy, our crown of rejoicing? Are not ye even in the presence of our Lord Jesus Christ at his coming? For ye are our glory and joy. These, I say, with many others of a like nature, have been great refreshments to me."

Not only before and after preaching was Bunyan accustomed to cry mightily to God for an effectual blessing, but also while he was in the exercise; for every word that he spake sprang out of an earnest desire by all means to save some. "When I have been preaching, I thank God my heart hath often, all the time of this and the other exercise, with great earnestness cried to God that he would make the word effectual to the salvation of the soul; still being grieved lest the enemy should take the word away from the conscience, and so it should become unfruitful; wherefore I should labour so to speak the word, as that thereby, if it were possible, the sin and person guilty might be particularized by it.

"Also, when I have done the exercise, it hath gone to my heart to think the word should now fall as rain on stony places: still wishing from my heart, Oh that they who have heard me speak this day did but see as I do, what sin, death, hell, and the curse of God is; and also, what the grace and love and mercy of God is, through Christ, to men in such a case as they are who are yet estranged from him. And indeed, I did often say in my heart before the Lord, that if to be hanged up presently before their eyes would be a means to awaken them, and confirm them in the truth, I should gladly be contented."

Justification by faith was Bunyan's great delight in preaching, as it was Luther's; and he had gone through a depth and power of experience in learning personally the nature of this doctrine, remarkably similar to the fiery discipline of Luther's own soul in coming to it. Hence it is not wonderful that there should be a striking similarity between Bunyan's style, thoughts, and expressions in preaching, and those of the great Reformer. For example, the following passages from his "Heavenly Footman," are such as might have been written down from Luther's own lips:—

"They that will go to heaven must run for it: because, as the way is long, so the time in which they are to get to the end of it is very uncertain. The time present is the only time; thou hast no more time allotted thee than that thou now enjoyest: 'Boast not thyself of to-morrow, for thou knowest not what a day may bring forth.' Do not say, I have time enough to get to heaven seven years hence; for I tell thee, the bell may toll for thee before seven days more be ended; and when death comes, away thou must go, whether thou art provided or not; and therefore look to it; make no delays; it is not good dallying with things of so great concernment as the salvation or damnation of thy soul. You know he that hath a great way to go in a little time, and less by half than he thinks of, he had need to run for it.

"They that will have heaven must run for it; because the devil, the law, sin, death, and hell follow them. There is never a poor soul that is going to heaven, but the devil, the law, sin, death, and hell, make after that soul. 'The devil, your adversary, as a roaring lion, goeth about seeking whom he may devour.' And I will assure you, the devil is nimble, he can run apace, he is light of foot, he hath overtaken many, he hath turned up their heels, and hath given them an everlasting fall. Also the law, that can shoot a great way, have a care thou keep out of the reach of those great guns, the ten commandments. Hell also hath a wide mouth; it can stretch itself farther than you are aware of. And as the angel said to Lot, 'Take heed, look not behind thee, neither tarry thou in all the plain (that is, any where between this and heaven), lest thou be consumed:' so say I to thee, Take heed, tarry not, lest either the devil, hell, death, or the fearful curses of the law of God, do overtake thee, and throw thee down in the midst of thy sins, so as never to rise and recover again. If this were well considered, then thou, as well as I, wouldst say, They that will have heaven must run for it.

"They that will go to heaven must run for it; because, perchance, the gates of heaven may shut shortly. Sometimes sinners have not heaven's gates open to them so long as they suppose; and if they be once shut against a man, they are so heavy, that all the men in the world, nor all the angels in heaven, are not able to open them. 'I shut, and no man can open,' saith Christ. And how if thou shouldst come but one quarter of an hour too late? I tell thee, it will cost thee an eternity to bewail thy misery in. Francis Spira can tell thee what it is to stay till the gate of mercy be quite shut; or to run so lazily, that they be shut before thou get within them. What, to be shut out! what, out of heaven! Sinner, rather than lose it, run for it; yea, and 'so run that thou mayest obtain.'"

Such preaching as this, such fire and life, coming from

such a spirit as was in Bunyan's heart, could not but be effectual; the Spirit of God attended it; crowds of people would flock together to hear it, and many who came to scoff went away with the fire of the preacher in their consciences. Bunyan enjoyed himself more in preaching on the subject of faith than on any other, though he proclaimed " the terrors of the Lord" with unequalled power and pungency. "For I have been in my preaching," says he, "especially when I have been engaged in the doctrine of life by Christ without works, as if an angel of God had stood at my back to encourage me. Oh! it hath been with such power and heavenly evidence upon my own soul, while I have been labouring to unfold it, to demonstrate it, and to fasten it upon the conscience of others, that I could not be contented with saying, I believe and am sure; methought I was more than sure, if it be lawful to express myself so, that those things which there I asserted were true."

Bunyan, from time to time, even in his preaching, experienced the assaults of his old adversary. "Sometimes," he says, "I have been violently assaulted with thoughts of blasphemy, and strongly tempted to speak the words with my mouth before the congregation." He was also tempted to "pride and liftings up of heart;" but it was his ever day portion to be so let into the evil of his own heart, and still made to see such a multitude of corruptions and infirmities therein, that it "caused hanging down of the head under all his gifts and attainments." Moreover, Bunyan had experience on this point from the word of God, which greatly chastened and humbled his spirit. " I have had also," says he, "together with this, some notable place or other of the word presented before me, which word hath contained in it some sharp and piercing sentence concerning the perishing of the soul, notwithstanding gifts and parts; as, for instance, that hath been of great use to me, *Though I speak with the tongues of men and angels, and have not charity, I am become as sounding brass and a tinkling cymbal.*

"A tinkling cymbal is an instrument of music with which a skilful player can make such melodious and heart-inflaming music, that all who hear him play can scarcely hold from dancing ; and yet behold the cymbal hath not life, neither comes the music from it, but because of the art of him that plays therewith ; so then the instrument at last may come to naught and perish, though in times past such music hath been made upon it.

"Just thus I saw it was, and will be, with them that have gifts, but want saving grace : they are in the hand of Christ as the cymbal in the hand of David ; and as David could with the cymbal make that mirth in the service of God as to elevate the hearts of the worshippers, so Christ can use these gifted men, as with them to affect the souls of his people in the church ; yet when he hath done all, hang them by, as lifeless, though sounding cymbals.

"This consideration, therefore, together with some others, were, for the most part, as a maul on the head of pride and desire of vain-glory. What, thought I, shall I be proud because I am a sounding brass ? Is it so much to be a fiddle ? Hath not the least creature that hath life more of God in it than these ? Besides, I knew it was love should never die, but these must cease and vanish ; so I concluded a little grace, a little love, a little of the true fear of God, is better than all the gifts ; yea, and I am fully convinced of it that it is possible for souls that can scarce give a man an answer, but with great confusion as to method,—I say it is possible for them to have a thousand times more grace, and to be more in the love and favour of the Lord, than some who, by the virtue of the gift of knowledge, can deliver themselves like angels."

LECTURE FOURTH.

Bunyan in Prison.

Illustrations of the Times of Bunyan.—Results of the spirit of persecution.—
The Puritans driven to America.—Baxter in the Parliamentary Army.—
The multiplicity of Sects, and Milton's opinion thereon.—Bedford Jail, and
Bunyan in it, with his little child.—The Plague in London, and the persecuting King and Court in Oxford.—Bunyan's conference with the Justice's
Clerk. —Interview of Bunyan's wife with the Judges. — Bunyan's prison
employments. – Suggestion and pursuit of the Pilgrim's Progress.

IN a former lecture, I have briefly sketched the principal movements of intolerance and persecution during the reign of those English monarchs who bore the name of Charles. In order the better to illustrate that persecuting spirit, which from the reign of James passed into this, and the glorious issues that grew out of it, through that omnipotent prerogative, whereby the Divine Being causes the wrath of man to praise him, we will call up several great separate scenes from the past, with the actors in them ; to note which will be better for our purpose, than would be a whole volume of historical dissertations. The first scene is in the great era of 1620, just eight years before the birth of Bunyan. It is a lowering winter's day; on a coast rock-bound and perilous, sheeted with ice and snow, hovers a small vessel, worn and weary like a bird with wet plumage, driven in a storm from its nest, and timidly seeking shelter. It is the May-flower, thrown on the bosom of Winter. The very sea is freezing ; the earth is as still as the grave, covered with snow, and as hard with frost, as iron ; there is no sign of a human habitation ; the deep forests have lost their foliage, and rise over the land like a shadowy congregation of skeletons. Yet there is a band of human beings on board that weatherbeaten vessel, and they have voluntarily come to this savage coast to spend the rest of their lives, and to die there. Eight thousand miles they have struggled across the ocean, from a land of plenty and comfort, from their own beloved country, from their homes, firesides, friends, to gather around an altar to God in the winter, in the wilderness! What does it all mean? It marks to a noble mind the invaluable blessedness of FREEDOM TO WORSHIP GOD! It means, that religious oppression is worse to bear, more hard, more intolerable to a generous mind, more insufferable to an upright conscience, than the war of the elements, than peril and nakedness, than cold and hunger, than dens and caves of the earth, than disease and the loss of friends, and the tomahawks of savage enemies! These men have fled from religious oppression; the hand of power has attempted to grasp and bind the conscience; and conscience, and an undying religious faith, have borne these men into the wilderness to worship God as freely as the air that breathes God's praises.

So noble, so grand, so holy, was the national birth of the best part of these United States of America! Well may we glory in the name of PURITAN. It is a synonyme for all that is holy in piety, unbending in moral rectitude, patient in self-denial, illustrious in patriotism, precious in liberty and truth. But the virtues of our Puritan ancestors, in their development, at least, grew out of oppression; they were good out of evil, the wrath of man turned into the praise of God. It was the touch of the iron sceptre of the Stuarts, laid upon that sacred thing, a pure, enlightened, religious conscience, and upon that sacred possession, a chosen, conscientious, religious faith and worship, that brought to pass all this glory; it was the tyranny of an Established Church, the daring usurpation by the King of England of the prerogative of Christ as the head of his people, that planted on this continent the germ both of civil and religious liberty, the elements of the purest religious faith, and of the freest political institutions in the world!

This is one of the most remarkable instances on record, of

the overruling sovereignty of God in its blessed purposes, by the instrumentality of his own enemies. The persecution, which in England threw John Bunyan into prison to write the Pilgrim's Progress, drove those holy men and women out of England into the wilderness, to form an asylum of liberty and religion for the whole world. It was one of King James's sayings, No Bishop, no King; and here, in this land, under the oppression of James, a church without a bishop, and a government without a king, secured and established that charter of civil and religious freedom, which king and prelate had alike violated and destroyed.

The colony of the Puritans was driven out of England, as the oppressed Hebrews were driven out of Egypt; and to this country they came, under just as sacred and holy an invisible guidance, as the Israelites of old to the land of Canaan. In the simple, striking language of the Bible, " It is a night to be much observed unto the Lord for bringing them out from the land of Egypt; this is that night of the Lord to be observed of all the children of Israel, in their generations." And so was the night of the departure of our pilgrim ancestors a night of the Lord; it was to them a night of sorrow, both when they came, and when they landed; but it was that night of the Lord; and it brought a day of glory, such as the world had not seen for ages, and of which, God grant the light may never go out.

> Ay! call it holy ground,
> The spot where first they trod!
> They left unstained what there they found,
> FREEDOM TO WORSHIP GOD!

We leave now this colony, growing, under God's protecting care, in numbers and in graces, and pass to another scene, about twenty years afterwards, when the conflict for liberty on the one side and tyranny on the other, was raging between King Charles I. and the Parliament with Oliver Cromwell.

The scene is in a church, and yet it looks like a camp, for it is crowded with soldiers, as well as with a village congregation. It is not the Lord's day, but a public talking day for sectarian controversy; and you might think the confusion of Babel had been there renewed, from the strife of tongues and opinions to which you listen. There are fierce Antinomians, and Free-willers, and Episcopalians, and Independents, and Anabaptists, and Presbyterians, and Nonconformists; all animated with zeal, and ready to contend for their peculiar opinions. The troopers of one regiment, and the soldiers of another, throw forth opinions and arguments with almost as much fury as they did musket-balls in war. But in the midst of all this confusion, there stands in the reading-pew under the pulpit, a plain man in a black dress, evidently a clergyman, with the Bible in his hand; a thin, pallid, but heavenly countenance, though indicating as great a sharpness in controversy as any of the soldiers in war; and he stands, and disputes, and discusses with the soldiers, without once quitting his post or relinquishing the contest, from morning till night. This is Richard Baxter, the holy, venerated author of the Saints' Rest. He served for a season as chaplain in the Parliamentary army; and in justice to that army, as well as to himself, I must describe in his own words something more of his position. "I was almost always," says he, "when opportunity offered, disputing with one or the other; sometimes upon civil government, and sometimes upon church order and government; sometimes upon infant baptism, often against Antinomianism and the contrary extreme. But their most frequent and vehement disputes were for liberty of conscience, as they called it; that is, that the civil government hath nothing to do to determine any thing in matters of religion by constraint or restraint; but that every man might not only hold, but preach and do, in matters of religion, what he pleased: that the civil magistrate hath nothing to do but with civil things, to keep the peace, protect the church's liberties, &c."

This is certainly a most striking testimony as to the character of Oliver Cromwell's army. Their very relaxations and amusements were chosen, not in the tap-room or the tavern, not in revelling and drunkenness, but in serious, hard-contested arguments with one another, and with the keenest disputant of the times, on some of the most important questions that can occupy the human mind. They were deeply interested, as no army ever was before, on the subject of religion; nor was it any wonder, that with such an army, Oliver Cromwell was invincible. Religious liberty was new to them; it was the grand *heresy* of the army; Richard Baxter pays the highest compliment to them in saying that they contended more vehemently for this than for any thing else. It was this precious possession and birthright of the Christian, which a persecuting religious hierarchy, in alliance with the despotism of the Stuarts, would have utterly destroyed.

A word seems necessary in regard to the multitude of sects existing in those days, and the causes and the nature of them. In the nature of the human mind there never can be a dead uniformity of opinion on any subjects;. there cannot be on political subjects, and on religious matters it was never intended by the great Head of the church that there should be. We may liken religious opinion in the church of Christ to the growth of a tree; there are ten thousand varying twigs and branches, and of the buds and blossoms you can find no two exactly alike, and in a million leaves there are a million varieties of outline, hue, veins, and fibres; and the fruit itself is different in shape, colour, fragrance, and taste. And for all this, the tree is incomparably more beautiful and wholesome. Now suppose, while that tree is growing, you should, for one season only, cover it over with some great crushing weight; it would still grow; the life of nature is too vigorous, too indestructible, except you uproot it, to be kept from shooting; but if you remove that weight in the autumn, what will you find as the result of compressed vital energy? Distortions, excrescences, monstrosities; knotted and contorted branches, uptwisted and inveterately convolved; leaves nested with worms, and overcurled, and grown in spasms and bunches; and fruit, if at all, hard and deformed, green, odious, and bitter. Precisely such is the effect of violently crushing the growth of opinion; sects, that would have spread into symmetrical varieties in twigs and foliage, with fair mellow fruit to suit all palates, are vermiculated, and pressed into inveterate deformities and perhaps poisonous monstrosities.

"They corrupt the discipline of Christ," says Baxter, "by mixing it with secular force. They reproach the keys, or ministerial power, as if it were a leaden sword, and not worth a straw, unless the magistrates' sword enforced it. What then did the primitive church for three hundred years? Worst of all, they corrupt the church, by forcing in the rabble of the unfit and unwilling; and thereby tempt many godly Christians to schisms and dangerous separations. Till magistrates keep the sword themselves, and learn to deny it to every angry clergyman who would do his own work with it, and leave them to their own weapons,—the word and spiritual keys,—the church will never have unity and peace. I disliked also," Baxter adds, "some of the Presbyterians, that were not tender enough to dissenting brethren; but too much against liberty, as others were too much for it; and thought by votes and numbers to do that which love and reason should have done." Ah! how much truth in this sad aphorism, as the habit of mankind; *votes and numbers, instead of love and reason.* "The poor church of Christ," Baxter curiously remarks, "the sober, sound, religious part, are like Christ, that was crucified between two thieves. The profane and formal persecutors on the one hand, and the fanatic dividing sectaries on the other, have in all ages been grinding the spiritual seed, as the corn is ground between the millstones."

And now, I must add to this the sensible remarks of the judicious and impartial biographer of Baxter, as to the period on which we have been dwelling. "It is worthy of observation," says Mr Orme, "that all attempts to produce uniformity have either been defeated or have occasioned fresh divisions. Under the appearance of outward unity, the greatest diversity of opinion generally prevails. And genuine religion flourishes most amidst what is commonly denounced as the contentions of rival sects. The soil whose rankness sends forth an abundant crop of weeds, will produce, if cultivated, a still more luxuriant harvest of corn. If the times of Baxter were fruitful of sects, and some of them wild and monstrous, they were still more fruitful in the number of genuine, holy, and devoted Christians. It was not an age of fanaticism only, but of pure and undefiled religion."

I am reminded also of that noble passage in Milton's Areopagitica: "For when God shakes a kingdom with strong and healthful commotions to a general reforming, it is not untrue that many sectaries and false teachers are then busiest in seducing; but yet more true it is, that God then raises to his own work men of rare abilities, and more than common industry, not only to look back and revise what hath been taught heretofore, but to gain further, and go on some new enlightened steps in the discovery of truth. And do we not see that while we still affect by all means a rigid external formality, we may as soon fall again into a gross conforming stupidity, a stark and dead congealment of wood, and hay, and stubble, forced and frozen together, which is more to the sudden degeneracy of a church than many sub-dichotamies (subdivisions) of petty schisms. Not that I can think well of every light separation; or that all in a church is to be expected gold and silver and precious stones; it is not possible for men to sever the wheat from the tares, the good fish from the other fry; that must be the angel's ministry at the end of mortal things. Yet, if all cannot be of one mind, as who looks they should be? this, doubtless, is more wholesome, more prudent, and more Christian, that many be tolerated, rather than all compelled."

The period on which we are dwelling might almost be termed a religious and political whirlwind; a hurricane of opinions, in which the elements of heaven and earth met and contended. But tyranny and unnatural restraint acting upon elements that in our human and religious nature must always exist, but that, if left to a quiet growth and development, will, under God's providence and grace, make a wholesome, transparent, circumfluent atmosphere for society; produced infernal mixtures, electric explosions, black thunder-clouds, charged at once with the fires of angry passion, and the tremendous energy of conscience, piety, and fanaticism together. Look over this, our own beloved land of liberty and religion; there are as many sects in it as there ever were on the borders, or in the heart of the period

of the Commonwealth of England; and if you were to put
upon them here those violent restraints, by which they had
then and there been made to chafe, and smoulder, and irritate
in confinement, and from which they broke loose with such
astounding developments, such flames, such indomitable life,
such exulting and contending fury, you would change the
calm and blessed aspect of our state into a hurricane of
anarchy and revolution; out of this all-surrounding atmosphere
of peace and freedom, in which every man sees clearly,
and breathes securely, you would evoke storms and lightning;
thunder-clouds would appear charged against each other,
and houses would be seen unroofed, and trees uprooted and
flying through the darkened air in tornadoes. Such is the
inevitable consequence of laying the hand of civil or religious
tyranny upon the liberty of opinion. It is like laying
a mountain without a crater upon a raging volcano. The
continent shakes with earthquakes; the thunder bellows
from its subterranean confinement; the lava breaks out in
plains, and pours and burns over smiling villages; and just
so, earth will be a symbol of the chaos of hell, if you lay
your mountain of civil or religious tyranny on the human
conscience. Leave it free, and it is like the atmosphere with
God to govern its elements; confine it, and it is like a pent
volcano, that will shake and devastate the world.

Fanaticism grows by opposition, in confinement, in constrained
silence and darkness; it may be thus produced,
where there was nothing of it before. This is but the Poet's
principle, that

> ———" Thoughts shut up want air,
> And spoil, like bales unopened to the sun."

It is especially so with religious opinion that is suffering
tyrannical restraint. It becomes a smouldering fire, that
burns inwardly; and as in a cotton-ship at sea, or a barn
crammed with wet hay, the combustion having once commenced,
if you open the hatches or cut the bundles to put it
out, it is ten to one that you are too late, and it all bursts into
a light flame together, so that houses and ships, and human
lives, are consumed in the conflagration; just so with restrained,
smouldering opinions in the civil and ecclesiastical

state. But if a bundle of wet hay were spread open with the rake, or tossed on the fork in the sun and air, it would speedily become dry and safe for your barns and cattle. Just so with swarming opinions, that by restraint would turn to fanaticism in the popular mind; give them the air; turn them, rake them, toss them, over and over again, in the bright sun, to the sound of free and merry voices; let all the world, if they wish, see what they are; let all the world, if they wish, help to turn and spread them; the mischief, if there were any, dies in such a process. Truth, liberty, justice, never fears the freedom of opinion, tossed out so in the open air, and spread beneath the sunlight; truth only asks the light and air, and the whole world to come and see every thing; but error, despotism, tyranny, fears such a tossing and spreading of the truth, and would rather shut it up in bundles and crowd it into a Bastile, or into the hold of a slave-ship. Such things have been, no doubt such things will be again. And we hope in God that in this country, by his word, and by his grace, his people will be prepared for the conflict. Nobly says Milton, "Though all the winds of doctrine were let loose to play upon the earth, so Truth be in the field, we do injuriously by licensing and prohibiting, to misdoubt her strength. Let her and Falsehood grapple; who ever knew truth put to the worse in a free and open encounter?" No man, ever; and where the Spirit of the Lord is, there is LIBERTY.

Pass we now to another scene, about twenty years later, during which time, save in the brief and glorious Protectorate of Cromwell, there had been an almost uninterrupted succession of arbitrary, persecuting measures in the Church and State of England. We enter the prison of John Bunyan. It is, you are aware, the common jail of Bedford. It is said to have been the damp and dreadful condition of this prison which first set Howard's philanthropic spirit in exercise for the improvement of the prisons throughout Europe. Bunyan's prison stood upon the Bedford bridge. It was a bridge of sighs to many, though, by God's grace, not to him; its walls were probably almost as damp as the dungeons in Venice, but it was not sea-water that washed its foundations, and trickled its rusty iron gates with moisture. There was no court-yard, no space for out-of-door work, or exercise in the open air; there were stone-walls and iron-bars, a bridge and a river. The window in his cell was grated, so that he could not look far or freely out of it; but he could see the sun-light, the water, the fields, and the clouds. The glimpses of sweet nature in this world were not so clear to him here, as were the perspective visions of the Holy City coming in upon his soul. His cell was small and comfortless, as was the whole jail; and when he would step farther than the few paces back and forth between the walls of that cell, he must go into the common room of the prison. In those times of persecution it was crowded; there were at one period more than sixty dissenters incarcerated along with Bunyan, some for hearing the gospel, some for preaching it. He had, it is said, the experience of some cruel and oppressive jailers, though others were very kind to him. Twelve years of imprisonment are long to bear,—

> Long years, it tries the thrilling frame to bear;

and for six or seven of those it has been said that there is no reason to believe that he ever was permitted to set his foot outside the rocky threshold. Perhaps he had died, says the continuation of his own life, which is supposed to have been written by a brother Baptist minister intimately acquainted with him—perhaps he had died, by the noisomeness and ill-usage of the place, had not his enlargement been procured from his hard and unreasonable sufferings. Unable to pursue the honest trade at which he had always hitherto wrought for the support of his family, he now learned—assisted, doubtless, by them—to make tagged thread laces, by the sale of which they might procure what must have been, at best, a scanty subsistence. A beloved wife and four children were dependent upon him, and were permitted at times to visit him; and that dear blind child, in regard to whom he has, in so artless and affecting a manner, related the trial of his feelings, was permitted to abide with him through the day, a solace to his heart, a companion in his work, and one to whom he could talk as artlessly as to his own soul; their conversation must have been often as the prattle of two children, for Bunyan had in him the freshness and simplicity of childhood, even in riper years; a mark of genius, which a great and profound writer has pointed out as one of its most precious and undoubted characteristics.

Now, let us enter his little cell. He is sitting at his table, to finish by sunlight the day's work for the livelihood of his dear family, which they have prepared for him. On a little stool his poor blind child sits by him, and with that expression of cheerful resignation with which God seals the countenance when he takes away the sight, the daughter turns her face up to her father, as if she could see the affectionate expression with which he looks upon her, and prattles to her. On the table and in the grated window there are three books, the Bible, the Concordance, and Bunyan's precious old copy of the Book of Martyrs. And now the day is waning, and his dear blind child must go home with the laces he has finished, to her mother. And now Bunyan opens his Bible, and reads aloud a portion of scripture to his little one, and then encircling her in his arms, and clasping her small hands in his, he kneels down on the cold stone floor, and pours out his soul in prayer to God for the salvation of those so inexpressibly dear to him, and for whom he has been all day working. So daily he prays for them and for her, and daily he prays *with her*, and teaches his blind child to pray. This done, with a parting kiss, he dismisses her to her mother, by the rough hands of the jailer.

And now it is evening. A rude lamp glimmers darkly on the table, the tagged laces are laid aside, and Bunyan, alone, is busy with his Bible, the Concordance, and his pen, ink, and paper. He writes as though joy did make him write. His pale, worn countenance is lighted with a fire, as if reflected from the radiant jasper walls of the Celestial City He writes, and smiles, and clasps his hands, and looks upward, and blesses God for his goodness, and then again turns to his writing, and then again becomes so entranced with a passage of scripture, the glory of which the Holy Spirit lets in upon his soul, that he is forced, as it were, to lay aside all his labours, and give himself to the sweet work of his closing evening's devotions. The last you see of him for the night, he is alone, kneeling on the floor of his prison; he is alone with God.

Hear him when he speaks of the blessedness he thus enjoyed:—" I never had, in all my life, so great an inlet into the word of God as now. Those scriptures that I saw nothing in before, are made, in this place and state, to shine upon me. Sometimes, when I have been in the savour of them, I have been able to laugh at destruction, and to fear neither the horse nor his rider. I have had sweet sights of the forgiveness of my sins in this place, and of my being with Jesus in another world. O the Mount Zion, the heavenly Jerusalem, the innumerable company of angels, and God the Judge of all, and the spirits of just men made perfect, and Jesus, have been sweet to me in this place! I have seen that here which I am persuaded I shall never, in this world, be able to express. I have seen a truth in this scripture, 'Whom having not seen, ye love; in whom, though now ye see him not, yet believing, ye rejoice with joy unspeakable and full of glory.'"

And where, and by whom, and for what, is this man imprisoned? In a Christian land, by an Established Church, for preaching the gospel to the poor, the ignorant, the destitute, and for not praying with a Common Prayer-Book! For this a heaven-commissioned minister of Jesus Christ languishes twelve years in prison! For this he is kneeling on the cold stone-floor of a narrow cell, in secret with his God, because he chose, without a commission from the government, to worship God in public, and to lead the devotions of others by the Scriptures merely, without the liturgical form imposed by the State upon the conscience. Yes! astounding as the fact may seem, John Bunyan is shut up within iron bars and stone walls, as men would shut up a wild beast or a murderer, because he would pray without a Common Prayer-Book! The only parallel instance of persecution is to be found in the case of Daniel, thrown by an oriental despot into the lions' den, for praying to God without the State liturgy. The cases are strikingly similar, the concoction of bigotry very much the same :—" All the presidents of the kingdom, the governors and the princes, the councillors and the captains, had consulted together to establish a royal statute, and to make a firm decree, that whosoever shall ask a petition of any god or man for thirty days, save of thee, O king, he shall be cast into the den of lions. Then Daniel, with his windows open towards Jerusalem, eschewing the king's liturgy, kneeled upon his knees without it three times a-day, and prayed and gave thanks before his God, as he did aforetime. Then these men assembled, and found Daniel praying and making supplications before his God; so they hasted with their accusation, and under the king's royal signet, caused Daniel to be thrown into the den of lions, because they found him praying and making supplications before his God."

And so did the sheriffs to Bunyan; they found him praying without the Common Prayer-Book, in a place not permitted by the decree of the king; they found him with the Bible in his hand, worshipping God in a conventicle, and forthwith, according to the king's decree, they threw him into prison, to remain there, for no crime whatever, twelve years, as a common malefactor! But they were years of mercy, comfort, glory. He has himself given some account of his own blessedness in this tribulation. "Many more of the dealings of God towards me," says he, "I might relate; but these, out of the spoils won in battle, have I dedicated to maintain the house of God."

And now we will turn to another scene during the same period, in the city of London. It is in the midst of the plague. The grass is growing in the streets. The red cross is marked upon the houses, the dead-cart is moving from street to street, with its melancholy bell, and the hoarse wailing cry of the grave's-man reverberates through the deserted passages, Bring out your dead! The pulpits have been forsaken of the established clergy; but holy men of God, persecuted of the Church and State, and forbidden to preach because of their Non-conformity, have entered the vacant churches, and are "holding forth the word of life" in the face of death, to trembling multitudes, in pulpits from which they had been driven with penal inflictions in a season of health! They preach as dying unto dying men; hearers one day, sick the next, and dead the next. They preach and listen, as though never to preach or listen again. But while God is consuming the people by these judgments, and the Non-conformists, fearless of death, are labouring to save men's souls, King Charles is revelling with his dissolute court at Oxford, and contriving with his Parliament and clergy, removed thither from London for fear of the Plague, an additional act of persecution, to drive these fearless ministers, whom death itself cannot stop from preaching, beyond the very limits of cities, towns, and villages! The impiety of such proceedings could not have been much greater, had they passed a law enacting that if any man attempted to be saved out of the Established Church, he should forthwith be consigned to eternal perdition. "So little," says Baxter, " did the sense of God's terrible judgments, or of the necessities of many hundred thousand ignorant souls, or the groans of the poor people for the teaching which they had lost, or the fear of the great and final reckoning, affect the hearts of the prelatists, or stop them in their way." It is a fearful picture of impiety, but nevertheless a picture of the times.

We return in the next scene to Bunyan's prison. The graphic dialogue forms so instructive a sketch in manner as in matter, that it shall be given in his own words. After he had lain in jail for some time, the justices sent their clerk of the peace, Mr Cobb, to admonish him and demand his submission. This man sent for Bunyan, and when he was come to him, he said,

Cobb. Neighbour Bunyan, how do you do?

Bun. I thank you, sir, said I, very well, blessed be the Lord.

Cobb. Saith he, I come to tell you that it is desired you would submit yourself to the laws of the land, or else, at the next sessions it will go worse with you, even to be sent away out of the nation, or else worse than that.

Bun. I said that I did desire to demean myself in the world both as becometh a man and a Christian.

Cobb. But, saith he, you must submit to the laws of the land, and leave off those meetings which you were wont to have; for the statute-law is directly against it; and I am sent to you by the justices to tell you that they do intend to prosecute the law against you, if you submit not.

Bunyan made answer to this, that the law by which he was in prison neither reached himself nor his meetings, being directed only against those who met for wicked treasonable purposes.

The clerk argued that Bunyan ought to consider it liberty enough, if permitted to speak to his neighbour privately and alone on the subject of religion; and added, that it was his private meetings that the law was against.

Bun. Sir, said I, if I may do good to one by my discourse, why may I not do good to two? And if to two, why not to four, and so to eight, and so forth? Bunyan's arithmetical progression would soon make a congregation. Ay, saith Cobb, and to an hundred, I warrant you.

Bun. Yes sir, said I, I think I should not be forbid, to do as much good as I can. If I, by discoursing, may do good to one, surely by the same law, I may do good to many.

Cobb. The law, saith he, doth expressly forbid your private meetings, therefore they are not to be tolerated.

Bunyan argued again that the law only intended mischievous meetings.

Cobb. But, goodman Bunyan, said he, methinks you need not stand so strictly upon this one thing, as to have meetings of such public assemblies. Cannot you submit, and notwithstanding do as much good as you can in a neighbourly way, without having such meetings! You may come to the public assemblies and hear. What though you do not preach, you may hear; do not think thyself so well enlightened, and that you have received a gift so far above others, but that you may hear other men preach.

Bunyan answered that he was as willing to be taught as

to give instruction, and that he looked upon it as his duty to do both.

Cobb. But, said he, what if you should forbear awhile, and sit still, till you see further how things will go?

And now comes into view one of the mighty impulses, which Bunyan had gained, doubtless from the Book of Martyrs, which had come sweeping down through the current of time and revolution, from John Wickliffe; Wickliffe's soul and Bunyan's meeting and communing together, across the gulf of more than two hundred years, in this passage, as Bunyan's and Luther's had done, to such powerful purpose, in the great Reformer's Commentary on the Epistle to the Galatians.

Sir, said Bunyan, as if he had been speaking scripture— and it shews what inspiring power the Book of Martyrs had over him—Sir, said Bunyan, Wickliffe saith, that he which leaveth off preaching and hearing of the word of God, for fear of excommunication of men, he is already excommunicated of God, and shall, in the day of judgment, be counted a traitor to Christ.

Cobb. Ay, saith he, they that do not hear.

Bun. But, sir, said I, he saith, he that shall leave off either preaching or hearing. That is, if he hath received a gift for edification, it is his sin if he doth not lay it out in a way of exhortation and counsel, according to the proportion of his gift, as well as to spend his time altogether in hearing others preach.

Cobb. But, said he, how shall we know that you have received a gift?

Bun. Said I, let any man hear and search, and prove the doctrine by the Bible.

Cobb. But will you be willing, said he, that two indifferent persons shall determine the case, and will you stand by their judgment?

Bun. I said, are they infallible?

There outspoke the true Protestant.

Cobb. He said no.

Bun. Then said I, it is possible my judgment may be as good as theirs; but yet I will pass by either, and in this matter be judged by the Scripture. I am sure that is infallible, and cannot err.

Cobb. But, said he, who shall be judge between you, for you take the Scriptures one way and they another ?

Bun. I said the Scriptures should, and that by comparing one Scripture with another ; for that will open itself, if it be rightly compared. As for instance, naming several passages.

Cobb. But are you willing, said he, to stand to the judgment of the Church ?

Bun. Yes, sir, said I, to the approbation of the Church of God ; the Church's judgment is best expressed in Scripture. This answer of Bunyan was admirable ; nor can any one do other than admire the wisdom, patience, and pertinency. as well as sometimes wit, and always calmness, of Bunyan's replies.

Well, neighbour Bunyan, said Mr Cobb, indeed, I would wish you seriously to consider of these things, between this and the quarter-sessions, and to submit yourself. You may do much good, if you continue still in the land ; but alas, what benefit will it be to your friends, or what good can it do to them, if you should be sent away beyond the seas into Spain or Constantinople, or some other remote part of the world ? Pray, be ruled.

Jailer. Indeed, sir, I hope he will be ruled.

Bun. I shall desire, said I, in all godliness and honesty, to behave myself in the nation whilst I am in it. And if I must be so dealt withal as you say, I hope God will help me to bear what they shall lay upon me. I know no evil that I have done in this matter to be so used. I speak as in the presence of God.

Cobb. You know, saith he, that the Scripture saith, The powers that be are ordained of God.

Bun. I said yes, and that I was to submit to the king as supreme, also to the governors, as to them that are sent by him.

Cobb. Well, then, said he, the king commands you, that you should not have any private meetings, because it is against his law ; and he is ordained of God, therefore you should not have any.

How was Bunyan to get over this? "I told him," said he, "that Paul did own the powers that were in his day to be of God; and yet he was often in prison under them for all that. And also, though Jesus Christ told Pilate that he had no power against him but of God, yet he died under the same Pilate; and yet, said I, I hope you will not say that either Paul or Christ did deny magistracy, and so sinned against God in slighting the ordinance. Sir, said I, the law hath provided two ways of obeying; the one to do that which in my conscience I do believe that I am bound to do actively, and where I cannot obey actively, then I am willing to lie down, and to suffer what they shall do unto me. At this he sat still, and said no more; which when he had done, I did thank him for his civil and meek discoursing with me; and so we parted. Oh, that we might meet in heaven!"

This was indeed a civil and meek discoursing, in comparison with the impious treatment Bunyan received from the justices in a preceding examination. And so they parted. But after this, Bunyan's wife, while he lay in prison, undertook to present a petition in his behalf to the judges. Three times she made the attempt, twice to Lord-chief-justice Hale, and nothing could daunt her, but she would receive a hearing. The scene is worthy the pencil of some great painter, where, without a creature to befriend or sustain her, this young and trembling woman, unaccustomed and abashed at such presences, entered the court-room, and stood before the judges, in the midst of the crowd of justices and gentry of the country assembled. She addressed herself, with a trembling heart, directly to Lord-chief-justice Hale, who wore in his countenance so clearly the lines of that gentleness and goodness for which he was illustrious, that the courage of the wife was somewhat supported, even amidst the frowns and wrathful words of the other justices.

My Lord, said she to Judge Hale, I make bold to come once again to your lordship, to know what may be done to my husband.

Bunyan loved to put these examinations in the form of a dialogue; it made every thing more vivid to his mind; and in this case he wrote down the account from the lips of his courageous wife, just as the scene was evolved in the court-room.

Judge Hale answered, Woman, I told thee before I could do thee no good, because they have taken that for a conviction, which thy husband spoke at the sessions; and unless there be something done to undo that, I can do thee no good.

Woman. My Lord, said she, he is kept unlawfully in prison; they clapped him up before there were any proclamation against the meetings; the indictment also is false; besides, they never asked him whether he was guilty or no; neither did he confess the indictment.

All this was true; but one of the justices, whom she knew not, said, My Lord, he was lawfully convicted.

Woman. It is false, said she; for when they said to him, Do you confess the indictment? he said only this, that he had been at several meetings, both where there was preaching of the word and prayer, and that they had God's presence among them.

Judge Twisdon. Whereat Judge Twisdon answered very angrily, saying, What, you think we can do what we list? your husband is a breaker of the peace, and is convicted by the law. Whereupon Judge Hale called for the statute-book.

Woman. But, said she, my Lord, he was not lawfully convicted.

Chester. Then Justice Chester said, My Lord, he was lawfully convicted.

Woman. It is false, said she; it was but a word of discourse that they took for conviction, as you heard before.

Chester. But it is recorded, woman, it is recorded, says Justice Chester. As if it must of necessity be true, because it is recorded. With which words he often endeavoured to stop her mouth, having no other argument to convince her, but it is recorded, it is recorded.

Woman. My Lord, said she, I was awhile since in London, to see if I could get my husband's liberty, and there I spoke with my Lord Barkwood, one of the House of Lords, to whom I delivered a petition, who took it of me, and presented it to some of the rest of the House of Lords for my husband's releasement; who, when they had seen it, they said that they could not release him, but had committed his releasement to the judges, at the next assizes. This he told me; and now I come to you to see if any thing can be done in this business, and you give neither releasement nor relief. To which they gave her no answer, but made as if they heard her not. Only Justice Chester was often up with this, He is convicted, and it is recorded.

Woman. If it be, it is false, said she.

Chester. My Lord, said Justice Chester, he is a pestilent fellow; there is not such a fellow in the country again.

Twisdon. What, will your husband leave preaching? If he will do so, then send for him.

Bunyan's wife remembered the sublime and noble answer of her husband, If I were out of the prison to-day, I would preach the Gospel again to-morrow, by the help of God. My lord, said she, he dares not leave preaching as long as he can speak.

Twisdon. See here; what should we talk any more about such a fellow; must he do what he lists? He is a breaker of the peace.

Woman. She told him again that he desired to live peaceably, and to follow his calling, that his family might be maintained; and moreover, my lord, I have four small children that cannot help themselves, of which one is blind, and have nothing to live upon but the charity of good people. This, with some other affecting distresses which she told, troubled Judge Hale. Alas, poor woman! said he.

Twisdon. But Judge Twisdon told her that she made poverty her cloak; and said, moreover, that he understood I was maintained better by running up and down in preaching, than by following my calling.

Hale. What is his calling? said Judge Hale.

Answer. Then some of the company that stood by said, A tinker, my lord.

Woman. Yes, said she, and because he is a tinker, and a poor man, therefore he is despised, and cannot have justice.

Hale. Then Judge Hale answered very mildly, saying, I

tell thee, woman, seeing it is so that they have taken what thy husband spake for a conviction, thou must either apply thyself to the king, or sue out his pardon, or get a writ of error.

Chester. But when Justice Chester heard him give her this counsel, and especially, as she supposed, because he spoke of a writ of error, he chafed, and seemed to be very much offended, saying, My lord, he will preach and do what he lists.

Woman. He preacheth nothing but the word of God, said she.

Twisdon. He preach the word of God! said Twisdon (and withal she thought he would have struck her), he runneth up and down, and doth harm.

Woman. No, my lord, said she, it is not so; God hath owned him, and done much good by him.

Twisdon. God! said he; his doctrine is the doctrine of the devil.

Woman. My lord, said she, when the righteous Judge shall appear, it will be known that his doctrine is not the doctrine of the devil.

Twisdon. My lord, said he to Jude Hale, do not mind her, but send her away.

Hale. Then, said Judge Hale, I am sorry, woman, that I cannot do thee any good; thou must do one of those three things aforesaid, namely: either to apply thyself to the king, or sue out his pardon, or get a writ of error; but a writ of error will be cheapest.

Woman. At which Chester again seemed to be in a chafe, and put off his hat, and, as she thought, scratched his head for anger; but then I saw, said she, that there was no prevailing to have my husband sent for, though I often desired them that they would send for him, that he might speak for himself, telling them that he could give them better satisfaction than I could, in what they demanded of him, with several other things, which now I forget. Only this I remember, that though I was somewhat timorous at my first entrance into the chamber, yet before I went out I could not but break forth into tears, not so much because they were so hard-hearted against me and my husband, but to think what a sad account such poor creatures will have to give at the coming of the Lord, when they shall there answer for all things whatsoever they have done in the body, whether it be good or whether it be evil.

Bunyan's wife was a partaker of his own spirit, a heroine, in this trying situation, of no ordinary stamp. This courageous woman, and Lord-chief-justice Hale, and Bunyan, have long since met in heaven, but how little could they recognise each other's character on earth! How little could the distressed, insulted wife have imagined, that, beneath the Judge's ermine, there was beating the heart of a child of God, a man of humility, integrity, and prayer! How little could the great, learned, illustrious, and truly pious judge have dreamed, that the man, the obscure tinker, whom he was suffering to languish in prison for want of a writ of error, would one day be the subject of greater admiration and praise than all the judges in the kingdom of Great Britain! How little could he dream, that from that narrow cell where the prisoner was left incarcerated, and cut off apparently from all usefulness, a glory would shine out, illustrating the government and grace of God, and doing more good to man, than all the prelates and judges in the reign of Charles II. put together had accomplished!

Twelve full years Bunyan remained in this prison. He wrote several works while there, besides the Pilgrim's Progress, among which was a work entitled, "A Confession of my Faith, and a Reason of my Practice." In this work, written but a short time before the end of his imprisonment, he makes a more distinct allusion to the sufferings of his incarceration than he was wont to do. "Faith and holiness," says he, "are my professed principles, with an endeavour, so far as in me lieth, to be at peace with all men. What shall I say? Let mine enemies themselves be judges, if any things in these following doctrines, or if aught that any man hath heard me preach, doth or hath, according to the true intent of my words, savoured either of heresy or rebellion. I say again, let they themselves be judges if aught they find in my writing or preaching, doth render me worthy of almost twelve years imprisonment, or one that deserved to be hanged, or banished for ever, according to their tremendous sentence. But if nothing will do, unless I make my conscience a continual butchery and slaughter-shop, unless putting out my own eyes, I commit me to the blind to lead me, as I doubt is desired by some, I have determined, the Almighty God being my help and shield, yet to suffer, if frail life might continue so long, even till the moss shall grow on mine eye-brows, rather than thus to violate my faith and principles."

When John Bunyan was first thrown into prison, he found a great friend in the jailer, through whose kindness his confinement, previous to his last examination, and the petition of his wife, was not at all rigorous. He was permitted to preach, to visit his friends, and even to go to London. It is related of him, that it being known to some of the persecuting prelates that Bunyan was often out of prison, they sent down an officer to talk with the jailer on the subject; and in order to find him out, he was to arrive there in the middle of the night. Bunyan was at home with his family, but so restless that he could not sleep. He therefore told his wife that he must return immediately. He did so, and the jailer blamed him for coming in at so unseasonable an hour. Early in the morning the messenger came, and said, "Are all the prisoners safe?" "Yes." "Is John Bunyan safe?" "Yes." "Let me see him." He was called and appeared, and all was well. After the messenger left, the jailer said to Bunyan, "Well, you may go out again when you think proper; for you know when to return better than I can tell you."

Bunyan made use of his liberty at this time to visit his fellow-Christians in London, which, says he, "my enemies hearing of were so angry, that they had almost cast my jailer out of his place, threatening to indict him, and to do what they could against him. They charged me also that I went thither to plot and raise division, and make insurrection, which, God knows, was a slander; whereupon my liberty was more straitened than it was before, so that I must not look out of the door." From this severe imprisonment it was that he wrote his Prison Meditations, dedicated to the heart of suffering saints and reigning sinners. From the character of these stanzas, we should deem it very probable that he had accustomed himself to scribble in verse before his imprisonment,—a habit with which he doubtless solaced not a few of the hours in his little cell. Some verses in his Meditations upon the four last things, Death and Judgment, Heaven and Hell, are not wanting in beauty. His meditation of Heaven sprung from its vivid foretastes.

> What gladness shall possess our heart,
> When we shall see these things!
> What light and life in every part
> Rise like eternal springs!
> O, blessed face; O, holy grace,
> When shall we see this day?
> Lord, fetch us to this goodly place,
> We humbly to thee pray.
>
> Thus, when in heavenly harmony
> These blessed saints appear,
> Adorned with grace and majesty,
> What gladness will be there!
> Thus shall we see, thus shall we be.
> O, would the day were come!
> Lord Jesus, take us up to thee,
> To this desired home.
>
> Angels we also shall behold,
> When we on high ascend,
> Each shining like to men of gold,
> And on the Lord attend.
> These goodly creatures, full of grace,
> Shall stand about the throne,
> Each one with lightning in his face,
> And shall to us be known.
>
> There cherubim, with one accord,
> Continually do cry—
> Ah, holy, holy, holy Lord,
> And heavenly majesty!
> These will us in their arms embrace,
> And welcome us to rest,
> And joy to see us clad with grace,
> And of the heavens possest.

Doubtless it was such music in his soul, such visions before him, and such panting desires after heaven, that set him to the composition of the Pilgrim's Progress. He wrote a book of poems entitled, "Divine Emblems, or Temporal Things Spiritualized, fitted for the use of Boys and Girls." Some of them are very beautiful, revealing the true poet;

passages there are, which would not dishonour Chaucer or Shakspeare, and which shew to what great excellence, as a poet, Bunyan might have attained, had he dedicated himself to the effort. What he wrote, he wrote with the utmost simplicity, and in the same pure, idiomatic language which is so delightful in the Pilgrim's Progress. Here is a ballad of the child with the bird on the bush; and as a child's ballad, it is one of the sweetest, most natural things in the language.

THE CHILD AND THE BIRD.

My little bird, how canst thou sit
  And sing amidst so many thorns?
Let me but hold upon thee get,
  My love with honour thee adorns.
Thou art at present little worth,
  Five farthings none will give for thee:
But prithee, little bird, come forth,
  Thou of more value art to me.

'Tis true, it is sunshine to-day,
  To-morrow birds will have a storm;
My pretty one, come thou away,
  My bosom then shall keep thee warm.
Thou subject art to cold o'nights,
  When darkness is thy covering;
At day thy danger's great by kites,
  How canst thou then sit there and sing?

Thy food is scarce and scanty too,
  'Tis worms and trash which thou dost eat,
Thy present state I pity do,
  Come, I'll provide thee better meat.
I'll feed thee with white bread and milk,
  And sugar-plums, if thou them crave;
I'll cover thee with finest silk,
  That from the cold I may thee save.

My father's palace shall be thine,
  Yea, in it thou shalt sit and sing;
My little bird, if thou'lt be mine,
  The whole year round shall be thy spring.
I'll teach thee all the notes at court,
  Unthought-of music thou shalt play,
And all that thither do resort
  Shall praise thee for it every day.

I'll keep thee safe from cat and cur,
  No manner o' harm shall come to thee
Yea, I will be thy succourer,
  My bosom shall thy cabin be.

But lo, behold, the bird is gone!
  These charmings would not make her yield;
The child's left at the bush alone,
  The bird flies yonder o'er the field.

COMPARISON.

The child of Christ an emblem is;
  The bird to sinners I compare;
The thorns are like those sins of theirs
  Which do surround them every where.
Her songs, her food, her sunshine day,
  Are emblems of those foolish toys,
Which to destruction leads the way,
  The fruit of worldly, empty joys.

The arguments this child doth choose
  To draw to him a bird thus wild,
Shews Christ familiar speech doth use
  To make the sinner reconciled.
The bird, in that she takes her wing
  To speed her from him after all,
Shews us vain man loves any thing
  Much better than the heavenly call.

Now, if this ballad had been found among the poems of Wordsworth, with one or two touches of his peculiar colouring, it would have been regarded as one of his happiest examples of the artless simplicity and truth of nature. But with Bunyan these things were thrown off without any elaborate effort, in such language as he might naturally command, not with *studied* simplicity, but in such simplicity of style, matter, and language, as his childlike musings naturally fell into. And this constitutes their charm. He says himself that he could have written in higher strains but he would not attempt it; and well for the poetry it was that he did not; instead of the childlike carelessness and naturalness, which pleases older minds as well as children, he might have fallen into a stiffness and affected elegance that would have pleased none. As it is, there is great genius and beauty in these hymns for infant minds. In the introduction to the courteous reader, Bunyan says, in a vein of vigorous and well-directed satire—

The title page will shew, if thou wilt look,
  Who are the proper subjects of this book;
They're boys and girls of all sorts and degrees,
  From those of age, to children on their knees.

Thus comprehensive am I in my notions,
They tempt me to it by their childish motions.
We now have boys with beards, and girls that be
Huge as old women, wanting gravity.

Then do not blame me, since I thus describe 'em,
Flatter I may not, lest thereby I bribe 'em
To have a better judgment of themselves
Than wise men have of babies on their shelves;
Their antic tricks, fantastic modes and way
Shew they, like very boys and girls, do play
With all the frantic fooleries of the age,
And that in open view as on a stage.
Our bearded men do act like beardless boys,
Our women please themselves with childish toys.

Our ministers long time by word and pen
Dealt with them, counting them not boys but men;
They shot their thunders at them, and their toys,
But hit them not, for they were girls and boys,
The better charged, the wider still they shot,
Or else so high, these dwarfs they touched not.
Instead of men, they found them girls and boys
To nought addicted but to childish toys.

I repeat it, that this is pleasant, good-natured, and instructive satire; its vein of strong sense and native humour may remind us of our elder, early poets, whom, indeed, Bunyan in his poetry resembles not a little, and with whom he would have taken the highest rank as a poet, had Divine Providence directed his native gifts to be developed that way. Bunyan apologizes for seeming to play the fool, that he might, like Paul, by all means, gain some, and he hopes that even men of graver fancies may possibly be taken by his homely rhymes.

Some, I persuade me, will be finding fault,
Concluding, here I trip, and there I halt;
No doubt some could those grovelling notions raise
By fine-spun terms, that challenge might the bays.
Should all be forced to lay their brains aside,
That cannot regulate the glowing tide
By this or that man's fancy, we should have
The wise unto the fool become a slave.
What though my text seems mean, my morals be
Grave, as if fetched from a sublimer tree!
And if some better handle can a fly,
Then some a text, wherefore should we deny
Their making proof or good experiment
Of smallest things great mischiefs to prevent.

> I could, were I so pleased, use higher strains,
> And for applause on tenters stretch my brains;
> But what needs that? The arrow out of sight
> Does not the sleeper nor the watchman fright;
> To shoot too high doth make but children gaze;
> Tis that which hits the man doth him amaze.
>   As for the inconsiderableness
> Of things, by which I do my mind express;
> May I by them bring some good things to pass,
> As Samson, with the jaw bone of an ass;
> Or as brave Shamgar with his ox's goad,
> (Both things unmanly, not for war in mode,)
> I have my end, though I myself expose,
> For God will have the glory at the close.

This was ever Bunyan's disinterestedness and forgetfulness of self. So he might glorify God, it was no matter what became of his own reputation, his own will. Human applause he sought not, and while writing the most original work of genius produced in his age, he wrote with an absolute unconsciousness of fame, and a disregard of it, such as marked the character of no other writer of the period. Baxter was an eminently holy man, and his mind wrought under holy influences, but never with such unconsciousness of greatness, such forgetfulness of self. Yet the maxim of both was, To God alone be the glory!

These Divine Emblems, of which I have spoken, are much in the manner of Quarles, whose poetry Bunyan may have been acquainted with, as the Puritans were fond of it, and who died while Bunyan was in prison. Some of them remind us of the significant things seen by Christian in the house of the Interpreter. It was thus that Bunyan filled up his vacant seasons, and with various sweetness recreated himself in prison. While he was musing, the fire burned. When he began his Pilgrim's Progress, he was surprised into it, for he was writing another book, which he had nearly finished; but as he was penning some things concerning the race of the saints in the day of the gospel, his thoughts fell suddenly into the form of an allegory in a number of particulars, which he put down; these grew into more, and again continued to multiply, as he was attracted from fancy to fancy, and still he wrote them down, till he said within himself, If I go on at this rate, it will be *ad infinitum*, and

I shall never finish the book I am already about. Wherefore my thick-coming fancies I'll put you by yourselves, and when I have leisure from the work I have undertaken, then I will return to you.

Thus his work, so produced, came to be the pure, artless, spontaneous creation of piety and genius. There was scarcely a conscious effort in the writing of it; nay, rather a restraint of its exquisite sweetness, till such moments as he could attend to and take down the lovely images, the fervent thoughts, that were crowding one another in his mind, and seeking for utterance. It was but for him to say the word, to say to himself, Now my favourite meditations I release you; and suddenly, as songsters from a cage, his thoughts flew from him, as has been beautifully said of Dr Payson's conversation, in every possible variety of beauty and harmony, like birds from a South American forest. His vivid imagination filled his lonely cell with these realities; and it would appear that only when he was alone did his genius brood over this sacred work; in secrecy and silence did he pursue it; it was a joy of his heart, with which heaven itself mingled, and lent its own blessedness, but with which no stranger could intermeddle.

That this was the manner of the suggestion and production of this great work of genius, is clear from Bunyan's own amusing and instructive preface; and it is one of the most curious things in all the history of literature, to be admitted thus into the secret developments of spontaneous genius in a great writer's mind, on a work, the subject of which possesses the writer as with the power of an angel, instead of being possessed by him; carries him away with its sweetness, bears him up upon its wings as a child in a dream, and moves him swiftly through the luminous air, gazing at the divinely coloured pictures painted upon it. So was Bunyan borne upward as on eagles' wings, both by the Spirit of God, and by the power of that natural genius, which was the gift of God; and I may add, by the exciting celestial beauty of a subject, which kindles the heart of the simplest Christian with enthusiasm, and shapes, for the time being, a poet in the plainest mind. All this, without difficulty, you may read under cover of Bunyan's rude rhymes, which are good, unadulterate Saxon, and full of genuine simplicity and humour, though he scorned attempting to make them more elegant.

> When at the first I took my pen in hand,
> Thus for to write, I did not understand
> That I at all should make a little book
> In such a mode; nay, I had undertook
> To make another; which, when almost done,
> Before I was aware, I thus begun.
> And thus it was: I writing of the way
> And race of saints in this our gospel-day,
> Fell suddenly into an allegory
> About their journey, and the way to glory,
> In more than twenty things, which I set down.
> This done, I twenty more had in my crown,
> And they again began to multiply,
> Like sparks that from the coals of fire do fly.
> Nay, then, thought I, if that you breed so fast,
> I'll put you by yourselves, lest you at last
> Should prove *ad infinitum*, and eat out
> The book that I already am about.
> Well, so I did; but yet I did not think
> To shew to all the world my pen and ink
> In such a mode; I only thought to make
> I knew not what; nor did I undertake
> Thereby to please my neighbour; no, not I,
> I did it mine ownself to gratify.
> Neither did I but vacant seasons spend
> In this my scribble; nor did I intend
> But to divert myself in doing this,
> From worser thoughts, which make me do amiss.
> Thus I set pen to paper with delight,
> And quickly had my thoughts in black and white.
> For having now my method by the end,
> Still as I pull'd it came; and so I penn'd
> It down, until at last it came to be,
> For length and breadth, the bigness which you see.
> Well, when I thus had put my ends together,
> I shew'd them others, that I might see whether
> They would condemn them, or them justify:
> And some said, Let him live; some, Let him die.
> Some said, John, print it: others said, Not so.
> Some said, It might do good; others said, No.
> Now I was in a strait, and did not see
> Which was the best thing to be done by me;
> At last I thought, since you are thus divided,
> I print it will: and so the case decided.

And how could it have been decided otherwise? Bunyan proceeds with an ingenious and amusing apology and justification for using similitudes. Gold, pearls, and precious stones worth digging for, he thought might fitly be put into an allegory; and truth, even in swaddling clothes, as a sweet laughing babe, might win upon the mind, inform the judgment, make the will submissive, and fill the memory with things pleasant to the imagination. There is refreshing water in dark clouds, when there is none at all in bright ones; and when there silver drops descend, then the earth yieldeth her ripe harvest. A fisherman goes patiently up and down the river-side, and engages all his wits to catch a few nibbles, with snares, lines, angles, hooks and nets; all stratagems he uses for the silly fish. So doth the fowler for the birds; one can scarce name the variety of his means, his gun, his nets, his lime-twigs, light and bell; one can scarce tell the variety of his postures: he creeps, he goes, he stands, he pipes and whistles. So shall he, who wisely seeks to catch men, speak dialogue-wise, parable-wise, in prose and poetry, in figures, metaphors, and meaning fables; in cunning cabinets and mantles he shall enclose truth's golden beams; he shall set his apples of gold in pictures of silver.

> Yea, let Truth be free
> To make her sallies upon thee and me,
> Which way it pleases God.

So Bunyan thought, and would not check the variety of his fancies, though some would-be critics laughed at their simplicity, and some were offended at their novelty. Yet he knew he might write in such a method, and not miss his end, which was the good of his readers; and so he wrote, and so he published, committing all to God. The close of his preface is very beautiful, and would to God that every man who reads, might, according to Bunyan's directions, lay the book, the head, and the heart together, and so follow the pilgrim from the City of Destruction to the City of Immanuel!

> This book will make a traveller of thee,
> If by its counsel thou wilt ruled be;
> It will direct thee to the holy land,
> If thou wilt its directions understand;
> Yea, it will make the slothful active be;
> The blind also delightful things to see.

BUNYAN IN PRISON. 135

Art thou for something rare and profitable?
Or wouldst thou see a truth within a fable?
Art thou forgetful? or wouldst thou remember
From new-year's day to the last of December?
Then read my fancies; they will stick like burrs,
And may be to the helpless comforters.
This book is wrote in such a dialect,
As may the minds of listless men affect:
It seems a novelty, and yet contains
Nothing but sound and honest gospel strains.
  Wouldst thou divert thyself from melancholy?
Wouldst thou be pleasant, yet be far from folly?
Wouldst thou read riddles, and their explanation?
Or else be drown'd in thy contemplation?
Dost thou love picking meat? or wouldst thou see
A man i' th' clouds, and hear him speak to thee?
Wouldst thou be in a dream, and yet not sleep?
Or, wouldst thou in a moment laugh and weep?
Or, wouldst thou lose thyself, and catch no harm;
And find thyself again without a charm?
Wouldst read thyself, and read thou know'st not what,
And yet know whether thou art bless'd or not,
By reading the same lines? O then come hither!
And lay my book, thy head, and heart together.

A great characteristic of original genius, perhaps its greatest proof, and one which Bunyan possessed in common with Shakespeare, is its spontaneous exertion; the evidence of having written without labour, and without the consciousness of doing any thing remarkable, or the ambitious aim of performing a great work. The thought, "how will this please?" has little or no power as a motive, nor is it suggested to such minds: the greatest efforts of genius seem as natural to it as it is for common men to breathe. In this view, Bunyan's work comes nearer to the inspired poetry of the Hebrews in its character, than any other human composition. He wrote from the impulse of his genius, sanctified and illuminated by a heavenly influence; and its movements were as artless as the movements of a little child left to play upon the green by itself; as if, indeed, he had exerted no voluntary supervision whatever over its exercise. Every thing is as natural and unconstrained as if there had been no other breather in this world but himself,—no being, to whose inspection the work he was producing could ever possibly be exhibited, and no rule or model with which it could ever be compared.

We can imagine this suffering Christian and unconscious poet in the gloom of his prison, solacing his mind with his own visions, as they came in, one after another, like heavenly pictures, to his imagination. They were so pleasant that he could not but give them reality, and when he found how they accumulated, then first did the IDEAL of the Pilgrim's Progress rise before his view. Then did he, with the pervading, informing, and transfusing power of genius, melt the materials, and mould them into shape. He puts the pictures into one grand allegory, with the meaning of heaven shining over the whole, and a separate interest and beauty in every separate part. It is an allegory, conducted with such symmetry and faithfulness, that it never tires in its examination, but discloses continually new meaning to the mind, and speaks to the heart of the Pilgrim volumes of mingled encouragement, warning, and instruction.

And how precious is the volume, which thus stores the nursery as well as the shelves of the theologian, with wholesome learning; which brings the divinest mysteries of grace into the quick conscience and soft heart of childhood, even before the understanding is prepared to receive and ponder their grave teachings! This is the point of Cowper's beautiful apostrophe to Bunyan.

> " O thou, whom, borne on fancy's eager wing,
> Back to the season of life's happy spring,
> I pleased remember, and while memory yet
> Holds fast her office here, can ne'er forget ;
> Ingenious Dreamer! in whose well-told tale
> Sweet fiction and sweet truth alike prevail ;
> Whose humorous vein, strong sense, and simple style,
> May teach the gayest, make the gravest smile ;
> Witty, and well employed, and like thy Lord,
> Speaking in parables his slighted word ;
> I name thee not, lest so despised a name
> Should move a sneer at thy deserved fame.
> Yet e'en in transitory life's late day,
> That mingles all my brown with sober grey,
> Revere the man, whose Pilgrim marks the road,
> And guides the Progress of the soul to God ;
> 'Twere well with most, if books that could engage
> Their childhood, pleased them at a riper age ;
> The man, approving what had charmed the boy,
> Would die at last in comfort, peace, and joy ;
> And not with curses on his heart, who stole
> The gem of truth from his unguarded soul."

LECTURE FIFTH.

Providence, Grace, and Genius,

IN BUNYAN AND THE PILGRIM'S PROGRESS.

Illustrations of Divine Providence in selecting Bunyan to write the Pilgrim's Progress.—Weak things chosen to confound the mighty.—The Author of the Pilgrim's Progress selected not from the Establishment, but from without it.—Signal rebuke of ecclesiastical exclusiveness and hierarchical pretensions, in the Pilgrim's Progress and the Saint's Rest.—More of Bunyan's Divine Emblems.—Bunyan's release from prison.—His release from life, and entrance into the Celestial City.—Dr Scott's opinion of the Pilgrim's Progress.—Its entire freedom from Sectarianism.—Its universality, both in genius and piety.—Comparison between Bunyan's Pilgrim's Progress, and Edwards on the Religious Affections.—Bunyan and Spenser.—Survey of the Events, Characters, and Scenery in the Pilgrim's Progress.—The Splendour of its conclusion.

WE meet in the life of Bunyan some of the most remarkable illustrations to be found anywhere on record, of the manner in which God has chosen the weak things of the world to confound the mighty, and base things of the world, and things which are despised, and things which are not, to bring to nought things that are; to abase the pride, and rebuke the pretensions of all human glory. Bunyan's preaching, which was the means of the conversion of so many souls, how utterly despised and counted like insanity was it, by all the wise, the noble, the esteemed of this world! And Bunyan's Allegory, when it first appeared, with how much contempt was it regarded, as a sort of story or ballad for the vulgar, by the lords, gentlemen, and ecclesiastics of the age. If any prophet in those days could have gone to the bishop and justices under whose jurisdiction Bunyan was thrust into the common jail, and left twelve years in prison, and could have said, My Lords, there is one John Bunyan, formerly a tinker, and now a tagged-lace maker in a cell in the prison of Bedford, imprisoned by your Lordships for preaching the gospel, who hath composed and published an allegory which shall work more to the accomplishment of God's counsels, and to the establishment of sound piety and morality, and to the usefulness and glory of the literature of this kingdom, than all that your Lordships, with all the preachers and authors in this civil and ecclesiastical circuit, shall have accomplished in your whole life-time; he would have been regarded as void of understanding, if not imprisoned for contempt of the higher authorities.

And yet, such a prophet would have spoken but the simple truth; for into how many languages this book hath been translated no man can tell, and how many editions it has passed through still less may any man enumerate, nor how many souls it may have guided to eternal glory. It has gone almost wherever the Bible has gone, and has left the stamp of the best part of English literature, where neither Milton nor Shakspeare were ever heard of. Indeed, it may doubtless be said of Bunyan as of that woman of sacred memory in the New Testament, Wherever this gospel shall be preached in all the world, there shall that, which this man hath done for Christ, be told for a memorial of him. The alabaster-box of very precious ointment which that woman poured upon the Saviour's head was an unutterably precious offering, because her heart went with it; but this alabaster-box of genius and piety, the fruit of these twelve years' imprisonment, was the work—both the offering itself, and the feelings with which it was offered—equally of Bunyan's heart, filled with love to the same Saviour. And wherever the Bible goes, doubtless, in all time, this book will follow it.

As the book itself is an illustration of this great principle of God's administration, so was his own selection of Bunyan as his instrument to do so mighty a work. Disregarding the claims of great establishments and mighty hierarchies, passing by the gorgeous state religions of the world and all their followers, passing the Archbishop of Canterbury, and the See of London, and the great consecrated shrines of applauded genius and piety, even the genius of Milton, and the pulpits of Jeremy Taylor, and Howe, and Usher, and the wise and mighty and noble together, he entered the prison cell in Bedford, and poured this unction of his Spirit upon John Bunyan, and touched his lips alone with this hallowed fire, and dipped his pen alone in these colours of heaven. There were as great boasts, if not of the apostolical succession, at least of the Ecclesiastical Establishment, in those days as in this; and God saw that a lordly hierarchy, and many a lordly bishop, were proclaiming to all the world this lie, that there could be no lawful worship of God, and no true church of Christ, without a prayer book and prelatical consecration, without episcopacy, confirmation, and a liturgy; but all this was as wood, hay, and stubble; and Divine Providence selected, to make the brightest jewel of the age as a Christian, a minister, and a writer, a member of the then obscure, persecuted, and despised sect of Baptists. He took John Bunyan; but he did not remove him from the Baptist church of Christ into what men said was the only true church; he kept him shining in that Baptist candlestick all his lifetime; for what is it to Christ whether a man be Baptist, Methodist, Congregationalist, Presbyterian, Independent, or Episcopalian, so he be but a true follower of the Saviour, so he lord it not over God's heritage, nor be guilty of schism in consigning to God's uncovenanted mercies, in defiance of all Christian charity, those whom the Saviour holds as dear as the apple of his eye? What are these sectarian shibboleths to Christ, if his people will but walk according to this rule, which was a text of favourite note with Bunyan, "By this shall all men know that ye are my disciples, if ye love one another!" MY DISCIPLES, not members of this or that sectarian persuasion, be it Episcopal, Baptist, Presbyterian, or what not. My disciples, not Church-men, nor Paul's-men, nor Rome's-men, but MY DISCIPLES.

All gorgeous and prelatical establishments God passed by, and selected the greatest marvel and miracle of grace and genius in all the modern age from the Baptist church in Bedford! If this be not a rebuke and a refutation of that absurd mockery, "the apostolical succession," and all pretensions like it, we know not how Divine Providence could construct one. It is just as clear as the Saviour's own personal rebuke of the same intolerant proud spirit in his day; and the feeling with which its application is received by the pretenders to the only true church in our day is remarkably similar. "I tell you of a truth, many widows were in Israel in the days of Elias, when the heaven was shut up three years and six months, when great famine was throughout all the land; but unto none of them was Elias sent, save unto Sarepta, a city of Sidon, unto a woman that was a widow. And many lepers were in Israel in the time of Eliseus the prophet; and none of them was cleansed saving Naaman the Syrian. And all they in the Synagogue, when they heard these things, were filled with wrath, and rose up, and thrust him out of the city, and led him unto the brow of the hill whereon their city was built, that they might cast him down headlong!" Why, what mighty evil hath our blessed Lord done to awaken this dreadful hell of wrath and malignity in this synagogue of Satan? He hath simply told them that their church was no longer to be the only true Church of Christ on earth, but that he was going to preach to the Gentiles! And the wickedness of this Jewish hierarchy is but a specimen of the wickedness which this pretence of being the only true church inevitably sets in motion and brings with it, wherever such a pretended true church can get the power to enforce its excommunications. It will lead our blessed Lord himself to the brow of the hill, and cast him down headlong, if he visit this earth in a conventicle, if he come to any other than an Established Church.

The same principle thus marvellously illustrated in the life of Bunyan, was that by which God passed by the many thousands of Israel of loftier genealogy and prouder claims, and fixed upon David the son of Jesse, the keeper of his father's flock in the wilderness, and anointed and crowned him King of Israel; passed by also the great towns and beautiful cities of Judea, and Jerusalem itself, and fixed upon Bethlehem as the birth-place of our Saviour; passed by also the learned and excellent, the princes and scholars of the land, when he would found a new spiritual kingdom to last for ever, and took the fishermen and the tax-gatherers; and to step out of sacred history once more, into common, in a case in some respects of great similarity to Bunyan's own, passed by the godliest learned men of honour, title, and rank, and chose a chaplain in Oliver Cromwell's parliamentary army to write the Saint's Rest. The two greatest, most important, most efficacious spiritual works the world has ever seen, written by men cast out, persecuted, imprisoned, as not being members of the true church, as not conforming to the will of the Established hierarchy! The world is full of these blessed instances of God's wisdom to cast down the pride of man, and abase his pretensions, that no flesh may glory in his presence. And as to these hierarchical arrogancies, it would seem that Divine Wisdom itself could resort to no expedient more sure to put them to shame, than when the Holy Spirit takes up his abode, and displays his glory, in beings cast out, persecuted, imprisoned, and burned, by such bigotry and violence. The great overshadowing, remorseless, hierarchical unity of the Church, when it is any thing else but unity in the possession and exercise of the Spirit of Christ, becomes a destructive unity of evil, a unity of ambition, consecrated under the name of religion, a unity of earthly power and aggrandizement, in which the passion of universal conquest, that like a chariot of fire whirled a Nimrod or Napoleon over the world, kindles in the bosom of churchmen, and makes out of the church itself the most perfect, awful form of despotism. It is such a dreadful unity that has anathematized and destroyed some of the brightest temples of the Holy Ghost, out of which God has shined in this world of darkness. It was indeed this remorseless, despotic, persecuting unity, to which our blessed Lord himself was sacrificed, to prevent a schism in the Jewish hierarchy. But under whatever form, save that of love to Christ, and participation in his Spirit, this unity is vaunted, it becomes an unhallowed, worldly, vain, ambitious boast; and powerfully, indeed, are its pretensions shewn to be vanity, when God raises up, beyond its precincts, such men as Baxter and Bunyan, Owen and Doddridge, Calamy and Howe, Brainerd and Edwards, Payson and Dwight. Rather let every Christian be in himself a separate sect, than the church of Christ a compulsory despotism.

And how may we suppose the great Head of the church regards such daring presumption, whether under pretence of apostolical succession or prelatical consecration, that shuts out such men from the church of Christ on earth, and gives them over even to God's uncovenanted mercies in heaven? Merely the statement of such pretensions is enough to shew how opposed they are to the spirit of the gospel. If a desire to spread that gospel, and to bring all men into the fold of Christ, had prevailed, or were now prevalent, we should hear nothing of such pretensions; if that unity of love existed, which our blessed Lord requires, and without which all other unity is worthless, there would be the kindest charity and piety, but no pride; Christians would, as Paul requires, receive one another, but not to doubtful disputations; and all sects would be found vying with each other, not to spread their own name, but the knowledge of the gospel; not to eject each other from the missionary field, but to fill the world with love and mercy. We trust in God that this spirit shall prevail over every other; and when it does, then will be the time when there shall be nothing to hurt nor destroy in all God's holy mountain.

The prison hours of such men as Bunyan have done much to bring the full blessedness of such a period, and out of Bunyan's prison shone much of that rosy light, that in the morning of the Reformation is more romantically beautiful, than even the clear shining of the sun at noon. His prison work was one of the stars, co-herald with the dawn, reflecting the Sun of Righteousness, but struggling with the darkness all night long. If, during his confinement, he wrote those Divine Emblems, of which I have spoken, as is very probable, there was calm, sweet light, shining out of the soul of the true poet, hidden, as by God's mercy, in a pavilion from the strife of tongues. As the tuneful bird of night sits even amidst the rain, and sings darkling, so the heart of Bunyan sang, while the storm raged round his prison; nay, it may be said of him, as of Luther, that he poured the music of truth from his soul as from a church organ. I could present some of his finished pieces in verse, that may well be compared with the best of our elder poets, and that, contrasted with the doggerel of his early days, shew an intellectual transformation as wonderful, almost, as his spiritual new creation. And yet, I must remark, in regard to those rude verses, which, with such inconceivably bad spelling, and with such cramped and distorted chirography, Bunyan used to write in the margin of his old copy of Foxe's Book of Martyrs, that they do not make upon the mind the impression of that word *doggerel;* the mint out of which they fall is too sacred for that, and the metal, though wrought with such extreme rudeness, manifestly too precious. As we gaze upon that chirography, in connection with the martyrdom that excited the passionate emotion of the writer, we seem to see the very soul of Bunyan impressing, as with the point of a diamond, in the only language he then knew how to command, the hieroglyphics of the martyr's spirit in his own bosom. Those verses are as Indian arrows, tipped with flint, in comparison with a rifle inlaid with gold. But they are more than curious; there is vigour in them, and fire of the soul.

If the following emblems (in addition to those I have before referred to) be taken as specimens of what fancies the poet could play with for the prisoner's amusement, there is no good critic but will recognise in them the elements of a true poetical genius. Who, for example, in Bunyan's stanzas upon the sun's reflection on the clouds in a fair morning, will not irresistibly be reminded of Milton's beautiful image in the Mask of Comus?

> Was I deceived, or did a sable cloud
> Turn forth her silver lining on the night?

Bunyan, certainly, never imitated any living creature, nor the writings of any genius, living or dead; yet there are passages, that, with the exception of the recurrence of "grace" or similar religious phrases, formed in a very different school from that of the poets of this world, might be deemed to have been cut directly from the pages even of such a writer as Shakspeare. Juliet, looking from her window, might have uttered the following lines, had her thoughts been upon such sacred things as the prayer of the saints.

> Look yonder! ah, methinks mine eyes do see
> Clouds edged with silver, as fine garments be!
> They look as if they saw the golden face
> That makes black clouds most beautiful with grace.
>
> Unto the saints' sweet incense of their prayer
> These smoky curled clouds I do compare;
> For as these clouds seem edged or laced with gold,
> Their prayers return with blessings manifold.

Remark also the beauty of the following lines upon the rising of the sun:

> Look how brave Sol doth peep up from beneath,
> Shows us his golden face, doth on us breathe;
> Yea, he doth compass us around with glories
> Whilst he ascends up to his highest stories,
> Where he his banner over us displays,
> And gives us light to see our works and ways.
>
> Nor are we now as at the peep of light,
> To question is it day, or is it night;
> The night is gone, the shadow's fled away,
> And now we are most certain that 'tis day.
>
> And thus it is when Jesus shews his face,
> And doth assure us of his love and grace.

Take also the following very beautiful moral upon the promising fruitfulness of a tree. Who could have written in purer language, or with more terseness and graphic simplicity?

> A comely sight indeed it is to see,
> A world of blossoms on an apple-tree:
> Yet far more comely would this tree appear,
> If all its dainty blooms young apples were;
> But how much more might one upon it see,
> If each would hang there till it ripe should be,
> But most of all in beauty, 'twould abound,
> If every one should then be truly sound.
>
> But we, alas! do commonly behold
> Blooms fall apace, if mornings be but cold,
> They too which hang till they young apples are,
> By blasting winds and vermin take despair.

Store that do hang while almost ripe, we see,
By blust'ring winds are shaken from the tree.

So that of many, only some there be,
That grow and thrive to full maturity.

COMPARISON.

This tree a perfect emblem is of those
Which do the garden of the Lord compose.
Its blasted blooms are motions unto good,
Which chill affections nip in the soft bud.

Those little apples which yet blasted are,
Shew some good purposes, no good fruit bear.
Those spoil'd by vermin are to let us see
How good attempts by bad thoughts ruin'd be.

Those which the wind blows down while they are green,
Shew good works have by trials spoiled been.
Those that abide while ripe, upon the tree,
Shew, in a good man, some ripe fruit will be.

Behold then how abortive some fruits are,
Which at the first most promising appear.
The frost, the wind, the worm, with time doth shew,
There flow from much appearance works but few.

I may add to these extracts the following emblem upon a snail, very much in the manner of our elder poets, and with an exquisite religious moral, which you might look far to discover in English poetry, and not find at all, or not find so simply and so well expressed.

She goes but softly, but she goeth sure,
 She stumbles not, as stronger creatures do ;
Her journey's shorter, so she may endure
 Better than they which do much further go.

She makes no noise, but stilly seizeth on
 The flower or herb, appointed for her food ;
The which she quietly doth feed upon,
 While others range and glare, but find no good.

And tho' she doth but very softly go,
 However slow her pace be, yet 'tis sure :
And certainly they that do travel so,
 The prize which they do aim at, they procure.

Altho' they seem not much to stir or go,
 Who thirst for Christ, and who from wrath do flee,
Yet what they seek for, quickly they come to,
 Tho' it does seem the farthest off to be.

One act of faith doth bring them to that flow'r
 They so long for that they may eat and live,
Which to attain is not in others' power,
 Tho' for it a king's ransom they would give.

> Then let none faint, nor be at all dismay'd,
> That life by Christ do seek, they shall not fail
> To have it; let them nothing be afraid:
> The herb and flow'r are eaten by the snail.

In the collection of Bunyan's poetical pieces in his works there are some very thoughtful and vigorous stanzas, entitled, "A Caution to Stir up to Watch against Sin." They may very probably be ranked along with the Divine Emblems, as the production of his prison hours. The following lines are powerful.

> Sin is the living worm, the lasting fire,
> Hell soon would lose its heat, could sin expire.
> Better sinless in hell, than to be where
> Heaven is, and to be found a sinner there.
> One sinless with infernals might do well,
> But sin would make of heaven a very hell.
>   Look to thyself then, keep it out of door,
>   Lest it get in and never leave thee more.
>
> No match has sin but God in all the world,
> Men, angels, has it from their station hurled;
> Holds them in chains, as captives, in despite
> Of all that here below is called might.
> Release, help, freedom from it none can give,
> But even he, by whom we breathe and live.
>   Watch, therefore, keep this giant out of door,
>   Lest, if once in, thou get him out no more.
>
> Fools make a mock at sin, will not believe
> It carries such a dagger in its sleeve;
> How can it be, say they, that such a thing,
> So full of sweetness, e'er should wear a sting?
> They know not that it is the very spell
> Of sin, to make men laugh themselves to hell.
>   Look to thyself then, deal with sin no more,
>   Lest he that saves, against thee shuts the door.

In the prose works of Bunyan there are here and there passages, which, had he put them into rhyme, would have made exquisite poems. Such, for example, is the following paragraph, which one might suppose to have been cut from the pages of the holy Leighton, so much do the spirit, the language, and the imagery resemble his. "I have thus written," says Bunyan, speaking of his work on Christian Behaviour, "because it is amiable and pleasant to God, when Christians keep their rank, relation, and station, doing all as becomes their quality and calling. When Christians stand every one in their places, and do the work of their relations, then they are like the flowers in the garden, that stand and grow where the gardener hath planted them, and then they shall both honour the garden in which they are planted, and the gardener that hath so disposed of them. From the hyssop in the wall to the cedar in Lebanon, their fruit is their glory. And seeing the stock into which we are planted is the fruitfulest stock, the sap conveyed thereout the fruitfulest sap, and the dresser of our souls the wisest husbandman, how contrary to nature, to example, and expectation we should be, if we should not be rich in good works. Wherefore, take heed of being painted fire, wherein is no warmth; and painted flowers, which retain no smell; and of being painted trees, whereon is no fruit. Whoso boasteth himself of a false gift, is like clouds and wind without rain. Farewell! The Lord be with thy spirit, that thou mayest profit for time to come."

In the same work on Christian Behaviour, he says beautifully, "It is the ordinance of God that Christians should be often asserting the things of God each to others, and that by their so doing they should edify one another. The doctrine of the gospel is like the dew and the small rain, that distilleth upon the tender grass, wherewith it doth flourish, and is kept green. Christians are like the several flowers in a garden, that have upon each of them the dew of heaven, which being shaken by the wind, they let fall their dew at each other's roots, whereby they are jointly nourished, and become nourishers of one another. For Christians to commune savourily of God's matters one with another is as if they opened to each other's nostrils boxes of perfume. Saith Paul to the church at Rome, I long to see you, that I may impart unto you some spiritual gift, to the end that you may be established; that is, that I may be comforted together with you, by the mutual faith both of you and me."

"Thus have I, in few words, written to you before I die, a word to provoke you to faith and holiness, because I desire that you may have the life that is laid up for all them that believe in the Lord Jesus, and love one another, when I am deceased. Though there I shall rest from my labours, and be in Paradise, as through grace I comfortably believe, but it is not there, but here, I must do you good. Wherefore I, not knowing the shortness of my life, nor the hinderance that hereafter I may have of serving my God and you, I have taken this opportunity to present these few lines unto you for your edification. Consider what hath been said, and the Lord give you understanding in all things. Farewell!"

How beautiful is the spirit here manifested, how full of the sweet charity of the gospel, and of what sweet simplicity and beauty are the thoughts and images here expressed! *It is not there in heaven, but here on earth, that I must do you good.* We are reminded of Paul's language, "To abide in the flesh is more needful for you." Infinitely desirable is such a blessed hope of heaven, as shall make the Christian desire to depart and be with Christ, and shall, at the same time, quicken and animate and fill with blessedness all his efforts for the good of others.

In that ingenious work of Bunyan, entitled "Solomon's Temple Spiritualized," there are passages of exquisite beauty and significancy. Take, for example, the two following extracts, the first in regard to the Gates of the Porch of the Temple, the second in regard to the Pinnacles of the Temple; and see the ingenuity and beauty of the author of the Pilgrim's Progress, in other modes of allegorizing besides that of the great admired production of his genius.

Of the Gates of the Porch of the Temple.

"The porch, at which was an ascent to the temple, had a gate belonging to it. This gate, according to the prophet Ezekiel, was six cubits wide. The leaves of this gate were double, one folding this way, the other that. Ezek. xl. 48.

"Now here some may object, and say, Since the way to God by these doors was so wide, why doth Christ say, the way and gate is narrow?

"*Ans.* The straitness, the narrowness, must not be understood of the gate simply, but because of that cumber that some men carry with them, that pretend to be going to heaven. Six cubits! What is sixteen cubits to him who would enter in here with all the world on his back? The young man in the Gospel, who made such a noise for heaven, might have gone in easy enough; for in six cubits breadth there is room: but, poor man! he was not for going in thither, unless he might carry in his houses upon his shoulder too, and so the gate was strait, Mark x. 17–23.

"Wherefore he that will enter in at the gate of heaven, of which this gate into the temple was a type, must go in by himself, and not with his bundles of trash on his back; and if he will go in thus, he need not fear there is room. *The righteous nation that keepeth the truth, they shall enter in.*

"They that enter at the gate of the inner court, must be clothed in fine linen; how then shall they go into the temple that carry the clogs of the dirt of this world at their heels? Thus saith the Lord, 'No stranger uncircumcised in heart, or uncircumcised in flesh, shall enter into my sanctuary.'

"The wideness therefore of this gate, is for this cause here made mention of, to wit, to encourage them that would gladly enter thereat, according to the mind of God, and not to flatter them that are not for leaving of all for God.

"Wherefore let such as would go in remember that here is room, even a gate to enter at, six cubits wide. We have been all this while but on the outside of the temple, even in the courts of the house of the Lord, to see the beauty and glory that is there. The beauty hereof made men cry out, and say, 'How amiable are thy tabernacles, O Lord of hosts! my soul longeth, yea, fainteth for the courts of the Lord;' and to say, 'A day in thy courts is better than a thousand.'"

Of the Pinnacles of the Temple.

"There were also several pinnacles belonging to the temple. These pinnacles stood on the top aloft in the air, and were sharp, and so difficult to stand upon: what men say of their number and length I waive, and come directly to their signification.

"I therefore take those pinnacles to be types of those lofty, airy notions, with which some delight themselves, while they hover like birds above the solid and godly truths of Christ. Satan attempted to entertain Christ Jesus with this type, and antitype, at once, when he set him on one of the pinnacles of the temple, and offered to thrust him upon a false confidence in God, by a false and unsound interpretation of a text, Matt. iv. 5, 6; Luke iv. 9, 10, 11.

"You have some men cannot be content to worship in the temple, but must be aloft; no place will serve them but pinnacles, pinnacles; that they may be speaking in and to the air, that they may be promoting their heady notions, instead of solid truth; not considering that now they are where the devil would have them be: they strut upon their points, their pinnacles: but let them look to it, there is difficult standing upon pinnacles; their neck, their soul, is in danger. We read, God is in his temple, not upon these pinnacles, Psal. xi. 4; Hab. ii. 20.

"It is true, Christ was once upon one of these: but the devil set him there, with intent to dash him in pieces by a fall; and yet even then told him, if he would venture to tumble down, he should be kept from dashing his foot against a stone. To be there, therefore, was one of Christ's temptations; consequently one of Satan's stratagems; nor went he thither of his own accord, for he knew that there was danger; he loved not to clamber pinnacles.

"This should teach Christians to be low and little in their own eyes, and to forbear to intrude into airy and vain speculations, and to take heed of being puffed up with a foul and empty mind."

In the same work, Bunyan says in regard to the ornaments carved upon the doors of the temple,

"There were also carved upon these doors open flowers; and that to teach us, that here is the sweet scent, and fragrant smell; and that the coming soul will find it so in Christ this door: *I am* saith he, *the rose of Sharon, and the lily of the vallies.* And again, *His cheeks are as beds of spices and several flowers, his lips like lilies drop sweet smelling myrrh.*

"*Open flowers.* Open flowers are the sweetest, because full grown, and because, as such, they yield their fragrancy most freely. Wherefore, when he saith, upon the doors are open flowers, he setteth Christ Jesus forth in his good savours as high as by such similitudes he could; and that both in name and office; for open flowers lay, by their thus opening themselves before us, all their beauty also most plainly before our faces. There are varieties of beauty in open flowers, the which they also commend to all observers. Now upon these doors, you see, are open flowers, flowers ripe, and spread before us to shew that his name and offices are savoury to them that by him do enter his house to God his Father, Song i. 1, 2, 3, 4.

"*All these were overlaid with fine gold.* Gold is most rich of all metals; and here it is said the doors, the cherubims, the palm-trees, and open flowers, were overlaid therewith. And this shews, that as these things are rich in themselves, even so they should be to us. We have a golden door to go to God by, and golden angels to conduct us through the world: we have golden palm-trees, as tokens of our victory and golden flowers to smell on all the way to heaven."

A man who, with the Bible and his Concordance for his only library, could write, and loved to write, in this manner, need be in no want of occupation or of solace in his prison hours. They fled swiftly and sweetly with Bunyan, notwithstanding all his cares; and never, since the beginning of the world, were twelve prison years made to yield a riper, more blessed harvest for his own soul's happiness and the world's good. Of them, as well as of his temptations, Bunyan could say, I have found a nest of honey in the carcass of the lion that roared upon me. Not only himself but all the world, are refreshed by its sweetness, and healed by it, as by a spiritual medicinal Nepenthé, in the midst of guilt and wretchedness. So, out of darkness God can bring forth light, out of evil good, out of the adversities of his people, the most precious of all manna for the nourishment of his church in the wilderness.

Bunyan's release from prison took place in the year 1672, or early in 1673; befriended, according to Bunyan's own grateful acknowledgments, by Dr Barlow, afterwards Bishop of Lincoln. His liberation is now said to have been obtained from Charles II., by Whitehead the Quaker. For two or three years the strictness of his imprisonment had been loosened, so that, probably through the kindness of his jailer, he used to meet with his church in Bedford, if not to preach to them. Indeed, it was even before his release from prison that he was chosen by that church, and ordained their pastor, in the year 1671, and that notwithstanding the revival and re-enactment of the barbarous Conventicle Act in 1670. This act was the means of a severe persecution of the members of Bunyan's church, from which he himself escaped only because he was already a prisoner, as he had been for near twelve years. In this there was at least a verification of Bunyan's own poetry in the Pilgrim's Progress:—

" He that is down needs fear no fall."

How he escaped afterwards, or how, without the slightest relinquishment of his principles, he should have been let out of prison, is almost inexplicable; only it was the good providence of God. He was thrown into prison as a preacher, and as a preacher he came out, in the full spirit of his first declaration, *that if he were out of prison to-day he would preach the gospel to-morrow by the help of God.*

He continued, for the rest of his life, writing, preaching, visiting, in Bedford and the region round about, often visiting London, and preaching there; preaching with such divine unction and power, that Owen, who heard him, made answer to Charles II., when the king ridiculed him for hearing an illiterate tinker prate, " Please your Majesty, could I possess that tinker's abilities for preaching, I would most gladly relinquish all my learning." With all the great learning of Owen, it would have been a good exchange; and the speech was in the highest degree creditable to that great and good man, and an admirable reproof to the king; for Bunyan's preaching was in demonstration of the Spirit, and with power; and his own account of his own exercises in preaching, with the wrestling and yearning of his soul for the conversion of men, shews something of the deep secret of that power. He preached in prison as well as out of it; and one of his biographers, who visited him while there, just after the prison was crowded with more than threescore dissenters newly taken, relates, " that in the midst of all that hurry which so many new comers occasioned, he had heard Mr Bunyan both preach and pray with that mighty spirit of faith, and plethory of divine assistance, that had made him stand and wonder." That is a graphic expression, that *plethory* of divine assistance.

Bunyan is said to have clearly foreseen the designs of King James in favour of popery, and " advised the brethren to avail themselves of the sunshine by diligent endeavours to spread the gospel, and to prepare for an approaching storm by fasting and prayer." For himself, he was always ready, but always labouring after a greater readiness. It was in the successful prosecution of a labour of love and charity that he died; having travelled to Reading to make peace between an alienated son and father. The gentle spirit of Bunyan prevailed to do away the alienation; but for himself, returning to London on horseback through the rain, he fell sick with a mortal fever, and died at the age of sixty on the 31st day of August 1688. On his dying bed, he acted the part of Hopeful in crossing the River of Death; for the Saviour was with him, and the songs of the Celestial City were ravishing his heart. The most ancient biography of Bunyan declares, that " He comforted those that wept about him, exhorting them to trust in God, and pray to him for mercy and forgiveness of their sins, telling them what a glorious exchange it would be, to leave their troubles and cares of a wretched mortality, to live with Christ for ever, with peace and joy inexpressible; expounding to them the comfortable scriptures, by which they were to hope and assuredly come unto a blessed resurrection in the last day. He desired some to pray with him, and he joined with them in prayer; and his last words, after he had struggled with a languishing disease, were these :—' Weep not for me, but for yourselves. I go to the Father of our Lord Jesus Christ, who will, through the mediation of his blessed Son, receive me, though a sinner, where I hope we ere long shall meet to sing the new song, and remain everlastingly happy, world without end.' "

So holy and blessed was the life, so happy was the death, but indescribably, inconceivably glorious the immortality of John Bunyan. Farther the pen traces him not, but the eye of faith follows him, and beholds him in glory.

"I saw in my dream that this man went in at the gate; and lo! as he entered he was transfigured, and he had raiment put on him that shone like gold. There were also that met him with harps and crowns, and gave unto him; the harps to praise withal, and the crowns in token of honour. Then I heard in my dream, that all the bells in the city rang again for joy; and that it was said unto him,

'ENTER THOU INTO THE JOY OF OUR LORD.'

I also heard the man himself sing with a loud voice, saying, 'BLESSING, AND HONOUR, AND GLORY, AND POWER, BE UNTO HIM THAT SITTETH UPON THE THRONE, AND UNTO THE LAMB FOR EVER AND EVER.'"

In remarking on the manner in which the truths of the Holy Scriptures come to view in the Pilgrim's Progress, and constitute its texture, it is important to remember that Bunyan was taught those truths not as a system, at second-hand, but by the Spirit of God, through his own experience in the word of God. His great work is as a piece of rich tapestry, in which, with the word of God before him as his original and guide, and with all his heaven-coloured materials tinged also in the deep fountain of feeling in his own converted heart, he wove into one beautiful picture the various spiritual scenery and thrilling events of his own life and journeyings as a Christian pilgrim. So, if it is all fresh and graphic from his own experience, vivid with real life, and not with speculation, it is also equally fresh and graphic from the word of God, and answering thereto as a counterpart, all that experience having been built throughout upon that word. We come to it with wrong criticism, therefore, if we look at it as a theological theory or system, though at the same time it is beyond measure interesting and delightful to recognise, while we read it as a book of life, the same great living elements of truth with which we are familiar in the Bible. The anatomy of speculation in the Pilgrim's

Progress, the bones, the vertebræ, and the articulations, aie, if I may so speak, the same with the anatomy of Divine Truth in the Scriptures; and hence the beauty and perfect symmetry of the body of life formed upon them.

The purity of the stream of the water of life, clear as crystal, flowing through these pages, is nowhere, in the Pilgrim's Progress, tinged or darkened with speculative error. Much the same remark may be made in regard to that beautiful, most ingenious, and instructive work, the Holy War in the Town of Mansoul. The theoretical system, and the practical spirit, can nowhere be separated, and both proceeded from the word and the Spirit of God in the understanding and the heart of the writer.

Dr Scott has said—and it is a remark sometimes quoted —that the Calvinistic system in theology has never been traced so unexceptionably as in Bunyan's Pilgrim's Progress. This remark, though unquestionably intended in the way of praise to Bunyan, may, nevertheless, in some respects, be regarded as doing him injustice; for he followed no man's theological system in the world. He knew almost as little, perhaps quite as little, about John Calvin as he did about Thomas Aquinas himself. He drew his theology from the Scriptures, under the teaching of God's Spirit, and thence only, and from no man's system in the world. And in his Pilgrim's Progress he delineates the theology of the Scriptures, and of the Scriptures only, and not of the Calvinistic system, nor of any other system, with any human name attached to it. If any man's name could with any justice be connected with Bunyan's system, it would perhaps more probably be that of Luther than Calvin, either of them being great and venerable; for Luther's Commentaries on Galatians had gone into Bunyan's soul like fire, whereas we are not aware that he ever read a page of Calvin in the world. No! It was one of God's providential disciplinary preparatives for him, that he might write the Pilgrim's Progress, that he was kept from the shackles of any human system. You cannot tell, from the perusal of that work, that Bunyan was of any religious persuasion, save that he was a living member of the church of Christ.

And this is one of its supremest merits. It belongs to no sect. It is Christianity, pure Christianity, and not churchism. You cannot say, from the perusal of that work, whether its author were a Presbyterian, or a Baptist, or a Congregationalist, or a Methodist, or an Episcopalian, or a Calvinist, or a Lutheran; only that he did not mean, in drawing his own portrait of a true Christian, that he should belong to any of these parties exclusively; or, if there were any one of these that approached nearest to the Bible, in its comprehensive, Christ-like, gentle, and forbearing spirit, it should be that. The portraiture was a compound of what was excellent in them all; for what was truly excellent they all drew from the Bible, and the Pilgrim's Progress was drawn from the Bible, and from no sect, from nothing at second-hand. There is no *ite*, nor *ian*, nor *ist*, that you dare put to Christian's name; no lisping, halting Shibboleth of a party; for he came from the mint of the Holy Scriptures, where no party names disgrace the glory of Christianity; where men are neither of Paul, nor Apollos, nor Cephas, but of Christ; and so, blessed be God, under his guidance Bunyan made Christian no Church-man, but Christ's-man. That is good, that is noble! as great a proof, almost, of the excellence of Bunyan's book, as it is of the divine origin of Christianity that to the poor the Gospel is preached.

And now, in very truth, if Dr Scott, or any other man of like candour, finds in this book, which is drawn only from the Bible, the pure outlines of the Calvinistic system, then, so far, there is a presumption in favour of the Calvinistic ystem; and it is a compliment which Dr Scott pays to that 'stem, when he says it is to be found in a book which is taken directly from the Bible. But in very truth, you can say no more of the Pilgrim's Progress, that it is the Calvinistic system, than you could say of Raphael's great picture of the Transfiguration, that it was copied from Washington Allston. You may say both of Bunyan and of Calvin that they were children of God, and drank at the fountain of the Holy Scriptures, and were fed and nourished by God's word; and that so far as their systems resemble each other, it is proof of their likeness to their divine original; but that either copied or contains the other, you cannot say. Just as you might say of both Raphael and Allston, that their genius was a gift from God; one far superior to the other, indeed, but neither an imitator, both original, both from God.

There has been in this world too much of the imitation of great names and great authorities in theology, and too little of exclusive adherence to the Bible; too much human nomenclature, and too little divine baptism. A Christian man may say, and ought to say, I would not give much for any compliment to my theology, nor thank you for any description of it, that likens it, and much less that links it, to Calvin's, or Luther's, or Archbishop Usher's, excellent though they all be; and much less to any man's system or authority nearer to my times, or contemporary with me. I follow Christ, Paul, and the Holy Scriptures, and not Emmons, or Edwards, or Jeremy Taylor, or the Prayer Book Homilies, nor any man's authority, be he Augustine or Tertullian, Cherubim or Seraphim. O for the spirit of combined independence and humility that characterized the noble company of martyrs and reformers! We need a greater independence of all human authority, church or individual, and a more entire dependence on the word and the Spirit of God. This makes a true theologian; and doubtless, if we could all be shut up in prison for twelve years, like Bunyan, with nothing but the Bible, and Foxe's old Book of Martyrs, we too should come out with a living theology, drawn from no man's system, but ready to set all men's hearts on fire. Indeed, indeed, this is what is needed in this day of the resurrection of rites and forms and apostolical successions, and patristical authorities, and traditions of the fathers, and of the rags of Judaism itself patched and gilded anew; this return to the Scriptures solely, and the Spirit of God, is what is needed.

And here let me say, in this connection, that it was a great thing in that personal experience, by which God prepared Bunyan to write the Pilgrim's Progress, that he could never say precisely at what time he became a Christian. So was he prevented from putting in his work what many men would have set up at its very entrance, a Procrustes' bed for tender consciences in the alleged necessity or importance of knowing the exact day or hour of a man's conversion. Bunyan always shrank from making his experience a test for others. His was one of the purest, humblest, noblest, least bigoted, most truly liberal minds that ever lived. Non-essentials he would never set up as standards. His Book, in its delineation of Christianity, differs from almost all uninspired records and systems, in that it has neither caricatures, nor extremes, nor marked deficiencies. Some men get a likeness, indeed, of Christian doctrine, but it is by making some feature predominate; you never think of some men's system, but you think of some peculiar tenet that stamps it, that throws the atmosphere, not of the cross, but of a particular dogma, around it. Other men have monstrous excrescences, which are imitated and adored as virtues, and even held sacred as the sign of a party; just as if a great commander, having an enormous wart upon his features, should have it painted on the shield of every one of his soldiers.

And here I am constrained to say, that this figment of the apostolical succession is just such a wart, of which, in the opinion of some, if there be not a true painting and proper veneration in a man's escutcheon, he is no minister of Jesus Christ. Now, if any such party-man in theology had had the making of the Pilgrim's Progress, be you sure he would never have suffered a single Evangelist to come in to guide his Christian, not even to pull him out of the Slough of Despond, without first painting him over with this wart of the apostolical succession, or giving him a diploma stating his descent, in a true line, down through the Antichristian church of Rome, clear across the monstrous corruptions of the dark ages, from one of the twelve apostles. Or he would have put up an exclusive church-sign over the wicket-gate; and that would have been making it strait and narrow indeed, in a way never contemplated by the Saviour. Yea, he would have let a soul wait there even to perishing, exposed to all the artillery of Satan, before he would have had even a porter to open the door, who was not of the true apostolical succession. And other men would have sprinkled their pages with conversations about the form of baptism, or the sign of the cross, or baptismal regeneration, or the Book of Discipline, or perhaps the Saybrook Platform, or one and another mark of party; letting the work be coloured in its progress, or rather discoloured by a thousand varying shades, through the prism of personal or party prejudice.

There is nothing of all this in Bunyan; in him you do not meet truth in fragments, or in parts put for the whole. You do not meet prejudice instead of truth, nor bigotries, nor reproaches, nor any thing in the sweet fields through which he leads you, that can drive away, or repel any, the humblest, most forgotten Christian, or the wisest, most exalted one, from these lovely enclosures. He is as a familiar friend, an angel from heaven, and not a partisan, walking with you through green pastures, and leading you beside still waters; and conversing with you all the way so lovingly, so instructively, so frankly, that nothing can be more delightful. You have in him more of the ubiquity, unity, and harmony of the divine truth, more of the pervading breath and stamp of inspiration, than in almost any other uninspired writer.

If I should compare Bunyan with other men, I should say that he was a compound of the character of Peter, Luther, and Cowper. He had Peter's temptations, and deep, rich experience; and Luther's Saxon sturdiness, and honesty, and fearlessness of as many devils as there were tiles on the roofs of houses, and not a little of Cowper's own exquisite humour, tenderness, and sensibility. And he had as little of the thirst of human applause as either Luther or Cowper.

As Bunyan's religious experience was not sectarian, but Christian, that it might be universal, so it was thorough and deep, that the colours might stand. In him there was a remarkable translucence of the general in the particular, and of the particular through the general. His book is to the religious sensibilities as the day-light to the flowers; from its rays they may imbibe what lasting colours are most suited to their peculiarities. So it is like the sun of God's word, in which the prism of each individual mind, under the influence of the Divine Spirit, separates the heavenly colours, and puts them in a new aspect, so that every Christian, in the rays of Divine Truth, becomes a new reflection of the Divine Attributes. Bunyan's book has the likeness of this universality, and Christians of every sect may take what they please out of it, except their own sectarianism; they cannot find that. In this respect it bears remarkably the divine stamp.

Bunyan's mind was long under the law, in his own religious experience, under a sense of its condemnation. This alone would never have prepared him to write the Pilgrim's Progress, though it must have prepared him to preach with pungency and power. It fitted him to sympathize with men's distresses on account of sin, wherever he found them. A man's religious anxieties are sometimes so absorbing, that they defeat their own end, they oppose themselves to his deliverance. Just as in a crowded theatre on fire, the doors of which open inward, the very rush of the multitude to get out shuts them so fast, that there is no unclosing them. Such at one time seemed to be Bunyan's situation; so it often is with the heart that has within it the fire of a guilty conscience; and in this case it is only the Saviour, who knocks for admittance, that can open the door, put out the flames, and change the soul from a theatre of fiery accusing thoughts into a living temple of his grace. The Pilgrim's Progress would never have been given to the world, except Bunyan had been relieved of his difficulties; but these difficulties were as necessary to furnish him with the experimental wisdom requisite for the author of that book as the relief itself.

There is one book in our language, with which the Pilgrim's Progress may be compared, as a reality with a theory, a personification with an abstraction, and that is Edwards on the Religious Affections. This book is the work of a holy, but rigid metaphysician, analyzing and anatomising the soul, laying the heart bare, and, I had almost said, drying it for a model. As you study it, you know it is truth, and you know that your own heart ought to be like it; but you cannot recognize in it your own flesh and blood. Edwards' delineations are like the skeleton leaves of the forest, through which, if you hold them to the sun, you can see every minute fibre in the light; Bunyan's work is like the same leaves as fresh foliage, green and glossy in the sunshine, joyfully whispering to the breathing air, with now and then the dense rain-drops glittering on them from a June shower. In Edwards' work you see the Divine life in its abstract severity and perfection; in Bunyan's work you see it assuming a visible form, like your own, with your own temptations and trials, touched with the feeling, and coloured with the shade of your own infirmities. Yet both these books are well-nigh perfect in their way, both equally adapted to their purpose. We love the work of Bunyan as a bosom friend, a sociable confiding companion on our pilgrimage. We revere the work of Edwards, as a deep, grave teacher, but its stern accuracy makes us tremble. Bunyan encourages, consoles, animates, delights, sympathizes with us; Edwards cross-examines, probes, scrutinizes, alarms us. Bunyan looks on us as a sweet angel, as one of his own shining ones, come to take off our burden, and put on our robe; Edwards, with the rigidity of a geometrician, as a sort of military surveyor of the king's roads, meets us with his map, and shews us how we have wandered from the way, and makes us feel as if we never were in it. Bunyan carries our sensibilities, Edwards our convictions. In short, Bunyan is the Man, the Pilgrim; Edwards the Metaphysician.

Bunyan was as great a master of allegory as Edwards was of logic and metaphysics; but not artificially so, not designedly so, not as a matter of study. He scarcely knew the meaning of the word allegory, much less any rules or principles for its conduct; and the great beauty of his own is that it speaks to the heart; it is the language of nature, and needs no commentator to understand it. It is not like the allegorical friezes of Spenser or of Dante, or like those on a Grecian temple, which may pass into darkness in a single generation, as to all meaning but that of the exquisite beauty of the sculpture, except there be a minute traditionary commentary. Bunyan's Allegory is a universal language.

D'Israeli has well designated Bunyan as the Spenser of

the people; every one familiar with the Fairy Queen must acknowledge the truth of the description. Johnson thought Bunyan must have read Spenser, and there are some passages in each writer surprisingly similar, especially in each writer's description of Despair. If it were not apparently incongruous, we would call him, on another score, the spiritual Shakspeare of the world; for the accuracy and charm with which he has delineated the changes and progress of the spiritual life, are not less exquisite than those of Shakspeare in the Seven Ages, and innumerable scenes of this world's existence. He is scarcely less to be praised than Shakspeare for the purity of his language, and the natural simplicity of his style. It comes, as I have said, even nearer to the common diction of good conversation.

The allegorical image of a Pilgrimage is beautifully adapted to express the dangers and hardships of the Christian Life: a Pilgrimage, with a glorious city at its end, into which the weary but faithful Pilgrim shall be received, to repose for ever from his toils. Every thing connected with the idea is pleasant to the imagination. It has been the origin of many beautiful hymns. " Jerusalem! my happy home," is a sweet one. The glories of the Celestial City, and the employments of its inhabitants, are the sources of many images in the Bible, and constitute much of the poetry in the Apocalypse. And these images always had a powerful effect upon the inmost soul of Bunyan. Spenser remembered them not a little. The following beautiful stanzas from the Fairy Queen are a picture in miniature of the close of the Pilgrim's Progress :

> From thence far off he unto him did shew
> A little path that was both steep and long,
> Which to a goodly city led his view,
> Whose walls and towers were builded high and strong
> Of pearl and precious stones, that earthly tongue
> Cannot describe, nor wit of man can tell;
> Too high a ditty for my simple song!
> The city of the Great King hight it well,
> Wherein eternal peace and happiness doth dwell.
>
> As he thereon stood gazing, he might see
> The blessed angels to and fro descend

> From highest Heaven in gladsome company,
> And with great joy into that city wend,
> As commonly as friend doth with his friend ;
> Whereat he wondered much, and 'gan inquire
> What stately buildings durst so high extend
> Her lofty towers into the starry sphere,
> And what unknowen nation there empeopled were.

We know of no other work in which we take a deeper sympathetic interest in all the circumstances of danger, trial, or happiness befalling the hero. The honesty, integrity, open-heartedness, humour, simplicity, and deep sensibility of Christian's character, make us love him : nor is there a character depicted in all English literature that stands out to the mind in bolder truth and originality. There is a wonderful charm and truth to nature in Christian's manifest growth in grace and wisdom. What a different being is Christian on the Delectable Mountains, or in the land Beulah, and Christian when he first set out on his pilgrimage ! And yet he is always the same being ; we recognise him at once. The change is not of the original features of his character, but a change into the character of the " Lord of the way," a gradual imbuing with his spirit ; a change, in Paul's expressive language, from glory to glory into the same image. In proportion as he arrives nearer the Celestial City he shines brighter, his character unfolds in greater richness, he commands more veneration from us, without losing any of our affection. As we witness his steadily increasing lustre, we think of that beautiful Scripture image, " the path of the just is as the shining light, that shineth more and more unto the perfect day." From being an unwary Pilgrim, just setting out with all the rags of the City of Destruction about him, and the burden of guilt bending him down, he becomes that delightful character, an experienced Christian ; with the robe given him by the Shining Ones, shining brighter and brighter, and the roll of assurance becoming clearer, and courage more confirmed and steady, and in broader and broader light Heaven reflected from his countenance. We go with him in his pilgrimage all the way. We enter the Interpreter's house ; we see all the varieties which the Lord of the Way keeps there for the entertainment of the Pilgrims ;

we solemnly gaze on that terrible picture of the Man of Despair ; we tremble as we listen to the Dream of the Judgment ; and the description of that venturous man that cut his way through the armed men, and won eternal glory, ravishes our hearts. Then we leave the house comforted and refreshed, and proceed on our way ; we climb the hill Difficulty, we rest in the Arbour, and lose our roll, and come back weeping and seeking for it ; in this much time is lost, and the night comes on, and we are fearful of the darkness We tremble and weep for Christian in his dreadful fight with Apollyon, in the Valley of Humiliation ; we rejoice in the radiant smile that at length breaks out from his distressed soul over his countenance ; then we plunge with him into the Valley of the Shadow of Death, and amidst all its gloom and horrors and hobgoblins, we think we hear a voice singing ; by and by we overtake Faithful ; we pass through Vanity Fair ; farther on we become tired of the way, and turn aside from the rough path to go in the soft meadow ; we are overtaken by the storm ; we fall into Giant Despair's Castle ; we are there from Wednesday noon till Saturday night ;—there never was a poem into which we entered so wholly, and with all the heart, and in such fervent love and believing assurance.

Now all this admirable accuracy and beauty Bunyan wrought seemingly without design. It was not so much an exertion, a labour of his mind, as the promptings and wanderings at will of his unconscious genius. He never thought of doing all this, but he did it. He was as a child under the power and guidance of his genius, and with a child's admiration he would look upon the creations which his own imagination presented to his mind. Thus Bunyan went on, painting that narrow way, and the exquisite scenery on each side of it, and the many characters crossing, appearing, and passing at a distance, and Christian and Hopeful on their way, and making every part of the picture, as he proceeded, harmonize with the whole, and yet add anew to its meaning, and all with as much quiet unconscious ease and simplicity, as an infant would put together a baby-house of cards, or as the frost on a winter's night would draw a picture on the window.

The minute passages of beauty, and the exquisite lessons of the allegory, are so many from beginning to end, that it is vain to make a selection. The whole description of the Slough of Despond, the character of Pliable, and his getting out on the side nearest the City of Destruction, and the reception he met from his neighbours when he came back, are rich in truth and beauty. The comparison of Christian's and Faithful's experience is beautiful; so is Faithful's description of a bold fellow he met in the Valley of Humiliation—Shame; so is their encounter with the plausible, gentlemanly, money-making Demas. The character of Talkative, and the way they took to prove him, are excellent. Their passage through Vanity Fair, and the whole trial in that town, with the names of the jurors and judges, and the characteristic speeches of each, are admirably described. The character of By-ends, who was for religion in her silver slippers, and the humour and keen satire in the dialogue between By-ends, Money-love, Save-all, and Hold-the-world, are equally admirable. Then we may remember that pleasant river, and the roughness of the road where it parted from the river, so that it made them not scrupulous to get over the stile, and walk in By-path Meadow, when that tempestuous night came on; and though amidst the darkness they heard a voice sounding, Let thy feet be to the King's highway, yet, with all the effort they made, they could not that night regain it, but trespassed on Giant Despair's grounds, and fell into his Castle. That night was a dreadful night for the Pilgrims. The Key of Promise, in Christian's bosom, while lying in the Dungeon, is a beautiful incident. It was a pleasant thing to see the Pilgrims, when they had escaped the giant, and got again to the King's highway, and so were safe, devising an inscription to keep those that should come after from falling, as they did, into the hands of Giant Despair. "Over this stile is the way to Doubting Castle, kept by Giant Despair, who despiseth the King of the Celestial Country, and seeks to destroy his holy Pilgrims." On the Delectable Mountains they saw some pleasant and admonitory sights. When the Shepherds unconsciously were telling Hopeful and Christian of Doubting Castle and Giant Despair, Christian and Hopeful looked meaningly on one another, but said nothing. It is also a beautiful incident, when, though they were bidden to look through the telescope at the Celestial City in the distance, their hands so trembled at the remembrance of the dangers they had seen, that they could not hold the glass so as to discern it with any clearness. The dialogue between Hopeful and Christian on Little-Faith's misfortunes, is exceedingly characteristic and full of humour. One of the most solemn and striking lessons is taught in the character of Ignorance, who met with none of the difficulties Christian passed through, and was even ferried over the river of Death in the boat of one called Vain-Hope. Then his disappointment at the gate of the city!

The scenery, and the countries all the way that lie on both sides the path, are in perfect keeping with the whole allegory. So are the paths that "butt down" on the king's highway, by which many enter, because the right way is too far round—not entering at the wicket-gate through which Christian, Faithful, and Hopeful entered, after sore difficulties encountered. The characters we meet here and there on the road, that have entered by such lanes and cross paths, are equally in keeping; and as they come successively under Christian's observation, it is amusing to see the manner in which, by turns, their real character is exposed in his honest, plain-dealing, rugged and humorous way. The conversation of Hopeful and Christian all along is truly delightful. It is as becometh saints; grave, sincere, full of good sense and discrimination, with much cheerful pleasantry; exhibiting Hopeful's youthful experience and ardour, and Christian's superior experience, richness of thought, frankness, and kindness. They walk together so lovingly, so sympathizing, so faithful to each other, that all must acknowledge they are a perfect example of the brotherly-kindness becoming the fellow pilgrims of that way.

Between the first and second parts of the Pilgrim's Progress there is a diversity that may be compared to that between the Paradise Lost and the Paradise Regained. Milton's genius, in his second effort, appeared not less than the excess of glory obscured. In the second part of Bunyan's work we readily recognise, and are pleased to follow, the footsteps of that original genius which has so delighted us in the first. Yet we feel that the region is inferior; there is more familiarity and humour, but less poetry; and though there is the same vigorous delineation of character, the allegory is imperfect. One of the most humorous and amusing portions of the whole work is the account of the courtship between Mercy and Mr Brisk, which took place while the parties were at the House-Beautiful. There are also some exquisitely beautiful snatches of melody in this second part of the pilgrimage.

Perhaps no other work could be named, which, admired by cultivated minds, has had at the same time such an ameliorating effect on the lower classes in society as the Pilgrim's Progress. It is a work so full of native good sense, that no mind can read it without gaining in wisdom and vigour of judgment. What an amazing effect must it have produced in this way on the mass of common minds brought under its power! We cannot compute the good it has thus accomplished on earth, nor tell the number of souls it may have been the means of guiding to heaven. It is one of the books, that, by being connected with the dearest associations of childhood, always retain their hold on the heart; and it exerts a double influence, when, at a graver age, and less under the despotism given to imagination in childhood, we read it with a serene and thoughtful perception of its meaning. How many children have become better citizens of the world through life, by the perusal of this book almost in infancy! And how many, through its instrumentality, may have been fitted after life to live for ever! The Christian warfare is here arrayed in the glow of imagination, to make it attractive. How many Pilgrims, in hours when perseverance was almost exhausted, and patience was yielding, and clouds and darkness were gathering, have felt a sudden return of animation and courage from the remembrance of Christian's severe conflicts, and his glorious entrance at last through the gates into the city!

As the work draws to its conclusion, the poet's soul seems to expand with the glory of the subject. The description of Christian and Hopeful's entrance up through the regions of air into the Celestial City, preceded by the touching account of their passing the River of Death, though composed of the simplest materials, and depicted in the simplest language, with scripture imagery almost exclusively, constitutes one of the finest passages in English literature. The Shining Ones, and the beauty and glory of their conversation; the Angels, and their melodious notes; the Pilgrims among them, in heaven as it were, before they come at it; the city itself in view, and all the bells ringing with joy of their welcome; the warm and joyful thoughts they had about their own dwelling there with such a company, and that for ever and ever; the letters of gold written over the gate; the transfiguration of the men as they entered, and the raiment put on them that shone like gold; the harps and crowns given them—the harps to praise withal, and the crowns in token of honour; the bells in the city ringing again for joy; the shout of welcome, "ENTER YE INTO THE JOY OF OUR LORD;" the men themselves singing with a loud voice, "BLESSING, AND HONOUR, AND GLORY, AND POWER BE UNTO HIM THAT SITTETH UPON THE THRONE, AND UNTO THE LAMB FOR EVER AND EVER!"

Now, says the Dreamer, just as the gates were opened to let in the men, I looked in after them, and behold the city shone like the sun; the streets also were paved with gold, and in them walked many men, with crowns upon their heads, palms in their hands, and golden harps to sing praises withal. There were also of them that had wings; and they answered one another without intermission, saying, Holy holy, holy is the Lord; and after that, they shut up the gates; *which, when I had seen, I wished myself among them.*

And who would not wish himself among them? or what man, reading of these things, or hearing of these things, can refuse to join them? In what attractive beauty of description are the life and the rewards of practical religion here delineated! The whole course of the Pilgrim's Progress shines with a light borrowed from its close. Just so it is in the reality. The splendours of the Celestial City, though rather to be dreamed of and guessed at, than distinctly seen, do nevertheless break from the clouds, and fall from mountain top to mountain top, flashing on forest and vale, down into the most difficult craggy passes of our mortal pilgrimage. At times, the domes and towers seem resting on our earthly horizon, and in a season of fair weather our souls have sight of the streets of gold, the gates of pearl, the walls of jasper. Then we walk many days under the remembrance of such a vision. At other times, the inhabitants of that city seem to be walking with us, and ministering to us; men do eat angels' food; melodious music ravishes the ear; listening intently, we think we hear the chimes of bells wafted across the sea; and sometimes the gales are laden with such fragrant spicy airs, that a single breath of them makes the soul recognise its immortal Paradise, and almost transports it thither.

When shall the day break, and the shadows flee away! It is night here, but there the sun shall never go down. *Light is sown for the righteous*, and in the harvest time it shall come up; but as Goodwin beautifully remarks in his "Child of Light Walking in Darkness," we must be content to let it lie under ground; and the longer it doth so, the greater crop and harvest will spring up in the end.

In the Pilgrim's Progress there is a charming passage descriptive of the Pilgrim's entertainment in the House Beautiful, which was thus:—"The Pilgrim they laid in a large upper chamber, whose windows opened towards the sunrising; the name of the chamber was Peace; where he slept till break of day, and then he awoke and sang." A great and thoughtful poet has written a poem with this description as its motto, which he has entitled "Day-break," and which closes with the following stanza:—

How suddenly that straight and glittering shaft
Shot 'thwart the earth! In crown of living fire

LECTURE FIFTH.

Up comes the day! As if they, conscious, quaffed
The sunny flood, hill, forest, city, spire,
Laugh in the wakening light. Go, vain Desire!
The dusky lights have gone; go thou thy way!
And pining Discontent, like them expire!
Be called my chamber PEACE, when ends the day.
And let me, with the dawn, like PILGRIM, sing and pray

ΘΕΩ ΜΟΝΩ ΛΟΞΑ.

LECTURE SIXTH.

The City of Destruction and Slough of Despond.

Locality of the City of Destruction.—Character of Christian.—The awakened sinner.—The sinner convinced of sin, and fleeing from the wrath to come.—Character of Pliable.—Difference between a burden and no burden.—Pliable and Christian in the Slough of Despond.—Mr Worldly Wiseman and his instructions.—Mr Legality and the town of Carnal Policy.—The terrors of the Law of God to an awakened conscience.—Christian's entrance at the Wicket Gate.

THE CITY OF DESTRUCTION! We are all inhabitants of it; no man needs ask, Where is it? What is it? Who are its people? Alas! our world of sin is the City of Destruction, and we know of a certainty from God's Word that it is to be burned up, and that if we do not escape from it, though we may die at peace in it before its conflagration, yet to be found with its spirit in our souls when we die, is to be for ever miserable. There is a blessed pilgrimage from the City of Destruction to the City of Immanuel. It is full of dangers, trials, difficulties; but the perils are not worthy to be named in comparison with the glory at its close. And indeed the pilgrimage itself, with all its roughnesses and trials, is romantic and delightful. As the author of this book has delineated it, he makes many a man wish that he were set out in it. And yet this delineation is not in the colouring of imagination, but of sober reality; there is nothing overdrawn, nothing exaggerated in it; the scenery along the way is not painted too beautiful, there are no ecstacies, or rapturous frames, or revelations in it; the colouring is sober, with all its richness, the experience is human, with all its variety ; the very angels are more like gentle sympathizing friends than glittering supernatural intelligences.

It is this charm of common sense and reality that constitutes in a great measure the power of this book. Its characters are not removed from our own experience ; the piety of Christian, though very rich and mellow, is progressive, and for every day's use, and for every saint's attainment. It is neither mystical, nor visionary, nor in extremes ; it is not perfection, nor ascetic sublimation from the world, nor contemplation, nor penance, nor the luxury of mere spiritual frames and exercises. It is deep, sincere, gentle, practical, full of the fruits of the Spirit, full of intelligence and kindness, of love, joy, peace, long-suffering, goodness, and truth. They are every day virtues which shine in Christian ; and his character is an example of what ours ought to be in our daily pilgrimage. His conflicts are such as every Christian may pass through, his consolations and enjoyments such as every Christian may experience, his knowledge of the Word of God, and indeed all his attainments, within reach of every pilgrim. He is indeed a model of excellence for all.

I think we shall observe, as we study the book through, that from first to last Bunyan has composed this character out of the most general and universally recognised traits belonging to the experience of a child of God. This, it is clear, was necessary, in order to its highest success and usefulness. And yet the individuality and originality of the character is as perfect, as striking, as graphic, as if it were the delineation from life of some person well known to Bunyan with all his peculiarities. Now, we do not suppose that Bunyan intended this in so definite a form of art and philosophy ; we do not suppose that he said within himself, I must make this Christian, in the absence of all peculiarities, a suitable model for all, and yet, in the translucence through his particular characteristics, of the general qualities belonging to our conception of a Christian, a character recognisable by, and the counterpart of, every individual. This would involve a greater degree of art and criticism than Bunyan

ever exercised; and yet his genius, under the guidance of
the Holy Spirit, did spontaneously work according to these
rules. Just so, Bunyan's own incomparable freedom from
all sectarianism, even in a sectarian age, has prevented the
character of Christian and of the whole Progress of the
Pilgrim, from being narrowed or disfigured by any thing
which could even be tortured to restrict its application, or
its preferences, to any religious party. Accordingly, the
more bigoted, exclusive, and sectarian a man is, the less he
will like this book; to a violent Churchman it wants a
bishop and the apostolical succession: to a rigid Baptist it
wants immersion at the Wicket Gate. But Bunyan was
wonderfully preserved from affixing to any part of this book
the seal of any such local or party distinctions. Though he
was himself a Baptist, yet he was an open communion
Baptist, and experienced the wrath of his more exclusive
Baptist brethren, because he laid no stress whatever on their
peculiarities. They had bitter controversies against him as
a deserter from the faith, because he would not pronounce
their Shibboleths, and was completely free from the unchurching spirit of his age.

Now here was a characteristic of the presence of the
Holy Spirit in him very remarkable; and his work accordingly has come from that school of heaven in which no
man is of Apollos, or Cephas, or Paul, but all of Christ.
Ah, this is delightful; and accordingly, in such a contro-
versial world as this, this work is like oil upon the waters;
it is as the very voice of the Saviour in the tempest, Peace,
be still; it is like the dove with her olive leaf, a prophet of
the garden of the Lord; it is like a white-robed herald with
his sacred flag, privileged to go every where, and admitted
every where, even amidst contending armies. This book
will remain, when there shall be nothing to hurt nor destroy
in all God's holy mountain, when Judah shall no more vex
Ephraim, nor Ephraim envy Judah; for it has come forth
from the mint of celestial universal love; it has no leaf in
it, which the Spirit of God may not sweetly mingle with
those leaves of the Tree of Life for the healing of the nations. We doubt whether there was another individual in

that age, except Leighton, whose piety could have produced so catholic, so unsectarian, so heavenly a work.

In accordance with what I have said, you will perceive how Bunyan commences with his Pilgrim. He begins with releasing himself and the position of the Dreamer from any positive locality; he does not suffer his personal situation or feelings to throw a single determinate shade upon the picture; he does not say (as many persons would very naturally have said), As I lay suffering for the Gospel in the prison of Bedford, but, As I walked through the wilderness of this world, I lighted upon a certain place where was a den, and laid me down in that place to sleep; and as I slept, I dreamed a dream. Ah, it was a wilderness indeed, and no small part of Bunyan's life was spent in the deserts and caves of it. It is a wilderness to us all, but to many a wilderness of sinful pleasures infinitely more dangerous than dens and caves, bonds and imprisonments. It is a wilderness to the soul, away from its God, surrounded by dangers, exposed to the wiles of its great adversary the devil, in peril of eternal ruin.

There are lions, chained and unchained, in the way, and temptations of every shape and name, and unseen dangers too, from which God alone can protect us. He only walks safely who walks as a stranger and a pilgrim.

> Yet the dear path to thine abode
> Lies through this horrid land;
> Lord, we would trace the dangerous road,
> And run at thy command.

And if we do this, then a blessed Faith comes in, and ours is a more cheerful, delightful, heavenly vision. We walk under the gracious care, and in the safe dominions of the King of the Celestial City; we travel the King's own highway; we come to the land Beulah;

> We're marching through Immanuel's ground
> To fairer worlds on high!

You will observe what honour, from his Pilgrim's first setting out, Bunyan puts upon the Word of God. He would give to no inferior instrumentality, not even to one of God's Providences, the business of awakening his Pilgrim to a sense of his danger ; but he places him before us reading his book, awakened by the Word. Now we know that it is often God's providence, in the way of sickness, the loss of friends, earthly disappointments, the voice and discipline of pain of various kinds, that awakens careless men in the first place, and leads them to the Word of God ; and kind and gracious providences are always, all through life, all through our Christian course, combining with the Word and the Spirit of God to help us on our pilgrimage, and make us wary in it ; but in general it is the Word of God, in some form, which God uses as the instrument in awakening men, as well as in converting them. And so Bunyan, with heavenly wisdom and truth, gives us the first picture of his Pilgrim, anxiously reading the Word of God. And he makes the first efficacious motive in the mind of this Pilgrim, a salutary fear of the terrors of that Word, a sense of the wrath to come, beneath the burden of sin upon his soul.

There is a passage so beautiful, in the pages of a great writer, on this very point, that it might have been written as a commentary on this very opening of the Pilgrim's Progress, and I shall set it before you. " Awakened," says Mr Coleridge, " by the cock-crow (a sermon, a calamity, a sick-bed, or a providential escape) the Christian Pilgrim sets out in the morning twilight, while yet the truth is below the horizon. Certain necessary *consequences* of his past life and his present undertaking will be *seen* by the refraction of its light: more will be apprehended and conjectured. The phantasms, that had predominated during the hours of darkness, are still busy. No longer present as forms, they will yet exist as moulding and formative motions in the Pilgrim's soul. The Dream of the past night will transfer its shapes to the objects in the distance, while the objects give outwardness and reality to the shapings of the Dream. The fears inspired by long habits of selfishness and self-seeking cunning, though now purified into that fear which is the *beginning* of wisdom, and ordained to be our guide and safeguard, till the sun of love, the perfect law of liberty, is fully arisen—these fears will set the fancy at work, and haply, for a time, transform the mists of dim and imperfect knowledge into determinate superstitions. But in either case, whether seen clearly or dimly, whether beheld or only imagined, the *consequences* contemplated in their bearings on the individual's inherent desire of happiness and dread of pain become *motives:* and (unless all distinction in the words be done away with, and either prudence or virtue be reduced to a superfluous synonyme, a redundancy in all the languages of the civilized world) these motives, and the acts and forbearances directly proceeding from them, fall under the head of PRUDENCE, as belonging to one or other of its three very distinct species. It may be a prudence that stands in opposition to a higher moral life, and tends to preclude it, and to prevent the soul from ever arriving at the hatred of sin for its own exceeding sinfulness (Rom. vii. 13); and this is an EVIL PRUDENCE. Or it may be a *neutral* prudence not incompatible with spiritual growth; and to this we may, with especial propriety, apply the words of our Lord, ' What is not against *us* is for us.' It is therefore an innocent and (being such) a proper and COMMENDABLE PRUDENCE.

" Or it may lead and be subservient to a higher principle than itself. The mind and conscience of the individual may be reconciled to it, in the foreknowledge of the higher principle, and with a yearning towards it that implies a foretaste of future freedom. The enfeebled convalescent is reconciled to his crutches, and thankfully makes use of them, not only because they are necessary for his immediate support, but likewise, because they are the means and condition of EXERCISE; and by exercise of establishing, *gradatim paulatim,* that strength, flexibility, and almost spontaneous obedience of the muscles, which the idea and cheering presentiment of health hold out to him. He finds their *value* in their present necessity, and their *worth* as they are the instruments of finally superseding it. This is a faithful, a WISE PRUDENCE, having indeed its birth-place in the world, and the *wisdom of this world* for its father; but naturalized in a better land, and having the Wisdom from above for its Sponsor and Spiritual Parent."

THE CITY OF DESTRUCTION AND SLOUGH OF DESPOND. 177

The Pilgrim is in rags, the rags of depravity and sin, and the intolerable burden of sin is bending him down; but the book is in his hand, and his face is *from* his own house. Reading and pondering, and full of perplexity, foreboding and a sense of sin, gloom and wrath, he cries out, What *shall* I do! This is his first exclamation. He has not as yet advanced so far as to say, What shall I do to be saved? And now for some days the solemnity, and burden, and distress of his spirit increases; his unconverted friends see that he is " becoming serious ;" they think it is some distemper of the mind or animal spirits; they hope he may sleep it away; they chide, neglect, deride him; carnal physic for a sick soul, as Bunyan describes it in the margin, is administered. But nothing answers. The sense of his mortal disease and danger, the painful sense of sin, and of what is to come on account of it, increases. Not even his wife and sweet babes can do any thing for him, but only add to his misery in a sense of their danger as well as his own. He pities and prays for those who deride him, and spends much solitary time in reading and praying. He looks this way and that way, as if he would run, and cries out in the anguish of his wounded spirit, What shall I do to be saved? This is the first stage of genuine conviction. " I perceive by the book in my hand, that I am condemned to die, and after that to come to judgment; and I find that I am not willing to do the first nor able to do the second."

And now he meets Evangelist, who gives him the parchment roll, Flee from the wrath to come! It is a godly minister of Christ, whom the Father of mercies has sent to help him. Bunyan has here put in the margin, Conviction of the necessity of fleeing. But which way shall I fly? Then said Evangelist, pointing with his finger over a very wide field, Do you see yonder Wicket Gate? The man said, No. He cannot see that yet, he is in such darkness. Then said the other, Do you see yonder shining light? *Thy word is as a lamp unto my feet, and a light unto my path.* He said, I think I do. Then said Evangelist, Keep that light in your eye, and go up directly thereto, so shalt thou see the gate; at which, when thou knockest, it shall be told thee what thou shalt do. Bunyan has here put in the margin, Christ, and the way to him cannot be found without the Word. So, if any awakened sinner will fill his eye with that light, and follow it, it will bring him to Christ.

And now the trembling Pilgrim, with fixed resolution, having a glimpse of the light, and a definite direction, begins to run ; it is an unutterable relief to his perplexities to run towards Christ ; though as yet he sees him not. But now the world clamours after him, yea, the dearest ones in it try to stop him ; but the fire in his conscience is stronger than they ; he stops his ears, and runs without looking behind him, and stays not in all the plain, but runs as swiftly as his burden will let him, crying, Life, life, eternal life !

And now he is fairly set out. But he becomes a gazing-stock to the world, and some of them set off after him to fetch him back. There is no telling the wiles which ungodly ridiculing companions have sometimes tried to turn their awakened friends from the way of life. There is nothing can stand against such enemies, but a resolute purpose like Christian's, a fire in the conscience, and a fixedness in the Word of God. These things will not, indeed, if he goes no further, make a man a Christian ; but these things, as long as they last, will make him despise the world's ridicule, and if he runs on, he will soon, by God's grace, get beyond the reach of ridicule, beyond all worldly harm.

Two of these City of Destruction men, who came to bring Christian back, Obstinate and Pliable, are portraitures of classes. They, together with Christian, constitute the representatives of most of the hearers of the Gospel, and of the manner in which they receive it ; they are either hardened against it, or are somewhat softened and disposed to set out, or they become real Pilgrims. Obstinate, finding Christian was not to be moved, tried to persuade Pliable not to give heed to him ; and then he went railing back, saying, I will be no companion to such misled, fantastical fellows.

And now Christian and Pliable went talking over the plain, Christian with a sense of sin and of the terrors of the Lord, with the fire in his conscience and the burden on his back, yet something of the light of life already within him.

and a resolute purpose never to give over seeking Christ;
Pliable, with some slight superficial sympathy and conviction, and somewhat moved with what Christian had told
him of the glories of the heavenly inheritance at the end of
their pilgrimage, but with no sense of sin, no knowledge of
his own heart, no desire after Christ, no feeling of his need
of a Saviour. In their talk, Christian speaks really like a
Christian already, though he is not one yet; and certainly,
his ravishing descriptions of the things that are to be enjoyed in heaven are very instructive, as shewing how far the
mind may be affected with a merely intellectual and imaginative sense of the beauty and excellency of the Gospel,
and the glory of its promises without regeneration. Nevertheless, it must be remembered, that where a work of grace
is really begun in the soul, though as yet it may not have
gone further than genuine conviction of sin, yet the sense
of divine things in such a soul is very different, even before
regeneration, from the views of the man, whom the Spirit of
God is not beginning to teach. Moreover, they are very
different in a man who has been accustomed to God's word,
and in one who has not. Pliable begs to be told more fully
what the glorious things are, and how to be enjoyed. So
Christian goes directly to his book. "I cannot describe
them," he says to Pliable, "so well as I can conceive them,
but I will read them to you in my book."

And now you see the difference between a man who has
been educated in the precious belief of the Gospel as the
word of God, and has been brought up in the habit of reading it, and the man who has all his life neglected it, and is
a stranger to it. You may see what a faint hold the Gospel
has over the one, and what a strong hold over the other.
Of these two men, neither of them as yet Christians, Pliable
is doubtful, Christian is as firm and unshaken as a rock.
Christian also, in the very sense of sin within him, begins
to have an irresistible proof and sense of the truth of God's
word, of which Pliable, without any such inward experience
and conviction, is entirely destitute. "I will read of them
in my book," says Christian. "And do you think," says
Pliable, "that the words of your book are certainly true?"

"Yes, verily," says Christian, "for it was made by him that cannot lie." There is a volume in those touches of Bunyan's pencil. What sweet simplicity of faith already in the Pilgrim! True? certainly it is true; for it is God's word, God that cannot lie.

Well said, answered Pliable, and what things are they? There is an endless kingdom to be inhabited, said Christian, and everlasting life to be given us, that we may inhabit that kingdom for ever. Well said, answered Pliable, and what else?

Chr. There are crowns of glory to be given us, and garments that will make us shine like the sun in the firmament of heaven.

Pli. This is very pleasant, and what else?

Chr. There shall be no more crying nor sorrow; for he that is owner of the place will wipe all tears from our eyes.

Pli. And what company shall we have there?

Chr. There we shall be with Cherubim and Seraphim, creatures that will dazzle your eyes to look on them There also you shall meet with thousands and ten thousands that have gone before us to that place; none of them are hurtful, but loving and holy; every one walking in the sight of God, and standing in his presence with acceptance for ever. In a word, there we shall see the elders with their golden crowns; there we shall see the holy virgins with their golden harps; there we shall see men that by the world were cut in pieces, burnt in flames, eaten of beasts, drowned in the seas, for the love they bore to the Lord of the place; all well, and clothed with immortality as with a garment.

Pli. The hearing of this is enough to ravish one's heart; but are these things to be enjoyed? How shall we get to be sharers thereof?

Chr. The Lord, the governor of the country, hath recorded that in his book; the substance of which is, if we be truly willing to have it, he will bestow it upon us freely.

Pli. Well, my good companion, glad am I to hear of these things; come on, let us mend our pace.

Here you have another volume of meaning in a single touch of the pencil. Pliable is one of those who are willing;

or think they are willing, to have heaven, but without any sense of sin, or of the labour and self-denial necessary to enter heaven. But now his heart is momentarily fired with Christian's ravishing descriptions, and as he seems to have nothing to trouble his conscience, and no difficulties to overcome, the pace of an honest, thorough inquirer, the movement of a soul sensible of its distresses and its sins, and desiring comfort only in the way of healing and of holiness, seems much too slow for him. He is for entering heaven at once, going much faster than poor Christian can keep up with him. Then, said Christian, I cannot go so fast as I would, by reason of this burden that is on my back.

Of poor Christian's burden of sin, Pliable was totally ignorant, and doubtless Christian was not a little grieved within himself, to see how lightly Pliable could step forward, while it was with much ado that he could take step after step beneath that great and heavy burden. So sometimes, they who are heartily and conscientiously, with a deep sense of sin, seeking after Christ, do almost look with envy and much surprise upon those others, who seem to run with so little difficulty, and sometimes, moreover, seem to find Christ without having any burden to be taken off by him. But Christian had the burden from his first setting out, and could by no means be rid of it.

However, Pliable's eagerness to get forward did not continue a great while. They were both walking somewhat heedlessly in the midst of their talk, as inquirers are very apt to do when they converse more than they pray, and missing the steps, or taking that for firm ground which was nothing but mud, they both fell into the Slough of Despond. This was especially sudden and unexpected to Pliable, who was not dreaming of difficulties, and it quenched his eagerness at once; and although Christian beneath his burden was sinking far deeper than he, yet he was filled with rage and discouragement. Is this the brave country you told me of? You may have it all to yourself for me; let me but get out with my life, and never again will I set out on a pilgrimage.

Now, it is not always that the Pliables of this world, who have some transitory sympathy towards heaven, and set out for a season in this pilgrimage, get so immediately tired, and turn back with such open rage and discouragement And yet this character, it is a most melancholy truth, is the representative of a class almost innumerable. Almost all men are, at some period of their lives, inclined to set out on this pilgrimage. Under God's Providence, Word, and Spirit, it cannot be otherwise; for men do and will feel that death and the judgment are before them; and all that pleasures and business and cares can do, they cannot utterly stifle the voice of conscience, nor the sense of sin, God, and eternity. And when these fires revive a little in the soul, and burst up out of the thick ashes, then men begin to think of this pilgrimage, then they begin to feel that they are inhabiting a City of Destruction, and must be getting out of it; then in fact, they do often set out for a little season; but not having much sense of sin, nor any purpose of renouncing it, nor any settled resolution, cost what it may, of becoming the disciples of Christ, they soon become wearied or discouraged, and turn back. Alas for them! Their case is worse when they get back to the City of Destruction than it was even while they were tumbling in the Slough of Despond. A sense of shame pursues them as long as they live, for their tergiversation. Oftentimes the inhabitants of that city do at first as stoutly ridicule those who turn back as those who set out; and oftentimes you will find those who have turned back become the loudest in their ridicule of the whole pilgrimage. Alas! the world is full of Pliables, who have not decision enough, in the face of contempt, trial, and danger, to run towards heaven; and yet they have many designs of doing so; but the word in their hearts is among thorns; the cares and pleasures and riches of this world, the lusts of other things, choke the word, although there be good designs; and hence the proverb, that "hell is paved with good intentions."

Farewell, then, to Pliable, who after a desperate struggle or two, got out of the mire on that side of the slough that was nearest his own house, and so Christian saw him no more for ever. If he had borne Christian's burden, at first setting out, that is, if he had had an awakened conscience, a view of his guilt, and of the wrath which he deserved, and had reason to dread on account of it, not forty Sloughs of Despond would have turned him back, nor all the ridicule in the world would have moved him. And you see, in the case of these two men, how much more powerful are the terrors of the law and a sense of sin, as motives in an unconverted mind, than any mere description of the glories of heaven. That is good in its place, good when there is also a sense of sin to accompany it; and as in the case of Christian, where there is this burden on the soul, then the description of those glories will have an effect deep and lasting; while in the case of one who does not feel that burden, does not see and feel his guilt, as with Pliable, the most ravishing description of heaven will be but as a sweet tune on a flute flung to the wind and forgotten,—it will make but a momentary impression, create only a transitory, superficial sympathy. There must be the preaching of the law and a law-work in the conscience, before men are likely even to set out resolutely for heaven, and without this law-work they do almost invariably turn back; unless, indeed, avoiding the Slough of Despond, and all the difficulties Christian met with, they take up with a false hope, as Ignorance did, and make a profession of religion; in which case they may, even as Ignorance, hold on to the last, and even at the river of Death be ferried over in the boat of one named Vain-Hope, not to find out their error, till on coming up and knocking at the gate, and crying, Lord, Lord, open unto us, the Lord shall answer, I never knew you.

And now is poor Christian left to struggle alone; and with the burden on his back, lamentable indeed is his case in the Slough of Despond. And here he would have remained and died, for he would struggle in no direction but that toward the Wicket Gate, the side farthest from his own house, had not a heavenly helper reached forth his hand to draw him out. Some men, like Pliable, endeavour to throw off their convictions of sin, by returning to worldly pleasures, getting out of the Slough on the side nearest the City of

Destruction; this, you remember, Bunyan himself did at one time; from his convictions he returned desperately to his sports. But the resolute Pilgrim, once fixed towards heaven, will not seek to be rid of his burden in any way but by going to Christ; in the midst of his distressing convictions, he will still struggle, as Christian did, toward the side farthest from the City of Destruction; and so doing he will find help.

In this Slough of Despond there were good and firm steps, sound promises to stand upon, a causeway, indeed, better than adamant, clear across the treacherous quagmires; but mark you, fear followed Christian so hard, that he fled the nearest way, and fell in, not stopping to look for the steps, or not thinking of them. Now this is often just the operation of fear; it sets the threatenings *against* the promises, when it ought simply to direct the soul *from* the threatenings *to* the promises. That is the object of the threatenings to make the promises shine, and to make the soul lay hold upon them, and that is the purpose and the tendency of a salutary fear of the divine wrath on account of sin, to make the believer flee directly to the promises, and advance on them to Christ. But in general, men under conviction of sin, having more desire to escape from hell than to get to Christ; more desire to be relieved of their distresses than to become holy; are blinded by the very fears which should have pointed out the promises, and without looking narrowly for those steps, they struggle for relief rather than holiness, for comfort rather than Christ, and so fall deeper into difficulty. Just so in all applications that we make of any remedies but the Gospel; in all directions that we go for relief but just to Christ, and with all the physicians we can have without him, our sickness of sin and misery never grows better, but rather grows worse. Flying from our fears, we fly only into greater guilt and fear, if we do not flee to Christ. Struggling to be rid of our burden, it only sinks us deeper in the mire, if we do not rest by faith upon the promises, and so come indeed to Christ. Precious promises they are, and so free and full of forgiveness and eternal life, that certainly the moment a dying soul feels its guilt and misery, that soul may lay hold upon them, and find Christ in them; and were it not for unbelief, there need be no Slough of Despond for the soul to struggle and plunge in its mire of depravity.

You see, said the dreamer's teacher, this Slough of Despond is a dreadful place, because unbelief and sin are such deep and dreadful evils. And as long as unbelief continues it cannot be mended; for still as the sinner is awakened about his lost condition there arise in his soul many fears and doubts, and discouraging apprehensions, which all of them get together and settle in this place; and this is the reason of the badness of this ground.

It is not the pleasure of the King that this place should remain so bad: his labourers also have, by the direction of his Majesty's surveyors, been above these eighteen hundred years employed about this patch of ground, if perhaps it might have been mended; millions of cartloads of wholesome instructions have been swallowed up in it, that have at all seasons been brought from all places of the King's dominions; the very best materials to make good ground of the place, if so it might have been mended; but it is the Slough of Despond still, and so will be, when they have done what they can. Nevertheless, the steps are there, if the burdened and terrified Pilgrims will but take them; and the ground is good, when they are once got in at the gate. There was also a heavenly Helper for poor Christian, as there always will be for one who is humble and sincere, even though, in the excess of his fear, he misses the steps, and seems to be sinking to destruction. The Lord will not leave him to perish, any more than he left Peter, because of his unbelief, to sink to the bottom. The Lord Jesus Christ can never resist that outcry of the sinking soul, Lord, save me, I perish!

And now you may think perhaps that Christian having got out of the Slough of Despond, and fairly on his way, it is all well with him; but not so, for now he comes into a peril that is far greater than the last, a peril through which we suppose that every soul that ever goes on pilgrimage passes, and a peril in which multitudes that get safely across the Slough of Despond, perish for ever. For now Christian meets, not with mud and mire, but with Mr Worldly Wiseman, from the great town of Carnal Policy, who besets and waylays him with another gospel. He directs him to a famous preacher of that gospel, Mr Legality, a gentleman whose parish is in the very respectable village of Morality, where there are nice, honest, and amiable neighbours, in credit and good fashion, where provision is cheap and good, where there are houses that stand empty to be had at a very reasonable rate, where Christian can get good and comfortable garments, and withal fashionable, instead of those rags that he has on his back; where also he can get rid of his burden, for Mr Legality hath great skill to take off the Pilgrim's burdens, and also to cure those that are somewhat crazed in their wits on account of them. He hath also a pretty young man to his son, Mr Civility, who can take off a burden, if need be, as well as the old gentleman; and moreover, to this very respectable village Christian can remove his wife and children, and so not be separated from them; and Mr Worldly Wiseman would have him do this by all means, and so not go back to the City of Destruction at all.

Now, is not all this very pleasant, a most comfortable prospect, rather than to forsake all that he hath, and go on in a pilgrimage begun with so many dangers! Here you see that Christian need no longer be in fear on account of the City of Destruction, for the town of Morality would keep him safe, even if that Sodom, which Mr Worldly Wiseman would certainly not advise him any longer to live in, should be burned up with fire on account of the sins of its inhabitants. Nevertheless, the comfort and respectability of this place would not have tempted Christian, had it not been for the advantage which Mr Worldly Wiseman had over him, because of his great desire and eagerness to be rid of his burden. The very first thing, when Mr Worldly Wiseman met him, and asked him whither he was going after this burdened manner, groaning and sighing so heavily, Christian made answer that he was going to get rid of his burden, and for that purpose was going to the Wicket Gate. Now see the advice of Mr Worldly Wiseman, and how it chimes in with the soul's desire for comfort rather than holiness. Christian was very impatient to get rid of his burden. Well, said Mr Worldly Wiseman, wilt thou hearken to me, if I give thee counsel? Certainly, said Christian, I stand in great need of good counsel. Well then, said Mr Worldly Wiseman, I would advise thee that with all speed thou get rid of thy burden; for thou wilt never be settled in thy mind till then; nor canst thou enjoy the benefit of the blessings which God hath bestowed upon thee till then.

This was counsel indeed! Get rid of thy burden, get rid of thy burden! This is the amount of the teachings of morality, this the perilous voice of all teachers that do not point the sinner to Christ, and his atoning sacrifice. Get rid of thy burden, it is a foolish thing; secure thy comfort by going to the town of Morality, and placing thyself under the pastoral care of that very judicious man and civil gentleman, Mr Legality. Evangelist had directed Christian to Christ; he had not told him to get rid of his burden, but to go to Christ, and Christ would remove it in good time. Now that was good counsel, all the counsel that Christian needed; but still he was very impatient to be rid of his burden, and so Mr Worldly Wiseman's counsels pointed to the same thing, and with great ingenuity he tried to prejudice Christian against Evangelist, and the strait and narrow way. Mr Worldly Wiseman, and all his connections, dislike the atonement; the Cross of Christ is foolishness unto them, except to make signs with it, and put it on the roofs of their houses and the outside of their churches. In all likelihood Mr Legality's own chapel, in that town of Morality, had a cross on the top of it; for so do men, who deny the atonement, cover up that denial by mingling the atonement and morality together, which answers the same purpose as denying it utterly; for if a man seeks to get rid of his burden by morality in part, he does not rest on the atonement at all. And just so, the men who hate the great truth of justification by faith, because that cuts off all worldly pride, and kills sin and self utterly, will often not avow that hatred plainly, but say that men must be justified by faith and works together; whereas it is the blood of Christ alone, and no works, though a man had a universe full of them to present to God, that can cleanse the soul from sin.

However, Mr Worldly Wiseman was very plump and bold in his condemnation of Evangelist and his doctrine. "Beshrew him for his counsel! there is not a more dangerous and troublesome way in the world, than is that into which he hath directed thee; and that thou shalt find, if thou wilt be ruled by his counsel. Thou hast met with something, as I perceive, already, for I see the dirt of the Slough of Despond is upon thee; but that Slough is the beginning of the sorrows that do attend those that go on in that way. Hear me, I am older than thou; thou art like to meet with in the way which thou goest, wearisomeness, painfulness, hunger, perils, nakedness, swords, lions, dragons, darkness, and in a word, death and what not. These things are certainly true, having been confirmed by many testimonies. And should a man so carelessly cast away himself by giving heed to a stranger?"

Mr Worldly Wiseman had read his Bible to some purpose, after all, for he almost gives Paul's exact catalogue of the evils he had met with in his pilgrimage. But Paul said, None of these things move me, and these things are not worthy to be compared with the glory that shall be revealed. Mr Worldly Wiseman could understand the catalogue of evils, and he thought to frighten Christian with them; but he could not understand the glory, and he had not calculated the power of genuine conviction of sin, to make a man despise death itself for the sake of deliverance from it. See now, says Bunyan in the margin, the frame of the heart of a young Christian. Why, sir, said Christian, this burden upon my back is more terrible to me than are all those things which you have mentioned; nay, methinks I care not what I meet with in the way, if so be I can also meet with deliverance from my burden.

How camest thou by thy burden at first?

By reading this book in my hand, said Christian.

And now, Mr Worldly Wiseman goes further, and shews, as Bunyan says in the margin, that he does not like that men should be serious in reading the Bible. I thought so, said he, and it is happened unto thee as to other weak men who, meddling with things too high for them, do suddenly fall into thy distractions; which distractions do not only unman men, as thine I perceive have done thee, but they run them upon desperate ventures, to obtain they know not what.

This conversation of Mr Worldly Wiseman is almost the exact counterpart of the dealings of those teachers who deny the Divinity and Atonement of Christ, and the truth of everlasting punishment. One of the most celebrated of those teachers in his day had been himself in early life under deep conviction of sin, had set out from the City of Destruction, but had turned into the town of Morality, and established himself as a preacher there. He used to say to those whom he ever saw in distress on account of Christian's burden, or Evangelist's counsel, I have been that way myself, and know all about it; I have passed through all that experience, and know that it is all nonsense. These distresses on account of sin are pure fanaticism, they are unmanly superstitions, which pleasant company, exercise, and recreation, will drive away.

Why wilt thou seek for ease this way of the Cross, said Mr Worldly Wiseman, seeing so many dangers attend it, especially since, hadst thou but patience to hear me, I could direct thee to the obtaining of what thou desirest, without the dangers that thou in this way wilt run thyself into; yea, and the remedy is at hand; besides, I will add, that instead of these dangers thou shalt meet with much safety, friendship, and content.

Now was Christian snared by these counsels, and taking Mr Worldly Wiseman's direction to Mr Legality's house, past Mount Sinai, for by that way he must go, he set out. But behold, when he was now got hard by the hill, it seemed so high, and also that side of it that was next the wayside did hang so much over, that Christian was afraid to venture further, lest the hill should fall on his head; wherefore, then he stood still, and wotted not what to do. Also, his burden now seemed heavier to him than while he was in his way. There came also flashes of fire out of the hill that made Christian afraid that he should be burnt; here therefore he did sweat and quake for fear. Poor Christian! he could not get past Mount Sinai! Nay, happy Christian! in that the terrors of the law got such hold upon him, that they would not let him pass; for if he had gone by, he too, like many thousand others, would have gone to the town of Morality, and got comfortably settled in perdition. He would have become a member of Mr Legality's parish, if he could have got past this mountain. But here Evangelist found him, half dead with shame, confusion, and terror. And here, with the most ingenuous simplicity and contrition, Christian made confession of his guilt. Yes, dear sir, I am the man! And now the reproofs and instructions of Evangelist are incomparably beautiful, and Christian, bemoaning his folly and sin in listening to the wicked counsels of the Deceiver, applied himself again to Evangelist in words and sense as follows :—

Sir, what think you? Is there any hope? May I now go back, and go up to the Wicket Gate? Shall I not be abandoned for this, and sent back from thence ashamed? I am sorry I have hearkened to this man's counsel; but may my sin be forgiven?

The mingling of reproof and encouragement with which Evangelist comforted the penitent, is exquisitely wise and beautiful. A rare pastor Bunyan found in holy Mr Gifford, to be able to draw so sweet and grave a character from real life. Evangelist kissed him, gave him one smile, and bid him God speed. And now you may be sure there was no more turning of Christian out of the way, no more inclination after Sinai, or Mr Legality, or the town of Morality, not though a hundred worldly wisemen had beset him. As an arrow to its mark, he went straight with haste, neither spake he to any man by the way; nor if any asked him would he vouchsafe them an answer. This experience of Sinai was enough for him, nor could he think himself safe, till in process of time he got up to the gate. There he knocked with trembling earnestness, for over the gate was written, KNOCK, AND IT SHALL BE OPENED UNTO YOU.

May I now enter here ? said Christian,

> May I now enter here? Will he within
> Open to sorry me, though I have been
> An undeserving rebel? Then shall I
> Not fail to sing his lasting praise on high.

Bunyan has put in the margin, The gate will be open to brokenhearted sinners ; and so it was, and Christian went in. But as he was stepping in, the kind Master gave him a sudden pull, at which Christian wondered ; but he was told that at a little distance from the gate there was a frowning castle, under command of Beelzebub, from whence they shot arrows at those that were entering the gate, or had come up to it, if haply they might die before they could enter. So Christian entered with joy and trembling.

This undoubtedly is an incident drawn from Bunyan's own experience ; for often when he himself was standing at mercy's gate, and knocking as for his life for entrance, he had been assaulted by these fiends ; when he was praying, then especially would there sometimes come a fiery storm of the darts of the Wicked One, so that often he thought he should have died indeed beneath them. Doubtless something like this is the experience of all who come up to this gate ; for sometimes the point of greatest difficulty and danger is just that point where the soul is summoning all its forces to come to Christ, or where it is just about sweetly to cast itself upon his mercy ; or where there is a great decisive struggle at the Wicket Gate, between good and evil in the soul, and where the perishing sinner is just able to say, Lord, I believe, help thou mine unbelief. All moments of decision are moments of danger, and when Satan, from his battlement, sees the soul knocking at the gate, then he says within himself, It is my last hope ; my archers must destroy him now or never. And so sometimes just the point of mercy is the point of greatest strife and danger.

A characteristic instructive conversation ensued between Christian and the Man at the Gate, in the course of which Christian, being questioned, told the man about his adventures in the Slough of Despond, and how Pliable had left him : and here Bunyan has put in the margin, A man may have company when he sets out for heaven, and yet go thither alone; but Christian also added, with sweet ingenuousness, that he was quite as bad as Pliable, for that he also turned aside to go in the way of death, being persuaded thereto by the carnal arguments of one Mr Worldly Wiseman. The Man at the gate comforted and encouraged him, and pointed out the strait and narrow way before him, so that he could not miss it; and now Christian was about to gird up his loins, and address himself to his journey; but O that heavy burden! Christian could not go without asking to be rid of his burden; so kind and skilful a man (thought he) may surely take it off, and I am sore weary with it. But the answer he received was memorable. As to thy burden, be content to bear it, until thou comest to the place of deliverance; for there it will fall from thy back of itself. Bunyan has here put in the margin, There is no deliverance from the guilt and burden of sin, but by the death and blood of Christ.

Now there is a vast deal of instruction and comfort in this last incident. Young Christians are very apt to expect entire relief from all their burdens, and a complete deliverance from sin, the moment they are got within the Wicket Gate, the moment they have come to Christ. But very often this expectation is not realized, and then they faint and become disheartened, or filled with gloomy doubts on this account. Now this experience of Christian having to bear his burden so long, and yet going on so patiently with it, for you will observe, he asked nobody after this to take off his burden, is very instructive and encouraging. The truth is, we are all more apt to be seeking for comfort than for Christ; whereas Christ should be our first object, and comfort will come of itself; Christ first, and all things else shall be added.

By the experience of Christian and Pliable in their commencement of this pilgrimage, we are taught some salutary lessons; as, *first*, The importance of a deep and thorough conviction of sin at first setting out; *second*, The importance of a resolute purpose in seeking salvation, so as not to be turned back; and, *third*, The importance of a hearty reception and thorough knowledge of God's word. The difficulties that Christian meets and overcomes in the beginning, do, instead of discouraging him, prepare him for constancy and conquest even to the end. It is no superficial Christian that Bunyan is describing, but a man of God, thoroughly furnished unto all good works; a soldier clad in armour of proof, the armour of righteousness on the right hand and on the left. He needed, as we shall see, a deep and thorough discipline from the beginning, in order to prepare him for the fiery ordeal through which he was to pass.

It is always thus that God deals with his people; the discipline of the Christian race and conflict is such, in its very nature, as best to prepare them for usefulness here, and for their place in glory hereafter. If there is to be endurance to the end, there must be thoroughness at the beginning; if victory at the end, a fight at the beginning; if rest at the end, a burden at the beginning. There must be fires to consume the dross here, if there is to be endless brightness and purity hereafter; self-denial and suffering in this world must prepare the way to glorify God and enjoy him for ever. There was a great connection between Christian's burden at first, and his delight in God afterwards; so there was between all the toils of his pilgrimage, and his panting desires after God; for certainly, if this pilgrimage were all the way a way of ease, then we should not much desire to hasten on in it, or to come to the end of it, or to see God in heaven; too much satisfied with the sweetness of the streams, we should stay away from the fountain. We having here no continuing city, seek one to come, that city which hath foundations, whose builder and maker is God.

> Jerusalem, Jerusalem,
>   Would God I were with thee!
> Oh that my sorrows had an end,
>   Thy joys that I might see!
> Thy walls are made of precious stone,
>   Thy bulwarks diamonds square;
> Thy gates are made of orient pearl;
>   O God, if I were there!
>
> O happy harbour of God's saints!
>   O sweet and pleasant soil!
> In thee no sorrows can be found,
>   No grief, no care, no toil.

No dimly cloud o'ershadows thee,
  No gloom nor darksome night,
But every soul shines as the sun,
  For God himself gives light.

Lord, in my forehead plant thy name,
  And take me hence away,
That I may dwell with thee in bliss,
  And sing thy praise for aye.
O mother dear, Jerusalem!
  When shall I come to thee?
When shall my sorrows have an end?
  Thy joys when shall I see?

LECTURE SEVENTH.

Christian in the House of the Interpreter

Meaning of the Interpreter, what great personage he stands for.—Richness and beauty of his instructions.—The Law and the Gospel as sweepers of the soul.—Passion and Patience, Sense and Faith.—How grace is sustained in the soul.—How the victory is gained by the Man in armour.—Misery of the soul in Despair.—Dream of the Judgment.—Power of Conscience.—Beauty of the Pilgrim's Progress as a book for Childhood.—Christian's deliverance from his burden.

It would be difficult to find twelve consecutive pages in the English language, that contain such volumes of meaning, in such beautiful and instructive lessons, with such heavenly imagery, in so pure and sweet a style, and with so thrilling an appeal to the best affections of the heart, as these pages descriptive of Christian's sojourning in the House of the Interpreter. This good man of the House, the Interpreter, we are, without doubt, to take as the representative of the Holy Spirit, with his enlightening and sanctifying influences on the heart. He is our Comforter, Guardian, and Guide through all our pilgrimage; our Instructor to take of the things which are Christ's, and to shew them to our souls; our Sanctifier, to lead us into all truth, and to make it the nourishing food of our souls, and with it and in it bringing Christ before us continually, to fasten our affections upon him, and make him, of God, unto us, our wisdom, righteousness, sanctification, and redemption. From the first moment of a Christian's setting out on his pilgrimage, this heavenly Comforter takes him under his peculiar guidance; so soon as he enters the Strait Gate, and puts himself under the care of the Great Shepherd, then the Spirit of God begins the work of discipline, instruction, refinement, and sanctification with him as a child of God. So you will observe that the very first thing which the Interpreter said to Christian was, Come in, and I will shew thee that which will be profitable unto thee. And then he bid his man light the candle, and brought Christian into a private room, where he shewed him the first of the beautiful and instructive visions that were to pass before him. Bunyan has put in the margin the word Illumination, and he might have added the text, Open thou mine eyes that I may behold wondrous things out of thy law. Or he might have referred us to the blessed walk of the two disciples with Christ in the way to Emmaus, when he opened their understandings, that they might understand the Scriptures; for such a work does the Spirit of God commence with us when he lights the candle of the Lord within our hearts.

But we are to observe that Christian did not get into the House of the Interpreter, nor obtain his precious guidance, without knocking, yea, and that earnestly. This is to signify that after Christ has let us in, as we hope, at the Wicket Gate, our great and immediate work must be to seek with most humble diligence and earnestness the gracious illuminating and sanctifying influences of his Spirit. In our first ignorance and darkness, how greatly they are needed no language can tell. The young convert will make but a poor soldier of Jesus Christ, but a weak and lagging pilgrim, if he does not go directly to the House of the Interpreter. Ah, what earnest prayer is needed, that the soul, having come to Christ, may be filled with the Spirit, be rooted and grounded in love, and built up in him and prepared to shew forth his praises! Be assured that the immediate time which passes after a soul's conversion is of indescribable importance for all after life. If it be passed in the House of the Interpreter, and under his divine instruction, if the soul is much in prayer for divine grace and illumination, then will there be a rich and precious preparation for a joyful and triumphant pilgrimage, in which the path of the soul shall be as a shining light, that shineth more and more unto the perfect day. But if joy come first, without the instruction and discipline of the Interpreter, then will there be trouble afterwards, a great many falls by the way, a great many Hill Difficulties, and perhaps a great many weeks instead of days passed in the Castle of Giant Despair. When a soul first comes to Christ, then for many days it ought to abide with the Holy Spirit: and when this is done, who shall say how many sights of glory may be seen, how many rich and refining experiences be enjoyed; how rapidly the soul may grow, and be transfigured, as it were, with the influences of divine truth, while thus it is alone with God; how it may be knit and strengthened for all future toils and combats, and prepared to go through the world almost as a seraph of light, prepared, at any rate, like Paul, so to run not as uncertainly, so to fight not as one that beateth the air.

The first sight which Christian saw was a "brave picture," an exquisite portrait of a grave and saintly man, who had his eyes lifted up to Heaven, the best of books in his hand, the Law of Truth was written upon his lips, the world was behind his back; it stood as if it pleaded with men, and a crown of gold did hang over its head. And whose portrait is Bunyan describing here? Again, we think he had holy Mr Gifford in his eye as a faithful minister of Christ; but Bunyan too had been the pleader with men, and over his own head the crown of gold was shining, and while he wrote these words, you may be sure that his spirit thrilled within him as he said, And I too am a minister of Jesus Christ! This picture was shewn by the Interpreter to Christian, in order that he might know the true from the false guide in the way to the City of Immanuel.

The next scene which the Interpreter shewed Christian, went, you may be sure, to his heart; for it displayed the inward corruptions of the soul, and the different effects, first of the Law, and afterwards of the Gospel upon them; and Christian, it must be remembered, had not yet got rid of his burden of sin, and had in his mind in great freshness the terrors of Sinai in the way to Mr Legality's house, and his distressing experience in the Slough of Despond, besides his deep convictions of sin and wrath in the City of Destruction. He had known most thoroughly what the Law could do with a burdened conscience; he had but begun to know what grace could do to ease it. The Interpreter carried him into a large parlour whereof the floor was thick with dust, because it had never been swept. So the moment a man began to sweep it, the dust flew about in such clouds that Christian was wellnigh stifled; but so soon as a damsel was called to sprinkle the room with water, then it was swept and cleansed easily.

The sweeper was the Law, stirring up the corruptions in the parlour of the heart; trying to sweep them, but only stirring them up, and raising a suffocating cloud in the atmosphere. This is the work of the Law in the conscience, to reveal sin, to make the sinner sensible of it; and this is all that the Law can do; it can only convince and condemn, for we have broken every one of its precepts, and the more its light shines in upon the soul, the more manifest our iniquities become. If we strive to keep it, and so to gain peace, we may keep it in some points outwardly, but inwardly we break it; we are defiled in every part, and our very morality condemns us, as not springing from the love of God. The voice of the law is, The soul that sinneth it shall die, and he that offendeth in one point is guilty of all; and what a broom this is to introduce into the heart to sweep it of its sins, you may well judge; every movement of it is as the besom of destruction; it is indeed condemnation and death perpetually. The law is holy, and just, and good; but its very holiness and goodness, laid alongside with our depravity, make the revelation within us appear like the uncovering of hell; it fills us with anguish and terror in the sight of what we are, and what we deserve.

Christian well knew this in his own deep experience; for the burden of sin was on him still, and sorely did he feel it while the Interpreter was making this explanation; and had it not been for his remembrance of the warning of the Man at the Gate, he would certainly have besought the Interpreter to take off his burden. The law could not take it off; he had tried that; and grace had not yet removed it; so he was forced to be quiet, and to wait patiently. But when the Damsel came and sprinkled the floor, and laid the dust, and then the parlour was swept so easily—there were the sweet influences of the gospel imaged, there was divine grace distilling as the dew; there was the gentle voice of Christ hushing the storm; there were the corruptions of the heart, which the law had but roused into action, yielding under the power of Christ; and there was the soul made clean, and fit for the King of Glory to inhabit. Indeed, this was a most instructive emblem. Oh that my heart might be thus cleansed, thought Christian, and then I verily believe I could bear my burden with great ease to the end of my pilgrimage; but I have had enough of that fierce sweeper, the Law. The Lord deliver me from his besom!

The next emblem was Passion and Patience, two little children, the very reverse in their characters, one of whom would have every thing now, the other would quietly wait. So Passion had his desire; and Christian looked and saw him with a bag of treasure exulting over Patience and laughing him to scorn; but Patience sat still, and answered nothing. So Christian looked again, and behold Passion had lavished all his treasure in a moment, and now had nothing but rags. This was a vivid and striking emblem, and one which in its general meaning a child could understand. Passion stands for the men of this world, Patience of that which is to come; Passion for those who will have all their good things now, Patience for those who are willing, with self-denial, to wait for something better; Passion for those who are absorbed in temporal trifles, Patience for those whose hearts are fixed upon eternal realities; Passion the things which are seen, and the impatient eagerness with which they are followed, Patience the things which are unseen, and the faith, humility, and deadness to the world exercised in order to enjoy them. Besides, Passion shews the scorn of Patience by prosperous men of this world in their bravery, Patience shews the gentle forbearance and endurance which the love of Christ, and the promise of eternal glory, do, by divine grace, enable the soul even of a persecuted Christian to exercise.

This beautiful passage is a good commentary on the seventy-third Psalm; it is good for those to read and meditate upon, who are at any time envious at the foolish, when they see the prosperity of the wicked; and there are times when the best of men fall into such a vein of murmuring and repining; they become foolish and ignorant, and as a beast before God, losing all sight and sense of eternal realities for a season, when they get to admiring the ungodly, who prosper in the world, who increase in riches. Ah, let them remember how as a dream when one awaketh, so the treasures and enjoyments of Passion are gone, and there is left nothing but rags and wretchedness! And let them remember those three sweet verses, which contain the very material out of which so gentle, yet noble a creature as Patience was made, and the very fire that as a flame of blessedness beforehand was burning in his heart, and making him care nothing at all for the braveries of Passion: "Thou shalt guide me with thy counsel, and afterward receive me to glory. Whom have I in heaven but thee? and there is none upon earth that I desire besides thee. My flesh and my heart faileth: but God is the strength of my heart, and my portion for ever."

It were well also to read along with this the account of Dives and Lazarus, of which again this emblem of Passion and Patience is a perfect representation. Dives was Passion, who would have all his good things in this life, and even doubted whether there was any life to come at all; at any rate, he would not be such a melancholy fool as to wait for it. Lazarus was Patience, who could not only wait, saying within himself, By and by it will be all right, and the crown of gold will keep its brightness for ever, but he could wait at the gate of the rich man full of sores, and yet singing and making melody in his heart unto the Lord, and thinking of the angels and of Abraham's bosom. And then the end, the eternal separation, the gulf of flame and the abode of glory! "Son," said Abraham, "remember that thou in thy lifetime receivedst thy good things, and likewise Lazarus evil things; and now he is comforted, and thou art tormented."

So the world goes! Passion says, A bird in the hand is worth two in the bush; give me good fortunes now, and you may have all your fine texts of Scripture, and all your glory in the world to come to yourself. Patience says, Wait a little, all is not gold that glitters, and a little that a righteous man hath, is better than the riches of many wicked. Passion says, Father, give me the portion of goods that belongeth to me; he will have them now, and he claims them as his right, and being indulged with them, away he goes and spends them to his own ruin; and then well for him it is, if amidst his rags and wretchedness his heart turns again to his father's house, and by the infinite mercy of divine grace he comes back as a lamenting, penitent, heart-broken Prodigal. Ah, thought Christian to himself, I was Passion once, Passion in the City of Destruction; and I should have been Passion still, Passion in rags and wretchedness, had not God had mercy on me. Now I will be Patience as long as I live.

The next bright instructive vision that the Interpreter shewed Christian, is one that sprung directly from Bunyan's own course of painful and blessed experience, mingled together. The Dreamer now is looking back and musing on the wonderful discipline of Divine Grace in his heart, and he says within himself, How marvellously, amidst all my terrible temptations, did my Divine Saviour, when I saw him not, and feared I never should see him, maintain his blessed, precious work of mercy in my heart! He has brought the blind by a way that they knew not; but now, blessed be God, how sweetly do I see it! When my spirit was overwhelmed within me, then thou knewest my path. "I saw in my dream," says Bunyan, "that the Interpreter took Christian by the hand, and led him into a place, where was a fire burning against a wall, and one standing by it, always casting much water upon it to quench it; yet did the fire burn higher and hotter." You will remember the sarcastic dialogue of the Tempter, the devil, with Bunyan's soul, when he had him near the entrance to the Valley of the Shadow of Death, and was torturing him with dreadful doubts and apprehensions. I will cool you yet, said Satan, though I take seven years to do it; you are very hot after mercy now, but you shall be cool enough by and by. And with what malignant wonder and disappointment must Satan have looked on to see all his efforts bootless, to see that the flame of love in Bunyan's heart was like the fire of guilt and despair in Satan's own conscience, unquenchable; to see, amidst all the torrents of rain and hail that he poured upon the soul of his apparently helpless victim, the fire of grace, to his utter desperation and astonishment, did only burn higher, and clearer, and brighter! Ah, the blind and guilty Fiend could not see the chariots and horsemen of heaven round about Bunyan; he could not see the Lord Jesus Christ continually pouring the oil of divine grace into Bunyan's heart, of which the Interpreter shewed Christian the emblem in the man on the other side secretly but continually pouring oil from a vessel into the fire.

So, said the Interpreter, by means of the oil of Christ's grace, notwithstanding what the devil can do, the souls of his people prove gracious still. And in that thou sawest that the man stood behind the wall to maintain the fire, this is to teach thee that it is hard for the tempted to see how this work of grace is maintained in the soul. My grace is sufficient for thee, for my strength is made perfect in weakness. Bunyan had had deep experience of the glory of this promise, for it was the passage of grace which did long strive with that of Esau, till at length the dreadful threatening grew dim and vanished away, while the promise grew brighter and brighter, till it filled his whole soul with its glory; till the Law had to give place to the Gospel, and Moses and Elias to leave Christ and his saints alone. Bunyan has put this sweet promise in a reference in the margin; and here I may remark, that as you pass along in the Pilgrim's Progress, if you will take the trouble to turn to your Bibles for references, you may see the very sources of the wisdom and inspiration of Bunyan's genius, the very channels through which the River of the Water of Life flowed in so many thousand deep beau-

CHRISTIAN IN THE HOUSE OF THE INTERPRETER. 203

tiful rills into these pages. The examination in such wise proves far more instructive.

The next sight which the Interpreter shewed Christian, is in many respects the most animating and ravishing passage to be found in all the Pilgrim's Progress. It set Christian's own heart on fire to run forward on his journey. Those who have read this book in early childhood, can well remember the powerful effect which this picture had upon the imagination. The Interpreter took Christian by the hand, and led him into a pleasant place, where was built a stately palace, beautiful to behold ; at the sight of which Christian was greatly delighted : he saw also upon the top thereof certain persons walking, who were clothed all in gold. So the Interpreter took Christian, and led him up towards the door of the palace ; and behold, at the door stood a great company of men, as desirous to go in, but durst not. There also sat a man at a little distance from the door, at a tableside, with a book and an ink-horn before him, to take the names of them that should enter therein ; he saw also that in the door-way stood many men in armour to keep it, being resolved to do to the men that would enter, what hurt and mischief they could. Now was Christian somewhat in amaze : at last, when every man started back for fear of the armed men, Christian saw a man of a very stout countenance come up to the man that sat there to write, saying, Set down my name, sir ; the which, when he had done, he saw the man draw his sword, and put a helmet upon his head, and rush towards the door upon the armed men, who laid upon him with deadly force ; but the man, not at all discouraged, fell to cutting and hacking most fiercely. So, after he had received and given many wounds to those who attempted to keep him out, he cut his way through them all, and pressed forward into the palace ; at which there was a pleasant voice heard from those that were within, even of those that walked upon the top of the palace, saying,

<blockquote>
Come in, come in,
Eternal glory thou shalt win!
</blockquote>

So he went in, and was clothed in such garments as they.

Then Christian smiled and said, I think verily I know the meaning of this.

Verily thou didst, noble Christian! And who is there that does not know the meaning of it, and what heart so cold as not to be ravished by it! Yea, we should think that this passage alone might set any man out on this pilgrimage, might bring many a careless traveller up to the gate of this glorious palace to say, Set down my name, sir! How full of instruction is this passage! What mingled encouragement and warning did it convey to Christian's mind to prepare him for the many trials before him. It was necessary that the Holy Spirit should shew him in some measure what he would have to encounter, should make him feel that if he gained heaven, it must be by a great conflict, and a great victory. Mr Worldly-Wiseman had predicted some of the dangers he was to meet with; but Mr Worldly-Wiseman could have no conception of the exceeding weight of glory that was to follow; but here the vision of the glory follows so close upon the sight of the conflict, that the conflict even adds to its charms, and makes it a thousand times the more exciting. Here is the sentence, " Through much tribulation," but here is also " the Kingdom of Heaven ;" and who so pitiful as not to be willing to undergo the tribulation, to encounter the hazard, to run the gauntlet of these armed men against him, for the glory of that kingdom ?

Yea, saith Christian, verily I think I can understand this. But here you will remark how great a multitude stood round the gate of this palace, fearing, yet desiring—desiring, yet fearing, to enter in. And you see that Christian found, while he was there, only one among them of like spirit with himself—only one who would come up and say, Set down my name, sir. Ah! what a multitude there are who have some faint desires after heaven, and half a mind, a thousand times, to set out in the way thither, but who never do it, who always shrink back. These men around the gate were so many Pliables, who were sure to go back to the City of Destruction; and we would say to those many persons in just their situation, unless you come to a fixed resolution, unless you step quickly and boldly to the gate, with your heart on fire, and say, Set down my name, sir, in a tone that shall make Christian rejoice, and the armed men tremble, you are not likely ever to fight your way into this palace, or ever to be walking with those upon its top in glory.

As for Christian, his whole heart went with the man of stout countenance, and went with every blow he gave; and he was so ravished with his courage, and with the pleasant voice and the glory, that as soon as that sight was done with, he was for starting at once upon his journey. Now, said Christian, let me go hence. How often does the young convert, in his moments of triumph, think he has got instruction enough, and grace enough, to last him all the way of his pilgrimage! But he needs, as I said, a great many sights, and much more heavenly discipline, in the House of the Interpreter, or his boasted courage will fail by the way. Christian thought he had received an impulse, under which his soul would shoot forward like an arrow, a gale of the Spirit filling his sails, that would carry his bark swiftly through all tempests to heaven. He felt, indeed, as if he were in heaven beforehand, he did so long to be there. Under this ravishing sight he scarcely felt the weight of his burden, and not a word was said to the Interpreter about removing it. But Christian needs more instruction still; and as these bright colours are apt to fade from the picture, or grow unnoticed, unless they be set off and heightened, and made more important by some dark shades beside them, the Interpreter did now, with heavenly skill, direct Christian's attention to a vision terribly instructive, which would both be fixed itself in his remembrance, and would make the bright vision more precious to him. Stay, said the Interpreter, till I have shewn thee a little more, and after that thou shalt go on thy way. When the Holy Spirit undertakes to illuminate and sanctify the soul, he will do it thoroughly; he will not dismiss a soldier to his work without his armour. Nor must the Christian be impatient of instruction, or of the time during which he seems to be detained in learning; for it is very precious to be thus in the House of the Interpreter, under the teachings of the Holy Spirit;

and he may be sure that all he can gain he will need. Warnings he needs, and solemn ones.

So the Interpreter took Christian by the hand again, and led him into a very dark room, where there sat a man in an iron cage. Now the man to look on seemed very sad; he sat with his eyes looking down to the ground, his hands folded together, and he sighed as if he would break his heart. Then said Christian, What means this? At which the Interpreter bid him talk with the man. Then said Christian to the man, What art thou? Christian's heart trembled as he put this question, and he said within himself, Alas! if I should ever be in this condition! The man answered, I am what I was not once. What wast thou once? said Christian. The man said, I was once a fair and flourishing professor, both in mine own eyes, and also in the eyes of others. I was also, as I thought, fair for the Celestial City, and had even joy at the thoughts that I should get thither. Well, said Christian, but what art thou now? I am now a Man of Despair, and am shut up in it, as in this iron cage. I cannot get out; O, *now* I cannot. But how camest thou into this condition? said Christian. I left off to watch and be sober; I laid the reins upon the neck of my lusts; I sinned against the light of the Word, and the goodness of God; I have grieved the Spirit, he is gone; I tempted the devil, and he is come to me; I have provoked God to anger, and he has left me; I have so hardened my heart that I cannot repent.

Then said Christian to the Interpreter, But are there no hopes for such a man as this? It was a dreadful sight to Christian, as it must be to us all; for what happened to this man may happen to any man who leaves off to be sober, and to watch unto prayer. It made Christian weep and tremble to see the deep misery of this man. But you will mark that the Interpreter does not give any answer to Christian, does not tell him whether there is yet hope or not, but refers him to the man himself for answer. Bunyan evidently did not mean to set it down as the judgment of the Holy Spirit, that such an one as this was past hope; and doubtless, men have conceived themselves in this condition for whom there was hope, and the door of whose cage has afterwards been opened, and they have come out. There may be a spiritual gloom, amounting, as it seems to the soul under it, to actual despair, from which there is at length a blessed deliverance. David was sometimes in prison in this way, and on account of his sins. Bring my soul out of prison, he cries; and in the eighty-eighth Psalm you have the statement of a case almost as bad as this of the Man in the Cage of Despair. The poet Cowper was thus in prison much of his time; but in his case it was a mind of exquisite sensibility thrown from its balance, and really insane in the belief of his being a lost soul. There are doubtless other causes of spiritual gloom besides sin, but unbelief and sin are the ordinary causes. Bunyan himself was sometimes in this gloomy state, without a ray of comfort, but never in such a state that he could not pray for mercy. Christian, when he fell into the dungeon of Giant Despair's Castle, was in this condition; and he must then have remembered this picture of the man in the iron cage with fearful vividness and keenness. The full sight and sense of any man's sins, without the sight and sense of a Saviour's mercy at the same time, would be sufficient to cast the soul at any time into utter despair; and we are inclined to think that Bunyan had in his memory, at the time of writing this description, that book which had so powerful an effect once upon his own mind, the despairing death of Francis Spira, the apostate, and especially that sentence, Man knows the beginning of sin, but who can bound the issues thereof? And Bunyan intended not to represent this man as actually beyond the reach of mercy, but to shew the dreadful consequences of departing from God, and of being abandoned of him to the misery of unbelief and despair.

So Christian, as the Interpreter bade him, accosted the man. Is there no hope, said he, but you must be kept in the Iron Cage of Despair? No, none at all, said the man. Why, said Christian, the Son of the Blessed is very merciful. Then said the man, I have crucified him to myself afresh; I have despised his person; I have despised his righteousness; I have counted his blood an unholy thing; I have done despite to the Spirit of grace; therefore I shut myself out of all the promises; and there now remains to me nothing but threatenings, dreadful threatenings, faithful threatenings, of certain judgments and fiery indignation, which shall devour me as an adversary.

For what did you bring yourself into this condition? asked Christian. For the lusts, pleasures, and profits of this world, in the enjoyment of which I did then promise myself much delight; but now every one of those things also bite me, and gnaw me like a burning worm.

But canst thou not now repent and turn? asked Christian. The man persevered in his gloomy awful answer. It is indeed a picture to the life, of a soul in incurable despair. God hath denied me repentance. His Word gives me no encouragement to believe. Yea, himself hath shut me up in this iron cage, nor can all the men in the world let me out. O Eternity! Eternity! How shall I grapple with the misery that I must meet with in eternity!

Then said the Interpreter to Christian, Let this man's misery be remembered by thee, and be an everlasting caution to thee. Well, said Christian, this is fearful! God help me to watch and be sober, and to pray that I may shun the cause of this man's misery. This was indeed a fearful lesson. The sight of this man in the iron cage was likely to remain with Christian at least as long as the preceding sight of the venturous man cutting his way to eternal glory. And the one sight is judged as important by the Holy Spirit as the other. This, after all, is nothing more than the reality must be, supposing a soul in the case described by Paul, "For it is impossible for those once enlightened, &c., if they shall fall away, to renew them again unto repentance." Woe unto them, says God, when I depart from them. There is no stoicism or philosophy can stand against God's departure. There is no harm can happen to a man, who has God for his friend; but there is no good can happen to a man abandoned of God. When he giveth quietness, who then can make trouble? and when he hideth his face, who then can behold him? whether it be done against a nation or against a man only.

Sir, said Christian, is it not time for me to be on my way

now? The Interpreter would have him tarry to see one thing more. So he took him by the hand, and led him into a chamber, where there was one rising out of bed; and as he put on his raiment he shook and trembled. This night, said he, as I was in my sleep, I dreamed, and behold the heavens grew exceeding black; also, it thundered and lightened in most fearful wise, that it put me into an agony. So I looked up in my dream, and saw the clouds rack at an unusual rate; upon which I heard a great sound of a trumpet, and saw also a man sitting upon a cloud, attended with ten thousands of heaven. They were all in flaming fire; also, the heavens were on a burning flame. I heard then a great voice, saying, "Arise, ye dead, and come to judgment!" and with that the rocks rent, the graves opened, and the dead that were therein came forth; some of them were exceeding glad, and looked upward, and some sought to hide themselves under the mountains. Then I saw the man that sat upon the cloud open the book, and bid the world draw near; yet there was, by reason of a fierce flame which issued out, and came before him, a convenient distance betwixt him and them, as betwixt the judge and the prisoners at the bar. I heard it also proclaimed to them that attended on the Man that sat on the cloud, "Gather together the tares, the chaff, and stubble, and cast them into the burning lake;" and with that the bottomless pit opened just whereabout I stood; out of the mouth of which there came, in an abundant manner, smoke and coals of fire, with hideous noises. It was also said to the same persons, "Gather my wheat into the garner." And with that I saw many catched up and carried away into the clouds; but I was left behind. I also sought to hide myself, but I could not; for the Man that sat upon the cloud still kept his eye upon me. My sins also came into my mind, and my conscience did accuse me on every side.

In this terrific dream, what terrified the Dreamer was the thought that the Day of Judgment had come, and that he was not ready for it; and also that the angels gathered up some for glory close by his side, but left him! and also that the pit of hell there opened where he stood; while conscience roused up and tormented him, and the Judge, with indignation in his countenance, always had his eye upon him.

This dream, so sublimely told, with such severe faithfulness to Scripture, there being no image in it but such as you may find in the Bible, was the recurrence of Bunyan's own early experience, chastened by Divine Truth. One of Bunyan's biographers has given us the record of some of his actual early dreams in such language as carries the stamp of Bunyan's own imagination upon it, and shews that the imagery in the Pilgrim's Progress was the combination anew, with a ripened art and wisdom, of realities which his own soul had experienced. Once he dreamed he saw the face of the heavens as it were all on fire, the firmament crackling and shivering as it were with the noise of mighty thunders, and an archangel flew in the midst of heaven, sounding a trumpet, and a glorious throne was seated on the east, whereon sat one in brightness like the morning star, upon which he, thinking it was the end of the world, fell upon his knees, and with uplifted hands towards heaven, cried, O Lord God, have mercy upon me! What shall I do? the day of judgment is come, and I am not prepared! Then he immediately heard a voice behind him, exceeding loud, saying, REPENT. Whereupon he awoke, and found it was a dream. Another time he dreamed that he was in a pleasant place, jovial and rioting, banqueting and feasting his senses, when immediately a mighty earthquake rent the earth, and made a wide gap, out of which came bloody flames, and the figures of men tossed up in globes of fire, and falling down again with horrible cries, shrieks, and execrations, while some devils that were mingled with them laughed aloud at their torments; and whilst he stood trembling at this sight, he thought the earth sank under him, and a circle of flame enclosed him; but when he fancied he was just at the point to perish, one in white shining raiment descended, and plucked him out of that dreadful place, while the devils cried after him to be left with them, to take the just punishment his sins had deserved; yet he escaped the danger, and leaped for joy, when he awoke and found it was a dream.

Now in these dreams of Bunyan's own soul you may see clearly the materials, afterwards put more visibly into the symmetrical mould of Scripture imagery, of that grand and awful Dream of the Judgment, which the man related to Christian in the House of the Interpreter. Almost all men have at times passed through something of the same experience; for conscience is often busy in the night-time, when the external business of the day prevented her work and claims from being attended to. We go about the world in the day-time, we see pleasant companions, we are absorbed in earthly schemes, the things of sense are around us, the world is as bright as a rainbow, and it bears for us no marks or predictions of the judgment, or of our sins, and it holds no conversation with us on those subjects, and conscience is retired, as it were, within a far inner circle of the soul. But when it comes night, and the streets are empty, and the lights are out, and the business and dancing and gaiety are over, and the pall of sleep is drawn over the senses, and reason and the will are no longer on the watch, then conscience comes out solemnly, and walks about in the silent chambers of the soul, and makes her survey and her comments, and sometimes sits down and sternly reads the record of a life that the waking man would never look into, and the catalogue of crimes that are gathering for the judgment And as conscience reads, and reads aloud, and soliloquizes, you may hear the still deep echo of her voice reverberated through the soul's most secret unveiled recesses. Imagination walks tremblingly behind her, and now they two alone pass through the open gate of the Scriptures into the future and eternal world; for thither all things in man's being naturally and irresistibly tend; and there, as conscience is still dwelling upon sin, imagination draws the judgment, and the soul is presented at the bar of God, and the eye of the Judge is on it, and a hand of fire writes, as on the wall of the universe, Thou art weighed in the balances, and found wanting! Then, whatever sinful thoughts or passions, words or deeds, the conscience enumerates and dwells upon, the imagination with prophetic truth fills eternity with corresponding shapes of evil. Our dreams sometimes reveal our character, our sins, our destinies, far more clearly than our waking thoughts; for whereas by day the energies of our being are turned into artificial channels, by night our thoughts follow the bent that is most natural to them; and as man is both an immortal and a sinful being, the consequences both of his immortality and his sinfulness will sometimes be made to stand out in overpowering light, when the busy pursuits of day and of the world are not able to turn the soul from wandering towards eternity.

A morning is coming, when we shall all awake out of the sleep of this world, but the Dream of the Judgment will then be no longer a dream. The friendly warning of the dream will have passed for ever, to give place to the reality. The thrones will be set, the dead will be raised, and we shall be judged; the Great White Throne, and him that sitteth thereon, and all nations gathered before him!

> Oh to be ready, ready for that day,
> Who would not give earth's fairest toys away?

So thought Christian, when, in mingled hope and fear on account of what he had seen, he began to gird up his loins, and to address himself to his journey. The Comforter be always with thee, said the Interpreter, to guide thee in the way that leads to the city! So he went musing on his way, grateful to the good Interpreter, meditating on what he had seen, drawing out the lessons, and soliloquizing over them, and praying for Divine grace to make them profitable. In truth, the things which he had seen were some of the most precious fruits of Bunyan's sanctified genius and deep religious experience. Whoever has read Bunyan's Divine Emblems for Youth, will see at once the same hand that placed these varieties for his Pilgrim's instruction in the House of the Interpreter. Bunyan might have added to them in verses wrought with the art of a true poet, had it pleased him so to exercise his skill.

It is difficult to overstate the importance for the mind in childhood of a book that contains such pictures at once so alluring, so solemn, and instructive. We speak from experience, and from what we have heard others describe of its effect upon their minds in early youth, when we suggest the importance of children early reading the Pilgrim's Progress. It never seems so beautiful, so fascinating a book, to those who read it first in later life, as to those who, having read it in childhood, when its power over the imagination is unbounded, read it afterwards with a grave perception and understanding of its meaning. It becomes a series of holy pictures engraven on the soul in its early, simple, childlike state; and though these pictures may be afterwards covered with sin, yet some time or other their covering may be swept off, and then outshine the pictures, in all their freshness and beauty. And what is true of the Pilgrim's Progress is much more true of the Bible. Where such early impressions are made upon the mind, it would seem as if Satan works hard to destroy them; he takes the tablet, and rubs out the inscription, just as the monks of old used to erase the classics, and write over them on the same parchment their own absurd legends; but God can restore the original inscriptions, and can utterly efface the writing of the Wicked One. And sometimes the original Builder of the mind is pleased to write his own name so deep there, that though it may be covered with depravity, in which Satan afterwards engraves his, and thinks it is written in the solid rock, yet God has a previous writing, and the Holy Spirit, in a season of trouble and conviction upon the sinner, can break away that covering of depravity, and Satan's name along with it, and there shall be God's name shining, and the whole temple of the mind shall be God's living temple. See that you write God's name upon your children's minds; and in order to do this, you must use the graving tools which God himself has given you, the diamond pen of the Word of God, sharper to write with, and to cut with, than any two-edged sword, and always successful, when used with faith and prayer.

Refreshed and instructed in the House of the Interpreter, Christian sets forward on his journey. His burden is still wearisome, and some of the sights which he has seen tend to make him feel it more sensibly, and to long for deliverance. Though the highway was fenced in on either side with the wall of Salvation, yet, as the way was ascending, Christian ran with great difficulty, because of the load on his back. But now he was near his deliverance, which indeed the instructions of the Holy Spirit had prepared him to experience and receive as a reality, a lasting, commanding reality, and not a mistaken, transitory, superficial joy. There is not a more important lesson taught in this book, than that growth in grace is not to be measured by sensible comfort, that joy is not to be sought as a test or proof of grace, and that a person may be in Christ, and yet a deep sense of the burden of sin may long remain upon the soul. The teachings of the Holy Spirit are needed, and new discoveries of the plan of salvation through Christ; and only in proportion as the soul sees clearly Christ and his Cross, and is filled and absorbed with the Saviour, does the burden of sin disappear, and the happiness of the soul become deep and lasting. All the direct efforts of Christian to get rid of his burden were of no avail, nor was it till he had the fullest view of the Cross, not till that salvation completely filled his soul, that the burden fell from him. He was not seeking to be rid of it when he lost sight of it; no, he was coming up to the cross and the sepulchre, his attention was occupied with Christ, his sufferings, his death, his atoning sacrifice for sinners; and as he ran and gazed, and saw these things more clearly, and came at length quite to the foot of the cross, then his burden fell from him while he was gazing, admiring, and loving, and rolled quite into the mouth of the sepulchre, so that he saw it no more. And very much surprised was he that the sight of the cross should thus ease him of his burden. It made him glad and lightsome, and he exclaimed with a merry heart, He hath given me rest by his sorrow, and life by his death. And so, as he stood and wondered, he wept, and wept again for gratitude, sorrow, and joy. And now came to him the Three Shining Ones, as he stood looking and weeping, and they all together saluted him, Peace be to thee. The first said to him, Thy sins be forgiven thee. The second stripped him of his rags, and clothed him with change of raiment. The third also set a mark on his forehead, and gave him a roll with a seal upon it, which he bid him look to as he ran, and that he should give it in at the Celestial Gate; so they went their way. Then Christian gave three leaps for joy, and went on singing.

LECTURE EIGHTH.

Christian on the Hill Difficulty.

Happiness of Christian with his roll.—His efforts to save others.—Simple, Sloth, and Presumption.—Christian's knowledge of Character.—Formalist and Hypocrisy.—Christian climbing the Hill.—The sleep in the arbour, and the loss of his roll.—Christian weeping and searching for it.—His thankfulness at finding it.

WE left Christian light of heart, and singing for joy of his deliverance from his burden. How lightly did he now step forward, with what pleasant thoughts in his soul, with what precious views of the cross and of the way of salvation! Now it seemed to him that he should never tire. He thought of that sweet Psalm, When the Lord turned again the captivity of Zion, we were like them that dream. Sometimes he could scarcely persuade himself that it was a reality; he was almost afraid it was a dream. But then, there was his roll that had been given him, and the new dress in which the Shining Ones had arrayed him, and his heart was full of gratitude and love. He thought "he could have spoken to the very crows that sat upon the ploughed land by the wayside," to have told them of his joy, and of the preciousness of his Saviour, if they could have understood it. His heart was like the blind man's restored to sight, and just as simple and unaffected.

> Now methinks I hear him praising,
> Publishing to all around,
> Friends, is not my case amazing?
> What a Saviour I have found!

Yes, and now Christian desires to save others. The joy in his soul was no transitory sympathy or selfish hope, that would subside into indolence. It led him to set himself to work at once to win others to Christ. This is very striking. Now he would neglect no opportunity of doing good, and he did not say, when he saw some ready to perish, I am but a young Christian, but just now converted, and must wait till I have more experience, before I try to persuade others. Not at all. But the very first opportunity Christian had after his release from his burden, he faithfully employed it. As he went on, singing and making melody in his heart unto the Lord, he came to a wide level place, where he saw, a little out of the way, three men fast asleep, with fetters on their heels. Their names were Simple, Sloth, and Presumption. The first thing Christian did was to go to them and endeavour to awake them, which he thought certainly he might easily do, for their danger was clear to him, though they themselves did not seem to see it. So he cried out to them to awake, telling them that they might as well sleep on the top of a mast, for that the Dead Sea was under them, a gulf without a bottom. Awake, said he, and come away, or you will perish for ever. He furthermore told them, that if they were but willing, he would help them off with their irons, but they manifested no anxiety. He told them that if he that goeth about as a roaring lion came by, they would certainly become a prey to his teeth. In fine, he used all proper and likely means to wake them up; and they were at length so far roused as to listen to him, and answer him.

Simple said, I see no danger. That was the voice of one-third part of the world in their sins. Tell them they are sleeping on the brink of perdition, and they say, We see no danger. Sloth said, yet a little more sleep. That was the voice of another third part of the world. A little longer indulgence in sin is pleaded for, a little more quiet, ease, and indifference; wait till we have a more convenient season; a little more folding of the hands to sleep! Presumption said, Every tub must stand on its own bottom. There outspoke at least another third part of the world in their sins. Take care of your interests, and I will take care of mine. You need not trouble yourself about my salvation, I am not at all concerned but that all will go well, and I am ready to take my chance. All these classes of men Christians have to encounter in their efforts to awaken the sinner and bring him to repentance; so Christian was earnest and faithful, but all his efforts were of no avail. These persons laid themselves down to sleep again, and Christian went sorrowfully on his way, being sad to think of the danger they were in, and their insensibility to it, and their utter indifference as to the help proffered them to get them out of it.

But now there met him persons of a different sort; for behold two men came tumbling over the wall, on the left hand of the narrow way; and they made up apace to him. The name of the one was Formalist, and the name of the other Hypocrisy. It looked very suspicious to see them tumbling over the wall; so Christian asked at once where they came from, and whither they were going. Their answer was very curious. We were born in the land of Vainglory, and are going for praise to Mount Zion. Christian asked them why they did not come in at the gate, for that they who came not in by the door, but did climb up some other way, were thieves and robbers. They told him, that in their country of Vainglory, that gate was considered too far round about, so that it was their custom to make a short cut, and get over the wall. Now you will remark that Bunyan had met these characters himself, and was well acquainted with them. He is here painting from real life; indeed in every part of the Pilgrim's Progress he had but to look back through the perspective of the way he had himself been travelling, and its characters started into life, thronging the path with such number and vividness, that the difficulty was not to find portraits, but to make choice of his materials. He had also only to look into his own soul, with the wonderful clearness and accuracy with which he remembered every part of his experience, and there he found within his own past self, before he became a Christian, the portraiture of many a character introduced in his pages; the portraitures of just such characters as he would himself have become, had he stopped where they did; had he stopped at the points where he sketched and painted these developments of classes.

This is, in truth, an illustration of the meaning of that passage, "Evil men understand not judgment, but they that seek the Lord understand all things." And also of that in 1 Cor. ii. 15. We see plainly that, as a clear-sighted Christian looks back upon his own experience, he sees himself in many aspects, and through the prism of his own nature he sees a thousand others; he sees, through and through, the motives, thoughts, feelings, veils, and hiding-places of every possible variety of the children of this world, because he has been one of them. He sees some stopping with their characters in perfection at one stage of his own experience, and some at other stages; some more advanced towards the point where he himself really set out to be a Christian, and some less; but many he sees, through the perfect knowledge he has of his own past refuges of lies, evidently trusting in the same refuges; refuges where he himself would have stopped and died as a pretended Christian, had not God had mercy on him.

On the other hand, a man of the world, a wicked man, an unconverted man, cannot see beyond the line of his own experience; the things of the Christian are hidden from him, for he has never gone into them; it is a world unknown, a world hidden by a veil that he has never lifted, a region of blessedness, knowedge, and glory, where his feet have never wandered; a region of sweet fields, and living streams, and vast prospects, of which he knows nothing, and can conceive nothing. It is all like the unseen future to him. But the Christian, you will perceive, is looking back; experience illumines the path that has been passed over, and the Christian sees that path clearly, and that path embraces all the world in it, just so far as it is the broad way, in which all characters in the world are travelling. So he which is spiritual judgeth all things, but he himself is judged of no man. So, in looking back, as Bunyan did, he says, Do you see such and such an one, travelling at such a pace, with such professions and conversations? A few years ago, I was just such a person; I know him perfectly. Do you see that thief going to prison, that murderer going to execution? Now but for the grace of God I was travelling the same way. But for the grace of God there goes John Bradford. So Bunyan said of himself, in describing these two fellows, Formalist and Hypocrisy, But for the grace of God there goes John Bunyan. Nay, in describing these characters, Bunyan was just cutting out two of the pictures of his own unconverted state, to insert them into this heavenly Mosaic of his Pilgrim's Progress.

For, in point of fact, he had been himself both Formalist and Hypocrisy; he had acted both these parts in his unconverted state; and, if he had stopped there, he had lived and died a formalist and a hypocrite. I do not mean that Bunyan ever had in his character the elements of such meanness, as would take to itself deliberately the cloak of religion to cover, conceal, and practise its wickedness; that is the extreme of hypocrisy, and marks the most abandoned of all villains. But formalism itself is hypocrisy, and where a man does only deceive himself, by the concealment from himself of his own true character as a sinner, and by trusting in some other refuge than Christ, that man is a hypocrite, for he pretends to be a great deal better than he is; nay, he pretends to have goodness enough for his salvation, without coming in by the door, when God knows it is all rottenness and a lie.

Now you will remember there was a time when Bunyan was a thorough-going Churchman, without one particle of religion in his soul. He would go to Church in the morning, and worship the minister's robes, and the altar, and in the afternoon he would make the air ring with his merriment at the game of Cat. At this time, you will remember, he neither cared nor knew whether there were any Saviour or not; the complete sum of his religion was Form; nor did he even attempt to go any farther. So, certainly, here was the Formalist in perfection. At another time, he was going to heaven by an external reformation, and thought he pleased God as well as any man in England. But he declared that every thing he either did or said, was done solely out of regard to human applause; for he was filled with delight to hear his neighbours speak so well of him. Here again, certainly, was the hypocrite in perfection. So that that answer, which Formalist and Hypocrite made to Christian, Bunyan wrote down out of his old, unconverted, vainglorious heart: We come from the land of Vainglory, and are going for praise to Mount Zion.

The right way by the gate, the way by Christ and his righteousness, was deemed too far. But, said Christian, will it not be counted a trespass against the Lord of the City whither we are bound, thus to violate his revealed will? Christian is always for Scripture. But they told him that they had plenty of examples for the way they came in, and testimony for more than a thousand years; yea, the antiquity of the custom was such that every impartial judge would admit it as a thing legal. The fathers would doubtless be brought to justify it, and all antiquity was in its favour; and when such multitudes had been justified by works for more than a thousand years, they would have been fools indeed, seeing that in the land of Vainglory there was plenty of that commodity, works done to be seen of men, if they should trouble themselves about faith and the gate. Besides, if we are in, we are in, said they. Thou art only in, who didst come by the gate; and we are also in, who came over the wall; so there is no difference.

Now here is depicted to the life that pretended liberality which you so often hear in men's conversation. All persuasions, it says, are right, and we are all travelling one way; they that reject eternal punishment, and they that believe in it; they that deny the atonement, and they that receive it; they will all get to heaven at last. Ah, but, said Christian, there is a Rule, and I walk by it, the Rule of my Master; but you walk by the rude working of your own fancies. You are thieves and robbers, by the Lord's own description; and as you come in by yourselves, without the Lord's direction, you will also go out by yourselves, without the Lord's mercy.

This was a plainness, honesty, and simplicity, characteristic of Christian. But the men told him to take care of himself, and they would take care of themselves; and as to laws and ordinances, they should keep them as conscientiously as he; and as to all his pretence of inward experience, the new birth, repentance, and faith, and all that, it might do for such a ragged creature as he had been. All the neighbours knew that he had been a worthless wretch, and it was well indeed that he had got such a coat to cover his nakedness; but they had always gone well dressed, and having never been so bad as he was, needed not so great a change; their laws and ordinances would save them. So Christian told them that this inward experience, this regeneration by the Holy Spirit, this faith in Christ alone as an atoning Saviour, and this evidence of that Saviour's mercy in a renewed heart and life, were as absolutely necessary for them as for him, and that if they had come in at the gate, they would certainly have had these things also; and that when they came to the Celestial Gate, they would be shut out without them. He told them, moreover, that the Lord of the place had given him that coat which was on his back, and not any of his neighbours; and that he did indeed give it to him to hide his nakedness, for that before he had indeed been a poor, miserable, ragged, guilty sinner; but now the Lord Jesus had given him for his garment his own wisdom, righteousness, sanctification, and redemption, and had thus sealed him by his grace in such a manner, that he would know him well when he came to give in his roll at the Celestial Gate. For all this, the men cared nothing at all, but looked at each other and laughed; it was so ridiculous to them to hear Christian talking of a new birth, and of grace and faith, and the love of the Saviour. All that cant may do very well for a conventicle, said they, but we abide by respectable antiquity and the forms of our church. So they all went on, and Christian communed with himself, seeing that they both laughed at him, and could not understand him. They thought he was a harmless mystic, probably weak in his mind, and very illiterate. So he went sometimes sighingly and sometimes comfortably, but much refreshed by reading in his roll.

Together therefore they went on, till they came at the foot of the Hill Difficulty; and this is about as far as Formalist and Hypocrisy will ever go in religion. You will always find them stopping at the foot of Hill Difficulty. Formalism and Hypocrisy may always be a ridiculing and persecuting religion, but never a suffering one. At the bottom of this hill there were two other paths beside the strait one, turning off one to the left, the other to the right; and there always will be such paths where there are difficulties; there always will be ways, by which persons so disposed may avoid difficulties, and indulge themselves; but when people turn aside to go in them, it were well to note distinctly that they are not the strait and narrow way, and do not lead to heaven. Over this Hill Difficulty must Christian go. But Formalist and Hypocrisy, seeing how high and steep it was, concluded between themselves that these two convenient paths, winding off so opportunely and invitingly at the bottom, must of course meet again in the strait and narrow way on the other side of the hill, and so determined to try them.

Mark you they did not intend to quit the strait way entirely, into which they came at first by tumbling over the wall, but to come into it again, after avoiding the Hill Difficulty. And so a great many persons intend to conform to the world, or to indulge in sinful things only in certain points, only for the present distress, and then come up again, just as a boat may strike her sails in being under a bridge, and then raise them again. And a great many persons intend to come at heaven without its costing them any thing. I will not undertake to say that if Formalist and Hypocrisy had known that these by-paths would never come again into the right way, they would not have gone over the hill; perhaps they might, and not have turned aside till they came to a more fearful evil. But Christian saw them no more. The names of these paths were Danger and Destruction, and they each took one, and wandered on till they came to dreary woods and dark mountains, where they stumbled and fell, and rose no more. And herein was fulfilled that in the one hundred and twenty-fifth Psalm, "As for such as turn aside into crooked ways, the Lord shall lead them forth with the workers of iniquity."

There was a cool delicious spring at the bottom of this

Hill Difficulty, as there generally is where the Lord's people have peculiar hardships to encounter, according to the promise, "As thy day is, so shall thy strength be." There are angels for Hagar in the wilderness, quails for Elijah pursued by his enemies, springs of water in the desert, where, when God pleases, the rain shall fill the pools to give drink to his beloved ones. Unto whatever conflict or labour God calls his people, he always gives the necessary preparation thereunto. So Christian went and drank of this precious spring at the bottom of the Hill Difficulty. From the eyes of Formality and Hypocrisy it seems to have been kept sealed, or, as it was pure cold water for a thirsty soul, they, having no spiritual thirst, cared not for it; but Christian drank thereof, and was sweetly refreshed; for God hath said, "He that hath mercy on them shall lead them, even by the springs of water shall he guide them." So with this draught of the water of life, Christian, animated and invigorated, addressed himself to the hill.

At first he ran, then he had to content himself with walking, and that very wearily and slowly; but at length it became so steep, that he was fain to clamber up on his hands and knees. Sometimes it is with the greatest labour and trial, that in our Christian course we make any progress whatever. We have to clamber from duty to duty, from prayer to prayer, from chapter to chapter in God's word. It is like an invalid climbing the pyramids, and with all the assistance we can get, it is slow work. Every thing within and without seems to be against us. We wait upon the Lord, but the heart is still heavy, the air seems heavy, and we do not mount up on wings as eagles, and though we walk we are weary, and we faint if we run. Many a Christian is climbing the Hill Difficulty when you cannot see his troubles.

But the Lord does not forget to be gracious. About midway of the Hill there was a pleasant arbour, for the refreshment of weary travellers, where Christian with thankfulness sat down to rest him. And now he began to look over his evidences, and to regard with great comfort and delight the garment that the Shining Ones had given him, so that he almost forgot that he was to go any farther, or that there was any more work for him to do. He forgot the exhortation to grow in grace, and in the knowledge of our Lord and Saviour, and to press forward towards the mark for the prize of the high calling of God in Christ Jesus; and he was so well satisfied with himself, his roll, his robe, his acceptance with God, that while he was resting, the spirit of slumber came over him, and what at first he intended should only be a moment's nap, like a man asleep during sermon time in church, became a thorough deep sleep, which endured even till the twilight; and in this sleep, Christian's roll fell out of his hand. Ah, if the great adversary had been there, ill would it have fared then with poor Christian. He is fast asleep, and his roll has fallen, and the night is coming, and he is only half-way up the hill, and still he sleeps on. He that sleeps is a loser, says Bunyan in the margin; that arbour was never designed to sleep in, but to rest in. But there is One who watches over him, who will not leave him, who helpeth our infirmities. This gracious Being whispered in his ear, "Go to the ant, thou sluggard; consider her ways and be wise!" Ay, that was a timely awakening and warning—so great is the Holy Spirit's faithfulness and mercy even when we lose ourselves in slumber.

Christian could now say, in that very striking verse of Watts, which those who have such a passion for altering our familiar hymns to make them correspond to their self-constituted musical judgment, have dephlogisticated in the hymn-book:

> The little ants, for one poor grain,
> Labour, and tug, and strive;
> But we, who have a heaven to obtain,
> How negligent we live!

Awakened thus by the Spirit of God, Christian started up, and ran as fast as he could, not yet knowing that he had lost his roll, till he came to the top of the hill. We sometimes fall into a state through our own heedlessness, in which assurance is gone, and the way is prepared for great gloom and anguish, if circumstances of trial come on. And yet we may run well, even without our roll, so long as there is nothing special to alarm us. Poor Christian had to endure a great deal of sorrow by that indulgence in sleep. As he was running on, Timorous and Mistrust met him, running full of terror the other way. What is the matter, said Christian, you run the wrong way? Why, said Timorous and Mistrust, the farther we go, the more danger we meet; we had but just conquered the Hill Difficulty, when just before us we discovered two lions in the way; so we turned, and are hurrying back as fast as possible. With that they ran down the hill.

Now was Christian himself greatly afraid, for there is nothing so takes away the courage as the consciousness of guilt; and Christian, on feeling for his roll, that he might have that to comfort and sustain him amidst these dangers, found that he had lost it. And now what should he do? What had become of it? Examining himself on this point, he remembered that he had slept in the arbour, and then at once falling on his knees, he asked of God forgiveness for that foolish sleep, and then with great heaviness and sorrow of heart went back to look for his roll. Thus, when the Holy Spirit brings to mind the sins of the Christian, as he is asking himself why he has so little heavenly evidence, there is no way for him to do but to seek forgiveness, confessing his guilt. But it is a fearful thing, when the night comes on, when danger and perhaps death are drawing near, and you need all the comfort, consolation, and support that you can possibly derive from a good hope in Christ, to find that that hope is gone from the soul, to find darkness where there ought to be light.

It is not to be doubted that Bunyan was writing this experience of Christian out of his own heart; it is almost the counterpart of his own inward trials about the time of his commitment to prison, when you will remember there was great gloom upon his soul, and the things of God were hidden from him, and neither sun nor stars appeared for many days. Then there were dreadful lions in the way, nor could he see that they were chained; then he felt afraid to die, because he had no spiritual comfort. Bunyan resolved to die for Christ, whether comfort came or not, whether he found his roll or did not find it. But Christian could not go on without his roll. Oh how did he chide himself for being so foolish as to fall asleep in that place, which was erected only for a little refreshment of his weariness! When he came to the arbour, the very sight of it renewed his sorrow and shame for that foolish sleep in the day-time and in the midst of difficulty; that he should have used that arbour of rest for ease to the flesh, which the Lord of the hill had erected only for the relief of the spirits of the Pilgrims. Alas, cried he, that I should have to tread those steps with sorrow, and thrice over, which I might have trodden but once, and with delight! This is what Christians are often doing, and this evil is certainly a great one, of using for indulgence and ease to the flesh what God has given us to minister to the advancement of our spirits. We are not anxious enough to be making progress towards heaven; we are too fond of comfort, and too averse from labour.

Oh, said Christian, that I had not slept! Oh that God would have mercy on me! And now the fifty-first Psalm came into his mind, and he cried out with David, "Cast me not away from thy presence, and take not thy Holy Spirit from me. Restore unto me the joy of thy salvation, and uphold me with thy free Spirit; then will I teach transgressors thy ways, and sinners shall be converted unto thee." But oh, thought Christian, without my roll I can never have the heart to speak to another person as long as I live. What shall I do? what shall I do? He knew now that it was an evil and bitter thing to depart from the living God; yea, this experience was as dreadful to him as that under Mount Sinai. Yea, says Doddridge, in his Rise and Progress of Religion in the Soul, the anguish of broken bones is not to be compared with the wretchedness of a soul that has departed from God, when it comes to be filled with its own way. Oh that God would have mercy upon me! said Christian. "Make me to hear joy and gladness, that the bones which thou hast broken may rejoice. Hide thy face from my sins, and blot out all mine iniquities. Create in me a clean heart, O God, and renew a right spirit within me."

Oh that I knew where I might find him! said Christian. "Behold I go forward, but he is not there; and backward, but I cannot perceive him." This must always be the case, when the child of God departs from God; and if it be not so, then there is great reason to believe that the person so wandering, and yet not troubled on account of it, is not a child of God. If Christian had said within himself, when he found his roll was missing, Well, it is not essential, or I shall find it again by and by; and so had gone on, indifferent and easy, it had been enough to shew that either he was not Christian, or that much sorer evil awaited him, and sharper discipline to bring him to repentance. But he could not go on in this manner, his conscience was too tender, and his sense of divine things too vivid; and so the sorrows of death compassed him, and the pains of hell gat hold upon him; he found trouble and sorrow; and back did he go, weeping and looking for his roll, and crying, O Lord, I beseech thee, deliver my soul.

Now God sees all this in his children, and permits them to endure this distress that they may gain a lesson from it, which will last them as long as they live. But he knows what he does unto them, and just what they need. "When my spirit was overwhelmed within me, then thou knewest my way." And just so, when Christian had wellnigh given up in despair, and was setting himself down to weep, disconsolate and broken-hearted, as kind Providence would have it, looking through his tears beneath the settle, there he espied the roll, and with what trembling, eager haste did he catch it up and secure it again in his bosom! Oh, who can tell how joyful he was when he had gotten his roll again! And now returning thanks to God for directing his eye to the place where it lay (and ever should the Christian who has been wandering from God, and so has gotten into darkness, be thankful for the least ray of returning light; and ever will he, for no deliverance is so grateful to the soul as that), Christian did with joy and tears betake himself again to his journey. But he had lost a great deal of time, and it was now growing dark, and now he began again to think of what Mistrust and Timorous had told him about the lions, a thing which his misery in the loss of his roll had driven at first from his mind, just as great griefs medicine the less. Now, said Christian to himself, these beasts range abroad in the night for their prey, and if I should meet them in the dark, how should I escape being torn in pieces ?

So he went on, troubling himself greatly with these thoughts, when suddenly there rose before him like a dream a very stately palace, close by the highway side, which being within the walls of salvation, and directly where he must pass by, he knew to belong to the Lord of the way, and therefore to the Pilgrims; or at any rate, that the Pilgrims would there be welcome. Now, if he might get to that palace, and be lodged there, he would care little for the lions. But as he went forward towards the narrow passage which led up to the gate, being very closely on the watch to see the lions of Mistrust and Timorous' description, there they were, sure enough, grim and terrible. And now he thought of going back, but the porter cried out to him, reproving him for his want of strength and faith, and telling him that the lions were chained, and were suffered to be there to try the faith of Pilgrims, if they had it, and to discover if they had none. With this was Christian greatly encouraged; but with all this he went trembling and afraid, and keeping to the middle of the path; and though he heard the lions roar on him, yet they did him no harm; and when he got past them he clapped his hands, and made haste up to the porter at the entrance to the Palace Beautiful. May I lodge here to night? said he. So he was told that the Lord of the Hill himself had built this house for the relief and security of pilgrims. The porter asked Christian several questions, as who he was, and where from, and what was his name, and whither he was going, and why he came so late; all which interrogatories Christian ingenuously answered, especially the last, confessing his sinful, sorrowful sleep.

There are some important lessons to be learned from this Hill Difficulty; as, first, the folly of thinking to gain heaven without trouble and self-denial. In nothing else in this world do men ever act on this principle. If there be any great thing to be gained in this life, all men are sure that it is going to cost great effort, and they are ready to make such effort; nor is it a light thing that will turn them aside. They will go up a Hill Difficulty, without drinking at any spring but that of their sanguine expectation, and without deigning to rest in any arbour by the way, much more without losing time by sleeping in it. And if there be lions in the way, they will go at them at once; yea, if a loaded cannon stood in their path, and a bag of gold beyond it, or the cup of sinful pleasure, they would go on. If there be mountains which they cannot overtop, they will dig through them; and they will suffer days of weariness and nights of pain; they will make long pilgrimages, will expatriate themselves for years, and suffer banishment from families, friends, firesides, into strange lands, will cross oceans, and encounter perils of every name and shape, to accomplish and realize the object of their earthly ambition. And after all, what is it? A dream, a straw, a bauble, a flake of foam on the surface of a river. They pluck it, it is gone, and they are gone with it. While they snatch at it they pass into eternity, and death finishes their plans for ever.

But even the poor things they seek for in this life, they do not expect to gain without labour. And shall we expect to gain heaven without labour? Is not heaven worth labouring after? And is it not the part of wisdom so to run, not as uncertainly; so to fight, not as one that beateth the air? Now, we ought soberly to say, I expect difficulties, and I mean, by God's grace, not to be discouraged when I meet with them. They are, in truth, the very means which God must use for my discipline. It is only by meeting and overcoming them that I can be fitted for heaven. And as to the dangers in the way, the best way of safety from them is to come up boldly to them. If we stand afar off and tremble, they seem much greater than they are. If we march straight on, confiding in Christ, we always find that the lions are chained, and can only roar at us and do no harm. At all events, it is better to go forward than backward. Be not like Mistrust and Timorous. It is more dangerous to run down the Hill Difficulty than to clamber up. And he that putteth his hand to the plough and looketh back, is not fit for the kingdom of heaven.

We see here, likewise, the repetition of that lesson that nothing is so hard to bear as a wounded conscience, a mind not at peace with God. There is nothing so hard for the Christian to bear as that. And when the light of God's countenance is hidden from him by reason of sin, be you sure that there is not a creature in the world so miserable as he. But if sin and conscience can make him so miserable, who has only fallen for a season into its power, as Christian did in the arbour, and who has a Saviour to go to, and will go to him, and stay at the foot of the cross even amidst the darkness, what work must it make in that man's soul who never asked forgiveness, never went to Christ— what work will it make when sin and conscience, long hidden, concealed, sleeping, are developed, roused up, and busy in the soul? Oh! if the fire that is thus kindled begins to be noticed first not until the soul enters on the eternal world, then it will never go out! So beware how you have conscience for an enemy.

> O Conscience! who can stand before thy power?
> Endure thy gripes and agonies one hour?
> Stone, gout, strappado, racks, whatever is
> Dreadful to sense, are only toys to this.
> No pleasures, riches, honours, friends, can tell
> How to give ease in this:—'tis like to hell.
>   Call for the pleasant timbrel, lute, and harp;
> Alas! the music howls! The pain 's too sharp
> For these to charm, divert, or lull asleep:
> These cannot reach it; as the wound 's too deep.
> Let all the promises before it stand,
> And set a Barnabas at its right hand;
> These in themselves no comfort can afford;
> 'Tis Christ, and none but Christ, can speak the word.
> There goes a power with his majestic voice,
> To hush the raging storm, and charm its noise.
> Who but would fear, and love, and do his will,
> Who bids such tempests of the soul be still?
>
> FLAVEL.

LECTURE NINTH.

Christian's Fight with Apollyon

IN THE VALLEY OF HUMILIATION.

Conversation with Discretion, Prudence, Piety, and Charity.—Blessedness of Christian Communion.— Too much sometimes anticipated.— Danger of making Church-Membership salvation.— Preparation for the Christian Conflict.—Apollyon's Assault upon Christian.—The fiery darts of the Wicked One.—Entering into temptation.—Christian's passage through this valley compared with the experience of Christiana, Mercy, and the children.— Pleasantness and grace of the Valley of Humiliation to a contented and submissive mind.

We left Christian, delivered from his dangers, and relieved from his distresses for a season, at the gate of the House Beautiful. But you will observe that the porter does not admit him at once, nor without inquiry. According to the rules of the house, Watchful, the porter, rings the bell, and commends Christian to the interrogatories of a grave and beautiful damsel, called Discretion. A number of questions were put to him, and sincerely answered; and so much affectionate kindness and sympathy were manifested on the part of Discretion, that Christian had nothing to fear as to his reception. Then Discretion called for Prudence, Piety, and Charity, and after this conversation, they welcomed him into the household of Faith. There, during his delightful abode with its happy inmates, he was entertained, as the Lord of the way had provided that all pilgrims should be in his house, with the most cordial hospitality and love. He was instructed with much godly conversation, and with many edifying sights; and he was clad in a complete suit of armour, to prepare him against the dangers of the future way. On his part, he entertained the household as much as they did him, by the account he gave of his own experience thus far. Piety made him tell all that had happened in his pilgrimage, from his first setting out to his arrival at the House Beautiful. Prudence asked him about his feelings now in reference to the land of his nativity, and the habits he used to be in at the City of Destruction.

And here Bunyan has left us in no doubt as to his own views in the exposition of the controverted passage in the seventh of Romans. He shews clearly that he regards the experience there recorded as a description of the conflict between good and evil still going forward in the Christian's soul. "Do you not," asked Piety, "still bear with you some of those things that you were conversant withal in the City of Destruction?" "Might I but choose mine own things," answered Christian, "I would choose never to think of those things more; but when I would do good, evil is present with me." Bunyan was too deeply experienced in the evils of the human heart, too severely had been disciplined with the fiery darts of the Wicked one, to suffer his Christian to make any pretence whatever to perfection. Too sadly did Christian find within himself the struggle between nature and grace, to suffer him to fall into any such dream or delusion. He made no pretence to have conquered all sin, or got superior to it; but his trust was in Christ, and his supreme desire was after holiness. "But do you not find sometimes," said Prudence, "as if those things were vanquished, which at other times are your perplexity?" "Yes," said Christian, "but that is but seldom; but they are to me golden hours, in which such things happen to me." Prudence then asked him how it was, by what means he ever succeeded in vanquishing his enemies, and getting free from the disturbers of his peace?

Christian's answer is very beautiful. "When I think what I saw at the cross, that will do it; and when I look upon my broidered coat, that will do it; and when I look at my roll that I carry in my bosom, that will do it; and when my thoughts wax warm about whither I am going, that will do it." Ah, yes! it is the cross by which we conquer sin; it is the remembrance of Him who hung upon it. And he that hath this hope in him, purifieth himself as he is pure. And having these evidences and these promises, faith gets the better of inward corruptions, and overcomes also the world. Nor, lastly, is there anything more powerful to give us the victory over sin than a clear view of heavenly realities, warm thoughts about the heaven to which we are going, visions of Mount Zion above, and the innumerable company of angels, and Jesus the Mediator, the assurance that we shall be like him, for we shall see him as he is. There is no death there, nor sin, nor weariness, nor disorder; and the Christian is weary of his inward sickness, and would fain be where he shall sin no more, and with the company that shall continually cry, Holy, Holy, Holy!

After this, Charity in like manner conversed with Christian, and all the while they were at table their talk was only of the Lord of the hill, and all his grace and glory, and what he had done and suffered for them, and all his amazing endless love to poor pilgrims, and his tender care in building that house for them; and so they discoursed even till late at night, for how could they ever be wearied with such a theme! And how did Christian's heart burn within him as they spake of his Saviour's love, and suffering, and glory! It may remind us of the poet Cowper's exquisitely beautiful description of the conversation in the walk to Emmaus:—

> Ah! theirs was converse such as it behooves
> Man to maintain, and such as God approves,
> Christ and his character their only scope,
> Their subject and their object, and their hope.
> The recollection, like a vein of ore,
> The farther traced, enriched them still the more.
> O days of heaven, and nights of equal praise
> Serene and peaceful as those heavenly days
> When souls drawn upwards in communion sweet,
> Enjoy the stillness of some close retreat.

Discourse, as if released and safe at home,
Of dangers past, and wonders yet to come,
And spread the sacred treasures of the breast
Upon the lap of covenanted rest!

This was a heavenly evening for Christian, a season of blessedness long to be remembered, and to walk in the strength of it. They closed their hours of sacred converse with the sweetness of family prayer, and then betook themselves to rest; the Pilgrim they laid in a large upper chamber, whose window opened towards the sunrising; the name of the chamber was Peace, where he slept till break of day, and then he awoke and sang.

Now, after all this, can any be at a loss to understand the meaning of the House Beautiful, or that era in the life of the Pilgrim at which Christian had arrived? We think every one will see drawn in these symbols, with great beauty and delightfulness of colouring, the institution and ordinances of the visible church of Christ on earth; the fellowship and divinely blest communion, the mutual instruction and edification, the happiness, hopes, promises, foretastes, enjoyments, growth in grace, and preparation for usefulness, peculiar to this sacred heavenly kingdom, belonging to the body of Christ, and growing out of a right use of its precious privileges.

'Tis a sweet tie that binds
Our hearts in Christian love,
The fellowship of kindred minds
Is like to that above.

This was indeed to Christian something like the Mount of Transfiguration; it was good to be there. It was like the day after those six days when Jesus took Peter, and James, and John, and went up into a mountain alone, and was transfigured before them. Bunyan himself had found such a season, about the time when he united with the church of Christ in Bedford, and this glory and refreshing comfort continued with him many weeks; and his own feelings were like those of Peter:—" And Peter answered and said to Jesus, Master, it is good for us to be here; and let us make three tabernacles, one for thee, and one for

Moses, and one for Elias. For he wist not what to say, for he was sore afraid. And there was a cloud overshadowed them, and a voice came out of the cloud, saying, This is my beloved Son, hear him." "Then I saw," says Bunyan, "that Moses and Elias must both vanish, and leave Christ and his saints alone." Mount Zion also was set before Bunyan, and his heart wandered up and down as in a labyrinth of glory, through the shining mazes of that passage, "Ye are come to Mount Zion, to the city of the living God, to the heavenly Jerusalem, and to an innumerable company of angels, to the general assembly and church of the first-born, which are written in heaven; to God, the Judge of all, and to the spirits of just men made perfect; and to Jesus, the Mediator of the New Testament, and to the blood of sprinkling, that speaketh better things than that of Abel." "Through this sentence," says Bunyan, "The Lord led me over and over again; first, to this word, and then to that; and shewed me wonderful glory in every one of them. These words also have oft since that time been a great refreshment to my spirit." It was in the memory of such experience that Bunyan composed his description of Christian's entertainment in the House Beautiful.

It is not, indeed, always the case that pilgrims find their anticipations realized in entering that house. Sometimes, it may be, because they expected miracles from it, because they relied more upon it than upon Christ, because they expected from an ordinance what is only to be got from grace, or because they came to it without that discipline of spirit in prayer, and that previous lowly walk with God, and that dwelling at the foot of the cross, which is requisite. But you will observe that this house is put quite far on the way; it is obvious that Bunyan would not have his pilgrims enter the House Beautiful so soon as they get within the Wicket Gate; between the Wicket Gate and the House Beautiful, between the cross of Christ and the visible communion of saints, there was much experience, much instruction, much discipline, much difficulty, much grace. Infinitely less would Bunyan have put the visible church, the House Beautiful, *before* the Wicket Gate, making church-membership the door of heaven, as some would do, to the destruction of multitudes of souls. Baptismal regeneration, and salvation by the Lord's supper, are two of the most unscriptural, ungodly, and pernicious figments, with which Satan ever succeeded in lulling men to security in their sins. Bunyan was so cautious of every thing like this, he had so much experience in his own heart of the dangerous, damning nature of a religion of forms, and he knew so well the wiles of Satan in that way, and the tendency of men, however warned and instructed, to rest in forms, that he almost went to the contrary extreme. He made one of his best pilgrims, as we shall see, go past the House Beautiful without stopping at it. You may be sure this was because in Bunyan's time there was such a hue and cry after the church, with its glory, and exclusive privileges and forms, its baptism, prayer-book, bench of bishops. and no salvation beyond. So he made his Martyr-Pilgrim belong to no visible church at all ; nor could he more quietly and powerfully have rebuked and resisted the fatal error that to enter the House Beautiful is to save the soul, nor the wicked intolerance that would restrict salvation to membership and obedience in the Church of England.

It is well to remark here that the House Beautiful stands beside the road ; it does not cross it, so as to make the strait and narrow way run through it, so as that there is no possibility of continuing in that way without passing through it. This would have been to make a union with the visible church necessary to salvation ; and the next step after this, and a very natural consequence of it, is that of making salvation an essential property of church-membership, that of making every member of the church a saved man ; and the next step, and quite as natural, is that of making a particular church the only church, THE church, to the exclusion of all others ; and the next step, and also very natural, is the excommunication of all dissenters, and the application of such penalties and persecutions as may benevolently operate to keep men from wandering, to the ruin of their souls, into conventicles ; such penalties and persecutions as may, with loving force, and out of pure regard to the salvation of souls, and pure compassion to those who are wandering from their Holy Mother Church, compel them to come in, that there may be one visible fold and one Shepherd.

Now, had this been the case with the House Beautiful, there would have been guards posted, and prisons erected, all along the way, to arrest self-willed dissenters, and bring them back into the house, saying to them, You are not permitted to be on the way to heaven, unless you go through the House Beautiful. There you must pay tithes, for it costs the servants of the Lord of the way a great deal to keep up this Establishment, and you, under pretence of being a dissenter and yet a Christian, are not to be suffered to pass without paying toll at this Establishment. This would be the House Shameful, and not the House Beautiful. It would be the house of pride, ambition, arrogance, and persecution; and not the house of love. But, blessed be God, there is no such house on the way of our pilgrimage. They arrested John Bunyan and threw him into prison, because he chose not to enter that house, but to worship with God's people among the Baptists.

The communion of saints was never more sweetly depicted, than in Christian's sojourning in the House Beautiful. But he staid not there for pleasure; that was not the end of his journey, nor the object of it; nor did he there, as in the Arbour, use for an indulgence to the flesh what was meant for the encouragement and refreshment of the spirit. He was up by day-break singing and praying, and then they had him into the study, to shew him the rarities of the place; and the next day into the armoury, to shew him all manner of warlike furniture, which the Lord of the way had provided for pilgrims, where also he was made to see ancient things, which, if Bunyan could be here to interpret, he would doubtless tell us were intended to symbolize that divine grace by which the servants of the Lord have done so many wonderful things,—that grace which, though to the world and the Goliahs in it, it looks as foolish as David's sling and pebble stones against a giant in full armour, is yet stronger than death, and shall overcome every thing; for " the foolishness of God is wiser than men, and the weakness of God is stronger than men." And the next day they shewed him from the top of the house a far-off view of the Delectable Mountains, Immanuel's land, woods, vineyards, fruits, flowers, springs, and fountains, where from the mountain summits they told him he should see the gate of the Celestial City. Faith, said they to Christian, is the substance of things hoped for, the evidence of things not seen; and the afflictions you meet with by the way will be but light things to you, if you keep the glories of heaven in your mind's eye, and the thoughts of what you are to meet with there warm in your heart.

> I love, by faith, to take a view
> Of brighter things in heaven;
> Such prospects oft my strength renew
> When here by tempests driven.

This view Christian could enjoy with increasing clearness, and found more and more the blessedness of it, the nearer he came to the Celestial City. For God, he could say,

> For God has breathed upon a worm,
> And given me from above,
> Wings such as clothe an angel's form,
> The wings of joy and love.
> With these to Pisgah's top I fly,
> And there delighted stand,
> To view beneath a shining sky,
> The spacious promised land.
> The Lord of all the vast domain
> Has promised it to me,
> The length and breadth of all the plain,
> As far as faith can see.

So when they had had much pleasant and profitable discourse with him, as Christian was eager to go on, they would detain him no longer, but had him again into the armoury, where they clothed him from head to foot in the armour of righteousness on the right hand and on the left, sword, shield, helmet, breast-plate, *all prayer*, and shoes that would not wear out, according to faithful Paul's directions:—" Put on the whole armour of God, that ye may be able to stand against the wiles of the devil. For we wrestle not against flesh and blood, but against principalities, against powers, against the rulers of the darkness of this world, against spiritual wickedness in high places. Wherefore take unto you the whole armour of God, that ye may be able to withstand in the evil day, and having done all, to stand. Stand, therefore, having your loins girt about with truth, and having on the breastplate of righteousness, and your feet shod with the preparation of the gospel of peace ; above all, taking the shield of faith, wherewith ye shall be able to quench the fiery darts of the Wicked One ; and take the helmet of salvation, and the sword of the Spirit, which is the word of God ; praying always and watching with all prayer and supplication in the Spirit."

So, in accordance with these directions, they harnessed Christian, and sent him away armed. But, indeed, he needed all his armour, for the hour of danger was near. Great helps from the Lord, great and sweet experiences of grace, are ordinarily granted when God has some great trial for his people to pass through ; so, when the Christian has been enjoying much sacred communion with Christ, and had much of the glory of God shining into his heart in the face of Jesus, he should say to himself, Now must I be watchful; this is not merely for my comfort, but to prepare me for what is to come, for labours and for conflicts ; and if I be not wary, my very spiritual enjoyments will put me off my guard and make me proud or self-indulgent. Now must I keep in my hand the weapon of ALL PRAYER. So was Christian in need, for Apollyon was near.

And first, he had to go down into the Valley of Humiliation, and this itself was hard and dangerous work, for the House Beautiful stood on a mount, as it were, even above the Hill Difficulty, and the humbling of the soul before God is as hard a work as climbing that hill. So Discretion, Piety, Prudence, and Charity, all must needs accompany Christian down into that Valley ; he had need of them all, and of their sweet discourses by the way ; and by their help, going warily, he got down to the bottom of the hill. Here, therefore, kindly giving him refreshments for the way, they bade him God speed, and he went on.

On very many accounts, this going down into the Valley of Humiliation is extremely difficult; and few indeed there be, who do not, like Christian, get some slips by the way. Satan here also hath an advantage in representing that, in going down so low, we are going out of the way of influence and usefulness. He tells us that great designs for God cannot be accomplished in the Valley, and he makes it appear as if we were going into darkness, or out of the world. He tells us that such a light as ours ought to be set on a very tall candlestick; and he sets that bold fellow Shame to work upon us, as upon Faithful, and sometimes to go with us quite through the Valley. And if he succeeds in creating an inward discontent and repining in Christian, then, a little further on, he is very likely to bestride the path as Apollyon, brandishing his flaming darts. So, in going down into this valley, a man must say within himself, What have I to do with dictating? It is God who knows what is best, and not I. He knows what is best for me, and what is most for his own glory. If I be submissive to him, he will make what use of me he can; and though I may miss my purpose, he will be sure not to miss his; and what more can I ask or wish for? My business now is SUBMISSION.

> But that thou art my wisdom, Lord,
>   And both mine eyes are thine,
> My mind would be extremely stirred
>   For missing my design.
>
> Were it not better to bestow
>   Some place and power on me?
> Then should thy praises with me grow,
>   And share in my degree.
>
> But when I thus dispute and grieve,
>   I do resume my sight,
> And pilfering what I once did give,
>   Disseize thee of thy right.
>
> How know I, if thou shouldst me raise,
>   That I should then raise thee?
> Perhaps great places and thy praise
>   Do not so well agree.
>
> Wherefore unto my gift I stand;
>   I will no more advise:
> Only do thou lend me a hand,
>   Since thou hast both mine eyes.
>
> GEORGE HERBERT.

This is all we need,—the Lord's guidance; then like little children to follow him, whether it be up the Hill Difficulty, or through the Valley of Humiliation. If it be he who raises us high, he also will keep us from falling; if it be he who lays us low, then we have no business to murmur, but simply to say to ourselves,

> How know I, if thou shouldst me raise,
> That I should then raise thee?

Now, good Christian, thou art no longer on the mount, and here, in the depth of this Valley, thou art to meet thine enemy, and try thine armour. Bunyan knew this from experience; and here, for the much better understanding of this conflict of Christian with Apollyon, the reader of the Pilgrim's Progress ought to turn to the history of Bunyan's own temptations in the Grace Abounding; for this passage, and that which follows it, of the Valley of the Shadow of Death, are written, as it were, out of Bunyan's own heart, and describe things which some Christians know not how to understand, but by the experience of others. You will find, from the perusal of Bunyan's own spiritual life, that he has here brought together, in the assault of Apollyon upon Christian, many of the most grievous temptations with which his own soul was beset, as also in Christian's answers against them, the very method of defence which he himself was taught by divine grace in the midst of the conflict. It is here condensed into a narrow and vivid scene, but it extended over years of Bunyan's life; and the wisdom that is in it, and the points of experience illustrated, were the fruit of many months of painfulness, danger, and desperate struggle with the adversary, which he had to go through.

This foul fiend, Apollyon, came across the field to meet Christian, just after he had had sweet evidence of his salvation from heaven, with many golden seals thereon, all hanging in his sight. "God," says Bunyan, "can tell how to abase us, and to hide pride from man. For after the Lord had in this manner thus graciously delivered me, and had set me down so sweetly in the faith of his holy gospel, and had given me such strong consolation and blessed evidence from heaven, touching my interest in his love through Christ, the Tempter came upon me again, and that with a more grievous and dreadful temptation than before." Now then, the question with Christian was, whether to go back or to stand his ground; but he considered, what it were well every Christian should remember, especially in times of danger, that though he was well armed in front, he had no armour for his back. God has given us a shield and a breastplate, and the command to stand; but no provision for flight, no defence in running, nor any safety even in looking back. So thought Christian, if it were only to save my life, I had better face my enemy; for if I run he is sure to follow, and so to pierce me. So forward he went, and Apollyon met him with his dragon wings and a disdainful smile, and a rough question where he came from, and whither he was going. Christian told him plainly that he came from the City of Destruction, which was the place of all evil, and that he was going to Mount Zion above. Apollyon told him he was a reprobate, and one of his subjects, and that he would certainly have him in his service.

Christian told him that his wages were such as a man could not live on, for that the wages of sin is death, and therefore he would not serve him. Apollyon told him that he would give him better wages, if he would go back and serve him. "Sometimes," says Bunyan of his own meeting with the Adversary, " he would cast in such wicked thoughts as these, that I must pray to him, or for him; I have thought sometimes of that, Fall down, or if thou wilt fall down and worship me." Christian told him that whereas he once walked according to the god of this world, he now, by divine grace, had become the servant of Christ, the Lord's freeman. Apollyon told him a great many had professed to do so, but had turned back, and if he would, then it should go well with him. Bunyan was, at one time, tempted to content himself with false opinions, as that there should be no day of judgment, that sin was no such grievous thing, and that present ease was all he need seek after. But then the thoughts of death and the judgment would come upon him. Christian told Apollyon that he could not go back from Christ's service and be forgiven; but that Christ would forgive all his sins in Satan's service ; and in fine, said Christian, I am his servant, and I love him, and will follow him. Then did Apollyon plead the hard lot and grievous ends of Christians in this life ; but Christian told him they had their glory in the life to come. Then did Apollyon accuse Christian of all the sins he had committed since setting out to be a Pilgrim ; and this distressed Christian greatly, but still he had faith to say that he had heartily repented of those sins, and that they would certainly be forgiven by the Prince of glory.

Then did Apollyon, with dreadful rage and blasphemies, set upon Christian, and launched a flaming dart at his breast; but Christian caught it on his shield. And now the fiery darts of the Wicked One fell as thick as hail, and poor Christian, wounded in many places, grew weaker and weaker, and was almost spent, his Enemy still pressing upon him, but still kept at bay by the Sword of the Spirit in Christian's hand. Among the flaming darts which Apollyon cast in, were whole floods of blasphemies against God, Christ, and the Holy Scriptures ; and many accursed suggestions, with such a fast seizure upon Christian's spirit, and so overweighing his heart with their number, continuance, and fiery force, that he felt as if there were nothing else but these from hour to hour within him, and as though there could be no room for any thing else ; and they made him conclude that God had, in very wrath to his soul, given him up to them, to be carried away with them, as with a mighty whirlwind. The only thing that prevented utter desperation was, that Christian could still perceive, by the hatefulness of these suggestions to his soul, that there was something in him that refused to embrace them. But this consideration he then only had, when Apollyon relaxed a little, for otherwise the noise, strength, and force of these temptations did drown, overflow, and, as it were, bury all such thoughts, or the remembrance of any such thing.

What made the fight a thousand times worse for poor Christian was, that many of these hellish darts were tipped by Apollyon's malignant ingenuity with sentences from Scripture, made to flame just like the fiery darts of the Wicked One, so that Christian could see no difference, and thought that all the sentences of Scripture stood against him. Yea, it seemed as if the air was full of wrathful passages of God's word, showering down as a fiery storm into Christian's soul. And now Apollyon, following up his advantage, threw a fiery dart, which made Christian think that he had committed the unpardonable sin; and the dart was tipped with this passage, "For you know how that afterwards he found no place of repentance, though he sought it carefully with tears." Also another great and dreadful dart with this, "It is impossible for those once enlightened, if they shall fall away, to renew them again unto repentance." Also another flaming dart with this, "He that shall blaspheme against the Holy Ghost hath never forgiveness, no, never."

Moreover, what weakened Christian more than any thing else, was the entrance into his soul of those dreadful suggestions against the Scriptures, so that by reason of unbelief he could not use with much power the Sword of the Spirit which was in his hand, notwithstanding that all this while these fearful sentences which Apollyon did cast at him burned in his soul like fire, so that Christian thought he should be bereft of his wits.

And now Apollyon, seeing his chance, gathered close to him, and wrestling with him, gave him a dreadful fall, so that his sword flew out of his hand. And now he was indeed gone; and now, said Apollyon. I am sure of thee; and he so pressed upon him that Christian was in despair. Darkness came over him, and he could see nothing but the dreadful face of the Fiend. But, as God would have it; (mind this, *as God would have it*, for it was only God's sovereign interposing mercy that could help Christian now;) as God would have it, just as Apollyon, with his knee on Christian's breast, was raising his arm to strike a dart quite through him, and make an end of him, Christian nimbly reached out his hand for his Sword, and caught it, saying, "Rejoice not against me, O mine Enemy! When I fall, I shall arise!" And with that he gave him so deadly and powerful a thrust, even while he was bending over him for his destruction, that Apollyon fell back, as one that had received his mortal wound. And then Christian sprang up, as a new man, and made at him again with this flaming promise, "Nay, in all these things we are more than conquerors, through him that loved us!" Then Apollyon, with hideous yelling and roaring, spread his dragon wings, and Christian saw him no more.

This was indeed a most terrific conflict. May God shield us all from such encounters with the great Adversary! With the delineation of Christian's own fight, I have mingled the descriptions of Bunyan's conflicts with the same Adversary, as recorded in the Grace Abounding. Christian, as well as Bunyan, was certainly brought to the very verge of perdition, but it was for the sake of after glory, and One there was who would not suffer him to be tempted beyond what he was able to bear, but stood by him, though invisible, and delivered him out of the mouth of the lion. But oh the sighs and groans that burst from Christian's heart in the fierceness of the conflict! "I never," says the Dreamer, "saw him all the while give so much as one pleasant look, till he perceived he had wounded Apollyon with his two-edged sword; then indeed he did smile and look upward; but 'twas the dreadfullest sight that ever I saw." Oh, with what tears of gratitude did Christian thank God for his deliverance; and then there came to him a divine hand, with leaves from the Tree of Life for his healing; and then having partaken of the refreshments given him in the House Beautiful, he addressed himself to his journey, for this was no place for delay, where such enemies were to be met with. So on through the Valley he went, with his drawn sword in his hand, the which, though he lost it once, had done him such mighty and precious service in the battle with Apollyon. It was best to be prepared, for who knows, thought he, what other enemy may be at hand. And indeed the place whence Apollyon came was very near, but Christian met with no other fiend or dragon quite through the Valley of Humiliation.

Now, terrible as this conflict is, it will never do to regard it in any other light than as an example of what every immortal soul has to encounter, that resolutely sets out for heaven. There is a conflict in this world between heaven and hell, sin and holiness, life and death, Christ and Satan, good angels and bad, good men, reprobates, and demons. There is a conflict between the hosts of heaven and the hosts of hell *for* the soul, and a conflict between grace and nature, good and evil, the Spirit of God and the spirit of worldliness *in* the soul. Eternal life or eternal death depends upon the issue. The soul's great Adversary is one of inconceivable power, skill, and malignity. There is but one other being who is able to cope with him, and even that Almighty and glorious Being, to accomplish his wondrous plan and purpose, became like one of us, yet without sin, and in our nature became obedient unto death, that he might destroy him that had the power of death, even the devil. There is therefore no way for Christ's disciples to overcome this Adversary but by the blood of the Lamb, and the word of their testimony in regard to redemption.

To some men Satan reveals himself more clearly than to others, assaults them more violently, and makes them feel more of his power and malignity. But all men know what it is to enter into temptation, and when that is done, Satan is not far off. Apollyon is near. Therefore our blessed Lord, in the prayer he has taught us, puts the two petitions in company, "Lead us not into temptation, but deliver us from the Evil One." And Satan is called the Tempter, and the shield of faith is given to the Pilgrim for this very purpose, that he may be able to quench all the fiery darts of the Wicked One. Now, there is enough of sin in every man's own heart to tempt him, and "every man is tempted when he is led away of his own lust and enticed." And when a man thus goes after his sins, he rather tempts Satan than Satan tempts him. There is no need for Apollyon to advance towards such a man, for such an one is coming over to Apollyon; he rather enters into the devil, than the devil into him. A man is waited for of Satan, when he enters into temptation; and there is much in that expression, *enter into*. Our blessed Lord never said, Pray that ye be not tempted, but, Watch and pray that ye enter not into temptation,—that ye enter not within it, as a cloud surrounding you and taking away your light, and leading you to deceive you,—that ye enter not into temptation, into its power, into its atmosphere, into its spirit, for when that is done, the soul is weakened and easily conquered.

Men that are led away of their own lusts, that are under the power of a besetting sin, or that are utterly careless and insensible, do not need to be tempted of the devil; he can safely leave them to themselves, for he has a friend within the citadel. He need look after such men only once in a while; for, going on as they do, they are sure of ruin. But good men, and especially eminently good men, such as Bunyan and Luther, he well knows cannot be safely left, inasmuch as the grace of God in them overcomes ordinary temptation, and therefore such ones are made to feel the power of his fiery darts. Apollyon attacked Christian, when Formalist and Hypocrisy, had they passed through that Valley, would have passed without any molestation at all. Moreover, Faithful passed through it without seeing or hearing any thing of Apollyon; and also all the Valley of the Shadow of Death beyond, Faithful passed in clear sunshine, so that Bunyan does not mean to represent every Christian as subject to such fierce temptations of the devil as he himself was called to endure.

Besides, it is proper to compare this passage of Christian through the Valley of Humiliation, and the dread conflict with Apollyon in it, with the sweet and pleasant passage of Mercy, Christiana, and her children, under the care of Mr Greatheart, through the same place. Bunyan evidently intends to represent that according to the degree of humility and contentedness with God's allotments in the heart of the Christian, will be the degree of ease, security, or delightfulness with which this Valley of Humiliation will be passed through. In going down into this Valley, Christian is represented as having had some slips, though accompanied by Discretion, Piety, Charity, and Prudence; and these slips are stated in the Second Part to have been the cause of his meeting with Apollyon; "for they that get slips there, must look for combats here; and the Scripture saith, He that exalteth himself shall be abased, but he that humbleth himself shall be exalted." If those slips were the fruit of discontent and self-exaltation, then it is evident that Christian needed the sore buffets of the Adversary, or something equivalent, to humble him; just as unto Paul was given a thorn in the flesh, the messenger of Satan, to preserve him from being exalted by the abundance of the revelations made unto him. But for whatever reason, the Pilgrims under Mr Greatheart found this Valley of Humiliation to be one of the most delightful places in all their pilgrimage.

There is also another character, exquisitely drawn by Bunyan in his Second Part—that of good Mr Fearing, who was so taken with the beauty, peacefulness, and security of this pleasant valley, that he would fain have spent his whole life there; it suited his deadness to the world, and his timid, retiring spirit, so aloof it was from all the cares and vanities of life, and all the temptations of the devil. " Yea, I think there was a kind of sympathy betwixt that valley and him; for I never saw him better in all his pilgrimage than he was in that valley. Here he would lie down, embrace the ground, and kiss the very flowers that grew in this valley. He would now be up every morning by break of day, tracing and walking to and fro in the valley. But when he was come to the entrance of the Valley of the Shadow of Death, I thought I should have lost my man: not for that he had any inclination to go back; that he always abhorred; but he was ready to die for fear. Oh, the hobgoblins will have me! the hobgoblins will have me! cried he; and I could not beat him out on't. He made such a noise and such an outcry here, that had they but heard him, it was enough to encourage them to come and fall upon us. But this I took very great notice of, that this valley was as quiet when we went through it as ever I knew it before or since. I suppose those enemies here had now a special check from our Lord, and a command not to meddle till Mr Fearing had passed over it."

Now it is manifest that however pleasant the Valley of Humiliation may be in itself, yet if a man may bring discontent in his own heart, and a proud mind into it, it will be filled, to him, with enemies, and Apollyon will be very sure to assault him there. But the passage of Christiana, Mercy, and the children, through this valley, was, as I have said, most delightful. And in the description of it, as they found it, Bunyan has, if possible, exceeded himself in beauty, that description being one of the finest chapters in either part of the pilgrimage, and sprinkled with snatches of true poetry. "Christiana thought she heard in a grove, a little way off on the right hand, a most curious melodious note, with words much like these :—

> Through all my life thy favour is
> So frankly shewn to me,
> That in thy house for ever more
> My dwelling-place shall be.

And listening still, she thought she heard another answer it, saying,—

> For why? the Lord our God is good:
> His mercy is for ever sure;
> His truth at all times firmly stood,
> And shall from age to age endure.

So Christiana asked Prudence who it was that made those curious notes. They are, said she, our country birds; they sing these notes but seldom, except it be in the spring, when the flowers appear, and the sun shines warm, and then you may hear them all day long. I often, said she, go out to hear them; we also ofttimes keep them tame in our house. They are very fine company for us when we are melancholy; also, they make the woods and groves and solitary places desirous to be in."

"We need not be so afraid of this valley, said Mr Greatheart, for here is nothing to hurt us, unless we procure it for ourselves. The common people, when they hear that some frightful thing has befallen such a one in such a place, are of opinion that that place is haunted by some foul fiend or evil spirit; when, alas! it is for the fruit of their own doing that such things do befall them there. But this Valley of Humiliation is the best and most fruitful piece of ground in all these parts. It is meadow-ground, and in the summer-time a man may feast his eyes with that which will be delightful to him. Behold how green this valley is, also how beautiful with lilies! I have known many labouring men that have got good estates in the Valley of Humiliation; for God resisteth the proud, but giveth grace to the humble; for indeed it is a very fruitful soil, and doth bring forth by handfuls. Some also have wished that the next way to their Father's house were here, that they might be troubled no more with hills or mountains to go over; but the way *is* the way, and there is an end.

Now, as they were going along and talking, they spied a boy feeding his father's sheep. The boy was in very mean clothes, but of a fresh and well-favoured countenance; and as he sat by himself, he sang. Hark, said Mr Greatheart, to what the Shepherd's boy saith: So they hearkened, and he said,—

> He that is down needs fear no fall;
> He that is low no pride;
> He that is humble ever shall
> Have God to be his guide.
>
> I am content with what I have,
> Little be it or much;
> And, Lord, contentment still I crave,
> Because thou savest such.
>
> Fulness to such a burden is
> Who go on pilgrimage.
> Here little, and hereafter bliss,
> Is best, from age to age.

Then said their guide, Do you hear him? I will dare to say this boy lives a merrier life, and wears more of that herb called hearts-ease in his bosom, than he that is clad in silk and velvet."

In this valley, says Bunyan, our Lord formerly had his country-house; he loved much to be here; he loved also to walk these meadows, for he found the air was pleasant. Besides, here a man shall be free from the noise and from the hurryings of this life; all states are full of noise and confusion; only the Valley of Humiliation is that empty and solitary place. Here a man shall not be so let and hindered in his contemplation, as in other places he is apt to be. This is a valley that nobody loves to walk in but those that love a pilgrim's life. And though Christian had the hard hap to meet here with Apollyon, and to enter with him on a brisk encounter; yet, I must tell you that in former times men have met with angels here, have found pearls here, and have in this place found the words of life.

Mercy thought herself as well in this valley as ever she had been in all their journey. "The place, methinks, suits with my spirit. I love to be in such places, where there is no rattling with coaches, no rumbling with wheels; methinks here one may, without much molestation, be thinking what he is, whence he came, what he has done, and to what the King has called him. Here one may think and break the heart, and melt in one's spirit. They that go rightly through this Valley of Baca, make it a well; the rain, that God sends down from heaven upon them that are there, also filleth the pools. To this man will I look, saith the King, even to him that is humble, and of a contrite spirit, and who trembleth at my word."

Mercy was right in her preference of this sweet valley. The few noises here heard were as the voices of heaven to shepherds watching their flocks by moonlight.

> Stillness, accompanied by sounds so soft,
> Charms more than silence. Meditation here
> May think down hours to moments. Here the heart
> May give a useful lesson to the head,
> And Learning wiser grow without his books.

This retired and lowly vale was a scene for a spirit like Cowper's to linger in; though his soul was long in the Valley of the Shadow of Death. Strange, that such a discipline should have been necessary for such a mind! This Valley of Humiliation, as Christiana and Mercy found it, Cowper has described more beautifully than any other writer that ever lived.

> Far from the world, O Lord, I flee,
> From strife and tumult far;
> From scenes where Satan wages still
> His most successful war.
>
> The calm retreat, the silent shade,
> With prayer and praise agree;
> And seem by thy sweet bounty made
> For those who follow thee.

> There, if thy Spirit touch the soul,
>   And grace her mean abode,
> Oh with what peace and joy and love,
>   She communes with her God!
>
> Then, like the nightingale, she pours
>   Her solitary lays
> Nor asks a witness of her song,
>   Nor thirsts for human praise.

Now if you wish for a commentary in plain prose on the sweetness of Bunyan's delineation of this Valley, you may find it in the Dairyman's Daughter, or in the Shepherd of Salisbury Plain. But it is very important to remember that those who would find a foretaste of heavenly rest in this Valley, must bring into it, in their own hearts, the spirit of Heaven; then, and not otherwise, is it a Valley of Peace. When God's discipline discloses to a man "the plague of his own heart," then he is very apt to lay the evil to the score of circumstances, instead of the inveterate diseased heart, which needed so much, and perhaps such violent medicine for its healing. Oh, cries one, if I were only in a different situation, how easy it would be to live near to God! Ah, cries another, if I were in the place of this or that happy individual, how easy it would be to adorn my profession! Every thing in my very circumstances would lead me to it! Oh, exclaims another, if I had the health of such an one, how easy it would be to rise above my difficulties and walk with God! And I, complains another, if my occupation did not so absorb me, could be as godly as I ought to be! Oh, if I were in the place of my minister, how holy I would become!

Ah! I would, and I would, and I would, if it were so, and if it were so, and if it were only so! Here, dear friend, is the very plague of your own heart revealing itself. You are discontented with your situation. You are not submissive to the trials God has laid upon you. And, instead of seeking to be delivered from your heart-plague, you are only casting about to find some position, if possible, where it will not have occasion to vex you; where you suppose, in fact, that it will be easier, that it will cost less self-denial to serve

Christ than it does now. But remember that you are not called to be holy in another's situation, but your own; and if you are not now faithful to God in the sphere in which he has placed you, you would not, probably, be any more faithful, let him place you where he might. For he that is faithful in that which is least, is faithful also in much; and he that is neglectful in that which is least, is neglectful also in much. And as to circumstances repressing the plague of your own heart, they would only change its exhibition a little. The plague is in your heart, and not in your circumstances. Prosperous circumstances might, it is true, hide that plague; in a different situation it might have been concealed from yourself, but would that be any gain? Would you really be any the better for that? The revelation of the evil might only be deferred till it should work your ruin. How much better it is to know it in season, and be humbled before God, though it be at the cost of ever so much suffering!

And remember that those whose happy lot you, under the influence of this envious plague in your own heart, deem so desirable, if they are really living near to God where they are, would also have been very holy in your situation. Take Mr Wilberforce, for example, a Christian in a sphere of life in society in all respects desirable and delightful in regard to this world, and living in that sphere to the glory of his Saviour. Now you may perhaps think if you could only change situations with such a man, O how easy it would be to conquer the plague of your own heart; how little should you feel it, how easy it would be, in such a conspicuous situation, with all your wishes gratified, to shine to the glory of your Redeemer. You could do it, you think, and it would cost you no self-denial at all. But in your present situation it is a hard thing to be a living Christian. Now remember that if a man like Mr Wilberforce could change situations with you, he would be a very holy and happy man where you perhaps are vexed and discontented, and you, in his place, might be a very worldly and ambitious man, where he was humble and prayerful. Be assured, it is not place, nor opportunities, nor circumstances, that make character or minister grace, but it is rather character that makes circumstances, and grace that makes place.

So the next time you detect your heart, under the influence of the plague that is in it, saying to you like a concealed devil, O if I were in such or such a one's place, how much good I could do, or how holy a person I could become, just think of some eminent saint, and say, If that person were in my place, how much nearer he would live to God than I do, how many opportunities that I waste he would use for his Master's glory, how he would fill my little sphere, that now is so dark, with brightness and happiness! And you, if you will, may do the same.

LECTURE TENTH.

Christian in the Valley of the Shadow of Death.

Sympathy with spiritual distresses.—The power of prayer.—Bunyan's own temptations depicted in Christian's distresses.—The similar experience of Job, and that of David.—The breaking of the light.—Comparison of the experience of Christian with that of Christiana and Mercy in this Valley.—The uses of trials.—Effect of the hiding of God's countenance from the soul.—Christian's meeting with Faithful.

We are naturally less affected with sympathy for men's spiritual distresses, than we are for their temporal or bodily evils. The reason is to be found in our want of spiritual experience, and in the fact that we habitually look at, and are moved by, the things which are seen, and not the things which are unseen. We are creatures of sense, and therefore a great battle, when a kingdom is to be lost or won, affects us more deeply than the far more sublime and awful conflict, where the soul and the kingdom of heaven are to be lost or won for ever.

I have stood upon the sea-shore, in a dreadful storm, and have watched the perils of a noble frigate, about to be cast upon the rocks, holding by only her last anchor, plunging and pitching amidst mountainous breakers, as if she would shoot like a stone to the earth's centre. One after another I have watched her masts cut away, to see if that would not save her. The shore was lined with spectators, trembling, affrighted, weeping, unable to do any thing, yet full of anxiety and sympathy.

Now, the sight of an immortal soul in peril of its eternal

interests, beset with enemies, engaged in a desperate conflict, with hell opening her mouth before, and fiends and temptations pressing after, is a much more sublime and awful spectacle. A spiritual bark in the tempest, on the ocean of life, struggling at midnight through furious gales and waves, that by the lightning flashes are seen every instant, ready to swallow her up, has nothing to compare with it in solemn interest. But of all those multitudes of intensely anxious spectators watching the frigate, on a rock-bound shore, ready to perish, there was scarcely here and there one, who could have been persuaded to look with the spiritual vision at spiritual realities, or to listen to the most vivid descriptions of the danger of the soul, amidst its struggle with its enemies: scarcely one, who would even understand the danger of the costly spiritual vessel about to be wrecked for eternity, and still less any who would sympathize with the distresses of such a soul.

And yet, for one spectator watching the ship in a storm on the Mediterranean, there were thousands tracing the course of such a soul as Bunyan's, out amidst the storms of sin and temptation, with fiends flying through the gloom, with fiery darts hurtling the air, with sails rent, and the sea making breach after breach over the vessel. Angels, that see from heaven to earth, are busy, though we are blind. Clouds of witnesses survey the course of the Pilgrim; and when he passes through a place like the Valley of the Shadow of Death, there are, we have reason to believe, more good angels than bad ones attending him, though he does not see them, by reason of the darkness. If he has not earthly sympathy, he has heavenly; and all the earthly sympathy he does get is heavenly, for it comes from God's own Spirit in the soul. They that have been new-born, understand his terrors: they know that there is nothing to be compared with the peril of the soul beset by its great Adversary on the way to heaven; nor any anguish to be mentioned along with that which is occasioned in the soul by the hiding of God's countenance. "When he giveth quietness, who then can make trouble, and when he hideth his face, who then can behold him? Whether it be done against a nation, or against a man only!"

LECTURE TENTH.

"Herein," says an excellent old writer, discoursing on the case of a child of light walking in darkness, "believers wrestle not alone with flesh and blood, and the darkness thereof, but do farther conflict also with those spiritual wickednesses, the Princes of Darkness, about their interest in heavenly privileges, even with Satan and his angels, whom the Apostle compares to a roaring lion, seeking whom he may devour. And like as when God makes the natural darkness, and it is night, then the young lions creep forth, and roar after their prey, as the Psalmist says, so do these roaring lions, now when God hath withdrawn the light of his countenance, and night comes on, and these damps and fogs of jealousies and guilt begin to arise out of a man's own heart, then come these forth and say, as David's enemies said in his distress, 'Come, let us now take him, for God hath forsaken him, let us now devour him, and swallow him up with darkness and despair.' And as God says of those enemies of his church, 'I was but a little displeased, and they helped forward the affliction;' so, when God is angry with his child, and but a little doth hide his face for a moment, yet Satan watcheth that hour of darkness, as Christ calls it, and joins his power of darkness to this our natural darkness, to cause, if possible, blackness of darkness, even utter despair, in us."

It is much such a picture as this, that Bunyan, our great master of spiritual allegory, hath set forth in such glowing colours, in the passage of his Christian through the Valley of the Shadow of Death. It is night; night in Christian's soul, and therefore night in this Valley. He is walking in the path of duty, and no forebodings of evil, though he had them abundantly, can turn him back; and yet, it is night in him, and night around him. Gloomy dark mountains shut in the horizon; the chill air penetrates his soul with images of the storm before it breaks on him; the path is exceedingly narrow, and on either side there are terrible pitfalls and quagmires, which must needs prove fatal to any that fall therein. What can Christian do? He is plainly in the case represented in the prophet Isaiah, being here, as I said, in the way of duty, and in the path direct to the Celestial

City. "Who is among you that feareth the Lord, that walketh in darkness and hath no light? Let him trust in the name of the Lord, and stay upon his God." There is but one thing for him to do, and that is, to grope his way forward with fear and trembling, remembering that God can, if he will, save him even here; and that, even if he were in kings' palaces, and God would not save him, he would be no better off than in the midst of that Valley. Besides, should a man whom God had delivered from the hand of Apollyon, be afraid of any of the fiends of darkness, or fear to trust God's mercy in the midst of them?

There are Christians, who, as Bunyan says, are strangers to much combat with the devil; and such cannot minister help to those who come, as Christian did, under his assaults. No man is introduced to the aid of Christian in all these severe conflicts; all the help he finds is in God only; direct to Christ he must go, for there is no other helper. This was Bunyan's own experience. While himself under the assaults of Satan, in the midst of this Valley of the Shadow of Death, he did at one time venture to break his mind to an ancient Christian. This was a good man, but not one of deep experience, and evidently unable to enter into Bunyan's difficulties or to understand his state of mind. Bunyan told this man that one of his dreadful fears was that he had sinned the sin against the Holy Ghost; and the man answered him that he thought so too! This was indeed but cold comfort, and the man that could administer it must have had a most narrow mind, as well as an insensible, unsympathizing heart; but you often meet with this want of tenderness among certain spiritual comforters, who take severity and want of feeling to be marks of faithfulness.

Poor Bunyan was forced again from man to God. "Wherefore I went to God again as well as I could, for mercy still. Now also did the Tempter begin to mock me in my misery;" and under this mockery, even the free, full, and gracious promises of the Gospel were as a torment to Bunyan, for the Tempter suggested that they were not for him, because he had sinned against and provoked the Mediator through whom they were given, and also that his sins were not among the number of those for which the Lord Jesus died upon the cross. He was as if racked upon the wheel; he was tossed to and fro like the locust, and driven from trouble to sorrow. Every part of the Word of God seemed against him; he was as one shut up in a house in flames, and running first to one door then to another for egress, but they are all fast barred against him. Nor could he, by reason of his own unbelieving fears, succeed, by any use he could make of the Scriptures, in driving the Tempter away from him. It was even suggested that it was in vain for him to pray; nevertheless, he kept crying out for mercy, and in answer to prayer, notwithstanding all that Satan could do, deliverance came. It must be this experience which Bunyan has in mind, when he makes Christian to pass hard by the mouth of hell in the midst of the Valley of the Shadow of Death, beset with fears and distresses, which he could put to flight by no use he could make of the Word of God. "Now, thought Christian, what shall I do? And ever and anon the flame and smoke would come out in such abundance, with sparks and hideous noises (things that cared not for Christian's sword, as did Apollyon before), that he was forced to put up his sword, and betake himself to another weapon, called All-Prayer; so he cried in my hearing, O Lord, I beseech thee, deliver my soul."

So did Bunyan cry unto God in the midst of his distresses. "Will the Lord cast off for ever? and will he be favourable no more? Is his mercy clean gone for ever? doth his promise fail for evermore? Hath God forgotten to be gracious? hath he in anger shut up his tender mercies?" And that promise sustained Bunyan, "My grace is sufficient for thee;" though it was long indeed before he could take fast hold upon it, or enjoy to the full its abundance of blessing. Long was he in passing through the Valley of the Shadow of Death; much longer than it seems to take Christian to grope his way out of its darkness. And, as you will observe, that Christian's conflict with Apollyon in the Valley of Humiliation lies in the stage immediately before the Valley of the Shadow of Death, so that he has to pass from the one directly to the other without any interval, save in the precious season in which the hand came to him with leaves from the tree of life for his healing; so it was with Bunyan himself: so it had been in his own experience. He had two distinct, long, and dreadful seasons of temptation to pass through, each of them lasting for more than two years,—the first more nearly resembling this dreadful conflict, hand to hand, with Satan, with Apollyon, and the second more fully depicted in Christian's fearful journey through this Valley of Death, after that conflict. There was but a short interval of ease and peace between them. "By the strange and unusual assaults of the Tempter," says Bunyan, " my soul was like a broken vessel, driven as with the winds, and tossed sometimes headlong into despair: sometimes upon the covenant of works, and sometimes to wish that the new covenant and the conditions thereof might, so far as I thought myself concerned, be turned another way and changed. But in all these I was as those that jostle against the rocks—more broken, scattered, and rent. Oh the unthought-of imaginations, frights, fears, and terrors, that are effected by a thorough application of guilt yielding to desperation! This is as the man that hath his dwelling among the tombs with the dead, who is always crying out and cutting himself with stones." " Now was the word of the gospel forced from my soul, so that no promise or encouragement was found in the Bible for me. I had cut myself off by my transgressions, and left myself neither foot-hold nor hand-hold among all the stays and props in the precious word of life. And truly I did now feel myself to sink into a gulf, as a house whose foundation is destroyed. I did liken myself in this condition unto the case of a child that was fallen into a mill-pit, who thought it could make some shift to scramble and sprawl in the water: yea, because it could find neither hand-hold nor foot-hold, therefore, at last, it must die in that condition. So soon as this fresh assault had fastened on my soul, that scripture came into my heart, ' This for many days;' and, indeed, I found it was so; for I could not be delivered, nor brought to peace again, until well-nigh two years and a half were completely finished."

This was the Valley of the Shadow of Death, and so did

Christian go trembling and astonished, and sighing bitterly by reason of his distress of spirit. The pathway was exceedingly narrow, with ditches on one side and quagmires on the other ; also, for a time it was pitch dark, except the lurid dreadful light of the flames that were reaching into the path towards him ; no other light did there seem to be,

> Save what the glimmering of those livid flames
> Cast pale and dreadful.

Also, in the midst of the darkness, there were doleful voices and rushings to and fro, as of mad companies, so that he thought he should be torn in pieces, or trodden down like mire in the streets. But what distressed and terrified Christian more than all other things that he met with in his passage through this dreary valley, was the horrid blasphemies that were whispered into his ear by the fiends coming up behind him, in such manner that he really thought they proceeded from his own mind ; but he had not the discretion either to stop his ears, or to know from whence these blasphemies came.

Here is a marked feature, drawn, as we have seen, directly from Bunyan's experience. This, with many other things, " did tear and rend" Bunyan himself in this Valley, out of which none but God could have delivered him. " These things would so break and confound my spirit," says Bunyan, " that I could not tell what to do ; I thought at times they would have broken my wits ; and still to aggravate my misery, that would run in my mind, You know how that afterwards, when he would have inherited the blessing, he was rejected. Oh, no one knows the terrors of those days, but myself." Yet others, doubtless, unknown to any but God and the soul's great Adversary, have passed through much the same conflicts. What battles are fought with Apollyon, and what victories gained through the blood of the Lamb, what dreary passages are made in every generation through this Valley of the Shadow of Death, will never be known till, amidst the disclosures of eternity, the saints saved shall reveal to each other, for the glory of the Redeemer, the wonders of his grace in their individual experience. It is but here and there that the trials and triumphs of faith come to view in this world in such instances as those of Bunyan and Luther; but eternity will be full of such spiritual epics. And in every man's experience, however humble, there will be something of peculiar glory to the Redeemer. Many are the pictures, unseen here, that are to be set in array in the eternal world, with the light of the Divine attributes in Christ shining in and through them, to be studied and admired for ever and ever.

One of the earliest recorded instances of a passage through this dark Valley is that of Job; and one of the sublimest instances of faith in the midst of it is his; for in almost the same breath in which he spake of the darkness in his paths, and of his hope removed like a tree, he exclaimed, " I know that my Redeemer liveth!" While you listen to the experience of Job, it seems as if you heard Bunyan himself bemoaning his spiritual distresses; and indeed the book of Job might, as well as the experience of Bunyan, be entitled " Grace Abounding to the Chief of Sinners." Who is this that is speaking? Is it not Christian in the Valley of the Shadow of Death? " He teareth me in his wrath who hateth me; he gnasheth upon me with his teeth; mine enemies sharpen their eyes upon me. They have gaped upon me with their mouth; they have smitten me upon the cheek reproachfully; they have gathered themselves together against me. God hath delivered me over to the ungodly, and turned me over into the hands of the wicked. I was at ease, but he hath broken me asunder; he hath also taken me by my neck, and shaken me to pieces, and set me up for his mark. His archers compass me round about; he cleaveth my reins asunder, and doth not spare; he poureth out my gall upon the ground. He breaketh me with breach upon breach; he runneth upon me like a giant. My face is foul with weeping, and on mine eyelids is the shadow of death. My breath is corrupt, my days are extinct, the graves are ready for me!" But what is the end of all this? " I know that my Redeemer liveth!" Fearful was the trial, glorious the triumph of this eminent servant of God!

There was another recorded instance of a journey through this Valley which Bunyan followed, and that was King

David's. For the bars of death were round about him also, laid in the lowest pit, in darkness, in the deeps. When he remembered God, he was troubled. "Thy wrath lieth hard upon me, and thou hast afflicted me with all thy waves. I am shut up, I cannot come forth. I am afflicted and ready to die. While I suffer thy terrors, I am distracted. Thy fierce wrath goeth over me; thy terrors have cut me off." But what was the end in the case of David? Deliverance and light, so signal and manifest in answer to prayer, that his example should be for encouragement to all that ever after him should have to pass through that Valley. "Thou forgavest the iniquity of my sin. For this shall every one that is godly pray unto thee in a time when thou mayest be found. I was brought low, and the Lord helped me. He restoreth my soul. Yea, though I walk through the Valley of the Shadow of Death I will fear no evil, for thou art with me."

This was a real Valley and no imaginary evil, but there were also real deliverances. The men whom Christian met making haste to go back did not at all exaggerate in their descriptions of its terrors; but they knew nothing of Him who would walk with all his true pilgrims through the midst of those terrors. They could see the fire of the furnace, and dared not think of entering into it; but they could not see the form like unto the Son of God walking with his people in the very flames. Why, what have you seen, said Christian?

"Seen! Why, the Valley itself, which is as dark as pitch: we also saw there the hobgoblins, satyrs, and dragons of the pit: we heard also in that Valley a continued howling and yelling, as of a people under unutterable misery, who there sat bound in affliction and irons; and over that Valley hang the discouraging clouds of confusion: Death, also, doth always spread his wings over it. In a word, it is every whit dreadful, being utterly without order."

This is almost a description of hell. And how much more afraid men are of the image of hell in this world, of the evils which here are a type of it, than they are of its reality in an eternal world! If these men had been as much afraid of losing the favour of God, and of being shut up in the prison of his wrath for ever, as they were of the terrors of this Valley, they would have gone through it, singing with David, " I will fear no evil." For what are all the difficulties that can be met with in this life, if in the end we may have the light of God's countenance ? A hearty desire after God, and a right fear of hell, will put to flight every other fear, will make every evil comparatively easy to be conquered, or light to be borne.

In this disconsolate situation, Christian was greatly encouraged, because he thought he heard the voice of another pilgrim singing before him, which turned out afterwards to be Faithful. He called out, but got no answer, for this other pilgrim deemed himself also to have been alone, and knew not what to make of it. In truth, when the soul is in this experience, it seems as though never a living creature had been in it before ; it seems to itself utterly alone, and desolate. Nevertheless, that sound of singing was a great comfort to Christian ; for he said within himself, Whoever this be, it is clear that he fears God, and that God is with him, for he could not otherwise go singing through this horrid Valley ; and if God is with *him*, why may he not be with *me*, though it is now so deep dark that I cannot perceive him ; yet, by the time I have gone a little further I may find him. By and by the day broke ; then said Christian, He hath turned the Shadow of Death into the morning.

Now, if you wish to trace Bunyan's own experience in a very striking manner in this sketch, you must turn to his own account in the Grace Abounding, of the first breaking of the dawn in his own soul after his dismal night in the pit, the prison, and the Death Valley ; you must note the manner in which he looked back upon the dangers through which he had been passing, the manner in which he began to approach and examine by the daylight, the fears and temptations that had been so terrible to him, that had so shaken and well-nigh distracted his soul. Just so did Christian look back upon the ditches and the quags, the hobgoblins, dragons, and satyrs of the pit, discoverable by the daylight ; according to that scripture, " He discovereth deep things out of darkness, and bringeth to light the Shadow of Death."

Now, as we have compared the experience of Christian in the Valley of Humiliation with that of the pilgrims under guidance of Mr Greatheart, so we ought to compare the two passages through the Valley of the Shadow of Death; and much instruction may be gained thereby. Christiana and her company were at one time in great darkness. "Their conductor did go before them, till they came at a place, where was cast up a pit the whole breadth of the way; and before they could be prepared to go over that, a great mist and darkness fell upon them, so that they could not see. Then said the pilgrims, Alas! what now shall we do? But their guide made answer, Fear not, stand still, and see what an end will be put to this also. So they staid there, because their path was marred. They then also thought that they did hear more apparently the noise and rushing of the enemies; the fire also and smoke of the pit was much easier to be discerned. Then said Christiana to Mercy, Now I see what my poor husband went through; I have heard much of this place, but I never was here before now. Poor man! he went here all alone in the night; he had night almost quite through the way; also, these fiends were busy about him, as if they would have torn him in pieces. Many have spoken of it, but none can tell what the Valley of the Shadow of Death should mean until they come in themselves. The heart knoweth its own bitterness; and a stranger intermeddleth not with its joy. To be here is a fearful thing."

"This, said Mr Greatheart, is like doing business in great waters, or like going down into the deep; this is like being in the heart of the sea, and like going down to the bottoms of the mountains; now it seems as if the earth with its bars were about us for ever. 'But let them that walk in darkness, and have no light, trust in the name of the Lord, and stay upon their God.' For my part, as I have told you already, I have gone often through this valley, and have been much harder put to it than now I am; and yet you see I am alive. I would not boast, for that I am not my own Saviour. But I trust we shall have a good deliverance.

Come, let us pray for light to Him that can lighten our darkness, and that can rebuke, not these only, but all the Satans in hell. So they cried and prayed, and God sent light and deliverance."

A remark pregnant with heavenly sense was dropped by one of the boys, which pilgrims beset with dangers and difficulties would do well to ponder. "It is not so bad," said he, "to go through here as it would be to abide here always; and for aught I know, one reason why we must go this way to the house prepared for us, is that our home may be made the sweeter to us." In this remark is much Christian wisdom and beauty. I am reminded of Wesley's hymn, or something like it:—

> The rougher our way, the shorter our stay;
> The ruder the blast,
> The sweeter our quiet when storms are all past.

We may also be reminded of those sweet expressive lines by Baxter,—

> Christ leads me through no darker rooms
> Than he went through before:
> He that into God's kingdom comes
> Must enter by that door.

But the best of all commentaries on the intent and meaning of this passage through the Valley of the Shadow of Death is to be found in Bunyan's thoughts and remarks upon other good men who have had to go through it, uttered while he himself was quite in darkness, and was looking to those bright examples, and wishing from the bottom of his soul that he also might thus be the favoured one of God. Poor Bunyan! this very darkness, these very desperate distresses, proved, in the end, that he was himself to be ranked among those favoured ones; for when his spirit was overwhelmed within him, then God knew his path; then was God leading the blind by a way that he knew not. "Oh, how my soul," says Bunyan, "did at this time prize the preservation that God did set about his people! Ah, how safely did I see them walk, whom God had hedged in! Now did those blessed places, that spake of God's keeping his people, shine like the sun before me, though not to comfort me, yet to shew me the blessed state and heritage of those whom the Lord had blessed. Now I saw that as God had his hand in all the providences and dispensations that overtake his elect, so he had his hand in all the temptations that they had to sin against him, not to animate them in wickedness, but to choose their temptations and troubles for them, and also to leave them for a time to such things only, that might not destroy, but humble them; as might not put them beyond, but lay them in, the way of the renewing his mercy. But oh! what love, what care, what kindness and mercy did I now see, mixing itself with the most severe and dreadful of all God's ways to his people! He would let David, Hezekiah, Solomon, Peter, and others fall, but he would not let them fall into the sin unpardonable, nor into hell for sin. O! thought I, these be the men that God hath loved; these be the men that God, though he chastiseth them, keeps them in safety by him, and them whom he makes to abide under the shadow of the Almighty."

Sweet are the uses of adversity! In God's hand indeed they are; when he puts his children into the furnace of affliction, it is that he may thoroughly purge away all their dross. A great writer has spoken with great beauty of the resources which God has placed within us for bringing good out of evil, or, at least, for greatly alleviating our trials, in the cases of sickness and misfortune. "The cutting and irritating grain of sand," he says, "which by accident or incaution has got within the shell, incites the living inmate to secrete from its own resources the means of coating the intrusive substance. And is it not, or may it not be, even so with the irregularities and unevenness of health and fortune in our own case? We too may turn diseases into pearls." But how much more wonderful are the wisdom and mercy of God, in making the spiritual temptations and distresses of his people their necessary discipline for their highest good, the means for the greatest perfection and stability of their characters. This indeed is a wonderful transmutation. "God," says the holy Leighton, "hath many sharp cutting instruments and rough files for the polishing of his jewels; and those he especially esteems, and means to make the most resplendent, he hath oftenest his tools upon."

Beautifully are the uses of temptations and trials, external and inward, illustrated in that old familiar hymn of Newton, so like in its language and spirit to some hymns which Cowper wrote from similar experience:—

> These inward trials I employ
> From self and pride to set thee free;
> To break thy schemes of earthly joy,
> And make thee find thine all in me.

It seems very strange that, with these truths so fully set forth in the Word of God, and so illustrated in the examples of many shining Christians, still generation after generation all men, all pilgrims, should have to learn them for themselves, should never be satisfied of them, till made to believe by their own experience. Every pilgrim expects of Christ that by his love's constraining power he will subdue the sins and hidden evils of the heart, and give the soul rest and relief from its corruptions all the way of its pilgrimage. Yet every pilgrim in turn has to go through this Valley, has to learn by himself both the dreadful evils of the heart, and the power of temptation, and the greatness of deliverance by the almighty power and love of the Saviour. He cannot learn this by hearing others tell it to him; God must teach him by the precious costly way of personal discipline. He can no more come to the stature of a perfect man in Christ Jesus without this discipline, than a babe could grow up to manhood without learning at first to creep, then to walk, then to speak, to read, to exercise all its faculties. The great discipline which we need as pilgrims is mostly the experience of our own weakness, and the art of finding our strength in Christ; but it is astonishing what severe treatment is oftentimes necessary to teach this, apparently the simplest and most obvious of all lessons, but yet the deepest and most difficult to be learned.

We are now to be introduced to a new Pilgrim, and Christian is no more to go on his way alone. The sweet Christian communion depicted in this book forms one of the most delightful features in it, and Faithful and Hopeful are both of them portraits that stand out in as firm relief as that of Christian himself. Faithful is the Martyr Pilgrim, who goes in a chariot of fire to heaven, and leaves Christian alone; Hopeful springs, as it were, out of Faithful's ashes, and supplies his place all along the remainder of the pilgrimage. The communion between these loving Christians, their sympathy and share in each other's distresses, their mutual counsels and encouragements, temptations and dangers, experience and discipline, their united joys and sorrows, and their very passing of the river of death together, form the sweetest of all examples of the true fellowship of saints, united to the same Saviour, made to drink into the same Spirit, baptized with the same sufferings, partakers of the same consolations, crowned with the same crown of life, entering together upon glory everlasting.

Here I cannot but speak again of God's tender love to his people in their spiritual distresses. It is but a little while, at the uttermost, that he lets any walk in darkness, and always this darkness prepares for greater light; and sometimes God darkens our room, that he may shew us with greater effect those visions of his own glory, on which he will have our attention to be fixed, and which we either will not or cannot see in the glare of the noonday of this world. But always his thoughts towards his afflicted people are thoughts of peace and mercy, and his language, even when they seem to be deserted of God, is of great tenderness. "For a small moment have I forsaken thee, but with great mercies will I gather thee. In a little wrath I hid my face from thee for a moment, but with everlasting kindness will I have mercy on thee, saith the Lord, thy Redeemer."

There are many things which may constitute a Valley of the Shadow of Death to the believer. There may be such an array of external evils as to do this. Sickness, poverty, want like an armed man, desertion and loss of friends, the disappointment and failure of all natural hopes and sources of enjoyment, the utter destruction of all schemes of usefulness and plans of life, the triumphing of the wicked, and the apparent prostration of the cause of God; all these things, or any of them, may almost overwhelm the soul, and be to it as a death-darkness. Elijah, Jeremiah, Job, David, were stricken down beneath such evils, sometimes accumulated together, so that they were ready to cry out for Death as a friend. But these things are not the real Valley; this is not the hiding of God's countenance; there may be all these things, and yet heaven's sunshine in the soul. But when God departs, or when the soul loses sight of him, then begins the Valley of the Shadow of Death. For, who can stand against such abandonment? Who can endure a sense of the wrath of God abiding on the soul?

> 'Tis Paradise if Thou art here;
> If Thou depart, 'tis hell!

This is the language of the believer's heart, and this too is the representation of the Word of God, and this is the reality of things. And men only need to see things as they are, and to feel things as they are, and they will see and feel that they cannot live without God; that without God, though every thing might be heaven in appearance, yet, in reality, it must be hell. I say, men only need to see and feel the truth, in order to realize this; for God is the only life of the soul, and if he be not in it, and it be not alive in him, then is its existence inevitable misery. The heart without God is at enmity against him, and the conscience without God is at enmity against the heart, and the thoughts without God are self-accusing, fiery, tormenting; and the imagination without God becomes a prophetic power in the soul, not only to start into fresher, fiercer life its present distress and sense of sin and desolation, but to image to it all fearful forebodings of future wrath, of interminable desolation and misery, to fill its horizon with upbraiding faces, sometimes with fiend-like forms waiting to receive it, and brandishing a whip of the twisted scorpions of remembered, known, unforgiven sins. The gate of the future, through which the soul must pass, is in such a case,

> With dreadful faces thronged, and fiery arms!

The sins of the soul, without God, without Christ, are the prophets of its coming woes; and its life, when surrounded by them, when under a sense of them, when conscience calls them up, and there is no sense of forgiveness, is the Valley of the Shadow of Death. This is the reality of things, even in this world, when the soul has a sense of its own true nature and accountability. And yet, in this world, it is but the prefiguring type of that Eternal Vale, where their worm dieth not and the fire is not quenched. Here, it is but the Valley of the *Shadow* of Death; once entered in eternity, once experienced there, it is Death itself, Death without God, say rather, Life without God, with all those revenging miseries as realities, which here at the uttermost were but predictions and merciful warnings to flee from the wrath to come!

Ah, many a man, who is not a Christian Pilgrim, enters this Valley in this world, has experience of its horrors, who never tells what he felt, never lets it be known that he was so far awakened as to see and feel what dreadful elements and faces were round about him, pressing upon his soul. Sometimes the souls of impenitent and hardened men are shaken with the terrors of God in this Valley, and wrapped in its gloom!

A very graphic writer (Mr Borrow, in his instructive book, The Bible in Spain) describes an interview with an imprisoned murderer, who, at the close of the conversation, " folded his arms, leaned back against the wall, and appeared to sink gradually into one of his reveries. I looked him in the face, and spoke to him; but he did not seem either to hear or see me. His mind was perhaps wandering in that dreadful Valley of the Shadow of Death, into which the children of earth, while living, occasionally find their way; the dreadful region where there is no water, where hope dwelleth not, where nothing lives but the undying worm. This Valley is the *fac-simile* of hell, and he who has entered it has experienced here on earth for a time, what the spirits of the condemned are doomed to suffer through ages without end."

Yes! there is much *foretaste* of this suffering, even in this world; and often, even amidst their guilty pleasures, the wicked are made to feel that they are themselves like the troubled sea, whose waters cast up mire and dirt. When Conscience takes a man in hand, and leads him up and down through the gallery of his own remembered sins, and stops at this picture and that, and points out shades and colourings that he never saw before, and sometimes darkens the room, and takes down a vivid transparency of guilt, and holds it before the fire to his vision, so that his past life seems to burn before him, it does not take long in such employment to make the room seem walled with retributive flames, and peopled with condemning fiends. Without the sense of God's forgiving mercy in Christ, such employment makes a man enter the Valley of the Shadow of Death; and there, though he may always have thrown ridicule upon these things among his boon companions, yet these, alone, with himself, the sights which he sees, and the sounds which he hears, are intolerable.

When the child of God, from whatever cause, wanders into this Valley, and has the face of God hidden from him, then the universe to him is covered with gloom; then the dead weight of anxiety, as the shadow of sepulchral mountains, is on his spirit; he enters into darkness, and is wandering on the borders of despair. God hides his face, and we are troubled. The gloomy, awful solemnity and coldness, that like a twilight pall enshroud the earth in a deep eclipse of the sun at noonday, making all nature to shudder, and the animals to cry out with terror, do faintly image forth the spiritual coldness and gloom of the soul, when the face of God is hidden from it. That eclipse forebodes to the soul the blackness of darkness for ever. Hence the earnest cry of David, "Hide not thy face from me, lest I become like them that go down to the pit."

At such times Satan may have much business with a child of God. "For although," as Mr Goodwin observes, " Satan cannot immediately wound the conscience, and make impressions of God's wrath upon it, (for as no creature can shed abroad God's love, and cause the creature to taste the sweetness of it, so neither the bitterness of his wrath, but God is equally the reporter of both), yet, when the Holy Ghost hath lashed and whipt the conscience, and made it tender once, and fetched off the skin, Satan then, by renewing the experimental remembrance of those lashes, which the soul hath had from the Spirit, may amaze the soul with fears of an infinitely sorer vengeance yet to come, and flash representations of hell-fire in their consciences, from those real glimpses they have already felt, in such a manner as to wilder the soul into vast and unthought-of horrors."

In the eternal world, there is no *living* without God, but a *dying*, an eternal dying. It is death in life, and life in death, for the soul to be without God ; and the discovery and sense of these things in the eternal world, amidst the convictions of despair, will be to the soul as if a man, who has been long time dead and buried, should suddenly come to life amidst enfolding slimy worms, a corrupt decaying carcass, in mould, gangrene, and putrefaction. What need of flames, if the sinner be left to the full sense and working of his own corruptions ? What man of sin is there, who, if he will judge candidly, can do otherwise than acknowledge that he finds within himself elements of evil, which, if left to work undisturbed, unimpeded, unmingled, will work absolute misery and ruin. Man of sin ! wilt thou stay in these corruptions, and die in them ; or wilt thou go for deliverance to Christ Jesus, to him who alone can put out these fires, can kill this undying worm, can drive the fiends from thy soul, can throw death itself into hell, and make the fountain of love, life, and blessedness to spring up within thee !

Just as Christian gets out of the Valley of the Shadow of Death, he passed by a place of bones, sculls, images, and crosses, the abode of Pope and Pagan, whom Bunyan most appropriately puts into the same cave together, though Pagan had been dead long time, and Pope now occupied his place alone. Popery and Paganism are two incarnations of depravity wonderfully similar, almost the same ; but Popery has, by far, the greatest dominion of "the blood, bones, ashes, and mangled bodies of Pilgrims." Christian passed by without harm, for now the living giant could do no more than grin and bite his nails, and growl at the passing pilgrims. "You will never mend till more of you be burned."

Possibly another burning is yet to come, for Giant Pope seems in some respects to be renewing his age, and he has now so many helpers, that it would not be surprising, if he should come out of his Cave, and once more, before the final fall of Antichrist, be seen arrayed in all the power and terrors of persecution. The proximity of this black Golgotha of Popery to the Valley of the Shadow of Death is very natural, considering the one as the emblem of the greatest external evils that can be met on the way of this pilgrimage, and the other as marking the opposite extreme of the horrors of inward desolation and spiritual misery in the soul.

After encountering all those dangers, there was a mount of vision, up which Christian with alacrity ascended, whence he could see far off over the prospect before him. The air was clear and bright, its reflection of all images distinct and certain, the mists of the Valley of the Shadow of Death were far below him, and came not to this border, the air was healthful and bracing, he seemed nearer to Heaven than he had been in all his pilgrimage, and so light and elastic for his journey, that it seemed as if he could have flown. Here was "an earnest of the Spirit," a refreshment after toil and danger. Here, as he looked onward, he saw Faithful before him, and shouted out to him to stay, for he would be his companion. But how should Faithful know that it was not the voice of some treacherous spirit from the Pit ? Faithful's answer shews the spirit of the future martyr. I am upon my life, said he, and the Avenger of blood is behind me; I may not stay. This nettled Christian; and now comes a beautiful and most instructive incident, for Christian, summoning all his strength, ran so earnestly, that he soon got up with Faithful; but not content with this, and being a little moved by spiritual pride at his own attainments, he did run on before him; so the last was first. *Then did Christian vain-gloriously smile!* Ah what a smile was that! how much sin, not humble spiritual gratitude and joy, was there in it! But now see how he that exalteth himself shall be abased, and how surely along with spiritual pride comes carelessness, false security, and a grievous fall. Not taking good heed to his feet, Christian suddenly stumbled and fell, and the fall was such, that he could not rise again, till Faithful, whom he had vain-gloriously outrun, came up to help him.

This is one of the most instructive incidents of the pilgrimage, and it might be applied to many things. Let the Christian, in pursuing the work of Christ, take care of his motives. Earthly ambition is a heinous sin, carried into spiritual things. Be not wise in your own conceits. Let us not be desirous of vain-glory, provoking one another, envying one another. See that you look not with self-complacency upon your own attainments. A man may vaingloriously smile within himself, at his own labours, at the applause of others, or in the comparison of others with himself, and when he does this, then he is in danger. When Christian did vain-gloriously smile, then did Christian meet a most mortifying fall. Peter's boasting of himself before the other disciples was not far off from Peter's fall. Let nothing be done through strife or vain-glory, but in lowliness of mind let each esteem others better than himself Yet, there is a right way of coming behind in no gift, enriched by Jesus Christ. Whoso seeketh this enriching for himself, seeketh it also for others. Let this lesson not be forgotten, *Then did Christian vain-gloriously smile*, and when he smiled, then he stumbled.

Now what happiness it was for these Christians to meet each other! What delightful comparison of each other's experience, what strengthening of each other's faith and joy! Each had not a little to tell peculiar to himself, for they had met with various dangers, temptations, enemies. They were both from the same City of Destruction; they were now dear friends going to the City of Immanuel; delightful indeed it was to call to mind former things, and trace the loving-kindness of the Lord thus far on their pilgrimage. Faithful had escaped the Slough of Despond, but he had fallen into worse dangers. The Old Man with his deeds had beset him. Then Discontent beset him in the Valley of Humiliation, and told him how he was offending all his worldly friends by making such a fool of himself. But of all his bold enemies, Shame, in that Valley, was the worst to deal with, the most distressing to Faithful's spirit, whom indeed he could scarce shake out of his company. The delineation of this character by Bunyan, is a masterly grouping together of the arguments used by men of this world against religion, in ridicule and contempt of it, and of their feelings and habits of opinion in regard to it. Faithful's account of him and of his arguments is a piece of vigorous satire, full of truth and life. Faithful was hard put to it to get rid of this fellow, but he met with no other difficulty quite through the Valley, and as to the Shadow of Death, to him it was sunlight.

The next character brought into view is that of Talkative, a professor of religion by the tongue, but not in the life, a hearer of the word, but not a doer, a great disgrace to religion, and in the description of the common people, a saint abroad, and a devil at home. But he was a great talker. He could talk " of things heavenly or things earthly ; things moral or things evangelical ; things sacred or things profane ; things past or things to come ; things foreign or things at home ; things more essential or things circumstantial :—provided that all be done to profit." Faithful was much taken with this man. What a brave companion have we got ! said he to Christian ; surely this man will make a very excellent pilgrim. Christian, who knew him well, related his parentage and character, and afterwards Faithful proceeded, according to Christian's directions, to converse with Talkative in such a way upon the subject of religion, as very soon proved what he was in reality, and delivered them of his company. Then went they on, talking of all that they had seen by the way, with such deep interest as made the wilderness, through which they were passing, appear well nigh like a fruitful field. And now they rejoiced again to meet Evangelist, and listen to his encouraging and animating exhortations, of which, as they were now near the great town of Vanity Fair, they would stand in special need. Indeed, it was partly for the purpose of forewarning them of what they were to meet with there, and to exhort them, amidst all persecutions, to quit themselves like men, that Evangelist now came to them. His voice, so solemn and deep, yet so inspiring and animating, sounded like the tones of a trumpet on the eve of battle.

The subject of the trials and temptations of the Christian in this part of the Pilgrim's Progress finds a beautiful commentary in the hymn to which I have referred, by Newton.

I ask'd the Lord that I might grow
In faith, and love, and every grace,
Might more of his salvation know,
And seek more earnestly his face.

'Twas he who taught me thus to pray
And he, I trust, has answer'd prayer;
But answer came in such a way,
As almost drove me to despair.

I hoped that, in some favour'd hour,
At once he'd grant me my request,
And, by his love's constraining power,
Subdue my sins and give me rest.

Instead of this, he made me feel
The hidden evils of my heart,
And let the angry powers of hell
Assault my soul in every part.

Yea more, with his own hand he seem'd
Intent to aggravate my woe;
Cross'd all the fair designs I schemed,
Blasted my gourds, and laid me low.

" Lord, why is this?" I trembling cried,
" Wilt thou pursue thy worm to death
" 'Tis in this way," the Lord replied,
" I answer prayer for grace and faith:

" These inward trials I employ,
" From self and pride to set thee free;
" And break thy schemes of earthly joy,
" That thou may'st seek thine all in me."

LECTURE ELEVENTH.

Christian and Faithful in Vanity Fair.

The Vanity Fair of this world.—Temptations to worldliness.—The deportment of the Pilgrims.—Their strange appearance to the men of Vanity Fair.—Their trial in the Fair.—The martyrdom of Faithful.—How this pilgrimage is regarded in our day.—Sketch of Vanity Fair in our time.—Visit to Giant Pope's Cave.—Characters of By-ends, Money-love, Hold-the-world, and Save-all.—Logic of Mr Money-love.—Temptations to filthy lucre.—Demas and the mines.—Danger of the love of money, and of conformity to the world.

VANITY FAIR is the City of Destruction in its gala dress, in its most seductive sensual allurements. It is this world in miniature, with its various temptations. Hitherto we have observed the Pilgrims by themselves, in loneliness, in obscurity, in the hidden life and experience of the people of God. The allegory thus far has been that of the soul, amidst its spiritual enemies, toiling towards heaven; now there comes a scene more open, tangible, external; the allurements of the world are to be presented, with the manner in which the true Pilgrim conducts himself amidst them. It was necessary that Bunyan should shew his pilgrimage in its external as well as its secret spiritual conflicts; it was necessary that he should draw the contrast between the pursuits and deportment of the children of this world, and the children of light, that he should shew how a true Pilgrim appears, and is likely to be regarded, who, amidst the world's vanities lives above the world, is dead to it, and walks through it as a stranger and a pilgrim towards heaven.

The temptations to worldliness are the strongest and most common in the Christian race; they are so represented in Scripture; we are told of the cares of this world, the deceitfulness of riches, and the lusts of other things choking the word, that becometh unfruitful; and in many passages we are warned against the love of the world, the imitation of its manners, and the indulgence of its feelings: especially in that striking passage in John, and the corresponding one in James. "Love not the world, neither the things that are in the world. If any man love the world, the love of the Father is not in him. For all that is of the world, the lust of the flesh, and the lust of the eyes, and the pride of life, is not of the Father, but is of the world." James is yet more severe. "Ye adulterers and adulteresses! know ye not that the friendship of the world is enmity with God? Whosoever therefore will be a friend of the world is the enemy of God."

Certainly, it was to illustrate these passages that Bunyan composed this portion of the Pilgrim's Progress. It was also to shew the truth of that saying, which the apostles and primitive Christians seem to have kept among the choice jewels of truth nearest their hearts, among their amulets of apples of gold in pictures of silver, that through much tribulation we must enter into the kingdom of heaven. "In the world ye shall have tribulation," said our blessed Lord to his disciples, "but be of good cheer, I have overcome the world. If the world hate you, ye know that it hated me before it hated you. I have chosen you out of the world, and ye are not of the world, even as I am not of the world, therefore the world hateth you." Bunyan would shew, by the treatment of the pilgrims in Vanity Fair, that this hatred is not gone out of existence. He would shew that the Christian life is not a pilgrimage merely of inward experiences, but that they who will live godly in Christ Jesus are a peculiar people, and must, in some sort or other, suffer persecution. They are strangers in a strange country. The world, its spirit and pursuits, are foreign from and hostile to their habits, inclinations, and duties, as children of the Saviour. To be conformed to the world is to depart from the way of life; the whole race of genuine pilgrims must therefore be a strange and singular people, a people of nonconformists, whose deportment rebukes and reproves the world, and convinces it of sin. It does this just so far as they live up to the rules of their pilgrimage.

It is not always the case, however, that simple-hearted godliness, travelling through the world, meets with such persecution as Christian and Faithful did in passing through Vanity Fair. This sketch of Bunyan borrows some shades from the severe aspect of his own times; yet the general picture is a picture of all times, the general lessons are lessons for the instruction of all pilgrims. The spirit of Foxe's old Book of Martyrs is here; the spirit of the Reformation, and the constancy and endurance of those who rode in the chariot of fire to heaven. Bunyan himself was almost a Martyr-Pilgrim, and he himself had passed through Vanity Fair with much the same treatment as Christian and Faithful experienced; this passage is a copy of his own life, not less than the passage through the terrors of the Valley of the Shadow of Death. Moreover, the picture of the Fair itself is drawn from scenes with which Bunyan was familiar in England; from those motley assemblages of booths, people, and sins, still to be witnessed in that country under the names of Greenwich Fair, Bartholomew Fair, and others; scenes where may be witnessed the world of sin in miniature. These places served Bunyan for the setting of his allegory, which is conducted with the utmost beauty, fulness of meaning, and truth to nature.

The merchandise of this Fair, comprising all conceivable commodities that can come under the categories of the Apostle John, the lust of the flesh, the lust of the eyes, and the pride of life, is described with great power of satire. The most abundant commodity was the merchandise of Rome, a sort of ware at present in greater demand in Vanity Fair than of long time, since Bunyan's day, it hath been. Through this place of Vanity Fair, once passed the Lord of life and glory, when the Prince and Owner of the Fair tempted him with the offer of all the kingdoms of the world, and the glory of them

In this Fair the garments of the Pilgrims were so strange, so different from the raiment of the men of the Fair; also their language, being "that of Canaan," was so unknown that they passed for barbarians, and were treated as such. Also, their utter indifference as to all the merchandise of the Fair, and their refusal to buy thereof, or to partake in the vain and sinful amusements of the place, made them to be considered as persons out of their senses. So there was a great hubbub in the Fair about them, and they were taken and confined in the Cage, and made a spectacle, and afterwards they were grievously beaten, as being the authors of such a disturbance. "These men, that have turned the world upside down, are come hither also." But their patience, forbearance, and gentleness of deportment did win them some friends even among the men of the Fair, which they of the contrary party being very much enraged at, it was at length resolved that these men should be put to death.

Now came on the trial; and here again, as in every part of the allegory, Bunyan's own experience served him in good stead; here again he draws his picture from real life, from his own life. Little could he have thought, when a few years ago amidst the taunts of his enemies, he himself stood at the bar to be examined for the crime of preaching the gospel, that the providence of God was then laying up in store materials of human life and character to be used with such powerful effect in his then unconceived imagined allegory. These phases of a world at enmity against God were indelibly impressed on Bunyan's mind, and now, in all the freshness of their colouring, he transferred them to the tablets of the Pilgrim's Progress.

Nothing can be more masterly than the satire contained in this trial. The Judge, the Witnesses, and the Jury, are portraits sketched to the life, and finished, every one of them, in quick, concise, and graphic touches. The ready testimony of Envy is especially characteristic. Rather than anything should be wanting that might be necessary to despatch the prisoner, he would enlarge his testimony against him to any requisite degree. The language of the Judge, and his whole deportment on the bench, are a copy to the life of some of the infamous judges under King Charles, especially the wretch Jeffries. You may find in the trial of the noble patriot Algernon Sidney the abusive language of the Judge against Faithful almost word for word. The Judge's charge to the Jury, with the acts and laws on which the condemnation of the prisoner was founded, are full of ingenuity and meaning.

But the best part of the trial is the heroic courageous deportment of Faithful. His answer to the charges and the witnesses against him, reminds us of Bunyan's answers to the arguments of his accusers. "As to the charge of Mr Superstition against me, I said only this, that in the worship of God there is required a divine faith ; but there can be no divine faith without a divine revelation of the will of God. Therefore, whatever is thrust into the worship of God that is not agreeable to divine revelation, cannot be done but by a human faith ; which faith will not be profitable to eternal life. As to what Mr Pickthank hath said, I say, (avoiding terms, as that I am said to rail, and the like,) that the Prince of this town, with all the rabblement his attendants, by this gentleman named, are more fit for being in hell than in this town or country ; and so the Lord have mercy upon me."

Well done, noble, resolute, fearless Faithful ! No doubt of death after such truth shot into the hearts of thine enemies ! Then was Faithful, after dreadful torments inflicted on him, burned to ashes at the stake, in the midst of the multitude. But behind the multitude there was a ravishing sight for any man whose eyes could have been opened to behold it, and which might have made any man willing to take Faithful's place at the stake for the sake of Faithful's place in glory afterwards. For there was a band of bright shining angels waiting for Faithful with a chariot and horses, in which, while the flames were yet cracking in the fagots which consumed his flesh to ashes, he was conveyed with the sound of trumpets up through the clouds to the Celestial City. This sight was enough to make Christian wish that, instead of taking him back to prison, they had burned him also on the spot,

Now this is a most exquisitely beautiful sketch; it is drawn to the life from many an era of pilgrimage in this world; there are in it the materials of glory that constituted spirits of such noble greatness as are catalogued in the eleventh chapter of the epistle to the Hebrews; trials of cruel mockings and scourgings, bonds and imprisonments, such as tortured and hardened the frames of men of whom the world was not worthy. Such was the stuff and discipline out of which the race of primitive Christians were moulded; and very much such was also the era of pilgrimage on which Bunyan himself had fallen. But is it an equally true sketch of the pilgrimage in our day? Is the world now regarded so much a wilderness and a world of enmity against God as it was? Certainly the pilgrims are now regarded with more favour. Is this because the world has grown kinder, better, more disposed towards godliness? or is it because the pilgrims have grown less strict in their manners, less peculiar in their language, and more accommodating and complying with the usages of Vanity Fair? Or is it from both these causes together, that the path of the pilgrimage seems so much easier now than it was formerly?

It is true that the more Christians there are in the world, the more delightful will this pilgrimage become, the fewer external enemies and difficulties will there be to be fought and conquered. There might be such a revival of religion in Vanity Fair itself, as should convert all its inhabitants, so that even my Lord Hategood would have to lay aside his name with his nature, and Malice and Envy would be changed into Love. Then would the lion lie down with the lamb, and the leopard would eat straw like the ox, and a little child might pass in white robes through Vanity Fair unhurt, unsoiled. Then would the merchandise of the Fair be changed, and no longer would the answer of the pilgrims, "We buy the truth," be deemed such a strange and barbarous answer; but godliness would be considered as gain, and not gain as godliness. That the world is coming into such a grand climacteric of innocence, happiness, and glory, there is no doubt, just in proportion as the gospel prevails, and the number of real believers is multiplied.

There is, however, an era of nominal Christianity. Vanity Fair itself may be full of profound pilgrims, and the pilgrimage itself may be held in high esteem, and yet the practice of the pilgrimage, as Christian and Faithful followed it, may almost have gone out of existence. With the increase of nominal Christians there is always an increase of conformity to the world; and the world appears better than it did to Christians, not so much because *it* has changed, as because *they* have changed; the wild beasts and the tame ones dwell together, not so much because the leopards eat straw like the ox, as because the ox eats flesh like the leopard. *Ephraim, he hath mixed himself among the people;* the people have not come over to Ephraim, but Ephraim has gone over to them; the people hath not learned the ways of Ephraim, but Ephraim hath learned the manners of the people. This is too much the case in the Vanity Fair of the world at the present time; there is not such a marked and manifest distinction between the church and the world as there should be; their habits, maxims, opinions, pursuits, amusements, whole manner of life, are too much the same; so that the pilgrims in our day have lost the character of a peculiar people, not so much because they have become vastly more numerous than formerly, as because they have become conformed to the world, not like strangers, but natives in Vanity Fair. The great temptation of the church in our day is that of entire, almost unmingled worldliness; formalism and worldliness are too sadly the types of our piety; we are in imminent danger of forgetting that our life is a pilgrimage, and that this is not our rest.

This being the case, what shall we say of this sketch of Vanity Fair, and of the treatment of the pilgrims in it, as applied to ourselves, to the Vanity Fair of our own era in the world, and of the society around us? Do the pilgrims of our day go as resolutely through Vanity Fair as Christian and Faithful did? Is it true that in simplicity and godly sincerity, not with fleshly lusts, we, as they did, have our conversation in the world? Is our merchandise the truth? or do we, as they did not, stop to trade in Vanity Fair, cheapening its commodities? And how many among us make Vanity Fair the end of our pilgrimage?

Let the Dreamer lie down, and dream again in the wilderness of the world, and surely a great change would come over the spirit of his dream, and the colouring also. Or let a man stand by the Dreamer, and recount to him what has happened since he passed this way before, what changes in the progress of two hundred years. Listen to him, if you please, as he speaks of Vanity Fair in your day. His account is somewhat as follows:—

The town was much altered since Christian and Faithful passed through it, and principally for the reason that a great multitude of Pilgrims who had set out on the pilgrimage had concluded, finding the air of the city much improved, and that by reason of the increase of refinement and knowledge among the inhabitants, the city itself was very profitable and pleasant to dwell in, to remain there for an indefinite season, and many of them for the residue of their lives. This began by some of them being allured to take part in the purchase and sale of the merchandise of the place, till at length a great part of the business came to be transacted by those who at first came to the place in the character of strangers and travellers to the Celestial City. They formed partnership with the natives and original owners of Vanity Fair, so that now no small part of the French Row, the German Row, and especially the English Row, was carried on under the profession of those who had thus settled in the place as pilgrims.

In process of time they had also appointed, as Lord Mayor of the place, a professor of the religion of the pilgrims, My Lord Know-the-World, whose grand entertainments and dinners, together with his courtly and affable manners, did much to render the name of the pilgrims respectable, and to put the whole place on good terms with them. Nay, it was a pleasant thing to the citizens that they could have so many of the pilgrims to stay with them, still preserving the profession of their pilgrimage; insomuch that at length it became fashionable among many of the native inhabitants of the city to take the same name and profession, without having ever once set out on their travels toward the Celestial City. And I observed that what aided this greatly was a certain thing that had got in vogue, which I was told was considered by many as involving the whole essence of the pilgrimage, and securing all its benefits, without the necessity of encountering its perils or labours, and which they called Baptismal Regeneration. There was also in the court end of the town a very large cathedral, builded of hewn stone, on which they had sculptured the image of the twelve apostles, and over the gate of it had engraven in large capitals these words, "No church without a bishop." I was told that it was in this building chiefly that the ceremony which they called Baptismal Regeneration was performed; and it was observable that most of those who entered this building and underwent the ceremonies there enacted, considered themselves safe for the Celestial City, although they had not Christian's roll, and never went a step beyond Vanity Fair.

There was also no small part of the court end of the city where the houses had crosses upon them; which I was told would prevent the growth of any such burden on the shoulders as Christian had borne with so much difficulty. There were also in various parts of the city places of worship erected, called Chapels of Ease, where the music was so fine, and the seats were so softly and beautifully prepared, and all the ceremonies were so pleasant, that most of the inhabitants became church-going people. In some of these places I was told that great care was taken to smooth down the rough places in the gospel, and that no alarms were ever suffered to be given to the consciences of the people who came there, and also that all those fiends, by which Christian had been so much vexed and alarmed, were considered as only imaginary beings, even Apollyon himself, and that the hell which had frightened so many pilgrims was regarded as a mere creation of the fancy.

Moreover, Mr Legality, from the town of Carnal Policy, had established a colony in this place, and by the aid of Mr Worldly-Wiseman, had gained no small number of the pilgrims, who had concluded to settle in Vanity Fair. I also observed that the pilgrims had thrived greatly in their business, and that their houses were among the most tasteful and costly buildings in the better parts of the city. When they first began to stop in Vanity Fair, they were of very small means, and of an humble exterior; but by degrees they acquired property, and moved up into the more airy and fashionable parts of the place, where they thought it important to make the name and profession of Pilgrim respectable in the eyes of the inhabitants. Some of them had great share in the various stocks in Vanity Fair, and were appointed directors and presidents of its banks, and had built themselves fine houses, and kept up large establishments, such as formerly none but the native men of Vanity Fair could build or reside in.

There was one Mr Genteel, who at first came into the place very dusty and poor from his pilgrimage (his name then being Rustic), and had resolved only to remain long enough in Vanity Fair to better his circumstances a little, and then to set out again, but who had such a tide of worldly prosperity upon him, that he became very rich, put up one of the finest houses in the place, changed his name, and concluded to remain there indefinitely. There was another man, Mr Worldly-Conformity, who followed this rich pilgrim's example; and they two, together with some others in the same neighbourhood, as Mr Luke-Warm, Mr Yielding, Mr Indifferent, Mr Expedient, and their families, constituted some of the most fashionable society in the region. They were not outdone by any of the merchants, or professional gentlemen, or nobility of Vanity Fair, in the costliness of their entertainments, and the richness of their style of living.

It is true that in some cases these professed pilgrims were found to have gone beyond their means, and to have built houses and supported this expensive mode of life at the expense of other people; but this did not prevent others from similar extravagance; and at length the world's people, as the original inhabitants at Vanity Fair were called, and the population of the pilgrims, could not at all be distinguished, the pilgrims having ceased to be a peculiar people, and engaging in the same amusements and pursuits as were generally deemed reputable. The pilgrims being so prosperous and well-esteemed, you may readily suppose there were very few new-comers but were persuaded to settle down in the same way, very few indeed, who, like Christian and Faithful of old, went strait through Vanity Fair, and would not be turned aside from their pilgrimage. Some who staid in the town retained the recollection of their pilgrim life a longer, and some a shorter time than others, and some would be ever and anon preparing to set out again; but there were certain persons of influence in the place, as Mr Self-Indulgence, Mr Love-of-Ease, Mr Creature-Comfort, Mr Indolence, My Lord Procrastinate, and My Lord Time-Serving, who, with fair speeches, did generally contrive to detain them, even to the day of their death. So that it was rare that any of those who stopped and became entangled in the cares and pleasures of life and business in Vanity Fair, ever again set out on pilgrimage. I have heard, however, that many of them, when they came to die, were found in great gloom and distress, and could get no peace whatever, crying out continually, " O that I had never ceased to be a pilgrim!"

There were some that had very grand country-seats, and spent their time in farming and gardening in the summer and were very busy at the Fair in large business operations in the winter. Some of these men were accustomed to give considerable sums to certain benevolent societies that were in the place, and also they would, as occasion offered, preside at their meetings, and give them countenance by their names. Nor was there any want of such societies now in Vanity Fair, for many persons seemed to think that the patronising of such societies rendered it unnecessary for themselves to go on pilgrimage. There were also many good books published in the place, and what seemed not a little surprising, the lives of some of the most noted pilgrims who had passed through Vanity Fair were put forth, and were greatly admired even by some of those who had settled in **Vanity Fair** because of its merchandise. There were also persons who might be heard to speak much of the necessity of living as strangers and pilgrims in the world, who, nevertheless, kept immense warehouses in **English Row** and **French Row**, and were very busy in increasing their estates and beautifying their establishments.

From all these things you may conclude, that whereas in Christian and Faithful's time the very name of a Pilgrim was enough to bring odium and disgrace, if not persecution, upon the men who entered the town in that character, it was now considered a very reputable thing, some of the very best society in Vanity Fair holding it in such esteem, that the persecution of Faithful was now thought to be the greatest disgrace that had ever befallen the inhabitants. The Cage in which the pilgrims were once confined as madmen was now never used, and some said that it had been broken in pieces, but others said that it had been consecrated for church purposes, and put under the Cathedral, in a deep cell, from which it might again be brought forth, if occasion required it. The old Lord of the Fair also, seeing how things were going on, now very seldom came thither in person, and was well content, it is said, to have the people appoint for their mayors and judges persons who had either been pilgrims themselves, or greatly favoured that part of the population.

There was another very singular thing that had happened in process of time; for a part of the pilgrims who remained in Vanity Fair began to visit the Cave of Giant Pope, which, you remember, lay at no great distance from the town; so, instead of going farther towards the Celestial City, there became a fashionable sort of pilgrimage to that Cave. They brushed up the Giant, and gave him medicines to alleviate the hurts from those bruises which he had received in his youth; and to make the place pleasanter, they carefully cleared away the remains of the bones and skulls of burned pilgrims, and planted a large enclosure with flowers and evergreens.

When this was done, they even denied that there had ever

been any such cruelties practised, as were demonstrated by the bones, when Christian and Faithful passed by. The Cave also they adorned, and let in just so much light upon it as made it appear romantic and sacred, so that some pilgrims, who came at first only to see the ceremonies, were so much attracted by them as to join in them.

What greatly aided to render this pilgrimage fashionable, was a large saloon erected about half-way between Vanity Fair and the Cave, where much good society from Vanity Fair were accustomed to stop for refreshment and social converse, where also they had little hermitages and altars, and a certain intoxicating refreshment, called Tracts for the Times, the effect of which was to make them feel, while pursuing their way to the Cave, as if they were stepping towards heaven. It was said also that there was an underground passage all the way between this Cave and the Cathedral, of which I have spoken, in Vanity Fair, where the twelve apostles were sculptured in stone, and the Cage was secreted; but this passage I never examined.

Is this a true or false report of some among many things that might be named in the state of society, and the reputation of the Christian pilgrimage now, in Vanity Fair? We will leave Conscience to answer this question, and pass on to the very instructive and exquisitely satirical sketches of character introduced by Bunyan, after Hopeful, rising out of Faithful's ashes, had joined Christian in the way. The martyrdom of Faithful had kindled a light in Vanity Fair that would not easily be put out, and many there were that by his example would themselves, as Hopeful did, become pilgrims. So, by the death of one to bear testimony to the truth, many were affected by that testimony, whose hearts might otherwise have remained hardened to the end of life. Foxe's Book of Martyrs, with the story of Latimer and Ridley, it must be remembered, was one of three books that constituted Bunyan's Prison Library.

There now pass before us in the Pilgrim's Progress a series of characters sketched with inimitable power and beauty, of whom Mr By-ends is the most remarkable, standing for a class of men of no small number and influence.

He got his estate by looking one way and rowing another, and he and his family, friends and relations, differed from the stricter sort in religion only in two small points; first, never striving against wind and water, and second, being always for Religion in his *silver slippers*, loving much to walk with him in the streets, of a sunshiny day, when the people applauded. It is very clear that there could be little or no communion between this man and Christian and Hopeful; for By-ends would hold to his own principles, they being, as he said, harmless and profitable, whereas the principles of Christian and Hopeful were in his view unnecessarily strict and rigid, compelling them to walk with Religion in rags and contempt, as well as in sunshine and silver slippers. When therefore they had met and conversed a little, they soon separated, and speedily after Christian had asked Mr By-ends what was his name.

But now By-ends meets a trio of more congenial companions, Mr Hold-the-World, Mr Money-Love, and Mr Save-all, the whole of them having formerly been schoolmates under Mr Gripe-man, in the town of Love-Gain. Their schoolmaster had taught them, among other things, the art of gaining by putting on the guise of Religion; and Bunyan seems to have designated in these men the characters of base, arrant cheats, and hypocrites. Their conversation with one another is a most amusing piece of satire, developing the sheer worldliness and selfishness of their principles, and the arguments by which such men justify the service of God and Mammon. The speech of Mr Hold-the-World is admirably characteristic, and for its string of earthly proverbs, with the selfish sagacity of which they are all the exponent, it rivals all the delineations of Sancho Panza, by Cervantes. Hold-the-World is indeed the very essence and personification of low worldly wisdom, and what is worse, he carries it all under the guise of piety; in this, it is to be feared, constituting an example of the real character of many who would not be willing to acknowledge such principles, either to themselves or others.

"For my own part," said he, "I can count him but a fool, who, having the liberty to keep what he has, shall be so unwise as to lose it. Let us be wise as serpents; it is best to make hay while the sun shines: you see how the bee lieth still in winter, and bestirs her only when she can have profit with pleasure. God sends sometimes rain and sometimes sunshine: if they be such fools to go through the first, yet let us be content to take fair weather along with us. For my part, I like that religion best that will stand with the security of God's good blessings unto us; for who can imagine that is ruled by his reason, since God has bestowed upon us the good things of this life, but that he would have us keep them for his sake? Abraham and Solomon grew rich in religion; and Job says that 'a good man shall lay up gold as dust.' But he must not be such as Christian and Hopeful, added Hold-the-World, if they be such rigid simpletons as you have described them."

Then By-ends proposed this question: Suppose a man, a minister or a tradesman, &c., should have an advantage lie before him to get the good blessings of this life, yet so as that he can by no means come by them, except, in appearance at least, he becomes extraordinarily zealous in some points of religion that he meddled not with before; may he not use these means to obtain this end, and yet be a right honest man?

Mr Money-Love undertook to answer this question, and the crooked policy of his conclusions jumped well, you may be sure, with the minds of his companions, first concerning ministers, second concerning tradesmen. Dr Paley would have done well to have read over this chapter in Bunyan before composing some of the chapters in his Moral Philosophy, and his sermon on the Utility of Distinctions in the Ministry. The philosophy of Money-Love and By-ends is that which the god of this world teaches all his votaries; and, alas, when motives come to be scrutinized, as they will be, at the bar of God, how much of our apparent good will be found to be evil, because in the root that nourished both the branches and the fruit, there was found to be nothing but self-interest carefully concealed! You seek me, not because of the miracles to be witnessed, or the grace to be gained, but because ye did eat of the loaves, and were filled.

"Suppose a minister," said Mr Money-Love, "a very worthy man, possessed but of a very small benefice, and has in his eye a greater, more plump and fat by far: he has also now an opportunity of getting it, yet, so as by being more studious, by preaching more frequent and zealously, and, because the temper of the people requires it, by altering of some of his principles: for my part, I see no reason why a man may not do this, provided he has a call, yea, and more a great deal besides, and yet be an honest man. For why?

1. His desire of a greater benefice is lawful; this cannot be contradicted, since it is set before him by Providence; so then he may get it if he can, making no question for conscience' sake.

2. Because his desire after that benefice makes him more studious, a more zealous preacher, &c., and so makes him a better man, yea, makes him better improve his parts; which is according to the mind of God.

3. Now, as to his complying with the temper of his people, by deserting, to serve them, some of his principles, this argueth: (1.) that he is of a self-denying temper; (2.) of a sweet and winning deportment; and (3.) so more fit for the ministerial function.

I conclude, then, that a minister who changes a *small* for a *great*, should not, for so doing, be judged as covetous; but rather, since he is improved in his parts and industry thereby, be counted as one that pursues his call, and the opportunity put into his hands to do good.

And now to the second part of the question, which concerns the tradesman you mentioned; suppose such an one to have but a poor employ in the world, but by becoming religious he may mend his market, perhaps get a rich wife, or more and far better customers to his shop; for my part, I see no reason but this may be lawfully done; for why?

1. To become religious is a virtue, by what means soever a man becomes so.

2. Nor is it unlawful to get a rich wife, or better customers to my shop.

1. Besides, the man that gets these by becoming religious,

gets that which is good, of them that are good, by becoming good himself; so then, here is a good wife, and good customers, and good gain, and all this by becoming religious, which is good; therefore, to become religious, to get all these, is a good and profitable design."

Now is not this logic of Money-Love very barefaced? And yet these men considered it perfectly triumphant, and an argument that Christian and Hopeful could not possibly contradict. Whereupon they resolved to propound the same question to them, and so puzzle and defeat them. But to their astonishment, Christian declared at once that none others than heathens, hypocrites, devils, and witches could be of their opinion, and then he went on to prove this so clearly and powerfully out of Scripture, with instances in point, that the men were completely staggered, and stood staring one upon another, unable to answer a word. What, said Christian to Hopeful, will these men do with the sentence of God, if they cannot stand before the sentence of men?

This passage in the pilgrimage is full of instruction, and we might dwell long upon it, and upon the danger of evil motives under the guise of a good cause, or of unholy motives in a holy cause. The motive is every thing; it makes the man. An eye single makes a single-minded man: an eye double makes a double-minded man. An eye single is good in whatever a man undertakes, considered even merely in reference to the things of this life, and as requisite to decision of character. In this view the children of this world are wiser in their generation than the children of light; what they do for this world they do with energy and whole-heartedness, which is just what, as pilgrims, we want for Christ. We want, in all things, an eye single for God, for his approbation, for his glory, and this is the precious motive that excludes every other, or keeps every other subordinate, and turns every thing to gold. "Whatsoever ye do, do it *heartily*, as to the Lord, and not unto men." The very drudgery and toilsomeness of our pilgrimage is turned into a divine and holy service, by this precious singleness of heart for Christ! Oh how desirable is this in every thing! This is the body of that beautiful composition by Herbert, which is perhaps the best series of stanzas he ever wrote, entitled The Elixir. It is good to drink this on our pilgrimage, especially after such a conversation with By-ends and Money-Love. By-ends are almost always bad ends, but love to Christ, singleness of heart for Christ, sets them at a distance, and shows them at once in their native hypocrisy and deformity.

> Teach me, my God and King,
> In all things Thee to see,
> And what I do in any thing,
> To do it as for Thee.
>
> Not rudely, as a beast,
> To run into an action;
> But still to make Thee prepossest,
> And give it thy perfection.
>
> A man that looks on glass
> On it may stay his eye;
> And if it pleaseth, through it pass,
> And then the heaven espy.
>
> All may of Thee partake;
> Nothing can be so mean,
> Which with this tincture for thy sake
> Will not grow bright and clean.
>
> A servant with this clause,
> Makes drudgery divine:
> Who sweeps a room as for thy laws,
> Makes that and the action fine.
>
> This is the famous stone,
> That turneth all to gold;
> For that which God doth touch and own
> Cannot for less be told.

Now we must go on with our Pilgrims. They had now a short interval of pleasant going, over a plain called Ease, but it was soon passed, and again they entered into danger. Bunyan has put in the margin, "The ease that Pilgrims have in this life is short." The temptation which they now encountered was that of filthy lucre, for they came to a silver mine in the side of a hill, and were invited by a very gentlemanly man, Demas, to turn aside for a little, and examine this mine, and perhaps undertake a small speculation for themselves. Hopeful was for going, but Christian held him back, while he examined Demas, who declared that the working in this mine was not very dangerous except to those who were careless. There are many pilgrims who reason thus, or are ensnared by such reasoning. They think that if other men have perished by the love of money, it was because they went too far; but for themselves, tney mean just to enter the mine, dig a little, and then come out again, satisfied to have neither poverty nor riches. But this is a temptation, where one step draws on another, so that no man can tell how far he is going; and the damps in this mine are such, that the further men go in, the greater danger they encounter, and the more incapacitated they are for turning back. "For they that will be rich, fall into temptation, and a snare, and into many foolish and hurtful lusts, which drown men in destruction and perdition. For the love of money is the root of all evil; which, while some coveted after, they have erred from the faith, and pierced themselves through with many sorrows."

In our day there are many such hills Lucre, and such men Demas, to be encountered in our pilgrimage. But the air of the mines, it is observable, is in all those regions, and the pilgrims who turn aside, generally get so infected with it that they are ever after either greatly hindered and weakened in their course, or entirely disabled from pursuing their pilgrimage. There are also certain wild lands stretching off behind the hill Lucre, where some pilgrims wandering in search of treasure have lost their way, and never been heard of more. By divine grace the vigilance of Christian carried him and Hopeful past this danger, though By-ends and all his company went into the mine at the first invitation from Demas, and these men were never more seen on their pilgrimage.

The habits of conformity to the world in Christians, and the love of money in the Church of Christ, are the two forms of sin and danger especially brought to view in this portion of the Pilgrim's Progress. There are certain passages of Scripture, certain declarations of our blessed Lord, which are "sharp arrows in the hearts of the King's enemies" on these subjects. "What shall it profit a man, if he gain the whole world, and lose his own soul?" This is a sum in profit and loss, which it will take eternity to cipher out. Therefore let no man try it; leave it to the Saviour. Turn you to him and say, Lord thou knowest; thou knowest perfectly what the soul is, and what eternity is, and I do not know either; and what it is to lose the soul, God grant I may never know. Lord, keep me from making this experiment. And yet, there are multitudes who *are* making it, multitudes who are playing at this game, working at this sum in arithmetic, What shall it profit a man, if he gain the whole world, and lose his own soul?

This is the arithmetic of a great part of the world in Vanity Fair. Now you may gain the world if you seek it. Its comforts, luxuries, sinful pleasures, may be yours, if you be willing to barter your soul for them; they almost always come at that price; so you may gain the world, you may know what that part of the sum is; but what it is to lose the soul, that computation you are to make, that column you are to add up, in eternity; and that is an experiment which you cannot make but by making it for ever.

Then there is that other passage, " Ye cannot serve God and Mammon!" Cannot! Yea, cannot; it is an absolute impossibility. Then the life of a great many persons is a perpetual strife after what is impossible, for many *are* striving to serve God and Mammon. Hard-working people they are; there are no greater drudges in the world than those By-ends and Money-Loves, and Demases, who, in the Christian church, are working away at this problem, to serve God and Mammon. That also is a tremendous sentence. " It is easier for a camel to go through the eye of a needle, than for a rich man to enter the kingdom of heaven." " Often as the motley reflexes of my experience move in long processions of manifold groups before me," says a great writer, and certainly not a cynical man, Mr Coleridge, " the distinguished and world-honoured company of Christian Mammonists appear to the eye of my imagination as a drove of camels heavily laden, yet all at full speed, and each in the confident expectation of passing through the eye of the needle, without stop or halt, both beasts and baggage!"

From such sad and fearful madness may the grace of our God deliver us!

> Fulness to such a burden is
> Who go on pilgrimage;
> Here little, and hereafter bliss,
> Is best from age to age.

LECTURE TWELFTH.

Doubting Castle and Giant Despair.

Beauty and wisdom of this delineation.—Many ways of getting into this Castle. —Only one way to get out.—By-Path Meadow, and its Allurements.—Enjoyment of Christian and Hopeful before they went into it.—Their discontent with the roughness of the King's highway.—Their four errors.—Their sleep amidst the storm, and the discovery of them by Giant Despair.—Their treatment and behaviour in the Castle.—A Sabbath-morning in prayer.— Discovery of the Key of Promise.—Their escape.—The mercy and faithfulness of God in Christ.—Consequences of the hiding of God's countenance.— Misery of being without God in eternity.—Solemn realities of this Allegory

WE are coming now upon a scene in this pilgrimage, which is drawn from the experience of all travellers towards the Celestial City, and is in a greater or less degree familiar to them all. What pilgrim does not know Doubting Castle, kept by Giant Despair ? Its huge keeps and moss-grown frowning battlements rise before us almost as familiar as the Wicket Gate ; and what pilgrims are there, that have not, at some time or another, seen the inside of the Castle ? They may not all have seen Giant Despair in person, but his wife Diffidence they have met with, and the underkeepers of his prison. They may not all have been thrown into the same horrible dungeon where Christian and Hopeful were confined, nor visited by the Giant with temptations to make away with themselves in their misery ; but in some cell or another they have had to bewail their sins, and to groan and suffer by reason of unbelieving doubts and fears. So, though the Dreamer, in the second part of his Pilgrim's Progress, gives an account of the destruction of the Castle, and the death of the Giant, yet no man believes that he is dead, and still from day to day the pilgrims are straying into his grounds, and finding to their cost the depth and terror of his prisons. Giant Despair will never die, so long as unpardoned sin remains, or a sense of it burdens the conscience; nor is there any security against falling into his hands, but in the care and mercy of One who is mightier than he, even Christ Jesus.

The personification of Despair is one of the most instructive and beautiful portions of Bunyan's Allegory. It appeals either to every man's experience, or to every man's prophetic sense of what may come upon him on account of sin. It is at once in some respects the very gloomiest and very brightest part of the Pilgrim's Progress; for it shews at once to what a depth of misery sin may plunge the Christian, and also to what a depth the mercy of God in Christ may reach. The colouring of the picture is extremely vivid, the remembrance of it can never pass from the mind; and as in a gallery of beautiful paintings, there may often be one that so strongly reminds you of your own experience, and carries you back into past life with such power, or that in itself is so remarkably beautiful, as to chain you before it in admiration, and keep you dwelling upon it with unabated interest, so it is with this delineation of Giant Despair, among the many admirable sketches of Bunyan's piety and genius. It is so full of deep life and meaning that you cannot exhaust it, and it is of such exquisite propriety and beauty that you are never tired with examining it.

It is easy for fallen beings to get into Doubting Castle; conviction of sin, unaccompanied by a sense of the mercy of Christ, will take any man there at once; and the last possession and abode of the soul hardened in sin and abandoned of God must be DESPAIR. There are many ways in which even a Christian may come there. Some men enter by unbelief, and whatever state of mind or habit of sin shuts out the Saviour, is sure to bring a man there at once. Some men enter by pride and self-righteousness; if a man trust in his own merits, instead of the blood and righteousness of

Christ, for justification, he may seem for a time to be at large ; but when he comes to know his own state, the bars of the prison will be round about him, and Giant Despair will be his keeper.

Some men enter this Castle by habits of self-indulgence, some by particular cherished sins, some by dallying with temptations, some by sudden falling into deep sins, some by neglect of watchfulness and prayer, some by a gradual creeping coldness and stupor in the things of religion, the dangerous spirit of slumber not being guarded against and resisted. Some get into this prison by natural gloom and despondency of mind, of which Satan takes an advantage ; others by brooding over the threatenings, and neglecting the promises ; others by going to penances and duties for the relief of conscience, and not to Christ. Neglect of duty takes most men to prison, but duties themselves may bring us there if we trust in duties for acceptance, and not in Christ. Neglect of God's Word will take men to this prison, and leaning to one's own understanding. Distorted views of Divine truth, speculative error, and the habit of speculation rather than of faith and life in divine things may shut up the soul in darkness. Some get into this prison by spiritual sins, others by sensual ; some by the lusts of the flesh, some by the lust of the eyes, some by the pride of life ; some by conformity to the world, and obedience to fashion ; some by the pressure of business, others by the cares of life and the deceitfulness of riches ; they that *will be rich* are always on the way to this Castle, if not in it.

There is a way to this Castle from the Arbour on the Hill Difficulty, and also from the Enchanted Ground, if a man sleeps there and loses his roll, and then, instead of going to Christ, pursues his journey without it. And if a Christian, when he has sinned against God, stays away from him, and keeps silence towards him, then he will be so shut up and beaten in this prison, that his bones will wax old through his roaring all the day long. This was once the case with David. David fell into this Castle by gross sin, and fearfully was he handled by Giant Despair. Asaph fell into this Castle by doubting and complaining of God's unequal dealings with the righteous and the wicked, so that he was as a beast before God. Job fell into this Castle by taking a wrong view of God's chastisements, and he only got out by this saying: "I know that my Redeemer liveth."

A child of God may fall into this Castle by making a wrong use, or rather by not making a right use, of trials, by not receiving them as a child should receive the corrections of a father. A repining disposition will very quickly bring the soul into this prison. Jonah fell into this prison by running away from known duty, and preferring his own will to God's will. He went down to the bottoms of the mountains, so that he had to cry out of the belly of hell; and God heard his voice. Thomas fell into the Castle by obstinate unbelief, so that all the prayers and tears of his fellow-disciples could not bring him out, and he came out only by that gracious voice of the Saviour, "Be not faithless, but believing!" Peter fell into this Castle, about the same time, and wept bitterly, and it was nothing but the mercy of the same Saviour that brought him out. Satan would have kept him there, had it not been for that wonderful prayer of the Saviour beforehand, "I have prayed for thee, that thy faith fail not."

Alas! alas! how many ways there are of getting into this gloomy prison! Oh, if Christ be not always with the soul, or if at any time it go astray from him, or if its reliance be on any thing whatever but his mercy, his blood, his grace, then is it near the gloom of this Dungeon; then may Giant Despair be heard walking in his grounds, and verily the echo of his footsteps oftentimes falls upon the soul before the grim form rises on the vision. And some who have once entered the Castle have staid there a great while, because they have tried many other means of escape, than by the blood of Christ; because they have used picklocks, and penances, and stratagems, and the help of friends outside the Castle, but not the Key of Promise, or not aright, not throwing themselves on the Saviour alone for pardon, peace, and justification. A man who gets into difficulty through sin, will never get out by self-righteousness; nor are past sins, nor the burden of them, to be ever removed by present morality;

nothing but faith, nothing but the precious blood of Christ, can take away sin, can remove the stain of it, can deliver the soul from its condemnation.

Perhaps, notwithstanding there are so many examples of great sins bringing men into his power, yet, with the majority of Christians, it is little sins neglected, and sins of omission, and duties undone, that shut them up in Doubting Castle, kept by Giant Despair. Duties undone are in reality great sins, but they do not strike the conscience with such immediate terror as open sins, and therefore perhaps they are the more dangerous. The soul gets sadly accustomed to such neglects, and there is always some plausible excuse in the first instance, in the beginnings, a man being always determined to repair the neglect immediately; but it soon grows into a habit, and then the conscience ceases to be so tender on that point, and at length there comes to be such an accumulation of neglects and omissions that there is no computing them.

Now, when this is the case, and yet a man attempts to keep on in his Christian course, beneath the burden of such neglect of duty, he is much like a man who has failed in business under a heavy load of debt, and attempts to set up again before his creditors have released him, so that if at any time they come upon him, all his new earnings are gone at once, and he is penniless. So a Christian, without coming to a reckoning with himself and Christ concerning such neglects of duty, and such habits of neglect, may think he is going on well, but the moment a sense of these sins comes to him, he finds himself in the grounds of Giant Despair, and is taken away to his Castle, and there he has to bewail his guilt and misery, sometimes many days before mercy comes to him. And never can he find mercy, but by casting himself, with all his accumulation and burden of sins upon Christ. And oh what mercy it is to be reclaimed from such habits of neglect to a habit of watchfulness, even at the expense of ever so many days and nights in this Castle! Better by far to be seized by Giant Despair while mercy may be sought, while Christ is, as it were, yet within hearing, than to be left to go on at ease amidst neglects of duty, and to become hardened in sin without meeting the Giant, without being wakened to a sense of guilt by his black countenance and his heavy club. Men sometimes neglect secret prayer for present business or pleasure; this is getting over the stile, and taking a few steps in By-Path Meadow; then a few steps farther are taken, and thus gradually the soul gets farther and farther from God, from Christ, from grace, from duty, and duty becomes more difficult, and the allurements of By-Path Meadow more dangerous, perhaps openly sinful; and then the night and storm come on, and in the morning, Giant Despair, prowling about his grounds, takes the trespassers, and shuts them under lock and key in his dungeon.

The pursuit of duty, though it be the way of self-denial, is without doubt the only way of peace and safety. But some pilgrims get into Doubting Castle by neglecting one set of duties while they perform others. In all our callings there are some duties more difficult than others, and some that are more pleasing to our natural inclinations. A merchant or tradesman loves to be diligent in his business, and all the active duties and even great fatigue in the course of it, are yet pleasing to him; but the word of God and prayer are not so naturally pleasing to him, and spiritual fatigue is not so readily encountered by him. A farmer loves the external occupations of his farm, and he must make hay while the sun shines, and he is not likely to get into By-Path Meadow by neglecting the making of his hay; but it is not so natural for him to pray, and he may possibly get into Doubting Castle by neglecting his prayers in August, that he may get in his hay in its season during the fair weather. A minister, who loves more to study, or to visit, than to pray, finds it very easy to study but very hard to pray; sometimes his very sermons may so occupy him, that he too may think he has not present time for prayer; nevertheless, by neglects and omissions in any way, he may fall into Doubting Castle, kept by Giant Despair. A prudent, busy housewife may love much better to be like Martha, anxious and troubled about many things, bustling and busy from morning till night, than to be like Mary, sitting at the feet of Jesus. Domestic avocations often constitute a By-Path Meadow, where spiritual duties are neglected, and so the soul wanders into the regions of Giant Despair.

The delineation of By-Path Meadow, with the experience of the pilgrims in it, is very affecting and very beautiful. Every man knows what By-Path Meadow means, as well as what Doubting Castle signifies. In general, some habit or mode of self-indulgence, some shrinking back from the hardness of the pilgrimage, and some departure from its duties, for indulgence to the flesh, is here shadowed forth. But it is observable that just before the pilgrims wandered from the right way into this Meadow, they had a season of great delight in the Word of God, great enjoyment in their Christian pilgrimage. After by divine grace they had been delivered from the temptations of Demas, they had sweet communion with God, reviving communications of the Holy Spirit, rich draughts from the Water of Life, delightful views of the preciousness of Christ, and such green pastures, such quiet meadows, with lilies and still waters, that it seemed as if all their conflicts were over, and they had nothing to do but to enjoy these abundant consolations. The passage in which Bunyan has described these earnests of the Spirit, these sweet foretastes of the heavenly rest, comprehends one of the most ravishing intervals in the experience of Christian and Hopeful.

"I saw then," says Bunyan, "that they went on their way to a pleasant river, which David the King called the River of God, but John, the River of the Water of Life. Now their way lay just upon the bank of the river; here therefore Christian and his companion walked with great delight; they drank also of the water of the river, which was pleasant and enlivening to their weary spirits. Besides, on the banks of the river, on either side, were green trees with all manner of fruit; and the leaves they ate to prevent surfeits, and other diseases that are incident to those that heat their blood by travels. On either side of the river was also a meadow, curiously beautified with lilies; and it was green all the year long. In this meadow they lay down and slept, for here they might lie down safely. When they awoke, they gathered again of the fruit of the trees, and drank again of the water of the river, and they lay down again to sleep. Thus they did several days and nights."

Here was a season of deep and exquisite enjoyment in the Word of God, and the exercises of the divine life. How could the pilgrims turn aside from it so soon? Perhaps it was by forgetting the Saviour's purpose in granting these enjoyments, taking that for their rest which was only meant to add to their holiness, and prepare them for labour. The truth is, that the active duties of the Christian pilgrimage are never in themselves so delightful as the River of the Water of Life flowing through the soul; that is, they require self-denial, and are attended with difficulty. When the affections are drawn out after Christ, and are warm towards God and heaven, and all external things go pleasantly, how easy and how sweet it is to wander up and down along the banks of the river, treading the soft grass, eating the wholesome and delicious fruits, and breathing the fragrance of the flowers. Do we not sometimes have such seasons? But they are given to us, as the Arbour was in the midst of the Hill Difficulty, not for indulgence to the flesh, but to invigorate and prepare us for active duty; not to constitute a rest, which we may quietly enjoy, but to fit us for remaining toil, for increasing activity and usefulness.

Now, then, if the pilgrims think too much of these comforts, if they are rather seeking after spiritual enjoyment, than for usefulness and growth in grace by active discipline and duty, it is possible that spiritual enjoyments themselves may become a snare, making the pilgrim unwilling to separate from such a blessed quietness of life, when the pilgrimage leads to a rougher road, where the river and the road part for a season. To read the Bible and to pray are easy duties, even for weak Christians, when the heart is full of love, and God's countenance is shining; but to go out into the highways and hedges, to visit the poor and afflicted, to do missionary work, to bear trials, to seek to win sinful men to Christ, as you have opportunity, this always requires self-denial; so that By-Path Meadow may be very attractive, and those very persons may be tempted to pursue it, who have been enjoying much in the Word of God and in prayer, but who, when trying times come on, and painful labours are necessary, listen to the voice of self-indulgence. This we are always apt to do, and nothing but divine grace can make us submit to divine discipline.

A spirit of discontent and repining amidst trials, a spirit of rebellion because God takes away our mercies, is likely at any time, if indulged, to bring the soul into the Castle of Giant Despair. If we have been enjoying much of God's goodness, both inward and external, and, then, because the path of duty leads through suffering, or because God sends us on errands humiliating to our pride, we shrink back from duty, and take some compromising course, we may seem to be travelling in a meadow, but the end thereof is danger and gloom. When a man refuses to undergo such labour and suffering for Christ as lie in the way of his duty, he will have to suffer far more inwardly than he ever could have done outwardly. The sufferings of Christian and Hopeful in the grounds and castle of Giant Despair were incomparably greater than all the fatigue they could have endured while travelling the rough road of their pilgrimage. Yet we often forget, when hardness comes, that our business is to "endure hardness, as good soldiers of Jesus Christ."

Our simple heavenly-minded pilgrims seem to have forgotten this for a season, and to have expected nothing but enjoyment all the rest of the way. But now the river and the way for a time parted, and the way was rough; so still as they went they wished for a better. Here were the first beginnings of discontent, and they ought to have repressed them. They should have said, It is true this way is not so pleasant as the Meadow, but it is the Lord's way, and the best, doubtless, for us to travel in; these trials are of God's making for us, and they come in the way of our duty; so we must still go on and be thankful. But they said, How very rough is the way, how painful, how fatiguing! I wish there were a better way; can we not find an easier way? When Christians thus allow themselves to wish for a better way than the way of God's appointment, Satan is generally at hand to point out some way that *seems* easier and better, and to tempt the soul to wander in it. A man speedily enters into temptation when he becomes discontented with God's allotments; then Satan presents allurements, and from wishing for a better way the soul goes into a worse. The discontented wish is father to a sinful will; *I wish for a better* is followed by *I will have a better;* and so the soul goes astray.

The pilgrims had no sooner wished for a better, than By-Path Meadow presented itself, with a convenient, tempting stile. This is very opportune, said they, just what we were wishing for; we'll not walk in the dust, when we can tread upon grass and flowers, especially if the meadow lies along the wayside. *So they went to the stile to see.* This was entering into temptation, this was looking on the wine when it was red, this was a wandering, sinful desire, not checked but dallied with. It is the same thing, said they, the meadow and the road go on together. But it is a dangerous thing to be trying the experiment how far we may sin safely. These pilgrims, contrary to their usual wont, were now trying the experiment with how little self-denial they could get along in their pilgrimage, and of course with how much self-indulgence it might consist. But this, I say, is very dangerous. It is like venturesome schoolboys trying how far they may make thin ice bend under them over a deep place without breaking through. This going as far as you can on debateable ground is a great injury to the tenderness of the conscience. A man who *will* go as far as he *may*, is sure to go farther than he ought; and then a tempestuous night and Giant Despair's Castle are not far off.

So deceitful are the ways of sin, that the first steps of travel in them seemed to these pilgrims but as an indulgence to wearied, sore-footed Virtue. True, there is no want of company in such a case. There as those who travel in By-Path Meadow without any scruple at all; so the pilgrims speedily espied a man going before them at a great rate, whose name was Vain-confidence, of whom (silly men) they asked if this were the way to the Celestial City; and he told them, Most certainly, he was straight in it himself!

So sometimes the real pilgrims take counsel and example of strangers, of worldly men, and of presumptuous, careless persons, who have little or no conscience. Vain-confidence is a sad guide anywhere, but especially when one has wandered out of the way.

Now, there were four capital errors which the pilgrims had already committed :—(1.) They had discontentedly wished for a better way ; (2.) They had gone up to the stile to look over it ; (3.) They had climbed over the stile ; (4.) They had taken encouragement by a wrong example, and followed Vain-confidence ; and what was strange, the older and stronger Christian had led the younger and weaker one out of the way. Now, when the night came on, and the storm, they began to find how evil and bitter a thing it is to wander from God. They heard the fall of Vain-confidence into a deep, dreadful pit, and they heard him groan, but could see nothing. And now they bemoan their folly, and though they are both in a sad case, yet Christian's is certainly the worse, for having led Hopeful out of the way; and most humbly and ingenuously does he beg his brother's pardon.

But why, in that tempestuous night, when the waters were rising around them, did they not obey the voice which they heard, and persevere, amidst all dangers, till they had gotten again into the King's highway ? Sometimes the pilgrims, who have thus wandered into darkness, seek relief by duties, and not by Christ ; and so conscience gets a temporary quiet, but a false one. There is no place of safety short of Christ. Some such relief these pilgrims seem to have gotten, in that they reached a rising ground, above the waters, and there being thoroughly tired, and not being able, or thinking they were not, to reach the King's highway that night, they there lay down and slept. But, ah, what sleep can there be until the soul has come back to Christ ? What sleep can there be amidst unforgiven sin ? They had better not have slept at all, but kept struggling amidst the storm all night long, for these grounds were the grounds of Giant Despair, and Giant Despair found them, not striving to get back, but fast asleep for sorrow and weariness. Ah, what safety can there be for sleepers away from Christ? This sleep was worse for Christian and Hopeful than that in the Arbour. So do Christians sometimes make an imperfect return to duty in their own strength; and conscience thus being imperfectly quieted, lulled by a sleep, and not sprinkled by the blood of Christ, Giant Despair after all finds them in his grounds, and carries them away to his castle.

Now were Christian and Hopeful in a dreadful case; deep down in darkness, the bars of the earth and of death around them, no food, nor drink, nor light, nor comfort, the weeds were wrapped about their head, and in this dungeon they cried as out of the belly of hell, bemoaning themselves to one another with groans and lamentations. The description which Bunyan has given of their treatment by the giant is exquisitely beautiful and affecting; no part of the Pilgrim's Progress makes a deeper impression than this; and the different manner in which the two pilgrims endure these trials, forms a development of character which in no other portion of the work is more profound and instructive. Hopeful continues hopeful, even in despair; Christian at one time abandons all hope, and listens seriously to the giant's infernal temptations to self-destruction. Hopeful had not fallen so far as Christian, for Christian had been the more eminent and experienced pilgrim of the two, and had also led his fellow astray. But this did not make all the difference. Hopeful's frame of mind was naturally more elastic than Christian's; he was of a more joyous temperament, and more apt to look on the bright side; not so deep, grave, and far-sighted as Christian, and not capable, in any case, of quite such deep trials of feeling. Hopeful's spirit soon rose again, but Christian, when he is down on account of sin, is brought even to the gates of hell. How affectingly instructive are Hopeful's arguments with Christian to dissuade him from suicide. Doubtless, good men have been tempted in this way, but strange enough, it seems that a sense of God's wrath and desertion on account of sin should tempt a man to plunge deeper into such wrath, nay, to incur it past redemption.

Christian never dreamed of destroying himself when he was fighting with Apollyon, in passing through the Valley of the Shadow of Death; but a sense of sin, and of God's wrath on account of it, quite unmans the soul. None can stand against God's terrors. A thousand fiends may easier be met with than the remembrance of one sin. Besides, in the conflict with Apollyon, and the passage of the Valley of the Shadow of Death, Christian was in the course of his duty; both these dangers lay directly in the path to the Celestial City, so that, though hard beset, and pressed out of measure, Christian was not despairing, for he knew he met those evils in the right way; but here he was out of the way. Giant Despair's Castle could not even be seen from the King's highway; it was so far off that he wandered a long distance before he came in sight of it, and here the pilgrims were far from the road, they knew not how far. They were in such desperation, that for a long time they could do nothing but brood over their gloomy thoughts, and they hardly dared to pray.

All this is related as a story, with such natural incidents, with such power of character and such vivid colouring, that no story of a life could be more graphic; and yet it is allegory, it is the experience of the mind alone; but allegory so perfect, the experience so touched into life, that each becomes either, and may be perfect story or allegory, as you please. The temptations to suicide, presented by Giant Despair, constitute a description so wonderfully similar to a passage in Spenser on the same subject, that it would seem as if Bunyan must have read the Fairy Queen. The effect of the vile arguments of Despair upon the knight in Spenser is very similar to that of the arguments used by the Giant upon Christian. The poor pilgrim was almost beside himself in his misery.

And yet, this is the man who overcame the Hill Difficulty, and passed through the Valley of the Shadow of Death, and passed so nobly through Vanity Fair. This is the hero of that dread conflict with Apollyon. And now he, whom the world could not overcome, nor fiends destroy, thinks of destroying himself! Oh, the intolerable misery of an accusing conscience! The sense of the guilt of our departure from God is far worse to bear than the mere hiding of God's countenance; it makes cowards and slaves of the bravest.

In this state did Christian and Hopeful remain day after day, night after night, though it was all night with them, and no light but to discover sights of wo. Yet, after all, they would not give way to the suggestions of Giant Despair. It is a curious picture which Bunyan has drawn of the intercourse between the Giant and his wife Diffidence. They form a very loving couple in their way, and the Giant takes no new step in the treatment of the pilgrims without consulting Mrs Diffidence over night; so that the curtain lectures to which we listen are very curious. But Mrs Diffidence ought rather to have been called Dame Desperation, or Desperate Resolution: for she seems, if anything, the more stubborn genius of the two; and when the Giant, very much astonished that "the sturdy rogues" hold out so long against his temptations and his beatings, brings the case to her at night for advice, she proposes his taking the pilgrims into the castle-yard to shew them the fearful heap of the sculls and bones of pilgrims who have been by him destroyed.

Nevertheless, all would not avail utterly to subdue the pilgrims; though in deep misery they waited still, and Hopeful would still be encouraging his brother, though it seemed to be hoping against hope. Like as in the Slough of Despond, at first setting out on the pilgrimage, they were unable to see the promises, or in dreadful, sullen unbelief, refused to take hold upon them, as being beyond their case. And this was partly because as yet, though bemoaning their sin and misery, they had not returned to prayer; a dreadful case, whenever it happens to the Christian; for when, from any cause, he is driven from the throne of grace, or yielding to temptation, stays away from that sure refuge, he is indeed in terrible danger, he is wellnigh lost. And this cannot remain, for he must either pray or *be* lost, and it is in prayer that he generally finds the first light after darkness. So Bunyan, with exquisite beauty and truth, makes his pilgrims resume this weapon of All-Prayer, compelled unto it by their very depth of guilt and misery.

It is Saturday night, and all night long they wrestle in prayer till the very break of day; all night long before they see the promise. The Sabbath, as it breaks, finds them in prayer; and now, as the dawn begins to make silvery gray the sky and the mountains outside the Castle, so the unwonted light is breaking on the soul in the pilgrim's Dungeon. All at once, as if it were a new revelation, Christian finds and applies the Promises: and indeed it *is* a new revelation, which none but the merciful Saviour could make; he it is, who has been watching over his erring disciples; he it is, who has known their path, when their soul was overwhelmed within them; he it is, who has kept back the hand of Despair from destroying them. They have gone astray like lost sheep; he it is, who leaveth the ninety and nine upon the mountains, and seeketh the hundredth one, until he findeth it; he it is, who binds up the broken in heart, and healeth all their wounds.

They were praying, "Restore unto me the joy of thy salvation, and uphold me by thy free Spirit; cast me not away from thy presence, and take not thy Holy Spirit from me;"— and now as the Sabbath dawns, when Jesus himself arose from the tomb, the star of Hope rises on the hearts of these prisoned ones, and they suddenly cried out, as a glimpse of the Saviour's long-hidden countenance broke through their gloom, There is forgiveness with thee, that thou mayest be feared, with thee there is plenteous redemption! What a fool am I, said Christian, to lie in this filthy dungeon, when I have a key in my bosom, that I am persuaded will open every lock in Doubting Castle! Yes, it was in his bosom; and it had been there ever since he entered the Wicket Gate. But who made him now feel it? Who made him remember it now, after so long forgetfulness, and who gave him skill and strength to use his golden key aright? It was God, against whom he had sinned; the Saviour, whom he had wounded; the merciful Spirit, whom he had grieved. But now, the key! the key! put it into the lock and try it! They trembled with fear and eagerness; the creaking of the rusty hinges made them tremble; they felt as if they could hear the breathing of the Giant after them, as if his grasp was upon their shoulders, and it was not till they had passed the outer gate of the Castle, and got into the clear open air, that they dared believe they were really escaping.

It was Sabbath morning. The sun was breaking over the hills, and fell upon their pale, haggard countenances. It was to them a new creation; they breathed the fresh, reviving air, and brushed, with hasty steps, the dew from the untrodden grass, and fled the nearest way to the stile, over which they had wandered. How much they had suffered! But they had learned a lesson by that suffering, which nothing else could have taught them, and which would remain with them to the day of their death. They had learned, from bitter experience, that any thing and all things had better be endured, than to depart from God and duty; and that whereas ease sought in the way of their pilgrimage might seem as a sweet meadow for a time, it would prove in the end a more intolerable evil than all the roughness and hardness of the King's highway.

They had learned also to value the light of God's countenance as they never did before, to watch as they never did before, against every thing that might interrupt that light, or shut out the Saviour from their souls. They had learned to distrust themselves more thoroughly, and to cast themselves on Christ more entirely; and these are the two great lessons which we need to learn from experience; our own weakness and Christ's strength. They had gained new proofs of the efficacy of a Saviour's blood, as well as new views, and a deeper sense, of the dreadful evil of sin, and in every way they were wiser, though perhaps sadder men than before. It was almost worth those fearful days and nights in Giant Despair's Castle, to learn so much more both of themselves and of Christ; but this bringing good out of evil was God's doing, and not theirs; they had perished in their sins, had not God had mercy on them.

And now they use, as all pilgrims should do, their own bitter experience for good to others. They mean to keep others, if possible, from falling into the same snare with themselves; and so, as soon as they are got safe into the Lord's blessed highway, and out of their enemies' jurisdiction, they proceed to nail up that famous inscription, " Over this stile lies the way to Doubting Castle, kept by Giant Despair." They thought, forsooth, that no pilgrim after them, reading this inscription, would dare go out of the way. But by a strange blindness, which happens to the pilgrims whenever they are bent on self-indulgence, they are so taken with the Meadow, that they do not read the inscription, and so they pass over the same stile, just as if no person had ever tried it before, and just as if there were no Giant Despair's Castle. Before Christian and Hopeful passed by, there had been just such inscriptions, but the pilgrims did not heed them. King David himself, who spent so long time in the Castle, put up just such an inscription, near three thousand years ago, and Solomon, from bitter experience, renewed it after him; but Christian and Hopeful themselves did not read it. Nor do any read it, except the Lord enlighten their darkness, and make them vigilant at the very moment temptation comes upon them. For the time when they enter into temptation is the time when this inscription disappears, and when they are once entered in as in a cloud, they can hear nothing, see nothing, but the temptation itself, and so they fall, and are afterwards made wretched. May the Lord keep us from such dreadful experience! Oh what dread meaning there is in those warnings of Christ, *Pray that ye enter not into temptation!* Watch and pray, *lest ye enter into temptation!* Entering *into* temptation is a very different thing from being assailed *by* temptation; but in neither case can we conquer or be delivered except by Christ.

There is nothing which God does, that he does not do freely, and like a God. When he pardons our sins, it is to remember them no more for ever; when he restores to us the joy of his salvation, his face shines upon us with a beautifying love, as if we had never offended him. " Only return unto me, and I will return unto you, saith the Lord." So we no sooner find the pilgrims got out of the Castle of Giant Despair, and their inscription over the stile finished, but we meet them in sweet instructive company on the top of the

Delectable Mountains. So great, so free, so abundant is God's goodness in Christ in the pardon of the penitent. Yet these mountains were not attained without climbing; none arrive at them but by much holy diligence in the pilgrimage; and Christian and Hopeful never walked more warily and prayerfully than now after their wonderful escape from the Castle of Giant Despair.

Here were gardens, orchards, vineyards, and fountains of living water, to reward their diligence and refresh their spirits. Here were Shepherds of Christ, appointed to feed and keep his flock on these mountains,—precious, holy men, named Knowledge, Experience, Watchful, and Sincere, who took the pilgrims by the hand, instructed them by their conversation, and led them about to shew them the wonders of these mountains, just as the good Interpreter had shewn them the rarities in his house. They were shewn where many men were dashed in pieces by carelessly climbing the Hill of Error, and falling in the midst of its speculations. They were shewn from the top of another mountain, called Caution, a number of blind men wandering and stumbling across tombs; and the Shepherds, little knowing or imagining the late fearful experience of the pilgrims in Doubting Castle, informed them that these were men who had had their eyes put out by Giant Despair, and were there by him thrown among these dark tombs; according to the saying of Scripture, "He that wandereth out of the way of understanding, shall remain in the congregation of the dead."

Oh, thought Christian and Hopeful, why were not we also left to such a dreadful fate! Who hath made us to differ? What mercy of God that he did not leave us also to be blinded and destroyed! They said not a word to the Shepherds, but looked on one another with a look that spoke volumes, and the tears gushed out. So, how many hair-breadth escapes have we all had amidst our sins, where others have stumbled and fallen to rise no more! What thankfulness should the remembrance of these mercies excite in us!

The good Shepherds also took the pilgrims to the top of the Hill Clear, from whence they could, in a fine day, see the Celestial City, through the telescope which the Shepherds kept by them. This perspective glass is Faith, but the pilgrims have not always equal skill in using it. However they managed to see something of the glory of the City; and that vision, imperfect though it was, was very ravishing to their spirits.

> We journey in a vale of tears;
>   But often from on high
> The glorious bow of God appears,
>   And lights up all our sky.
> Then through the breaking clouds of heaven
>   Far distant visions come,
> And sweetest words of grace are given,
>   To cheer the pilgrim home.
>
> Then doubt and darkness flee away,
>   And shadows all are gone:—
> Oh! if such moments would but stay,
>   This earth and heaven were one.
> Too soon the vision is withdrawn;
>   There's only left, "He saith;"
> And I, a lonely pilgrim, turn,
>   To live and walk by faith.
>
> Yet e'en for glimpses such as these
>   My soul would cheerful bear
> All that in darkest days it sees,
>   The toil, the pain, the care.
> For through the conflict and the race,
>   Whatever grief my lot,
> If Jesus shews his lovely face,
>   All troubles are forgot.
>
> My quickened soul, in faith and love,
>   Mounts up on eagles' wings,
> And at the City Gates above
>   Exulting sits and sings!
> 'Tis through thy sufferings, O my Lord,
>   I hope that world to see,
> And through those gates, at thy sweet word,
>   To enter into Thee!

After going through the conflict with Apollyon, the Valley of the Shadow of Death, the scenes in Vanity Fair, and the dread experience of the pilgrims in Giant Despair's Castle, it is well to note what a Gallery of solemn REALITIES is here, what a system of Divine Truth, commending itself to all men's consciences. It is not so much the richness of imagination, nor the tenderness of feeling here exhibited, nor the sweetness and beauty of the imagery, with which this book is filled, as it is the presence of these REALITIES, that constitutes the secret of its unbounded power over the soul.

Walk up and down in this rich and solemn Gallery. How simple are its ornaments! How grave, yet beautiful, its architecture! Amidst all this deep, serene beauty to the imagination, by how much deeper a tone do these pictures speak to the inner spiritual being of the soul! When you have admired the visible beauty of the paintings, turn again to seek their meaning in that light from eternity by which the Artist painted them, and by which he would have all men examine their lessons, and receive and feel the full power of their colouring. In this light the walls of this Gallery seem moving with celestial figures speaking to the soul. They are acting the Drama of a Life which by most men is only dreamed of; but the Drama is the reality, and it is the spectators only who are walking in a vain show.

The Pilgrim's Progress shews an immortal being journeying in the light and under the transforming power of these realities. They are such ever-present truths, that you cannot read this work, without discovering them, any more than you could read aloud the pages of a book, without pronouncing its words; any more than one could travel through a magnificent city, and not behold its streets and palaces; any more than one could look at the rainbow without seeing its colours, or at the sun without beholding its light. It is by the power of these truths that the Pilgrim's Progress, like the sword of the Spirit, which is the Word of God, proves itself *a discerner of the thoughts and intents of the heart.*

The whole foundation on which the author of this work, which of all other books stands the nearest after the Bible to the overpowering light of eternity, has built the structure of its realities, is his view (taken from the Bible and the Spirit of God) of sin, of God, of Christ, of the eternal world, and of the relations of man, as a fallen being, to that world and to his Maker. The gloom in this book, if gloom it can be called, where the light of the Cross so irradiates it, arises from the immutable dread nature of sin, and not from any dark views of the Gospel. It is not a gloomy book; no man ever thought of bringing against it such an accusation; it is one of the most cheerful books in the language. And yet it is a solemn array of the realities of spiritual truth. The way of our pilgrimage is from gloom to grace and glory; gloom at first, but afterwards glory everlasting; but they who will reject the element of gloom from their theology in this world are not likely to have the element of glory spring from it hereafter.

LECTURE THIRTEENTH.

The Delectable Mountains and Enchanted Ground, with the Characters of Ignorance and Little-Faith.

View of the Celestial City.—The importance of such visions on our pilgrimage.—Character of Ignorance.—False views of Justification.—Denial of the doctrine of Justification by Faith.—Salvation by our own merits in any way impossible.—Christ, a whole Saviour or none at all.—To say that a man is saved by his works is just the same as to say that he is saved by his sins.—Character of Little-Faith.—The Enchanted Ground and the Flatterer.—The delusions of self-righteousness.—The religious experience of Hopeful.—The renewed heart a mirror of Divine Truth.

On the Delectable Mountains, the pilgrims had a sight of the Celestial City. No matter if it was but a glimpse, still they saw it, they really saw it, and the remembrance of that sight never left them. There it was in glory! Their hands trembled, their eyes were dim with tears, but still that vision was not to be mistaken. There, through the rifted clouds for a moment, the gates of pearl were shining, the jasper walls, the endless domes, the jewelled battlements! The splendour of the city seemed to pour, like a river of light, down upon the spot where they were standing. We may adopt the imagery of the poet Wordsworth, attempting to convey the idea of a material vision which he beheld in the clouds after a storm, in order to shadow forth something of that glory which might have been seen from the summit of the Delectable Mountains.

> Glory beyond all glory ever seen
> By waking sense, or by the dreaming soul '
> The appearance, instantaneously disclosed,
> Was of a Mighty City,—boldly say
> A wilderness of building, sinking far,
> And self-withdrawn into a wondrous depth,
> Far sinking into splendour without end !
> Fabric it seemed of diamond and of gold,
> With alabaster domes and silver spires,
> And blazing terrace upon terrace, high
> Uplifted: here, serene pavilions bright,
> In avenues disposed ; there, towers begirt
> With battlements, that on their restless fronts
> Bore stars,—illumination of all gems !

Now this sight did ravish the hearts of the pilgrims, though they could not look steadily through the glass. Sometimes this vision is revealed to pilgrims much more clearly than at other times ; but no language can describe the glory of the vision, whenever and however it is manifested to the soul ; for eye hath not seen, nor ear heard, neither hath it entered into the heart of man to conceive the things which God hath prepared for them that love him. But God reveals them by his Spirit, and sometimes doubtless with such a revelation as language cannot compass.

Much depends upon the weather in our soul's horizon. Sometimes, even when ascending the Delectable Mountains, the pilgrims are enveloped in joy all the way up. They climb and turn to see the prospect, but can see nothing ; it is like ascending the Alps on a misty day. But still they climb. And now, all unexpectedly and suddenly, they rise out of the cloud and beyond it ;—the sun is shining, the mountains are flashing like pure alabaster ;—they seem to have angels' wings, they come to the Hill Clear, the Celestial City breaks upon them. Ah, how glorious, how merciful is such a vision ! Worth all the climbing, all the fatigue, all the mist, rain, and darkness. Now the soul can go on its way rejoicing ; now it can say to Athiest, What ? No Celestial City ? Did I not see it from the Delectable Mountains ? Shall not my soul remember thee, O God, and the sweet glimpses of thy glory which thou hast caused to pass before me ? Yea, my soul followeth hard after Thee, and thy right hand upholdeth me ; and as long as I live will I praise the Lord for his goodness, and pant for his abode.

> Jerusalem! Jerusalem!
> Name ever dear to me!

Such glimpses of Heaven, though they be but glimpses, are inexpressibly blessed and sustaining in our pilgrimage. They help to wean the affections from earth, they strengthen us against temptations, they make us see in the most striking light, the emptiness and vanity of the things of the world, and the folly and sinfulness of the love of the world; they make us feel, while confined to the world, what shadows we are, and what shadows we pursue; they make trials also seem very small and transitory, and easy to be borne. Moreover, they quicken the heart after God; for the renewed heart well knows that God is the glory of that City, "for the Lord God Almighty and the Lamb are the temple of it; and it has no need of the sun, neither of the moon to shine in it; for the glory of God doth lighten it, and the Lamb is the light thereof." When the heart is filled and purified with such desires after heaven, as in Paul's case, then it doth desire to depart and to be with Christ; it would lay by these garments of mortality, that it may put on Christ, and be clothed upon with our house which is from heaven. Sometimes, when God, by his grace, puts the heart in such a holy frame, discloses so much of himself in Christ to it, every day is counted, as it passes, for joy, as a step nearer heaven; so that Death seems no longer the King of Terrors, but the Angel of a Father's love; and the day when he comes is the Christian's BIRTH-DAY OF ETERNITY. So Time itself, the most fleeting of all things, seems sometimes long, because it separates the soul from the Saviour!

> For this it is makes life so long
> While it detains us from our God:
> E'en pleasures here increase the wrong,
> And length of days lengthens the road.
> Who wants the place where God doth dwell,
> Partakes already half of hell.
>
> HERBERT.

O how desirable is such a frame! But the pilgrims are not always in it; so Christian and Hopeful must go down from the Delectable Mountains, and be on the common way of their pilgrimage ; for these happy experiences and visions of heaven are given, as I said, not to constitute our rest, but to make us long after it, to make us willing to endure hardships as good soldiers of Jesus Christ. The Crown of Life is after Death, and no man can be crowned, till, through Christ, he has gained the victory. The Lord, in mercy, grant us that grace, that we, through him, may gain that victory, being made faithful unto death !

The pilgrims must go on, and though they have been where they could see the Celestial City, yet there are dangers and labours still to go through, and no chariot, nor bright cloud, nor way through the air, to convey them insensibly, or without fatigue to heaven. So they bade the kind Shepherds a loving farewell. Methinks, after all their past experiences and visions, they breathed, as they went, the very spirit of those sweet verses of Baxter, in which he poured forth, with such simplicity, the breathings of his soul after heaven, and the quiet spirit of resignation to God's will.

> Lord, it belongs not to my care,
>   Whether I die or live ;
> To love and serve thee is my share,
>   And this thy grace must give.
> If life be long, I will be glad,
>   That I may long obey ;
> If short, yet why should I be sad,
>   That shall have the same pay ?
>
> Christ leads me through no darker rooms
>   Than he went through before ;
> He that into God's kingdom comes,
>   Must enter by this door.
> Come, Lord, when grace hath made me meet
>   Thy blessed face to see ;
> For if thy work on earth be sweet.
>   What will thy glory be !
>
> Then I shall end my sad complaints,
>   And weary sinful days ;
> And join with the triumphant saints,
>   That sing Jehovah's praise.
> My knowledge of that life is small,
>   The eye of faith is dim ;
> But 'tis enough that Christ knows all,
>   And I shall be with him !

After the pilgrims are set out from the Delectable Mountains, there pass before us a succession of scenes of great beauty, and characters of great interest, mingled with so much instructive and delightful conversation by the way, that it is a good type of that growth in grace and that heavenly wisdom, which should more and more mark the pilgrims, the nearer they come to the Celestial City. The first character we meet is that of Ignorance, from the town of Conceit; then Little-Faith passes before us with his story; then the character of Great-Grace. Next comes the Flatterer, then the Atheist, then the Enchanted Ground, and Hopeful's instructive relation of his religious experience, then the farther development of the character of Ignorance, then the course of an apostate. Next comes the picture of the land Beulah, and last of all, the river of Death and the Celestial City.

Ignorance was a very brisk lad, that came out of the country and was going to enter heaven "as other good people do," by his goodness and not by Christ. He was a man of morality, a payer of his debts, a faster, a tithe-payer, an alms-giver; and to this catalogue of his worthy qualities, by which he was to be received in at the Gate, he also added, *that he had left his own country for whither he was going.* Here, then, was a professor of religion, who meant to be saved by his own merits, and yet deemed himself to have forsaken all for Christ, at least to have left his native country of Conceit. But he had still, unknown to himself, all the manners and feelings of his native land, and though he seemed to himself to be travelling towards the Celestial City, yet he was a stranger both to himself and to Christ, and of course had never entered by the Wicket Gate, and was destitute of Christian's roll of assurance. How many professed followers of Christ there may be, who are entirely ignorant of their own depraved nature, and of their need of a Saviour's righteousness, we cannot tell, but we are all *natives* of this country of Conceit; and if we expect to attain salvation by our own works, prayers, fastings, merits in any way, and not by the all-sufficing merits, the all-atoning sacrifice, and the all-renewing grace of Christ, we are utterly ignorant of what be the very first principles of the Cross of Christ. Where there is this ignorance of the Cross, there is very likely to be enmity against it, or a light esteem of it. So Mr Ignorance did not think that there were "any men in all our parts who knew the way to the Wicket Gate," and for his part, he did not think there were any need of knowing it, since there was a much nearer way.

So Ignorance and the pilgrims parted for a season, but afterwards they renewed their conversation, and Ignorance gave the pilgrims to know more particularly what were some of the grounds of his own assurance in regard to his good estate. The main thing seemed to be his comfortable hopes of heaven, and the good things that his own heart was telling him about himself. He seems never to have known the desperate wickedness of his own heart, nor to have thought of distrusting it; and when good Christian explained to him that by the judgment of the word of God the heart is naturally altogether sinful, then did Ignorance break out with this speech, saying, I will never believe that my heart is thus bad. Therefore, said Christian, thou never hadst one good thought concerning thyself in thy life.

This good opinion of Ignorance concerning himself was a radical, blinding evil, a great delusion, as it is with many professed pilgrims; for, not seeing his own desperate sinfulness, of course he saw not his need of Christ as a Saviour, and had never fled to him, nor known what it was to rely upon him for mercy. Yet, he spake of Christ, and expected to be saved only by him, but it was in such a way as if Christ died to give to the sinner's own works a saving efficacy.

The case of Ignorance shews that there must be deep conviction, knowledge, and hatred of one's own guilt, to make one fully see, feel, and know the preciousness of Christ, and then indeed the soul rests upon him; but it cannot rest upon him and upon its own works or merits together. Christ will be an only Saviour, or none at all. But there are many, who, like Ignorance, profess to rest upon Christ, but make him only half their Saviour, relying on their own holiness also for acceptance before God. This is a very dangerous error, as in the instance of Ignorance, for it proceeds from self-conceit, and even while under its influence men still think that they hold to the fundamental doctrine of Justification by Faith.

This was the case with Ignorance, yet his description of Faith would sound very plausible to many minds. I believe, said he, that Christ died for sinners, and that I shall be justified before God from the curse, through his gracious acceptance of my obedience to the law. Or thus, Christ makes my duties, that are religious, acceptable to his Father, by virtue of his merits, and so I shall be justified. Now this faith was truly, as Christian said, a fantastical, false, deceitful faith, nowhere described in the word of God, although, having a great shew of scriptural truth, it was wonderfully adapted to mislead and delude the simple and ignorant.

But who does not see that such a faith as this makes Christ not a Saviour of ourselves, but of our duties? it makes Christ die in order to constitute for us a self-righteousness, in order to make what we do the ground of our salvation. But Christ himself is our salvation, or we have none at all. He himself, and not our duties for his sake, is our wisdom, righteousness, sanctification, and redemption. He died to save our souls, and not to save our righteousness, nor to make our obedience fit for us to rest upon for salvation, for it never can be fit, but always needs to be forgiven. But this faith of Ignorance would make Christ a justifier not of the believer, but of his actions, and a justifier and Saviour of the believer for the sake of his actions! That is, it makes Christ die for the justification of the believer's duties, which thus, it is pretended, become merits, and may be presented, through Christ, to God, as the purchase of salvation!

Now, when Christian explained the real nature of justifying faith in Christ, as relying solely upon him and his merits, the self-righteousness of Ignorance cried out against it. What, said he, would you have us trust to what Christ in his own person hath done without us? This conceit would loosen the reins of our lusts, and tolerate us to live as we list; for what matter how we live, if we may be justified by Christ's personal righteousness from all sin, when we believe it?

This was the common outcry and reproach of Antinomianism thrown against the doctrine of justification by faith, on the part of those who reject it. Ignorance was equally prejudiced against the declaration of Christian from the Bible, that no man can know Jesus Christ but by revelation from the Father; and this was simply the common unwillingness of our proud hearts to admit such truth as throws us entirely on the sovereignty and mere good pleasure of God.

The idea of justification by works, in any way, when we look at our own depravity, must appear to every sound mind as irrational as it is unscriptural. The best works, performed by the best man, are imperfect and mingled with sin, and therefore need to be forgiven; so that to say that a man is justified by his works is no better than saying that a man is justified by his sins; and how great an absurdity this is, there is no man who will not acknowledge. Every true Christian deeply feels that the best duties he ever performed, the best services he ever offered to God, the most unmingled spiritual sacrifices he ever laid upon the altar of a Saviour's love, need to be sprinkled with a Saviour's blood, and cannot otherwise be accepted of God. How then can he, in any sense whatever, be justified by his works, seeing that his works themselves need to be forgiven? The utmost that his best works can do is to prove the existence, in manifesting the fruits of that saving faith, through which the soul is united to Christ, and by his blood justified; but if our works all partake of sin, then, so far from being in any sense justified by works, we are condemned by them, and without other justification must perish everlastingly.

In this view what can be more offensive to a believer in Christ than that spurious mixture of faith and works as a reliance for justification, which in our day is so common, but which robs the Saviour of his glory, and the atonement of its efficacy, and which, so far from excluding boasting, produces pride, and sustains the most subtle and destructive form of self-righteousness. Justification by faith is a precious doctrine, because it exalts the Saviour and cuts up human pride. Justification by works is an abominable Popish perversion of the Gospel, which, whether in the form of penances or prayers, ministers to human pride, lays another foundation than that which Christ hath laid, introduces another Saviour, and so provides for the ruin and not the redemption of the soul. A church may have justification by faith among its articles, and yet may go over upon Popish ground in justification by forms and works, and so may desert and betray this fundamental living truth of Christ. And many a man, like Ignorance, unacquainted with his own heart, and with Christ as his Physician, may be taken unawares by a show of scriptural truth, and instead of really building on the Rock Christ Jesus, may be led to build his house upon the sand. One of the most subtle poisons of the age is the doctrine of human merit, which, like a cloud from the bottomless pit, or thick vapour from the caves of Antichrist, darkens the gospel, and sends the soul wandering in the mazes of pride and error. Christ is our Saviour, and not our works; Christ alone, and not works in any sense; Christ must be all, and in all, or we have no Saviour; wherefore, let us be sure that we rest on him, for no righteousness can save us but his, nor is there any thing but his blood that can cleanse the soul from sin.

> Since the dear hour that brought me to Thy foot,
> And cut up all my follies by the root,
> I never trusted in an arm but Thine,
> Nor hoped, but in Thy righteousness divine.
> My prayers and alms, imperfect and defiled,
> Were but the feeble efforts of a child.
> Howe'er performed, it was their brightest part
> That they proceeded from a grateful heart.
> Cleansed in thine own all-purifying blood,
> Forgive their evil, and accept their good.
> I cast them at Thy feet—my only plea
> Is what it was, DEPENDENCE UPON THEE!
>
> COWPER.

The character of Ignorance is a type of many, who, having never been truly convinced of sin, remain unconscious of the desperate wickedness of their own hearts, and of their utter helplessness in themselves as to salvation. As Hopeful said of him, there are abundance of such as he in our town, whole families, yea, whole streets, and that of pilgrims too; and if there be so many in our parts, how many, think you, must there be in the place where he was born! Something like his was the character of Temporary, who was awakened once, and resolved to go on a pilgrimage, but suddenly becoming acquainted with one Save-self, he gave up the labour of it. This is what a great many persons do; instead of despairing in themselves, and going to Christ alone to save them, they go to duties and pretended merits of their own, and when they do this, then farewell to Christ and his righteousness, and so, in reality, farewell to the hope of heaven.

This spirit of self-righteousness is a fearful delusion and snare to many on first setting out in this pilgrimage. It seems to be the most difficult thing in the world for the heart to come to Christ just as it is, wholly bankrupt, and to receive Christ, and to understand him, and to rest upon him, just as he is, our only, all-sufficient Saviour. It is the most difficult thing to come and buy the wine and milk of the gospel without price; the sinner thinks he must bring something in his hand to purchase with, some duties, some merits, prayers at least, if nothing else, to buy forgiveness. And, in truth, the act of resting on Christ is taught only of God; a right appreciation and reception of Christ comes only from God's Spirit. So it is made for us the greatest, most important of all prayers, that the God of our Lord Jesus Christ, the Father of glory, *would give unto us the spirit of wisdom and revelation in the knowledge of* HIM. Without this revelation of Jesus to the soul as a Saviour, a man may talk ever so devoutly of the cross of Christ, and yet be a mere Save-self after all. *Redemption made easy, or every man his own saviour*, was a label which Mr Coleridge, with great justness and severity of satire, once wrote over a collection of Socinian Tracts; but in our day, the doctrine of justification by faith seems to be abandoned not only by those who deny the atonement and divinity of Christ, but by many who make a boast of those doctrines. Their theology is such a mixture of self-righteous morality, with something like the gospel plan of salvation, as effectually destroys the saving efficacy of the gospel, and yet satisfies the soul with the pretence and form of it. They make

Christ a mere endorser, on the ground of his own death, of the bill of merits which the sinner presents on the ground of his own morality; they make Christ merely a helper, and not a Saviour. But the gospel must be every thing or nothing, and he that comes to Christ thinking that he only needs him to make up his own deficiencies, does not believe in him as a Saviour at all, does not come to him as such.

Nevertheless, it is not merely Ignorance who is pleased with the delusions of self-righteousness; but real disciples sometimes, who think themselves rooted and grounded in faith and love, are led away by the same temptations. This the pilgrims found to their cost, when they encountered the Flatterer, by whom there can be little doubt that Bunyan intended to represent another enemy of justification by faith, under the guise of spiritual pride, a good opinion of themselves, and a reliance for salvation upon their own duties and degree of advancement in the spiritual life. This Flatterer led them in a way so like the right way at first, that they thought it *was* the right way; but so adroitly and insensibly did he deceive them, that at length their faces were turned from instead of towards the Celestial City, and then the white robe fell from his back, and disclosed his native blackness and deformity. Then also he threw a strong net over them, and left them to struggle in it, unable to get out. By such difficulties do men always become entangled, who leave the way of simple reliance on Christ and his righteousness.

There is also in our day a flattering delusion, by which this black man in white may be represented, which is the doctrine of perfection attained by saints in this world, which doctrine, by its fostering of pride and self-righteousness, has set many a man with his face from instead of towards the Celestial City. A man eager after spiritual attainments does certainly seem to be in the high road to heaven; but if he makes those attainments, instead of Christ, his Saviour, then certainly his face is turned, and his feet are tending the other way. So we need to be upon our watch against any thing and every thing, though it should come to us in the shape of an angel of light, which would turn us from a sole reliance upon Christ, or tempt us to a high opinion of ourselves. A broken heart and a contrite spirit are in the sight of God of great price; but if any man thinks himself to have attained perfection, he is not very likely to be in the exercise of a broken heart or of a contrite spirit, nor indeed in the exercise of true faith in Christ for justification.

You will observe that this flatterer, robed in white, pretending to great strictness, spirituality, and holiness, carried the pilgrims seemingly onwards towards the Celestial City, but left them with their faces direct *from* Zion, instead of heavenward. Now this has been the case with so many persons who have at first professed to have attained perfection, and believed that they sought it, that it would seem as if Bunyan must have had in his eye the very error we are contemplating. From the belief in one's own perfection, it is often but a single step to the monstrous conclusion that the soul cannot sin; that whatever the body does, the soul cannot be defiled thereby, or made guilty; that the law of God is no more a rule of conduct, and that its commands may be broken at pleasure without sin. This is doubtless one tendency of a self-righteous spirit. They who trust simply and solely in Christ and his righteousness for salvation have often been accused by self-righteous moralists of "making void the law;" but, in point of fact, it is they only who establish the law; it is nothing but the love of Christ, and faith in his merits, in his blood, that ever produces any morality required by the law. On the other hand, they who trust in their own merits, and they who pretend to a perfection of their own, are always perverting, and so making void, both the law and the gospel, and sometimes they do openly and plainly trample all its requisitions under their feet. So true it is, that "pride goeth before destruction, and a haughty spirit before a fall."

Our entire reliance upon Christ as himself our Saviour, our only Saviour, is beautifully expressed in one of Herbert's sweet though quaint pieces, entitled, The Hold-Fast. Christ is the Hold-Fast; he is the fast and firm holder of what is ours; but what is ours is his, and ours only as it comes from him, so that we have nothing in ourselves, even to trust in him being his. What is ours in ourselves is weakness and sin; what is ours in him is strength and righteousness; so he is our Hold-Fast.

> I threatened to observe the strict decree
> Of my dear God with all my power and might:
> But I was told by one it could not be:
> Yet I might trust in God to be my light.
>
> Then will I trust, said I, in him alone,
> Nay, e'en to trust in him was also his:
> We must confess that nothing is our own.
> Then I confess that he my succour is.
>
> But to have nought is ours, not to confess
> That we have nought. I stood amazed at this,
> Much troubled, till I heard a friend express,
> That all things were ours by being his.
> What Adam had, and forfeited for all,
> Christ keepeth now, who cannot fail or fall.

While Christian and Hopeful were struggling in this net, there came a bright Shining One, with a whip of small cord in his hand, who questioned them as to how they came there, and what they were doing. When they had told all, and had been reminded that if they had diligently perused the note of the way given them by the Shepherds, they would not have fallen into this snare; this Shining One made them lie down, and submit to a sore, though loving chastisement. By this is figured the discipline of the good Spirit of the Lord with his children, when they in any manner go astray, and also the loving-kindness of the Lord, even in the chastisement of his people. "As many as I love, I rebuke and chasten." "He restoreth my soul," saith David, "and leadeth me in the paths of righteousness for his name's sake." So were these two erring disciples, who had now insensibly been beguiled away from Christ and his righteousness into flattering, delusive opinions of their own attainments, whipped back by the Shining One into the path of humility faith, truth, and duty. So great is "the love of the Spirit," so sweet and long-suffering the patience and the mercy of the Lord.

Few passages are more instructive than that which in

this stage of the pilgrimage contains the character of Little-Faith, and the story of the robbery he suffered. This man fell asleep in Dead-Man's Lane, not far from Broadway Gate. He had certainly no business in that place, where so many murders were committed, and to sleep there was above all unsafe. So three desperate villains, Faint-Heart, Mistrust, and Guilt, set upon him, and robbed him of all his ready money, and left him half-dead. There are a great many Little-Faiths in our pilgrimage, and though they do not all sleep in Dead-Man's Lane, yet they go doubting and trembling through life. Faint-heart, Mistrust, and Guilt clog their footsteps, and their faith in Christ is not strong enough to triumph over these enemies and make them flee. So they go burdened with sin, and literally mourning after Christ, rather than believing in him. Yet this mourning after Christ is something precious; it is infinitely better than hardness and indifference of heart, or false security, and infinitely better, also, than a dangerous, false confidence, or a joy that has not a scriptural foundation.

Little-Faith had a tender conscience, which made him bewail his sinful sleep, and all his failings by the way. Little-Faith's spending money, that is, almost all the present comfort of a hope in Christ, with those foretastes of heaven, which are the earnest of the Spirit, was taken from him by those desperate robbers; but his costly jewels they did not find, or else did not value them, as they were good only at the Celestial City; that is, these robbers, Faint-heart, Mistrust, and Guilt, did not take away those graces of the Spirit, by which Little-Faith's soul was really united to Christ, though they did steal from him his own present evidences, so that he went on distressed and troubled in his pilgrimage, and a beggar to the day of his death.

There was one good thing about Little-Faith, and that was his sincerity; he had indeed little faith, but what he had was real faith, and no trust in his own merits. Now, if from our faith as Christians, all foreign ingredients were abstracted, all mixture of self-righteousness and vain-confidence, it is to be feared very few of us would be found with much to boast above Little-Faith; if every thing were taken from the grace which we hope is in our hearts, but only what is "believing, true, and clean," what is sincere, without offence, and pure before God, the residue might be found a very small modicum. Should all the wood, hay, and stubble be burned up, which we have builded on the foundation that is laid for us, how much gold, silver, and precious stones would be found remaining, we might fear to know. If Guilt, Mistrust, and Faint-Heart were to set upon us as they did upon Little-Faith, would they take merely our spending money, and leave us our jewels, or would they take jewels and all?

Hopeful seemed to think if he had been in Little-Faith's place, he would not have given up so easily; but Christian bade him beware of self-confidence, for it was a very different thing to hear of these villains who attacked Little-Faith, and to be attacked by them one's self. No man could tell the wonderful fearfulness of that combat, but he who has been in it. Great-Grace himself, by whose coming up the desperate rogues were frightened away from Little-Faith, though excellent good at his weapons, would very likely get a fall, if Guilt, Faint-Heart, and Mistrust got within him, not being kept at his sword's point; and when a man is down, and three such wretches upon him, what can he do? Peter once thought he would never give up; he was ready to try what he could do, even to go to prison and to death, but when these grim robbers came upon him, "though some do say that he is the Prince of the Apostles, they handled him so, that they made him at last afraid of a sorry girl." So there is no help, trust, strength, or safety for us but in Christ, in his great grace in us, upon us, and for us. Great-Grace must be our champion, as he was Little-Faith's, or it is all over with us.

Little-Faith dwelt in the town of Sincere, and his sincerity was a very precious thing in him, for the Lord looketh on the heart, and on the man who trembleth at his word. Moreover, our blessed Lord hath said, that he will not break the bruised reed, nor quench the smoking flax; and where there is smoke, as with Little-Faith, there was but little else, so that he was under a cloud all the while, stifled as it were with the smoke of his evidences, and seeking in vain to find his own fire, yet there is hope of a blaze; it will break out at last, and burn brightly. So if a man can but say, "Lord, I believe, help thou mine unbelief," if he says this sincerely, he need never be discouraged; let him hope in the Lord. Little-Grace can trust in Christ, and Great-Grace can do no more; and if "one promise doth belong to thee," says an excellent old writer, "then all do; for every one conveys a whole Christ; and Christ will acknowledge hee to be his, if he sees but one mark of his child upon thee in truth and sincerity. For God brings not a pair of scales to weigh your graces, and if they be too light refuseth them; but he brings a touchstone to try them; and if they be pure gold, though never so little of it, it will pass current with him; though it be but smoke, not flame, though it be but as a wick in the socket, (as the original hath it,) likelier to die and go out, than continue, which we used to throw away; yet he will not quench it, but accept it." This is a sweet comforting truth, but let it not be turned to indolence or licentiousness; for if a man would have God to work out his salvation for him, he must also be willing and industrious to work it out himself with fear and trembling.

The next character which the pilgrims met with in their way to the City, after, by the help of the Shining One, they had escaped the net of the Flatterer, was an open, broad, blaspheming Atheist. He pretended to have been twenty years seeking the Celestial City, and had not found it, and now he knew there was no such thing in existence, and was determined to take his full swing of the pleasures of this life, to make amends for all the labour he had undergone. There is no doubt that Bunyan had met with such characters; they are to be found sometimes now; and dangerous indeed they are to the young and inexperienced. This man Atheist reminds me of a professed preacher of the Gospel, but a denier of our Lord's Divinity and Atonement, to whom I referred as having been settled over one of Mr Legality's parishes, who had been in early life the subject of many and strong religious impressions, but had denied the faith, and become worse than an infidel. This man used to say, just as Atheist to Christian and Hopeful, though not that there was no Celestial City, yet that there was no need of such a laborious pilgrimage to come at it, for that he had been through all this pretended religious experience, and knew it to be all nonsense, a perfectly needless and foolish trouble. "The lips of a fool will swallow up himself. The beginning of the words of his mouth is foolishness, and the end of his talk mischievous madness. He knoweth not how to go to the City." This fool Atheist lost his labour with Christian and Hopeful, for they had seen the Gate of the Celestial City from the top of the Delectable Mountains. So when temptations to unbelief and Atheism beset the Christian, he may very properly throw himself back upon his past experience of God's loving-kindness, when the candle of the Lord shined upon him, and he could see afar off. So David, in trouble and darkness remembered God from such and such a place, when he had commanded deliverance, and he knew he would command it again.

But now the pilgrims enter on the Enchanted Ground. The air of that region tends to such drowsiness, that it disposed the pilgrims to lie down at once and sleep; and Hopeful would have done so, had it not been for the warnings of Christian, who bade his brother remember what the good Shepherds had told them. Hopeful was inclined to say with Paul, "I only and Barnabas, have not we power to forbear working?" May I not lie down and take a short nap? said Hopeful. Sleep is refreshing to the labouring man, and I can scarcely hold my eyes open. Ah, these short naps for pilgrims! The sleep of death, in the Enchanted Air of this world, usually begins with one of these short naps.

Sleeping here, there is no safety; for if you give way to your almost irresistible inclination, it becomes more irresistible, you are in imminent danger of the lethargy of spiritual death. Wherefore, beware of spiritual indolence; it is a gradual, but fearful and powerful temptation. "Wherefore, let us not sleep, as do others; but let us watch and be sober." O beware of a lukewarm formality in your spiritual exercises, especially in prayer, in family prayer, in secret prayer. And rest not in the form, but pray earnestly to God to infuse more life and earnestness in your devotions, to give you a more vivid view and sense of eternal realities, to wake you up, and to shake from you this sloth, and to make you vigorous and fervent in spirit. This is what is needed, for in this Enchanted Ground of indolence and spiritual slumber you must, though it crucify your own flesh, resist this dangerous inclination to sleep.

This desire to slumber is sometimes an indication of spiritual coldness, rather than of spiritual fatigue, for those who have been exercising themselves vigorously are not apt to feel it: so that it indicates a state in the soul, like that which takes place in the body, when a person is near perishing in the snow. There is an account in the voyages of some of our early circumnavigators about the globe, of a danger of this kind that came upon them when travelling in a certain frozen region, which I always think of when I come to this place in the Pilgrim's Progress. The surgeon of the company, a man of great skill and firmness, warned his companions that they would feel a great inclination to sleep, but that so sure as they gave way to it, they would die in it, for no power on earth could wake them. But if I remember right, this very surgeon, Dr Solander, was one of the first to be overcome with this irresistible desire to sleep; and had they not, by main force, kept him from it, he would have lain down in the cold, and slept, and died. Now, when this inclination to spiritual slumber is the result of spiritual coldness, a man is in danger indeed. It is time to bestir yourself, for if you yield to this propensity, it is most likely that death will overtake you in it. Wherefore, rouse up, and walk on, and beat yourself, if need be, and call earnestly upon God to save you, and Christ will be your guide.

The way Christian and Hopeful took to avoid this danger was excellent and very instructive. They sang and conversed together, and Hopeful related to Christian the deeply interesting account of his own Christian experience. While they were thus amusing, singing, and talking, the fire burned, and the danger grew less and less, the more they became interested. So sweet is heavenly conversation between Christians, so good to warm and enliven the heart. No wonder, where there is so little of it, and so much and constant vain and trifling talk on the vanities of this world, that there should be so much spiritual coldness. Some men are all ear and tongue in earthly things, conversable and social in the highest degree on the business, arts, and manners of this world, but when it comes to things of spiritual experience, when it comes to that exhortation, "Let your speech be always with grace, seasoned with salt," ah, how little salt is there! *Attic* salt, as the world calls it, there may be plenty of it; wit and learning, and common gossip in abundance; but of the salt of grace, hardly enough to keep the talk from the dunghill. This is sad, and yet true. But Christian conversation, warm from the heart, is a precious means of life, and the means, sometimes, of opening the prison doors, and bringing out a sleeper. Bunyan's lines are as true as they are pithy:

> Saints' fellowship, if it be managed well,
> Keeps them awake, and that in spite of hell.

Such conversation as that of Christian and Hopeful is full of awakening and edifying power.

Hopeful gave Christian an account of his own conversion, and seldom indeed has there ever been a description of the workings of conscience, and the leadings and discipline of Divine Providence and Grace with an individual soul bringing it to repentance, in which the points and main course of conviction, conversion, and Christian experience, have been brought out with such beautiful distinctness and power. It is very instructive to trace them in Hopeful's relation. He was first awakened by the life and death of Faithful in Vanity Fair. Many a conscience can answer to the truth of his enumeration of the occasions and times in which, even in his unconverted state, he used to remember God, and be troubled. Heart-frightening hours of conviction he had upon him, and many things would bring his sins to mind; as, if he did but meet a good man in the streets, or if he heard any one read in the Bible; or if his head did begin to ache; or if he were told that some of his neighbours were sick; or if he heard the bell toll for some that were dead ; or if he thought of dying himself ; or if he heard that sudden death happened to others ; but especially when he thought of himself, that he must come to judgment. So there was continually, as with all wicked men, a dreadful sound in Hopeful's ears. The truth is, the Ocean of Eternity will make itself heard. And there is a low wailing sound, as of spirits in torment, always wafted across it to the inhabitants of this world, as well as the voice of the spirits in bliss, saying, " Come up hither ! "

These things set Hopeful upon an effort to amend his life, for otherwise, thought he, I am sure to be damned. So he betook himself to praying, reading, weeping for sin, speaking the truth to his neighbours, and many other things, and thus, for a little season, succeeded in lulling and satisfying conscience. But again his difficulties were renewed, and his trouble came tumbling upon him, and that over the neck of all his reformation. Such sentences as these sounded in his ears : " By the works of the law shall no man be justified ;" and " He that offendeth in one point is guilty of all." Moreover, Hopeful found that no present reformation would wipe off the score of past sins, and indeed he could get no relief but in Christ. By Faithful's directions, he went to the mercy-seat, and pleaded with God to reveal Christ unto him ; and though he was tempted to give up praying, an hundred times twice told, yet he persevered, till in that saying, " Believe in the Lord Jesus Christ and thou shalt be saved," he found peace ; he found that coming to Christ and believing on him are all one. He found then to whom he must look for righteousness, and what it was to trust in the merits of Christ, and what was meant when it was said that " Christ is the end of the law for righteousness to every one that believeth."

Hopeful's experience stands in a fine instructive contrast with that of Ignorance ; the first shews the relish of the renewed heart for pure divine truth, and the secret of it ; the second shews the secret of the opposition of the unrenewed heart against that same divine truth in its purity. The pride of our nature is one of the last evils revealed to ourselves, and whatever goes against it, we do naturally count as our enemy. But Humility, learning of Christ, makes a different estimate, and counts as precious, beyond price, all that truth and virtue in the Gospel which abases self.

> The soul, whose sight all-quickening grace renews,
> Takes the resemblance of the good she views,
> As diamonds, stripped of their opaque disguise,
> Reflect the noonday glory of the skies.
> She speaks of Him, her Author, Guardian, Friend,
> Whose love knew no beginning, knows no end,
> In language warm, as all that love inspires,
> And in the glow of her intense desires,
> Pants to communicate her noble fires. COWPER.

On the other hand, those who do not love God cannot expect to find in his word a system of truth that will please their own hearts. A sinful heart can have no right views of God, and of course will have defective views of his word; for sin distorts the judgment, and overturns the balance of the mind on all moral subjects far more than even the best of men are aware of. There is, there can be, no true reflection of God or of his word from the bosom darkened with guilt, from the heart at enmity with him. That man will always look at God through the medium of his own selfishness, and at God's word through the colouring of his own wishes, prejudices, and fears.

A heart that loves the Saviour, and rejoices in God as his Sovereign, reflects back in calmness the perfect view of his character, which it finds in his word. Behold on the borders of a mountain lake, the reflection of the scene above received into the bosom of the lake below! See that crag projecting, the wild flowers that hang out from it, and bend as if to gaze at their own forms in the water beneath. Observe that plot of green grass above that tree springing from the cleft, and over all, the quiet sky reflecting in all its softness and depth from the lake's steady surface. Does it not seem as if there were two heavens? How perfect the reflection! And just as perfect and clear and free from confusion and perplexity is the reflection of God's character, and of the truths of his word from the quietness of the heart that loves the Saviour and rejoices in his supreme and sovereign glory.

Now look again. The wind is on the lake, and drives forward its waters in crested and impetuous waves, angry and turbulent. Where is that sweet image? There is no change above: the sky is clear, the crag projects as boldly, the flowers look just as sweet in their unconscious simplicity; but below, banks, trees, and skies are all mingled in confusion. There is just as much confusion in every unholy mind's idea of God and his blessed word. God and his truth are always clear, always the same; but the passions of men fill their own hearts with obscurity and turbulence; their depravity is itself obscurity, and through all this perplexity and wilful ignorance they contend that God is just such a Being as they behold him, and that they are very good beings in his sight. We have heard of a defect in the bodily vision, that represents all objects upside down: that man would certainly be called insane, who, under the influence of this misfortune, should so blind his understanding, as to believe and assert that men walked on their heads, and that the trees grew downwards. Now, it is not a much greater insanity for men who in their hearts do not love God, and in their lives perhaps insult and disobey him, to give credit to their own perverted misrepresentations of him and of his word. As long as men will continue to look at God's truth through the medium of their own pride and prejudice, so long they will have mistaken views of God and eternity, so long will their own self-righteousness look better to them for a resting-place than the glorious righteousness of Him, who of God is made unto us our Wisdom, Righteousness, Sanctification, and Redemption.

Such an one is the mere "natural man (who) receiveth not the things of the Spirit of God: for they are foolishness unto him: neither can he know them, for they are spiritually discerned." He has not the proper discipline and preparation of heart—the pure and fitting tastes for these higher and better things. He has dwelt in a low earthly region until his whole being has become conformed to low and earthly objects; and his dimmed and distorted vision cannot see the bright heaven above him. As well might the untutored eye of him who hath always been labouring in the dark and dusty mines under ground, attempt to judge of the beauty of colours and to determine the rules of art. Such an one is justly called Ignorance, and his self-confidence only serves the more to set off the barrenness and grovelling tastes of his soul. The more confident and dogmatical he is, the more an object of pity does he become to good angels and spiritual men, and of contempt and mockery to lost spirits. His boastfulness is only the strong symptom of his insanity, and the sure token of his perdition.

On the other hand, he who hath renounced his self-righteousness, and, with a broken and contrite heart, hath fled for refuge to the righteousness of Christ, he hath found a clear vision and noble and rational tastes. Now he despises and loathes the objects which he before admired and loved, and lifts up his rejoicing eye to behold the beautiful scenery of the green and smiling earth, and the quiet lake reflecting the happy heavens, and he sees the happy heavens themselves, from whence the reflection comes. Justly is this one called Hopeful. The things which he hath chosen are not in the present, but they open to him the blessed future. He hopes for them, and he hopes not in painful doubtfulness, but in the sweet assurance of the faith which hath brought him to Christ.

Abba, Father! send forth the spirit of thy dear Son into our hearts, that we, being made humble, believing, and holy, may ever give back a serene, unsullied reflection of thy Truth and Love! Blessed is that Spirit of adoption! Grant that we all, in its possession, may be made the children of God by faith in Christ Jesus. May we, through the Spirit, wait for the hope of righteousness by faith : remembering that in Jesus Christ neither circumcision availeth any thing, nor uncircumcision, but FAITH, which worketh by LOVE. For we are made partakers of Christ, if we hold the beginning of our confidence steadfast unto the end.

> Oft as I look upon the road,
> That leads to yonder blest abode,
> I feel distressed and fearful :
> So many foes the passage throng,
> I am so weak and they so strong,
> How can my soul be cheerful !

But when I think of Him, whose power
Can save me in a trying hour,
  And place on Him reliance,
My soul is then ashamed of fear;
And though ten thousand foes appear.
  I'll bid them all defiance.

The dangerous road I then pursue,
And keep the glorious prize in view,
  With joyful hope elated;
Strong in the Lord, in Him alone,
Where he conducts, I follow on,
  With ardour animated.

O Lord, each day renew my strength,
And let me see thy face at length,
  With all thy people yonder;
With them in heaven thy love declare.
And sing thy praise for ever there,
  With gratitude and wonder.

LECTURE FOURTEENTH.

The Land Beulah and the River of Death.

Gradual progress of the Pilgrims from strength to strength.—Their enjoyment in the Land Beulah.—Similar experience of Dr Payson.—Beauty and glory of the close of the Pilgrim's Progress.—Fear of Death by the Pilgrims.—Bunyan's own experience.—Why Death is the King of Terrors.—Dying is but going home for the Christian.—Death-beds of believers and unbelievers contrasted.—Christian instances in Fuller, Pearse, Janeway, Payson, and others.—Blessedness of such a death.—Necessity of a preparation for it in life.—What constitutes the Land Beulah.—Sweetness and preciousness of a close walk with God.—Solemn lesson from the fate of Ignorance.—No safety but in Christ.

WE are come now, in our pilgrimage, as far as to the Land Beulah. Would that we were all there in reality, and could abide there while we stay this side of the River of Death! But the Land Beulah, lovely as it is, is only one stage in our pilgrimage, and that a very advanced stage. And it is observable how Bunyan makes his pilgrims go from strength to strength, by a gradual progress, from one degree of grace, discipline, and glory to another, in accordance with that sweet scripture image, "The path of the just is as the shining light, that shineth more and more unto the perfect day." So the pilgrims go from strength to strength, every one of them in Zion appearing before God. They first, from the House Beautiful, had a view of the Delectable Mountains; then from the Delectable Mountains, they had a view of the Celestial City; then in the Land Beulah, they even meet with the inhabitants of that City. In this land they also hear voices coming out of the City, and they draw so near to it that the view of its glory is almost overpowering. Would to God that we all did better know the meaning of these images by our own blissful experience; for certainly the imagination alone cannot interpret them to us. A very near, deep, blissful communion with God is here portrayed, and that beholding as in a glass the glory of the Lord, by which daily the soul is changed more and more into the same image. Here the ministering spirits that do wait upon us are more frequent and full in their companies. Here the Spirit of adoption is breathed over the soul, and it walks and talks with Christ, almost as Moses and Elias in the mount of transfiguration.

No other language than that of Bunyan himself, perused in the pages of his own sweet book, could be successful in portraying this beauty and glory; for now he seems to feel that all the dangers of the pilgrimage are almost over, and he gives up himself without restraint so entirely to the sea of bliss that surrounds him, and to the gales of heaven that are wafting him on, and to the sounds of melody that float in the whole air around him, that nothing in the English language can be compared with this whole closing part of the Pilgrim's Progress, for its entrancing splendour, yet serene and simple loveliness. The colouring is that of heaven in the soul, and Bunyan has poured his own heaven-entranced soul into it. With all its depth and power, there is nothing exaggerated, and it is made up of the simplest and most scriptural materials and images. We seem to stand in a flood of light poured on us from the open gates of Paradise. It falls on every leaf and shrub by the way-side; it is reflected from the crystal streams, that between grassy banks wind amidst groves of fruit-trees into vineyards and flower-gardens. These fields of Beulah are just below the gate of heaven; and with the light of heaven there come floating down the melodies of heaven, so that here there is almost an open revelation of the things which God hath prepared for them that love him.

During the last days of that eminent man of God, Dr Payson, he once said, "When I formerly read Bunyan's description of the Land of Beulah, where the sun shines and the birds sing day and night, I used to doubt whether there was such a place; but now my own experience has convinced me of it, and it infinitely transcends all my previous conceptions." The best possible commentary on the glowing descriptions in Bunyan is to be found in that very remarkable letter dictated by Dr Payson to his sister a few weeks before his death :—" Were I to adopt the figurative language of Bunyan, I might date this letter from the Land Beulah, of which I have been for some weeks a happy inhabitant. The Celestial City is full in my view. Its glories have been upon me, its breezes fan me, its odours are wafted to me, its sounds strike upon my ears, and its spirit is breathed into my heart. Nothing separates me from it but the River of Death, which now appears but as an insignificant rill, that may be crossed at a single step, whenever God shall give permission. The Sun of Righteousness has been gradually drawing nearer and nearer, appearing larger and brighter as he approached, and now he fills the whole hemisphere; pouring forth a flood of glory, in which I seem to float like an insect in the beams of the sun; exulting, yet almost trembling, while I gaze on this excessive brightness, and wondering with unutterable wonder, why God should deign thus to shine upon a sinful worm."

There is perhaps, in all our language, no record of a Christian's happiness before death, so striking as this. What is it not worth to enjoy such consolations as these in our pilgrimage, and especially to experience such foretastes of heaven as we draw near to the River of Death; such revelations of God in Christ as can swallow up the fears and pains of dying, and make the soul exult in the vision of a Saviour's loveliness, the assurance of a Saviour's mercy. There is no self-denial, no toil, no suffering in this life which is worthy to be compared for a moment with such blessedness.

It is very remarkable that Bunyan has, as it were, attempted to lift the veil from the grave, from eternity, in the beatific closing part of the Pilgrim's Progress, and to depict what passes, or may be supposed to pass, with the souls of the righteous, immediately after death. There is a very familiar verse of Watts, founded on the unsuccessful effort of the mind to conceive definitely the manner of that existence into which the immortal spirit is to be ushered.

> In vain the fancy strives to paint
> The moment after death,
> The glories that surround the saint
> In yielding up his breath.

The old poet, Henry Vaughan, in his fragment on heaven in prospect, refers to the same uncertainty, in stanzas that, though somewhat quaint, are very striking.

> Dear, beauteous Death, the jewel of the just,
> Shining no where but in the dark,
> What mysteries do lie beyond thy dust,
> Could man outlook that mark!
> He that hath found some fledg'd bird's nest may know
> At first sight if the bird be flown,
> But what fair field or grove he sings in now
> That is to him unknown.
> And yet, as angels in some brighter dreams
> Call to the soul when man doth sleep,
> So some strange thoughts transcend our wonted themes,
> And into glory peep.

Indeed, our most definite view of that glory is but a glimpse, a guess, a look as through a dim glass darkly, and what we *know* of the intermediate or immediate state of untabernacled souls is but little and in part. Perhaps the most general conception is that of an immediate, instantaneous transition into the vision and presence of God and the Lamb. But Bunyan has with great beauty and probability brought in the ministry of angels, and regions of the air, to be passed through in their company, rising, and still rising, higher and higher, before they come to that mighty mount, on which he has placed the gates of the Celestial City. The angels receive his Pilgrims as they come up from the River of Death, and form for them a bright, glittering, seraphic, loving convoy, whose conversation prepares them gradually for that exceeding and eternal weight of glory, which is to be theirs as they enter in at the Gate. Bunyan has thus, in this blissful passage from the River to the Gate, done what no other devout writer, or dreamer, or speculator, that we are aware of, has ever done; he has filled what perhaps in most minds is a mere blank, a vacancy, or at most a bewilderment and mist of glory, with definite and beatific images, with natural thoughts, and with the sympathizing communion of gentle spirits, who form, as it were, an outer porch and perspective of glory, through which the soul passes into uncreated light. Bunyan has thrown a bridge, as it were, for the imagination over the deep, sudden, open space of an untried spiritual existence, where it finds ready to receive the soul that leaves the body, ministering spirits, sent forth to minister unto them who are to be heirs of salvation.

These ministering spirits he can describe, with the beauty and glory of their form and garments, and the ravishing sweetness of their conversation; he can also describe the feelings of the pilgrims in such company, and their glorious progress up through the regions of the air to their eternal dwelling-place. He can image to us their warm thoughts about the reception they are to meet with in the City, and the blessedness of beholding "the King in his beauty," and of dwelling with such glorious company for ever and ever; but Bunyan goes no farther; he does not attempt to describe, or even shadow forth their meeting with the Lord God Almighty and the Lamb in that Celestial City. This would have been presumption. He has gone as far as the purest devotion and the sweetest poetry could go, as far as an imagination kindled, informed, and sustained by the Holy Scriptures, could carry us; he has set us down amidst the ministry and conversation of angels, at the Gate of the City, and as the Gate opens to let in the pilgrims, he lets us look in ourselves; but farther nor revelation nor imagination traces the picture.

But in all the untrodden space which Bunyan has thus filled up, he has authority as well as probability on his side. For our blessed Lord said of the good man Lazarus, that when he died he was carried by the angels into Abraham's bosom, that is, into the abode of the blessed. It is not said that the instant Lazarus died he was with Christ in glory, but the mind has an intermediate transaction, a passage, a convoy, to rest upon; "*he was carried by angels;*" there is time occupied, and a passage from this existence to the sight of God and the eternal life of glory, which passage Bunyan has filled up with the utmost probability, as well as with an exquisite warmth and beauty of imagery, which finds no rival in the language. The description comes from the heart, and from an imagination fed, nourished, and disciplined by the Scriptures; and this is the secret of its power, the secret of the depth and heavenly glow of its ravishing colours, and of the emotions with which it stirs the soul even to tears. For it is almost impossible, in a right frame of heart, to read this description without weeping, especially that part of it where Christian and Hopeful pass the River of Death together.

How full of sweet feeling and Christian wisdom is this passage! How gentle, and tenderly affectionate are Hopeful's efforts to encourage his fainting brother! And how instructive the fact that here the older and more experienced Christian of the two, and that soldier in the Christian conflict who had the most scars upon him for Christ, should be the one to whom the passage of the River of Death was most difficult — instructive as shewing us that safety does not depend upon present comfort, but upon Christ, and that it is wrong to measure one's holiness and degree of preparation for death by the degree in which the fear of death may have departed. The pilgrims, especially Christian, began to despond in their mind when they came to the River. Notwithstanding that the angels were with them, and though they had been for many days abiding in the Land Beulah, and though they were now in full view of the Celestial City, and though they heard the bells ringing, and the melodious music of the City ravishing their hearts, yet were their hearts cast down as they came to the borders of this river, and found no means of being carried across it.

> For timorous mortals start and shrink,
> To cross that narrow sea,
> And linger, shivering on the brink,
> And fear to launch away.

They looked about them on this side and on that, and inquired of their shining seraphic companions if there were no other way of getting over the river, and they must go into it: and when told there was none, they were at a stand With all the glory before them, it was *death's cold flood* still. The fear of death is not always taken away, even from experienced and faithful Christians, nor is the passage without terrors. Christian had much darkness and horror, while to Hopeful there was good ground all the way. Christian was wrong when he said, If I were right, He would now arise to help me; for he had, as Hopeful told him, forgotten that it was of the wicked that God saith, " There are no bands in their death." However, it is observable that Christian's darkness did not last quite over the River. The Saviour was at length revealed to him, the clouds and darkness fled away, the evil spirits, and the shades of unbelief that had invited and strengthened their temptations, were subdued and put to flight for ever, and the Enemy after that was as still as a stone, and the rest of the River was but shallow.

" Brother, I see the gate," Hopeful would say, while Christian was sinking, " and men standing by to receive us." But Christian would answer, " It is you, it is you, that they wait for; you have been hopeful ever since I knew you." " And so have you," said he to Christian. What affecting simplicity, and faith and love in this last, stern, dark scene and conflict of their pilgrimage! The great Tempter and accuser of the saints was busy now with Christian, as he had been under the form of Apollyon, and in the Valley of the Shadow of Death. But this was his last opportunity for ever, and his last desperate assault.

If Bunyan, throughout this work, had been unconsciously throwing into his delineation of Christian's character the features of his own religious experience, we may suppose that he drew this death-scene also with a foreboding that his own soul would have to experience in the last mortal hour, another fearful conflict with the Adversary. But could he have returned into life, to paint the conclusion of his own passage of the River of Death, there would have been little or no gloom in the colouring, for his own death was full of peace and glory; his forebodings, if he had them, were never realized. We may suppose that in general the children of

God find this passage much easier in reality than they had anticipated; but it is only because Christ is with them: he is with them in death, by a manifestation not granted in life, because not necessary. Yet, if there were as great conflicts to pass through in life, there would be as great and sustaining manifestations of the Saviour. In life and in death he knoweth how to succour them that are tempted. To those who live by the grace of Christ during life, dying grace will be vouchsafed in a dying hour; for he hath said, "My grace is sufficient for thee."

"It is appointed unto all men once to die, and after that the judgment." It is this judgment which sinful men dread; it is this which makes Death the KING OF TERRORS. The future is indeed an unknown region, but the judgment is as certain as the present life, and even beyond the judgment the sinner's conscience and the Word of God combined, fill the unknown future with definite scenes and images. The elements of retribution are there, and also the subjects of retribution, living, moving, acting, speaking, suffering. Our blessed Lord, in that mighty spiritual drama of the rich man and Lazarus, has raised before us, as it were, a vast, graphic, living transparency, where the glories of heaven and the terrors of hell flash upon the soul. Death stands between the sinner and the eternal world; death hands him over to the elements of eternal retribution. The agonized conscience, not sprinkled with the blood of Christ, sees the fires of eternity glimmering through the grim monarch's shadowy skeleton form, as it rises and advances on the soul's horizon. Death, in such a case, *is* the KING OF TERRORS. He marshalls them at pleasure. He has but to stand before the frame of the unprepared mortal, and he curdles the blood and blanches the cheek, even of the atheist. He has but to touch the frame of the boldest of God's enemies, and they are brought into desolation as in a moment; they are utterly consumed with terrors. The poet of The Grave has depicted, in a powerful and never-to-be-forgotten passage, the terrors of the unprepared soul in such a moment.

How shocking must thy summons be, O Death!
To him that is at ease in his possessions;

> Who, counting on long years of pleasure here,
> Is quite unfurnished for that world to come!
>   In that dread moment, how the frantic soul
> Raves round the walls of her clay tenement,
> Runs to each avenue, and shrieks for help,
> But shrieks in vain! How wishfully she looks
> On all she's leaving, now no longer hers!
> A little longer, yet a little longer,
> O might she stay to wash away her stains,
> And fit her for her passage! Mournful sight!
> Her very eyes weep blood; and every groan
> She heaves is big with horror. But the Foe,
> Like a stanch murderer, steady to his purpose,
> Pursues her close through every lane of life,
> Nor misses once the track, but presses on,
> Till, forced at last to the tremendous verge,
> At once she sinks to everlasting ruin!

This is indeed dreadful. And yet, let Christ come in, let Christ stand by the King of Terrors, and there comes a death of which there is no fear, no terror connected with it. There are souls on whose horizon, though Death's skeleton form comes striding, the light from eternity does but invest the form with glory. It is rather like the light of a clear sunset seen through the bars of a prison window, or through the foliage of a tree in the horizon. It is no more Death the Skeleton, but Death the Angel, a messenger of peace, mercy, love, glory. There are souls that welcome him, for he opens the prison door, out of which they are to pass into a world of light; out of a prison of flesh, sin, fear, doubt, and bondage, into a celestial freedom in the perfection of holiness; into love, praise, and blissful adoration, without any mixture of sin, any cloud or shadow of defilement, or any thing, for ever and ever, to mar or change the perfect peace and blessedness of the soul. To such souls, Death is but the Messenger, to take them before the throne of God in his likeness, to present them "without spot, or wrinkle, or any such thing." Death is life to such; it is the being born out of a state of sinfulness, darkness, and wretchedness in fallen humanity, into a condition of purity, light, and happiness, in a City where the glory of God doth lighten it, and the Lamb is the light thereof. There is no future terror, of which Death is King, in such a case. Dying is but going home. It was such a death of which Paul spake, when he said that he desired "to depart and to be with Christ." He was not then contemplating any images of terror. The future was to him filled with a glory, towards which his soul was pressing, and into which death was to introduce him.

> If you, O Man! of Death are bound in dread,
> Come to this chamber, sit beside this bed.
> See how the name of Christ, breathed o'er the heart,
> Makes the soul smile at Death's uplifted dart.
>
> The air to sense is close that fills the room,
> But angel forms are waving through the gloom;
> The feeble pulse leaps up, as 'twould expire,
> But Christ still watches the Refiner's fire.
>
> Life comes and goes,—the spirit lingers on;
> 'Tis over! No! the conflict's not quite done;
> For Christ will work, till of life's sinful stain
> No spot nor wrinkle on the soul remain.
>
> He views his image now! The victory's won!
> The last dark shadow from his child is drawn.
> The veil is rent away. Eternal Grace!
> The soul beholds its Saviour face to face!
>
> Is this Death's seal? Th' impression, O how fair!
> Look, what a radiant smile is playing there!
> That was the soul's farewell: the sacred dust
> Awaits the resurrection of the just.
>
> Call not the mourners, when the Christian dies,
> While angels shout him welcome to the skies.
> Mourn rather for the living dead on earth,
> Who nothing care for his Celestial Birth.
>
> Death to the bedside came, his prey to hold,—
> All he could touch was but the earthly mould :—
> This to its native ashes men convey ;—
> The freed Soul rises to eternal day !

And yet, in itself, death is the self-same thing to the righteous as to the wicked. It is the same painful, convulsive separation between soul and body, sometimes attended with greater suffering, sometimes with less, but always constituting the supreme last strife of agony endurable in this mortal tenement. But what an infinite difference, when all the circumstances of death, all forms and processes of disease, every kind and degree of pain and suffering, are ordered by the Saviour for the good of the soul; when he sits over this furnace into which his child is cast, removing the dross, and watching for his own image! What an infinite difference, when disease and pain are but as graving tools in his hand, with which he is giving symmetry and a perfect polish to the living stones which he is to set in his temple, removing every imperfection, every wrinkle, every stain! Death, in such a case, is but the last act of a Saviour's loving discipline with his people, the perfection and consummation of his mercy.

Some wicked men have suffered much less in dying than some righteous men. "One dieth in his full strength, being wholly at ease and quiet; another dieth in the bitterness of his soul. They shall lie down alike in the dust, and the worms shall cover them." It would be interesting to draw a comparison between the deaths and the deathbeds of a number of the most remarkably wicked men, with an equal number of the most remarkably righteous men. The circumstances of disease, of mere material evil, are much the same, except that as material evils they are always aggravated by spiritual distress; the pangs of conscience giving sharpness to the pangs of dissolving nature. Compare even the deathbeds of Hume, Voltaire, and Paine, with those of Edwards, Brainard, Henry Martyn, and Payson, and you will find that there is not much to choose as to the physical pain of dying. Take the deaths of Herod and of Paul, the one eaten of worms, consumed inwardly, and the last in all probability crucified, and there was about as much physical suffering and terror in the one death as in the other. Take the deaths of Nero and of John; the one is a suicide, the last dying quietly at an hundred years of age; the pangs of dissolution in both cases were probably very nearly equal. The death of the righteous is no more exempt from physical distress and suffering than that of the wicked.

Nor is the physical distress of suffering that ingredient in death which men particularly regard or fear. In reading of the death of a Christian, how little are our feelings distressed as to the depth and intensity of his bodily sufferings, so long as we have the conviction that God was with him, that Jesus Christ was his support. But in reading of the death-sufferings of a wicked man, or in witnessing such a deathbed, you are terribly affected by the spectacle of such physical pain. It is because the misery of the soul is there; there is nothing in this latter case to bear up the body, to proclaim the blessedness of the immortal part, even amidst the suffering of mortality; on the contrary, mortality borrows suffering from the soul; the body is doubly tortured in the hour of dissolution by the pangs of a wounded conscience.

Hume would have died an easy death had his soul been at peace with God, and resting on his Saviour, although the disease and suffering of his body had remained the same. As it was, there was that ingredient in the suffering of his last hours which made his nurse ever after refuse attendance at the sick-bed of a philosopher! Voltaire would have suffered little, even had his physical sufferings remained the same, if in his last moments, instead of inward wrath of conscience, and forebodings of wrath to come, there had been the Christian's faith and sense of pardoned sin; if instead of alternate blasphemies and prayers, there had been love to that Saviour, whom the infidel, amidst the admiration of his fellow-infidels, had dared to deride. But the stings of a wounded conscience give a sharpness to all mortal diseases, that nothing else can give, making even the common sufferings of sickness an intolerable weight of misery.

On the other hand, to a mind at peace with God, there is very little terror in physical sufferings;—I had almost said there is very little pain. Sometimes, indeed, the dying pains of a holy man will be so great as for a season to absorb all his attention; but even then, you feel that all this is nothing in comparison with the presence of Christ now, and the glory which shall be revealed. When Andrew Fuller was dying, he said to those around him, "It seems as if all bodily torture were concentrated in my frame." That was but for a moment, and it was outweighed by the faith of his soul, even while so concentrated and intense that the powers of his being could fix on nothing else intently. When Payson was dying, his bodily sufferings were what would have been intense, had it not been for the flood of glory and happiness with which his soul was filled. His faith gave even to suffering a glory. When Mr Pearce was dying, he said, after a restless night, "I have so much weakness and pain that I have not had much enjoyment; but I have a full persuasion that the Lord is doing all things well." Now, here was a case in which the pain of dying, the pain of the mortal disease, was so great, as materially to interfere with the positive enjoyment of the soul, but yet it added no terror; the pain was sensibly experienced, but with such trust in God and such sweet resignation, that it gave Death, as the King of Terrors, no advantage. But if this same degree of pain had been experienced by a man without the consolations of the gospel—a man dying unprepared for eternity—the anguish of the bodily suffering would have been incalculably more intense. The terrors of death do not belong necessarily to the pains of death; they do to the wicked, but not to the righteous.

Were the universe at the command of the soul, it would not be worth a grain of sand to a man dying without the consolations of the Gospel. Friends can do nothing in such a case; the strongest affection, though it be stronger than death, can be of no avail. But Christ can do every thing. The presence of Christ can overcome the sense of pain, and fill the soul with blessedness in the midst of it. Instances are not wanting of this even amidst the unimaginable sufferings of being burnt to death at the stake.

I have before me two instances of this glory and the power of Christ's presence in death; the one in a very young Christian, the other in a saint of more advanced age and experience. When young Mr Janeway, in England, was dying, his language was as follows:—" O my friends, stand by and wonder; come, look upon a dying man. What manifestations of rich grace! *If I were never to enjoy more than this, it were well worth all the torments that men and devils could invent, worth coming through even a hell to such transcendent joys as these.* If this be dying, dying is sweet. Let no true Christian ever be afraid of dying. Christ's smiles and visits, sure they would turn hell into heaven. Oh that you did but see and feel what I do! Come and behold a dying man more cheerful than ever you saw any healthful man in the midst of his sweetest enjoyments." "Methinks I stand, as it were, with one foot in heaven, and the other upon earth. Methinks I hear the melody of heaven, and by faith I see the angels waiting to carry my soul to the bosom of Jesus, and I shall be for ever with the Lord in glory. And who can choose but rejoice in all this ?" The pangs of death in this man were strong, but the exceeding and eternal weight of glory was so much stronger, that it quite absorbed his soul, and filled him with triumphant praises.

Now what can an unbeliever do with such a case ? Here is no opportunity for enthusiasm or mistake from animal sympathy or excitement, nor any external sources of support or happiness whatever, nor any anodyne that can overcome the present sense of pain, or give buoyancy to the spirits, or provide material for the dreams of a youthful imagination, or set it in play in the presence of the King of Terrors. To the blind eye and gloomy reasoning sense of unbelief, here is nothing but pain, weakness, darkness, relinquishment of all the blessings of life, and a blank, drear vacancy in prospect. And yet, there is a mysterious, unseen, supernatural presence and power, a power of life and joy so upspringing, deep, and inextinguishable, so certain, sensible, and ecstatic, that this dying man, convulsed with pain, can say, "If I were never to enjoy more than this, it were well worth all the torments that men and devils could invent, worth coming through even a hell, to such transcendent joys as these!" And this is CHRIST ! This it is to have a SAVIOUR ! This is that Saviour's omnipotency and mercy ! Gloomy, self-torturing, unhappy infidel, what hast thou to say to this ?

Our second instance is the case of Dr Payson. He once said, in his last illness :—I have suffered twenty times,— yes, to speak within bounds,—twenty times as much as I could in being burnt at the stake, while my joy in God so abounded, as to render my sufferings not only tolerable, but welcome. The sufferings of this present time are not worthy to be compared with the glory that shall be revealed. God is my all in all. While he is present with me, no event can in the least diminish my happiness; and were the whole world at my feet, trying to minister to my comfort, they could not add one drop to the cup." On another occasion he said, " Death comes every night and stands at my bedside in the form of terrible convulsions, every one of which threatens to separate the soul from the body. These continue to grow worse and worse, until every bone is almost dislocated with pain, leaving me with the certainty that I shall have it all to endure again the next night. Yet, while my body is thus tortured, the soul is perfectly happy, perfectly happy and peaceful, more happy than I can possibly express to you. I lie here, and feel these convulsions extending higher and higher, but my soul is filled with joy unspeakable. I seem to swim in a flood of glory which God pours down upon me."

This is wonderful. And so the dying Evarts exclaimed, borne down, or rather I should say, borne up by such a weight of glory. " Wonderful! wonderful!" But here again there is nothing external, nothing visible, no earthly thing conceivable, as a source of such joy amid suffering. These are the consolations of Christ, and in the presence of these infidelity stands stunned, aghast, and silent. They are not always granted so abundantly in such triumphant, overpowering measure even to the Lord's most faithful servants; but if need be, they are. But even a little measure of them, a glimpse of the Saviour's countenance, and an assurance of his mercy, is enough to deprive death of his sting, to take away all his terrors, and to swallow him up in victory. " O Death! where is thy sting? O Grave! where is thy victory? The sting of death is sin, and the strength of sin is the law; but thanks be to God who giveth us the victory, through our Lord Jesus Christ!"

It might, on some accounts, seem strange that so few, if any, death-scenes of the apostles or primitive disciples are left on record by divine inspiration. They must have been eminently animating and instructive. But their whole life was a living death; they died daily, and when we see them daily serving Christ, and daily desiring to depart and to be with Christ, the death-scene could add little to this testimony.

St Paul has given us, at the close of the fifteenth chapter of the First Epistle to the Corinthians, and also throughout the eighth chapter of the Epistle to the Romans, a picture beforehand of the blessedness of Christ's servants in death. And the death-scene of the first martyr is given us in the Acts of the Apostles, with heaven opened, and the glory of God visible, and Jesus standing on the right hand of God; and in the view of this vision, the dying Stephen is praying for his murderers. This was an example for all that should come after, both of the divine consolations, of which they might be sure in the hour of suffering and death, and of that divine spirit of forgiveness, in the exercise of which they must glorify their Saviour.

That the divine glory in the death of Christians is the object of our Lord's particular regard, may be gathered from what is said when Jesus gave an intimation concerning the death of Peter, in one of his last interviews with his disciples:—" This spake he, signifying by what death he should glorify God." This too is partly the meaning of that expression in the 116th Psalm,—" Precious in the sight of the Lord is the death of his saints." Every peaceful, every triumphant deathbed is a commentary on this passage; for the glory, the faithfulness, the mercy, and love of the Saviour, and the love of his dear disciples to him, stronger than death, and the greatness of his atoning sacrifice, and the power of his blood to cleanse from sin and give peace to the conscience, are here exhibited, as they are nowhere else. Here the cross shines in its saving power and glory. Every precious thing in the character of Christ and the scheme of redemption, all the lovely attributes of God, and the unspeakable blessedness of those who have their portion in him, are here manifested together. All the lessons of the law and the gospel seem brought to a point; but above all, the preciousness of Christ to the soul that rests on him is so illustrated, and the necessity of faith so demonstrated, that it seems as if the sight of one such death-scene, if all men could behold it, would draw all men to the Saviour. It does make all men exclaim, " Let me die the death of the righteous, and let my last end be like his ! "

Let us now turn the light of Death upon our own life, for Death is the great Enlightener, in whose presence we see things as they really are, all delusions being withdrawn, all dreams having vanished, and an overpowering flood of light being thrown back upon the vanities through which we have been treading. Let us flee to Christ, and, by his grace, live the life of the righteous, and so our last end *shall* be like his! Of true peace in death there is no possibility but by being IN CHRIST; but even the peace of a true Christian may be greatly obscured and troubled if he has been willing to live at a distance from his Saviour. But where the soul is in Christ, relying on his precious blood and righteousness, and the affections are habitually fixed upon the things which are above, where Christ sitteth on the right hand of God, then indeed dying is but going home; and such blessedness is worth all the daily watchfulness in life, that can possibly be given for it. Such blessedness makes the soul live on the borders of heaven, in the Land Beulah; for to be in the Land Beulah is to be spiritually-minded, and that is the secret of all the blessed visions to be seen in that land. To be spiritually-minded is life and peace; and they who are eminently so, are eminently happy. Nor is any labour to be accounted painful, in comparison to the sweetness of so resting upon God. The way to such blessedness may be trying, the steps to be taken may cost much self-denial, but the results are unspeakably glorious and delightful. Nor is there any happiness to be compared with that which is enjoyed by a growing Christian, a saint, whose life is truly hid with Christ in God. The happiness of walking with God daily is very great. It is blessed to breathe after God, to hunger and thirst after righteousness, and to long for the communication of his Spirit. It is blessed to feel with the Psalmist that the soul thirsteth for God, thrice blessed to cry out "As the hart panteth after the waterbrooks, so panteth my soul after thee, O God!"

And if the experience of such *desires* is blessed, much more is the fruition of them, when God reveals himself to the soul that waiteth on him. "Blessed are they that do hunger and thirst after righteousness, *for they shall be filled.*" A watchful, earnest attention to the increase of one's personal piety makes every part of Christian experience animated and delightful. There is a divine relish in all the exercises of the Christian life, a savour of heaven, a foretaste of the enjoyment of the saints in glory. The word of God is precious, the duty of prayer is precious, the vision of faith is clear and strong, and heavenly realities come in with vivid power upon the soul, and the peace of God, which passeth all understanding, keeps the heart and mind through Christ Jesus.

" The secret of the Lord is with them that fear him, and he will shew them his covenant." He will hold it up to their view, unfold its rich blessings in their sight, and shew them that they have a part and a place in it. He will open and expound its glories, its glories of wisdom and knowledge in the revelation of Christ, its glories of spiritual things, into which the angels desire to look, its glories in the purchased possession of the saints and the riches of their heavenly inheritance, and the wonders of that infinite love, by which such celestial, everlasting treasures were procured. All this, and infinitely more than can be described, is the heritage of them that fear the Lord, that rest upon the Saviour, and who earnestly endeavour, renouncing every sin, to maintain daily that close walk with him which he requires, and to follow on after that perfection which he has exhibited as the only right standard of the soul.

Is not this a life to be chosen, to be greatly desired, to be laboured after with exceeding great diligence, perseverance, and earnestness? Is it not worth a great deal of self-denial and fervent energy in prayer, and a great deal of time given to the word of God, and to all the secret exercises of the Christian life? Is it not worth a great many sacrifices of external ease and comfort, if that were necessary, and of external business, if that presses too urgently? Is it not worth every thing, and are not all things else laid in the balance with it empty and worthless? Is it not the pearl of great price which he that is wise will readily sell all that he hath to be master of ? the one thing needful, for the attainment of which all other things may well be given up, and forgotten as of no moment ?

Yea, it is the kingdom of God and his righteousness, without which the universe cannot make you happy, but with which all things else shall be added unto you. Give what God will, without that you are poor, but with that rich, take what he will away. For when he gives himself, he gives all blessings. Who would not rather be the poorest wanderer that walks the earth, the most down-trodden and despised outcast of creation, and have his daily meals at God's spiritual table, his daily walks with his Redeemer, his daily visits of refreshment at the full fountain of his love, than without that refreshment to possess the riches of all kingdoms, or be the worshipped idol of the world! Yea, who would not rather be perishing for want of daily bread, or begging from door to door, if that were necessary, and yet daily faithful in prayer, growing in grace, and having his life hid with Christ in God, than surrounded with all affluence and at ease amidst all luxuries, and yet living in that worldly frame and at that distance from the Saviour, and in that gloomy coldness of spirit, which worldly prosperity, without great secret diligence in walking with God, so invariably produces!

The close of the Pilgrim's Progress is rendered exceedingly instructive, solemn, and admonitory by the fate of Ignorance. It is as if the writer had interposed a check to the gushing fulness of our feelings excited by the heavenly splendours of the preceding description, and had said to us, as we were thinking ourselves almost in heaven beforehand, "Beware!"

"While I was gazing at all these things," says the Dreamer, "I turned my head to look back, and saw Ignorance come up to the river side; but he soon got over, and that without half the difficulty which the other two men met with. For it happened that there was then in that place, one Vain-hope, a ferry-man, that with his boat helped him over; so he, as the others I saw, did ascend the hill to come up to the gate; only he came alone, neither did meet with any the least encouragement. When he was come up to the gate, he looked up to the writing that was above, and then began to knock, supposing that entrance should have been quickly administered to him; but he was asked by the men that looked over the top of the gate, Whence come you? and what would you have? He answered, I have eat and drank in the presence of the King, and he has taught in our streets. Then they asked him for his certificate, that they might go in and shew it to the King. So he fumbled in his bosom for one, and found none. Then said they, Have you none? But the man answered never a word. So they told the King; but he would not come down to see him, but commanded the two Shining Ones that conducted Christian and Hopeful to the City, to go out and take Ignorance, and bind him hand and foot, and have him away. Then they took him up and carried him through the air, to the door that I saw in the side of the hill, and put him in there. Then I saw that there was a way to hell even from the gates of heaven, as well as from the City of Destruction."

Now, can any thing be more solemn than this? You will remember that this man Ignorance was ignorant both of himself and of his Saviour, and yet he had been long a traveller towards the Celestial City. His case is described by the Saviour, with the addition that "Many shall say unto me in that day, Lord, Lord, open unto us; to whom I will say, Depart from me, I never knew you, ye that work iniquity." Now may God in mercy keep us from such self-deception! Nevertheless, it would be nothing strange, should it be found in the great day of trial, that this age was distinguished as an age of self-deception; and if we take not great heed to ourselves, we shall glide on with the same general current. And it is the saddest, most dreadful mistake that ever man fell into, to dream on of heaven, only to awake and find himself in hell. We had better do any thing most hard, be pressed with the greatest evils, encompassed with the most painful difficulties, endure all labours, undergo all suffering, practice every self-denial of the good soldier of Jesus Christ, than remain in such danger. What is it not worth to be unalterably safe in Christ, to have constant experience of his preciousness, to be making constant additions to our knowledge of him, to be nourished daily by his grace, and to be animated constantly by his love? Oh if we had any thing in this world of a value in the least to be compared with the blessedness of a well-grounded hope in Christ, we would not leave it for a single day in such risk as we do our hope of heaven, by living at such a distance from our Saviour!

What shadows we are, and what shadows we pursue! absorbed with vanities! a vision made for eternity, blinded by the shadows of time! A soul made for God, and the boundless realities of everlasting ages, absorbed with earth, and the poor worthless trifles of transitory years! Is this the manner in which Christ would have his people live! Or is the prize of heaven's eternal inheritance of so little value, that we can run the hazard of losing it with so little concern? Ah, no! The crown of righteousness is not of so little worth. "The kingdom of heaven suffereth violence, and the violent take it by force."

Nor is there any safety but in Christ, and in a constant effort after an increase of that holiness, with which alone the soul can be fitted to overcome the dangers of its mortal pilgrimage, or to enjoy the crown laid up in heaven. There is safety where Christ is. There is safety where there is watchfulness and growth in grace. There is safety where there is much secret prayer. There is safety in giving all diligence to make your calling and election sure. There is safety in lying low at the feet of the Saviour. There is safety and blessedness unspeakable, even here, in a world of darkness and trial, amidst temptations and dangers. There is safety and blessedness now, there is triumphant glory at the close, in so walking with Christ, so resting on him, so pursuing his pilgrimage.

And then the usefulness which is the result of all this! For there is no picture more lovely, than of that external activity which grows out of inward holiness. A zeal that is the result of secret humility, gentleness, prayer, love to Christ, sorrow for sin, is ever blessed and successful. The world even of hardened opposers bow to so lovely a spirit as that which Henry Martyn and Harlan Page exhibited. It is a spirit which grows out of secret faithfulness in the Christian life. Let any disciple dwell with Christ in secret, and that disciple will assuredly be like unto Christ in public. Let him prayerfully, anxiously, weepingly, attend to his own private growth in grace, let him make the increase of his personal holiness a steadfast object, and the fruits of holiness will presently appear. While he is watching and praying, and watering the plant in his own heart with tears, the tree will be growing, with green leaves, and fair perpetual blossoms, and ripe, rich fruit, to the admiration and benefit of every beholder.

It is a blessed life, but a close how transcendently glorious, which we have been tracing in this precious book. Looking at its close, every man wishes to enter on just such a pilgrimage. Let us then stand at the Gates of the Celestial City, as they are flung wide open to admit the transfigured pilgrims, and then, with the light shining on us, let us turn to the prayerful, patient prosecution of our own earthly pilgrimage, our own work for Christ. "Now, just as the gates were opened to let in the men, I looked in after them, and behold the City shone like the sun; the streets also were paved with gold, and in them walked many men with crowns on their heads, palms in their hands, and golden harps to sing praises withal. There were also of them that had wings; and they answered one another without intermission, saying, 'Holy, holy, holy is the Lord.' And after that, they shut up the Gates; which, when I had seen, I wished myself among them."

Turn now, dear fellow-pilgrim, animated and encouraged on thy way. Thou hast heard the songs of the redeemed; in the Apocalypse thou hast gone with John into the Celestial City; in the Pilgrim's Progress thou hast wished thyself with Bunyan among the crowned and shining ones, that cry Holy! Holy! Holy! Go then, and be faithful. Live in and upon Christ. Knock and weep, and watch and pray; but in all thy darkness (and darkness thou mayest have to encounter), never let the light of this Vision be forgotten.

Hie thee on thy quiet way,
 Patient watch the breaking dawn:
For the shadows flee away,
 And the night will soon be gone.

Thy pilgrimage lies through the wilderness,—a wilderness indeed; but the dear path to Christ's abode is there, and His light is shining. No pilgrim's *rest* is in this world, but there *is* a REST that remaineth for the people of God. Here we have no continuing city, but we seek one to come, a city which hath foundations, whose builder and maker is God. Go, then, on thy way, singing as thou goest,—

How happy is the Pilgrim's lot,
How free from every anxious thought,
 From worldly hope and fear!
Confined to neither court nor cell,
His soul disdains on earth to dwell,
 He only sojourns here.

This happiness in part is mine;
Already saved from low design,
 From every creature-love!
Blessed with the scorn of finite good,
My soul is lightened of its load,
 And seeks the things above.

The things eternal I pursue,
A happines beyond the view
 Of those that beastly pant
For things by nature felt and seen;
Their honours, wealth, and pleasures mean,
 I neither have nor want.

No foot of land do I possess;
No cottage in this wilderness;
 A poor wayfaring man;
I lodge a while in tents below,
Or gladly wander to and fro,
 Till I my Canaan gain.

Nothing on earth I call my own;
A stranger to the world, unknown,
 I all their goods despise:
I trample on their whole delight,
And seek a city out of sight,
 A city in the skies.

There is my house and portion fair,
My treasure and my heart are there,
 And my abiding home;

> For me my elder brethren stay,
> And angels beckon me away,
> And Jesus bids me come.

BLESSING, AND HONOUR, AND GLORY, AND POWER, BE UNTO HIM THAT SITTETH UPON THE THRONE, AND UNTO THE LAMB FOR EVER AND EVER.

LECTURE FIFTEENTH.

Christiana, Mercy, and the Children.

Comparison between the First and Second Parts of the Pilgrim's Progress.—Cheerfulness of the Second Part.—Beauty of its delineation of the female character.—Its great variety.—Characters of Mr Great-heart and Standfast.—Character of Mr Fearing.—Instructive lessons from the Enchanted Ground.—Reigning traits of the Pilgrimage as delineated by Bunyan.—Closing lesson.

If only the Second Part of the Pilgrim's Progress had been written, it may well be doubted whether it would not have been regarded in a higher light than it is now. The First Part is so superior to the Second, that this loses in the comparison, and gains not so much admiration as it really deserves. Just so, the Paradise Regained would have been esteemed a nobler Poem, had it not stood after the Paradise Lost, the splendour of Milton's genius in the first effort quite eclipsed its milder radiance in the second. Yet the Second Part of the Pilgrim's Progress is full of instruction and beauty, and exhibits varieties of the Christian Life delineated with such truth both to nature and grace, that though there is less elevation both in thought and style, and more familiarity and homeliness, we are still delighted with our journeyings, and love to listen to the voice of our accustomed teacher. There is not such purity and severity of taste, not such glowing fire of sentiment and feeling, not such point and condensation, not such unity and power, in the Second Part as in the First. The conversations do not possess the same richness and fulness of meaning, nor the same deep solemn blissful tones of warning and of heaven; there is sometimes almost all the difference that is found between the garrulity of men at ease, and the earnest, thoughtful talk of men pondering great themes and set upon great enterprises. Not that the journey ever ceases to be the Christian pilgrimage, but it becomes so very sociable, and at times so merry and gossiping, that it almost passes into comedy.

Perhaps the Second Part of this pilgrimage comes nearer to the ordinary experience of the great multitude of Christians than the First Part; and this may have been Bunyan's intention. The First Part shews, as in Christian, Faithful, and Hopeful, the great examples and strong lights of this pilgrimage; it is as if Paul and Luther were passing over the scene. The Second Part shews a variety of pilgrims, whose stature and experience are more on a level with our own. The First Part is more severe, sublime, inspiring; the Second Part is more soothing and comforting. The First Part has deep and awful shadows mingled with its light, terribly instructive, and like warnings from hell and the grave. The Second Part is more continually and uninterruptedly cheerful, full of good nature and pleasantry, and shewing the pilgrimage in lights and shades that are common to weaker Christians.

So there is a sweet tone and measure of gentleness and tenderness, in accordance with that passage, "Lift up the hands which hang down, and the feeble knees, and make straight paths for your feet, lest that which is lame be turned out of the way; but rather let it be healed." We have before us a company of the maimed, the halt, the lame, the blind, and a merry party it is, after all, through the magic of faith and Christian sympathy. Here are Mr Ready-to-halt, Mr Feeble-mind, Mr Despondency, and his daughter Much-afraid, and others of like frame and mould, as well as old father Honest, resolute Mr Standfast, discreet Christiana, and the lovely Mercy. Here are canes, crutches, and decrepitude, as well as young limbs, well-set sinews, and fresh, elastic, tripping feet of childhood. The Canterbury Tales themselves have scarcely a greater variety in their pilgrimage. And all these characters are touched with great originality and power of colouring. They are separate, individual, graphic portraitures of classes.

Perhaps the most delightful portion of the Second Dream of Bunyan, is its sweet representation of the female character. There never were two more attractive beings drawn than Christiana and Mercy; as different from each other as Christian and Hopeful, and yet equally pleasing in their natural traits of character, and under the influence of divine grace, each of them reflecting the light of heaven in an original and lovely variety. His own conception of what constitutes a bright example of beauty and consistency of character in a Christian woman, Bunyan has here given us, as well as in his first Dream, the model of steadfast excellence in a Christian man. The delineation, in both Christiana and Mercy, is eminently beautiful. We have, in these characters, his own ideal of the domestic virtues, and his own conception of a well-ordered Christian family's domestic happiness.

I know not why we may not suppose this picture to have been drawn from the experience of his own household, as well as that the picture of Christian in the First Part was taken from his own personal experience; and if so, he possessed a lovely wife and a lovely family. Wherever he may have formed his own notions of female loveliness and excellence, he has, in the combination of them in the Second Part of the Pilgrim's Progress, presented two characters of such winning modesty and grace, such confiding truth and frankness, such simplicity and artlessness, such cheerfulness and pleasantness, such native good sense and Christian discretion, such sincerity, gentleness, and tenderness, that nothing could be more delightful.

The matronly virtues of Christiana, and the maidenly qualities of Mercy, are alike pleasing and appropriate. There is a mixture of timidity and frankness in Mercy, which is as sweet in itself as it is artlessly and unconsciously drawn; and in Christiana we discover the very characteristics that can make the most lovely feminine counterpart, suitable to the stern and lofty qualities of her husband. The characters of her boys, too, are beautifully delineated, with her own watchfulness over them as a mother. The catechising of the children is full of instruction, and every thing shews the principles of a good Christian education. The boys themselves are children of good sense and affectionate dispositions; and on the whole, this domestic picture of a family travelling towards heaven is one of the most beautiful and instructive delineations drawn by Bunyan's genius.

There are two traits that ought to be particularly noted, which are, first, the uninterrupted Christian cheerfulness of the whole party, so that there is " music in the heart, music in the house, and music in heaven," because of them; and second, the exquisite beauty of affectionate kindness and care exercised towards them, the compassionate and joyful tenderness with which they were received; and the openhearted hospitality and love with which they are helped forward on their journey. The "meekness and gentleness of Christ," with the " love of the Spirit," and the lowly sweetness of the Gospel, especially in its condescension to the smoking flax and the bruised reed, were never more beautifully and successfully depicted. Mr Feeble-Mind is gently carried up the Hill Difficulty. At the House of the Interpreter, when Mr Fearing stands without in the cold, long time trembling and afraid to knock, good father Honest is sent forth by the Lord of the Way to entreat him to come in. In the significant rooms of the House of the Interpreter, there are discovered new varieties to please and instruct the women and children, and beautiful indeed are some of them. Also, the Lord of the Way is constantly sending refreshments to his beloved ones, and he grants them a heavenly Conductor to fight for them all along their pilgrimage. Sweet dreams wait on them, the peace of God keeps them, and when the boys go astray by eating of the fruit of " Beelzebub's orchard," the skill and efficacy of their physician are not greater than his kindness and gentleness.

As to the notable cheerfulness of this part of the pilgrimage, it is to be remarked, that it springs from the prevalence of Hope and Love. There is such constant Christian benevolence, such mutual humility, such each esteeming other better than themselves, such watchfulness for each other's good, such a Christian spirit to each other's failings, such sympathy in each other's joys and sorrows, such unselfish, unworldly hearts are mingled together, that there can hardly be a sweeter example of that Christian conversation which is always instructive, because always with grace, seasoned with salt; and always cheerful, because always singing and making melody in the heart to the Lord. The terrors of the law are not present in this second pilgrimage, so much as the consolations of the Gospel; there is constant, serene enjoyment, and not by any means so many difficulties in the way as there are pleasures.

And it is observable that all the pilgrimage wears an aspect reflected from the gentle retiring character of the pilgrims. The very dangers that were so frightful in the First Part, have a gentler cast when Christiana and Mercy pass through them; the very fiends lose something of their ugliness and terror; in passing through Vanity Fair they meet with some good men, and are entertained with Christian hospitality in the house of a true pilgrim; and when they come to the close of their pilgrimage, the River of Death itself, for them and for good Mr Fearing, becomes almost dry. When they pass through the Valley of Humiliation, it is to them a sweet and quiet place, because their own spirit is so sweet and contented; no sight or semblance of Apollyon is there; they could live there and be happy all their life long.

When they pass through the Valley of the Shadow of Death, Christ's rod and his staff do so comfort them, and they so cling together amidst their fears, and encourage each other by their holy conversation, that it is no more the dread valley which Christian passed through alone; it is a place where they are bid stand and see the Lord's deliverance. Their company is constantly increasing as they go, and they are all so ready to bear one another's burdens, they obey so perfectly the Apostle's injunction to put on, as the elect of God, holy and beloved, bowels of mercies, humbleness of mind, and the gentlest forbearance, that a more alluring picture of the pilgrimage could scarcely be drawn, and yet a most perfectly correct one, wherever the blessed Spirit of Christ prevails. The pilgrims all act according to this divine rule, "Let every one of us please his neighbour for his good to edification, for even Christ pleased not himself."

All this is delightful. It suits the pilgrimage to the walks of humble life, and holds up an example neither too high for the common multitude of Christians, nor in any way restricted to great stations or opportunities, nor at all removed from the familiar occasions and occurrences of our every-day existence. We have here a picture of the pilgrim in society, and how entirely it stands contrasted with the monkish and monastic piety once in fashion, and now again in some quarters beginning to be revered, I hardly need say. There is nothing severe, or stiff, or formal in it, nothing ascetic or morose, but every thing good-natured and sociable, joyful, charitable, and kind. As a picture of the pilgrim in domestic life, of the pilgrim as the mother of a family, and of the pilgrim, though in the world, yet living above the world, the description is as pleasing and attractive as it is true and valuable. It is what the humblest minds can understand, while the most elevated may dwell upon it with profit and delight. Perhaps to the minds of children, the Second Part proves even more attractive than the First; a striking proof of its merits, since Bunyan wrote it for child-like minds and for the common people.

One of its greatest beauties is its rich and vigorous delineation of character, and that not merely in the case of pilgrims, but of opposers and evil-minded persons. The sinful women who beset Christiana and Mercy at the outset to dissuade them from becoming pilgrims, are portraits of the kind of character which those generally bear who oppose and revile any that may be fearing God and seeking the salvation of their souls. Mrs Timorous, Mrs Bats-eyes, Mrs Light-mind, Mrs Inconsiderate, Mrs Know-nothing, and others still worse, make up the character of those, who either do not themselves become pilgrims, or who endeavour to turn friends or acquaintances from the ways of righteousness. But Christiana and Mercy are too much in earnest, too deeply convinced of sin, and too sincerely bent upon securing their salvation to be turned aside in the least by such opposition. So it always is where there is sin in the conscience and the motion of God's Spirit on the heart. Not all that men or devils can do, not all the power either of temptation, or persuasion, or ridicule, can have the least effect where the conscience is once thoroughly awakened and burdened with a sense of guilt. To be in earnest on first setting out in this pilgrimage is a great thing, and the explicit promise of God is, " Ye shall find me when ye shall search for me with all the heart."

Next to the characters of Christiana and Mercy stands that of Mr Great-heart, their conductor, a man of great faith, a man of the same spirit as Christian, Faithful, and Hopeful. There is a combination of energy and gentleness in his character, a union of the fearless warrior and the kind and careful Shepherd. He can fight with Giant Grim, can talk with the children, can condescend to Mr Feeble-mind, can carry the Lambs in his bosom, and gently lead those that are with young. His portrait is drawn with remarkable freedom, as a frank, fearless, noble, open character, with neither severity nor prejudice to mar those confiding and attractive qualities.

Mr Honest, Mr Valiant-for-truth, and Mr Standfast, are men of a kindred greatness of spirit. It is a beautiful incident, when they find Mr Standfast at prayer on the Enchanted Ground, and the manner of his introduction to our knowledge suits well the close of his life, which was very triumphant. There was a great calm at that time in the River of Death; and when Mr Standfast was about half way over, he stood firm, and spoke to those who had accompanied him to the bank of the river, in language of such glowing love to Christ, and such unshaken faith, as was enough to ravish the hearts of the survivors with joy for the prospect of the glory before him. The deaths of the pilgrims in this Second Part are all either quiet or triumphant, and some, who had passed all their life under a cloud, beheld it break, and the mist to disperse, and the sun to shine brightly at the last hour.

The character of Mr Fearing is also an admirable portrait. In every country where pilgrims are sojourning, there are just such men as he is to be met with on the pilgrimage. If we all possessed Mr Fearing's tenderness of conscience, and his dread of sinning against God, it would be well for us; and yet, if all Christians were in all respects like him, there would not be so much good done in the world, though there might be less evil committed. Good Mr Fearing needed confidence in God, and the spirit of adoption and of freedom in his service. There was in him so great a degree of humility and self-abasement, so great a sense of his own unworthiness, that, being unaccompanied by a corresponding sense of the free mercy of Christ to the chief of sinners, it went over into unbelief and fear. He feared to apply to himself the promises, feared that he was too unworthy even to pray for an interest in them, feared that he should not be accepted of Christ, feared to make a profession of religion, hardly dared shew himself among Christians, or permit himself to be considered as one of them. These fears and despondencies went so far in his mind, that they prevented a right view of his duties; they made what are the duties of the Christian appear to him as such great privileges, of which he was altogether unworthy, that he hardly dared take upon himself to perform them.

Yet he was ready for difficulty and self-denial, and was sometimes prompt and bold, where pilgrims that were stronger than he found themselves drowsy and fearful. The Hill Difficulty he did not seem to mind at all, and in Vanity Fair his spirit was so stirred within him at the sins and fooleries of the place, that father Honest had much ado to keep him within the bounds of prudence, and feared he would have brought the whole rabble of the Fair upon them. Then on the Enchanted Ground, where many are so sleepy, he was wakeful and vigilant; so that he was always giving good evidence to others of being a true child of God, even while he had very little hope for himself, and many, very many fears, lest he should at last be refused admittance at the gate of the Celestial City.

The humility of Mr Fearing was good, and a precious,

rare grace it is; but it is no part of humility to distrust the mercy of the Saviour, or to shrink from active duty for want of reliance on the strength of Christ, for want of resting on that sweet promise, "My grace is sufficient for thee." Mr Fearing's unbelief was a source of great distress to him, and deprived him of much enjoyment all the way of his pilgrimage. Persons like him, though truly fearing God, often go under a cloud all their life long, and sometimes even refuse to make a profession of religion, and to join themselves with other Christians, because of their prevailing gloom. Mr Fearing himself, though he had much comfort in the House Beautiful, was with difficulty persuaded to enter. "I got him in," said father Honest, "at the House Beautiful, I think before he was willing; also when he was in, I brought him acquainted with the damsels that were of the place, but he was ashamed to make himself much for company. He desired much to be alone, yet he always loved good talk, and often would get behind the screen to hear it: he also loved much to see ancient things, and to be pondering them in his mind. He told me afterward that he loved to be in those two houses from which he came last, to wit, at the Gate, and that of the Interpreter, *but that he durst not be so bold as to ask.*"

He had much joy in the Valley of Humiliation, but he was a man of few words, and had a habit of sighing aloud in his dejection. He was very tender of sin, and so afraid of doing injuries to others, that he would often deny himself that which is lawful, because he would not offend. This is a very precious trait, but so extreme in him, that by the lowness of his spirits his life was made burdensome to himself, and not a little troublesome to others. They had need of great patience with him, and tenderness towards him. He carried a Slough of Despond in his mind, and was always foreboding evil to himself, especially when he saw the fall and ruin of others. When they came to where the three fellows were hanged, he said he doubted that that would be his end also; and he was always fearing about his acceptance at last. But it is very clear that he was a person described in that passage where God says, "To this man will I look, even to him that is poor, and of a contrite spirit, and who trembleth at my word." It is evident also that he would come under the saying of the Saviour, "Blessed are the poor in spirit, for theirs is the kingdom of heaven." Wherefore, says Bunyan, the Lord of the Way carried it wonderfully loving to him, for his encouragement. "For thus saith the high and lofty One, that inhabiteth Eternity, whose name is Holy, I dwell in the high and holy place, with him that is of a contrite and humble spirit, to revive the spirit of the humble, and to revive the heart of the contrite ones." This character of good Mr Fearing, in the Second Part of the Pilgrim's Progress, stands in a striking and instructive contrast with the characters of Talkative and Ignorance in the First, as also with the character of Self-will as described by father Honest.

In the pilgrimage of the Second Part, Bunyan has introduced a most instructive variety and change in his treatment of the same subjects that came under his notice with Christian and Hopeful. The happiness of the Valley of Humiliation to a quiet and contented mind is described with great beauty. The timid pilgrims had daylight through the Valley of the Shadow of Death, and yet they saw enough to convince them of the terrors of that place, and of the reality of Christian's fearful experience in passing through it. The ugly shapes that they saw were indistinct, but the rushing of the fiends, the roaring of flames, and the fire and smoke of the pit, were easy enough to be discerned, so that the place was a Vale of Horrors still. Among other things, "Mercy, looking behind her, saw, as she thought, something almost like a lion, and it came a great padding pace after; and it had a hollow voice of roaring; and at every roar that it gave it made the Valley echo, and all their hearts to ache, save the heart of him that was their guide. So it came up; and Mr Great-heart went behind, and put the pilgrims all before him. The Lion also came on apace, and Mr Great-heart addressed him to give him battle. But when he saw that it was determined that resistance should be made, he also drew back and came no farther." The pilgrims might have thought of what Peter says concerning this Roaring Lion, "Whom resist stedfast in the faith;" and also of that of James, "Resist the devil, and he will flee from you."

There is also a very instructive variety in the delineation of the Enchanted Ground, a region which wears a very different aspect according to the varying condition, circumstances, and habits of the pilgrims. Christiana and her party did here encounter much mist and darkness, with mire underfoot, and a forest of briers and thorns entangling and painful. What made this the more dangerous was the alluring and refreshing arbours, green, soft, and beautifully wrought, where the very weariness of the pilgrims did urge them to rest and sleep, though they might never again wake in this world. It has been thought that here are delineated the circumstances and temptations of those pilgrims who are deeply engaged in business, and perhaps became wealthy, and are ensnared by advantageous offices, schemes, and worldly connections, so that they are overwhelmed by the cares of life, the deceitfulness of riches, and the lusts of other things. The arbours that are prepared for them by worldly prosperity they are very apt to slumber in, to the great detriment if not ruin of their souls. Amidst the thorns and briers the word of God becomes unfruitful, and in the Arbour it will not take root. If real Christians are in this condition and view their situation aright, they will be as much troubled as the pilgrims were on this Enchanted Ground, and will find it full of mire, perplexity, and vexation of spirit. But if worldly prosperity be hailed by them for enjoyment, as an arbour to sleep in, instead of being watched against as a snare, and employed for usefulness, then they are sleepers on the Enchanted Ground, nor can any tell if ever they will awake.

In the midst of their mist and darkness the pilgrims came to a place where a man is apt to lose his way. So Mr Great-heart struck a light and examined his map; and well was it for them that he did so, for just at that point, a little before them, and that at the end of the cleanest way too, there was a deep pit, none knows how deep, full of mud and mire, made there on purpose to destroy the pilgrims in. But Mr Great-heart, by narrowly consulting his map, with the light that was lighted, by taking heed to God's word, with earnest prayer for the teachings of the Holy Spirit, discovered at once what was the right way, and so they were saved from this danger.

So is the word of God a lamp unto our feet, and a light unto our paths, if we will walk thereby. And it becomes us diligently to pray with the Psalmist, "Open thou mine eyes, that I may behold wondrous things out of thy law." The word of God is a precious, heavenly map, in which we have not only the right way, the way of salvation, clearly laid down, as a path that shineth more and more unto the perfect day, but also the cross-paths and the by-paths, which Satan and wicked men, and deceivers, have traced along this pilgrimage, and which they have sometimes made to look so much like the right way, that the pilgrims may easily be deceived, if they do not closely study this map, seeking at the same time the guidance of the Holy Spirit. In a place of darkness especially, like this Enchanted Ground, they must take heed to the word of God, as to a light that shineth in a dark place, until the day dawn, and the day-star arise in their hearts. The watchful pilgrims did thus with Mr Great-heart, and besides, they cried unto him that loveth pilgrims, that he would enlighten their darkness, and so a wind speedily arose that drove away the fog, and the air became more clear.

This was one of those blessed "gales of the Spirit," that do breathe upon the pilgrims in answer to prayer; and then, in what a sweet, clear atmosphere they travel on, in a pure air, in the light of heaven, with all the prospect distinct and fresh around them! Ah, it is not the word of God alone that we need, but the Spirit of God to go with it; and his precious influences and teachings will surely be granted to all who humbly seek for them. There is much meaning in these incidents, especially in that point, that it was the way which seemed to be the cleanest, that led in the end to a pit of mud and mire.

This reminds us of the way of the flatterer, whom the pilgrims, in the First Part, met with, and by whom their faces were turned away from the Celestial City, while they seemed to themselves to be going directly towards it. Can any thing be more plainly indicated by this than that pretence to sinless perfection, by which so many have been flattered and allured, and which in so many cases has led directly, in the end, to the deepest pollution. What seems the cleanest path leads to the pit; it leads pilgrims thither by pride, self-righteousness, and the pretence of a holiness superior to God's law, and releasing them from its obligations. It is not the way of Christ's righteousness, nor of reliance upon him; and so, though it may seem at first to be a morality and sanctification of the highest tone, it ends in licentiousness. The men that devised this path, and that lead unwary souls in it, are described by Peter. "For when they speak great swelling words of vanity, they allure through the lusts of the flesh, through much wantonness, those that were clean escaped from them who live in error. While they promise them liberty, they themselves are the servants of corruption, for of whom a man is overcome, of the same is he brought in bondage."

It was amidst this Enchanted Ground that good Mr Standfast, whom the pilgrims there found upon his knees, was so hard beset and enticed by Madam Bubble; and indeed it is by her sorceries that the ground itself is enchanted. Madam Bubble is the world with its allurements and vanities; and whosoever, as Mr Great-heart said, do lay their eyes upon her beauty are counted the enemies of God; for God hath said that the friendship of the world is enmity against God; and he hath said furthermore, "Love not the world, nor the things of the world; if any man love the world, the love of the Father is not in him." So Mr Standfast did well to betake him to his knees, praying to him that could help him. So if all pilgrims, when worldly proposals and enticements allure them, and they feel the love of the world tempting them and gaining on them, would thus go to more earnest prayer, and be made more vigilant against temptations, Madam Bubble would not gain so many victories.

"Set your affections on things above, and not on things on the earth." The spirit of the Pilgrim's Progress is every where in admirable accordance with this divine injunction. There is an incident recorded of Christiana's boys, which very beautifully inculcates an instructive lesson on this subject, and shews Bunyan's opinion as to the manner in which Christian parents should educate their children in regard to the pleasures of the world. There was, on the other side of the wall that fenced in the way of salvation, a garden, with fruit trees that shot their branches over the wall; and the fruit, being very mellow and tempting, and hanging down into the way, would often allure passengers to pluck and eat. The boys did this, as boys are apt to do, and as older boys had done before them; and, though their careful mother did chide them for so doing, still they went on.

Now this was Beelzebub's orchard, and the fruit was his fruit; but Christiana at the time only knew that, being out of the way of salvation, it was none of theirs; for had she known to whom it belonged, she would have been ready to die with fear. The fruit produced a serious illness in the boys, a good while after, which illness did not shew itself indeed, till they had left the house of the Interpreter, and gone over the Hill Difficulty, and dwelt some time in the House Beautiful; and then Matthew, the eldest boy, who had eaten the fruit against the advice of his mother, fell grievously sick.

Now when Christiana learned from the Physician that it was Beelzebub's fruit that Matthew had eaten, she was sore afraid, and wept bitterly over her own carelessness, as well as her boy's naughtiness. And ever will the Christian mother have to bewail in her children the mistakes into which, through carelessness and want of prayer, she may have fallen, in their education, and the improper indulgences and amusements, in which, through a vain fondness to be fashionable, or through the example of worldly families and friends, she may have allowed her children. There are pleasures, amusements, and gratifications, which are so thoroughly and solely worldly, so entirely on the other side of the wall of salvation, that they must be considered as belonging to Beelzebub's orchard, and therefore the pilgrims and their families should have nothing to do with them.

Nevertheless, the fruit hangs over so temptingly into the pilgrim's way, and so many are in the habit of considering Beelzebub's mellow apples as *innocent* amusements, that many pilgrim families do partake of them, to the injury of the cause of Christ, and to their own great spiritual harm. There is decision as well as affectionate kindness needed in every Christian parent, to keep his children from the fruit of those trees that grow on Beelzebub's side of the wall.

It is very instructive to see how long after the fruit was taken, the evil broke out in Matthew's system. Sin may be carelessly or wilfully committed, and yet at the time the conscience may be blinded or quiet in regard to it, even with those who are true believers; but such sin may be the cause of great darkness, discouragement, and distress, when the conscience, though late, is made to feel it; and it may be the cause of the withdrawal of the consolations of God's Spirit, and the cause of great gloom in the soul, even while the sin is not remembered, and the believer does not know why God is contending with him. In such a case the pilgrims must say with Jeremiah, "Let us search and try our ways, and turn again to the Lord."

The skilful Physician in this allegory proposed such questions to Matthew and his mother, that they soon discovered the cause of his illness; and when the cause was known, then by the medicines of Christ, by the blood of Christ, with the tears of faith and repentance, the cure was easy. But concealed sin must sooner or later work distress in the conscience, and so must every sinful habit, and every wrong worldly indulgence, however it may have been pleaded for and allowed under the guise of an innocent gratification. Forbidden fruit is dangerous fruit, and works ruin, whether children take it, or grown people. The heart of persons who live upon it becomes, in Bunyan's expressive phrase, good for nothing but to be tinder for the devil's tinder-box. Just so combustible are the passions even of children, where sin is not restrained.

There are two characteristics that reign both in the First and Second Parts of the Pilgrim's Progress; the most important, and the one which is diffused through the whole work, constituting its spirit, and pervading it like a warm, clear, sunny atmosphere, is the love of Christ and the Cross. This was the grand trait in Bunyan's Christian character, and all his writings are deeply penetrated with it. The blood of the slain Lamb is every where present; this is the precious hue that suffuses the work, and gives to all its colours such depth, such power and richness. The heart of the work is Christ; Christ's love, Christ's atoning sacrifice, Christ's righteousness, Christ's precious intercession, Christ's meekness and gentleness, Christ's ever-present grace, Christ's prevailing merits, Christ the victory over sin, Christ our wisdom, righteousness, sanctification, and redemption. This secures to the book the ever-present influences of the Holy Spirit; this makes it a stream of the Water of Life, clear as crystal, flowing through the world; this makes it a book beloved by the heart of the pilgrim, just in proportion as every thought and feeling are brought into captivity to the love of Christ.

The second reigning trait of the whole work is its sober practical, and affectionate wisdom. It is the wisdom that cometh from above, pure and peaceable, gentle and easy to be entreated, full of mercy and of good fruits, without partiality and without hypocrisy. The views of the Christian life here inculcated are judicious; its trials and its dangers not at all concealed, yet never overrated; its enjoyments tinged with a sober colouring, though rich; the King's highway often rough and beset with difficulties, yet passing through scenes of inexpressible loveliness, and provided here and there with deep springing wells of comfort. The practical spirit of this book is of indescribable value and importance. An allegory like this, one might suppose, would make rather an imaginative than a working pilgrim; and in some hands it would have tended to produce a dreaming mystic, instead of a sober, experienced Christian. But there is hardly a book of greater practical wisdom in the world, and certainly, with all its imagination, no more correct map of the Christian Pilgrimage. Its wisdom is that of dearly bought experience, heaven-taught and heaven-descended. Along with this wisdom there mingles at the same time, a vein of the purest, most genuine cheerfulness and humour. It is as a part of that wisdom, that Bunyan has introduced the domestic constitution so beautifully, so happily, so sacredly, in the course of the pilgrimage. It has made his pilgrims marry and give in marriage, in accordance with the inspired declaration that "marriage is honourable in all, and the bed undefiled," and in opposition to that asceticism and fanaticism of celibacy, which would proclaim a single state as the holiest, and which in the Roman Church has wrought such a frightful career of abominations. But Bunyan also makes his pilgrims marry according to the Apostolic injunction, "only in the Lord."

In the course of this delineation in the Second Part there occurs a passage, which, for exquisite humour, quiet satire, and naturalness in the development of character, is scarcely surpassed in the language. It is the account of the courtship between Mercy and Mr Brisk, which took place at the House Beautiful.

"Now by that these pilgrims had been in this place a week, Mercy had a visitor that pretended some good-will unto her, and his name was Mr Brisk, a man of some breeding, and that pretended to religion; but a man that stuck very close to the world. So he came once or twice or more to Mercy, and offered love unto her. Now Mercy was of a fair countenance, and therefore the more alluring. Her mind also was to be always busying of herself in doing; for when she had nothing to do for herself, she would be making of hose and garments for others, and would bestow them upon them that had need. And Mr Brisk, not knowing how or where she disposed of what she made, seemed to be greatly taken, for that he found her never idle. I will warrant her a good housewife, quoth he to himself."

Mercy then revealed the business to the maidens that were of the house, and inquired of them concerning him, for they did know him better than she. So they told her that he was a very busy young man, and one that pretended to religion; but was, as they feared, a stranger to the power of that which is good.

"Nay, then, said Mercy, I will look no more on him; for I propose never to have a clog to my soul.

"Prudence then replied that there needed no great matter of discouragement to be given to him; for continuing so, as she had begun, to do for the poor, would quickly cool his courage.

"So the next time he comes, he finds her at her old work, a making of things for the poor. Then said he, What, always at it? Yes, said she, either for myself or for others. And what canst thou earn a-day? quoth he. I do these things, said she, that I may be rich in good works, laying a good foundation against the time to come, that I may lay hold of eternal life. Why, prithee, what dost thou do with them? said he. Clothe the naked, said she. With that his countenance fell. So he forbore to come at her again. And when he was asked the reason why, he said that Mercy was a pretty lass, but troubled with ill conditions." Not a word of comment is necessary on this exquisitely humorous passage.

The snatches of poetry in this Second Part are certainly superior to those which are sprinkled in the pages of the First. The song of Mr Valiant-for-truth is so much after the manner of our old English Melodists, and so valuable in itself, that it would make a gem, even in the pages of Shakspeare. There is an old melody to which this poetry is set, which has been said likewise to have been composed by Bunyan; how true this may be we know not; but the spirit of the music is in excellent harmony with the stanzas, the melody being such an one as any cheerful, resolute pilgrim, fond of music, might hum to himself upon his journey, and greatly solace himself thereby.

> Who would true valour see,
>   Let him come hither;
> One here will constant be,
>   Come wind, come weather.
> There's no discouragement
> Shall make him once relent
> His first avowed intent
>   To be a Pilgrim.

> Who so beset him round
> With dismal stories,
> Do but themselves confound;
> His strength the more is.
> No Lion can him fright,
> He'll with a Giant fight,
> But he will have a right
> To be a Pilgrim.
>
> Hobgoblin nor foul fiend
> Can daunt his spirit;
> He knows he at the end
> Shall life inherit.
> Then, fancies, fly away;
> He'll not fear what men say,
> He'll labour night and day
> To be a Pilgrim.

This song brings into view another reigning trait of the pilgrimage as depicted by Bunyan, which is the passionate intensity and steadfastness of purpose requisite for its successful pursuit. In the experience of Bunyan's pilgrims, especially the most faithful among them, there is realized that holy thirsting for God, and that earnest effort after him, of which the Psalmist speaks in so many and such striking passages, but especially in the 63d and 42d Psalms. "My soul followeth hard after thee; thy right hand upholdeth me. As the hart panteth after the water-brooks, so panteth my soul after thee, O God!"

The work of finding God is justly represented in this pilgrimage as being great and arduous; and the pilgrims are represented as pursuing it with a single eye, and a holy intensity of purpose. If a Christian would be at all successful in this great pursuit, there must be such a habit of intensity and perseverance; for God hath said, "Ye shall seek me, and ye shall find me, *when ye shall search for me with all the heart.*" In this there is brought to view what ought to be the passion of the mind, its daily, unceasing, unbroken effort, the habitual bent of its energies, the struggle of its powers. This is just as necessary to a Christian's success in the Divine Life, as enthusiasm in any path of science, or of acquisition, is necessary to success in the pursuits of this life.

But it is not so common among Christians as it ought to

be. In Bunyan's own experience, and in that of his favourite pilgrims, there was a holy fixedness of purpose, and a fervent breathing of the soul after the accomplishment of that purpose, and a perpetual return of the soul with undiminished freshness to its work, which are rarely beheld in exercise, and in the want of which it is to be feared that the piety of our own age is greatly defective. As an earthly enthusiasm it exists in men of the world; in the pursuits of this world you may find it; and the existence or the absence of this persevering intensity of effort is the great cause of the different success which men meet with in the pursuits of life.

The children of this world are wiser in their generation than the children of light. And it is precisely this enthusiasm of soul, exhibited by men who have become great in particular occupations in this world, that we speak of, as essential to success in the search after God and eternal greatness. Look over the life, for example, of a man like Sir Isaac Newton, or Sir Humphrey Davy, and what intense devotion do you find to their particular pursuits. Day and night the thirst for knowledge occupies their souls. They despise weariness, temptations, the seductive allurements of the senses, even the natural calls of appetite. They undergo what in the pursuits of religion would be accounted martyrdom; but with their enthusiastic love of science, it is nothing, it is pleasure. They encounter dangers, and subject themselves to hazardous experiments and painful toils, all submitted to with ease and even delight, in prosecution of the ruling passion of the soul, the business to which the whole energies of the being have been devoted with so much enthusiasm, that it has become a second life and nature.

Now it is just this which is needed in the effort after God. It is this turning of the whole passion and power of the soul into the business of seeking God. It is this making an acquaintance with God, and a greater love of him, and a greater knowledge of him, the passion and the business of existence. It is this passionate pursuit after holiness, never intermitted, but returned to with the recurrence of each day, and maintained with an habitual perseverance of feeling and effort, that at length shall wear the channels of blessedness so deep in the soul, that all its energies of sensibility and activity shall pour into them; that shall make the hungering and thirsting after righteousness as inseparable a movement of the daily tide of life, as undying a passion of the heart's daily experience, as is any form whatever of this world's idolatry in the souls of its worshippers.

It is this which was David's experience when his soul was following hard after God. It is this to which he refers when he breaks out, "As the hart panteth after the water-brooks, so panteth my soul after thee, O God!" It is this which has constituted the secret of the eminent attainments of all eminent saints, in the Scriptures and in all history. It is this which feeds the secret fire of men's souls, who have still sought God amidst terrors, sufferings, and deaths. It is this which has constituted the secret power of assurance; not so much the consciousness or the belief of holiness already attained, as the experience of this inextinguishable, unquenchable thirst, and daily intense effort of the soul after it. It is this which in an eminent degree is its own reward, and its own blessedness. It fulfils in its own exercise the promises of God before hand. It is a well of water springing up to everlasting life. It brings God and heaven near to the soul day by day, in the very intensity of the effort after him. It is accompanied with a great promise, that the soul, so seeking him, shall find him,—that he that thus hungers and thirsts after righteousness, shall be filled.

And this promise is fulfilling with every increase in the earnestness of the soul's desires after God, with every addition to the power of that passion, and the immutability of that habit, which binds the soul to the business of seeking God. The very intensity of this search after God is an element of power. It puts every thing else at a distance, every interference aside, every earthly glory into darkness. Its keen gaze sees God, and all things else are shadows. It gives great superiority to the world and to temptation, great clearness of view, great power to faith, great nearness to the unseen world, a great victory over things seen and temporal. It touches all experience with glory, converts all events into ministers of grace and goodness, making even sore trials the means of still greater nearness to God, and earthly disappointments but so many steps in the ladder, up which the soul is mounting to its Maker.

The positive happiness of such a life is greater than the Christian in the ordinary frame of custom can conceive. The very effort of thus seeking after God is itself positive blessedness. And we would ask any Christian, and especially any one just setting out in the Christian life, whose habits for life therefore are now forming, Had you not better be employed in such an effort, even though you seem to fail, even though your soul be much discouraged by the way, and you seem to meet with enemies of which others are entirely unconscious? Would not that life be infinitely happier which is so spent? If you do not meet with those enemies, it is not because they do not exist; and if you be at peace without this holy effort after God, it is not because these enemies are overcome, or that sin is dead within you, or that your vision is bright toward heaven. It is rather because sin is alive, and you know it not, or care very little for it: it is because sensibility is dead, and not sin; it is not because you are really secure that enemies do not trouble you, but because they are secure of you, and quietly waiting till they shall have full possession of you. Now again, in regard to this pilgrimage, it is clear that there is great blessedness in this search after God, and certainly no blessedness without it, although in it the earnest pilgrim may see his sins and his enemies with a clearness of which they that are at ease can have no conception, and though he may have to pass through conflicts which they that sleep know nothing of. Better by far to have these conflicts now, and rest and triumph at the end, than rest and peace now, and a conflict with sin and its consequences for ever and ever. It were better to be all one's lifetime in the Valley of the Shadow of Death, to emerge from it into light and life eternal, than to be walking in a false light here, to be followed by the blackness of darkness for ever.

It cannot be denied that the way of this pilgrimage is a straight and narrow way. The difficulties, and hardships, and terrors, have not been magnified in the Allegory of Bun-

yan. It is a strictly scriptural representation. Nor can it
be denied that the world spreadeth in our way many alluring
baits, and that the sense hath for the time exquisite and intoxicating delights. So that, in becoming a pilgrim, one
seems to turn his back upon a present and positive enjoyment, and to choose self-denial, painfulness, and sorrow. But
at the very outset we are met by the tremenduous question,
" What shall it profit a man, if he gain the whole world and
lose his own soul ?"

We cannot unmake our being or annihilate its conditions.
We must die, and die only to be immortal. If while we live
we live to the world, when we come to die and leave the
world, we shall die to all blessedness. But if while we live,
we die to the world, then when we come to die and leave the
world, we shall live to blessedness perfect and eternal. So
let the world be as pleasant as it may, and the pilgrimage
as toilsome and forbidding as it may, in choosing between
them we must remember we are choosing between heaven
and hell. If we would laugh now, we must do it at the
cost of weeping for ever ; if we would laugh and rejoice for
ever, we must consent to be weeping pilgrims now. Now
what will it profit you to gain the whole world at the cost
of your soul ?

But when the choice is once made under the strong principle of duty, and the conviction of substantial and eternal
gain ; and the man with violent resistance shuts out the
alluring voices of the world, by putting his fingers in his
ears, and its alluring prospects by turning his back upon
them, and runs for the entrance into the narrow way, crying out Life ! Life ! Eternal Life !—then there springs up
the excitement, enthusiasm, and joy of a new and glorious
interest. What has he to do now ? To become holy, like
God ; to lead the life of Love, like God in Christ ; to win
heaven for ever and ever ? Having turned from the world,
its fascinations depart from his soul like a light vapour and
vanish into nothingness. And fixing now all the energies
and insight of his being upon the work and prospects before
him, the life of the pilgrim and the crowning rewards stand
out continually in increasing beauty and glory. And thus

is he more and more conformed to that which he seeketh after; and gaineth, even in the winning of heavenly blessedness, a taste of it, which maketh the keenest delight of the world appear utterly insipid. The pilgrim has a precious reward as he goes along; it meets him at the cross, at the hill of difficulty, in the valley of humiliation, in the valley of the shadow of death; it meets him most abundantly when to the world he appears most wretched; it is an inward light and love which enables him to see, and draws him towards the gate of heaven—it is the promise and the earnest of the world to come. And when at last his flesh and heart faileth, then God becomes the strength of his heart and his portion for ever.

THE END.

www.ingramcontent.com/pod-product-compliance
Lightning Source LLC
Chambersburg PA
CBHW032020220426
43664CB00006B/308